W9-BJH-628

ENGLISH
FOR FOREIGN LANGUAGE SPEAKERS

THE
EASY
WAY

Christina Lacie, M.A.

BARRON'S

All inquiries should be addressed to:
Barron's Educational Series, Inc.
250 Wireless Boulevard
Hauppauge, New York 11788
www.barronseduc.com

ISBN-13: 978-0-7641-3736-5
ISBN-10: 0-7641-3736-0

Library of Congress Control No. 2007025834

Library of Congress Cataloging-in-Publication Data

Lacie, Christina.
    Barron's English for foreign language speakers : the easy way / by Christina Lacie.
        p. cm.—(Barron's Educational series) (The easy way)
    Includes bibliographical references and index.
    ISBN-13: 978-0-7641-3736-5 (alk. paper)
    ISBN-10: 0-7641-3736-0 (alk. paper)
    1. English language—Textbooks for foreign speakers. 2. English language—Examination—Study guide. 3. English language—Ability testing   I. Title.
II. Title: English for foreign language speakers.

PE1128.L336 2008
428.2'4—dc22   2007025834

PRINTED IN THE UNITED STATES OF AMERICA
9 8 7 6 5 4 3 2 1

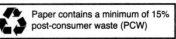

Paper contains a minimum of 15%
post-consumer waste (PCW)

CONTENTS

INTRODUCTION

Developing or improving skills in a new language is challenging. When learning a different language, practice is vital. In fact, it is through practice, practice, and more practice that we refine our skills and become more proficient. Reading, writing, grammar, vocabulary development, listening, speaking and pronunciation are all integral parts of absorbing a language. This book will guide the second (or third or fourth) language learner through the ins and outs of the English language. Chapter 1 of this book contains a preliminary skills test. It is a general test that will allow you to evaluate your strengths and weaknesses. Use it to focus on the areas that need more study and as a review for those areas of strength. The last chapter of the book contains a comprehensive English exam that encompasses the major skills presented in *English for Foreign Language Speakers: The Easy Way*. It will be a good tool to measure your comprehension of the material presented.

Each chapter of *English for Foreign Language Speakers: The Easy Way* is written in an order that builds one skill upon another. For instance, you must know nouns, verbs, subjects, and predicates before you can understand simple sentences. The chapters incorporate these skills either through direct instruction, practical activities, and review quizzes or as additional out-of-the-book and into the real world applications.

Additionally, all but the exam chapters contain a list of vocabulary words. These words are an unusual mix and for the most part are intended to broaden the reader's vocabulary scope. When possible, the words are used in examples throughout the chapter. Unfortunately, incorporating all of them into the context of the chapter does not always work. However, review the words and learn them. A comprehensive exam on the vocabulary is at the end of the book. Use it to evaluate your vocabulary strengths.

Keep These Suggestions in Mind

• You are what you read, write, and speak. The more you read, the more you write, and the more you work on developing vocabulary and applying grammar skills, the easier the new language becomes. As a word of advice, in the beginning, read nonfiction. Newspapers, news magazines, science articles, sports articles, or any area of nonfiction that you are interested in are good choices. Some fiction is good. Often, though, novels are written in regional dialects or the author uses colloquialisms (slang) or other grammatical oddities artistically that might cause confusion for new speakers of English. However, the most important thing to remember is that you read—it will help you in all areas of language development—comprehension, grammar, speaking, and writing.

• Throughout your studies of English, keep a log or journal of words that are unfamiliar to you. Look up the definitions and pronunciations. Write a sentence using the word correctly. Review these words frequently and try using them in daily conversations.

• Listen carefully and regularly to news programs, and apply the activities suggested in this book to listening skills.

Chapter 1

ENGLISH PRETEST

A pretest will allow you to consider your strengths and weaknesses. Take the following exam, which encompasses all areas covered in this book. Use the results to focus on your weaknesses and provide you with a guideline for more intense study. Use the chapters covering your areas of strengths as a review. The answers are in the appendix at the end of the book.

Nouns

1. _____ A noun names _____.
   a. an action
   b. a description
   c. a person, place, thing, or idea
   d. a preposition

2. _____ Identify the proper noun.
   a. Bobby
   b. carpet
   c. armoire
   d. stamp

3. _____ Identify the concrete noun.
   a. raspberry
   b. peace
   c. English
   d. sensitivity

4. _____ Which of the following is an indefinite noun?
   a. chef
   b. friend
   c. doctor
   d. all of the above

5. _____ A gerund is a verb that is used as a noun and ends with an _____.
   a. apostrophe *s*
   b. *-ing*
   c. *-ed*
   d. *-que*

Pronouns

6. _____ A pronoun is a word that takes the place of a _____.
   a. verb
   b. preposition
   c. noun
   d. adjective

7. _____ Identify the pronouns.
   a. Rene, Mark, Taris
   b. general, tailor, soldier
   c. gender, possession, collection
   d. they, we, ours

8. _____ Identify the sentence below with the underlined antecedent.
   a. <u>Maria</u> said her mother was a great cook.
   b. Yesterday Basem sent his <u>skateboard</u> to the repair shop.
   c. Colin laughs his head <u>off</u> on a daily basis.
   d. Sarah can <u>spend</u> money like crazy.

9. _____ Identify the interrogative pronoun.
   a. she
   b. them
   c. who
   d. us

10. _____ The "person" of a pronoun includes _____.
    a. first, second, and third
    b. nominative, possessive, and objective
    c. personal pronouns
    d. none of the above

Verbs

11. _____ Identify the action verbs below.
    a. swim, giggle, eat
    b. dog, cat, porcupine
    c. sweet, sour, bitter
    d. lovingly, bitterly, utterly

12. _____ True or False? Verbs describe nouns.
    a. True
    b. False

13. _____ Verbs have _____ tenses in English.
    a. two
    b. three
    c. four
    d. six

14. _____ A verb used in the _____ mood gives a command.
   a. imperative
   b. indicative
   c. subjunctive
   d. all of the above

15. _____ Irregular verbs form their past and past participle in some other way than by adding _____.
   a. *-ing*
   b. apostrophe *s*
   c. *-d* or *-ed*
   d. all of the above

Subjects and Predicates

16. _____ The subject of the sentence is the _____ part of the sentence.
   a. verb
   b. indirect object
   c. direct object
   d. noun or pronoun

17. _____ The predicate is the _____ part of the sentence.
   a. verb
   b. indirect object
   c. direct object
   d. noun or pronoun

18. _____ True or False? A simple sentence must have a subject and a predicate.
   a. True
   b. False

19. _____ The _____ usually answers the question *what* or *whom*.
   a. verb
   b. indirect object
   c. direct object
   d. noun or pronoun

20. _____ The _____ usually tells *to whom* or *for whom*.
   a. verb
   b. indirect object
   c. direct object
   d. noun or pronoun

Subject/Verb Agreement

21. _____ True or False? Subjects should never agree with verbs in number.
   a. True
   b. False

22. _____ Singular subjects require _____ verbs.
   a. plural
   b. many
   c. singular
   d. less

23. _____ Identify the sentence with the correct subject/verb agreement.
   a. Mrs. Snodgrass have three blonde children.
   b. Your neighbor Ann has two brunette daughters.
   c. Juli, who lives down the hill have two blonde daughters with freckles.
   d. The woman over there named Vicki have two blonde sons who like to surf.

24. _____ Plural subjects have _____ verbs.
   a. plural
   b. many
   c. singular
   d. less

25. _____ Pronouns must agree in number and _____.
   a. strength
   b. integrity
   c. gender
   d. none of the above

Adjectives

26. _____ A definite article is _____.
   a. a
   b. an
   c. the
   d. all of the above

27. _____ Common adjectives are adjectives that are NOT _____.
   a. capitalized
   b. underlined
   c. highlighted
   d. circled

28. _____ Proper adjectives are _____ capitalized.
   a. never
   b. sometimes
   c. frequently
   d. always

29. _____ Identify the noun that is used as an adjective.
   a. large boots
   b. giant boots
   c. rubber boots
   d. slippery boots

30. _____ Which of the following is the positive form of the word *fast*?
   a. fast
   b. faster
   c. fastest
   d. all of the above

Adverbs

31. _____ Adverbs modify or describe _____.
   a. nouns
   b. prepositions
   c. articles
   d. verbs

32. _____ Identify the adverbs of degree.
   a. entirely, almost, greatly
   b. red, yellow, purple
   c. dusty, friendly, sadly
   d. here, there, everywhere

33. _____ Identify the three forms of adverbs.
   a. superlative, comparative, lacking
   b. superlative, comparative, overdone
   c. superlative, comparative, positive
   d. superlative, comparative, negative

34. _____ Identify the sentence below that contains an adverb that modifies another adverb.
   a. Chicago was almost completely destroyed by a fire in 1871.
   b. It is situated on the shore of Lake Michigan.
   c. Chicago attracted many settlers and industry with the opening of the Erie Canal.
   d. The world's first skyscraper, the Sears Tower, was built in Chicago in 1885.

35. _____ Identify the adverbs of manner.
   a. yesterday, today, tomorrow
   b. entirely, highly, totally
   c. badly, kindly, gentlemanly
   d. none of the above

Prepositions/Conjuctions/Interjections

36. _____ True or False? A preposition is a word that shows the relationship between a noun and a pronoun to another word.
   a. True
   b. False

37. _____ Identify the sentence that begins with a preposition.
     a. An albino is a person or animal with a hereditary condition.
     b. Albinos lack pigment in their skin, hair, and eyes.
     c. With albinos, the hair is white and the skin is pink because blood vessels are visible.
     d. The albino's eyes are highly sensitive to light.

38. _____ Interjections are usually punctuated with a(n) _____.
     a. period
     b. question mark
     c. exclamation point
     d. comma

39. _____ Conjunctions are words that connect individual words or _____.
     a. groups of words
     b. adjectives
     c. prepositions
     d. verbs

40. _____ There are three types of conjunctions: _____.
     a. coordinate, cooperative, and uncooperative
     b. coordinate, uncoordinated, subordinate
     c. coordinate, correlative, and uncreative
     d. coordinate, correlative, and subordinate

Phrases and Clauses

41. _____ A phrase is a group of related words that _____ contain both a subject and a verb.
     a. do
     b. do not
     c. will
     d. cannot

42. _____ A clause is a group of words with a _____ and can often stand alone.
     a. subject and predicate
     b. verb and adverb
     c. preposition and noun
     d. verb and adjective

43. _____ Identify the sentence with an appositive phrase.
     a. A wombat is nocturnal.
     b. The wolverine, a ferocious mammal native to pine forests, is the largest member of the weasel family.
     c. A woodchuck has sharp front teeth.
     d. A wolffish has powerful jaws and teeth that it uses to catch other fish.

44. _____ Infinitive phrases usually begin with the word _____.
     a. Sara
     b. this
     c. that
     d. to

45. _____ A gerund phrase includes _____.
     a. life experiences
     b. a gerund
     c. the entire alphabet
     d. three clauses

Sentence Structure and Classification

46. _____ There are _____ different categories of sentence structure.
     a. three
     b. four
     c. five
     d. six

47. _____ Compound sentences have _____ or more independent clauses.
     a. two
     b. three
     c. four
     d. five

48. _____ True or False? There are NO dependent clauses in a compound sentence.
     a. True
     b. False

49. _____ A complex sentence has _____.
     a. a subject and predicate and a preposition
     b. an independent clause and a dependent clause (or more)
     c. two dependent clauses
     d. three simple sentences combined

50. _____ The most complicated of the sentences is the_____.
     a. simple sentence
     b. compound sentence
     c. complex sentence
     d. compound-complex sentence

Punctuation

51. _____ Periods are used to end a sentence that makes _____.
     a. a statement
     b. a question
     c. an exclamation
     d. a quotation

52. _____ Exclamation points are used following a word or group of words that express _____.
   a. hope
   b. despair
   c. strong feelings
   d. laughter

53. _____ The _____ is used before a list of items.
   a. semicolon
   b. period
   c. question mark
   d. colon

54. _____ Apostrophes are used _____.
   a. for contractions
   b. for possessive case
   c. to form plurals
   d. for all of the above

55. _____ True or False? Quotation marks are used to punctuate song titles, poems, short stories, lectures, chapters of books, episodes of a radio or television program, as well as articles in periodicals, newspapers, or encyclopedias.
   a. True
   b. False

Sentence Purpose

56. _____ Identify the exclamatory sentence below.
   a. Where are you going?
   b. I don't believe that!
   c. Let's go to France.
   d. Take the bus home.

57. _____ Declarative sentences end with a _____.
   a. exclamation point
   b. comma
   c. question mark
   d. period

58. _____ Identify the interrogative sentence.
   a. Where are you going?
   b. I don't believe that!
   c. Let's go to France.
   d. Take the bus home.

59. _____ Interrogative sentences _____.
   a. make statements
   b. express strong emotion
   c. ask questions
   d. give commands

60. _____ Identify the imperative sentence below.
    a. Where are you going?
    b. I don't believe that!
    c. Let's go to France.
    d. Take the bus home.

Capitalization

61. _____ Which of the following should be capitalized?
    a. chilean
    b. Guatemalan
    c. Gaelic
    d. Honduran

62. _____ Identify the sentence that is incorrectly capitalized.
    a. Take a U-turn at that sign.
    b. The nfl will repeat the best of the season this summer.
    c. The PTA will fund our end-of-the-year party.
    d. I'm going to be taking History 101.

63. _____ True or False? The pronoun *I* is ALWAYS capitalized.
    a. True
    b. False

64. _____ Which of the following should NOT be capitalized?
    a. holidays
    b. names of ships
    c. common nouns
    d. historical events

65. _____ Identify the incorrectly capitalized sentence.
    a. Blaise Pascal is a French scientist and mystic.
    b. The Parthenon is a temple dedicated to the goddess Athena.
    c. The Jewish festival of Passover commemorates the Exodus from Egypt.
    d. a parsnip is a root vegetable native to eurasia.

Writing Paragraphs

66. _____ Topic sentences are located at the _____ of the paragraph.
    a. end
    b. beginning
    c. middle
    d. none of the above

67. _____ Support sentences add_____ to the paragraph.
    a. detail and interest
    b. fluff
    c. transitions
    d. conclusions

68. _____ A transitional sentence_____.
      a. ends a paragraph completely
      b. ends a paragraph but moves it smoothly into the next
      c. begins the paragraph
      d. adds supporting detail

69. _____ _Thereafter, despite,_ and _although_ are examples of _____.
      a. topics
      b. support details
      c. concluding sentences
      d. transitional words

70. _____ Each paragraph should have one _____.
      a. clause
      b. phrase
      c. idea
      d. noun

Pronunciation

71. _____ Identify the word that has a long _a_ sound.
      a. flea
      b. goat
      c. jade
      d. tan

72. _____ Identify the word that has a short _o_ sound.
      a. goat
      b. tote
      c. soap
      d. top

73. _____ True or False? Words with vowel digraphs are words that have two vowels together but have only one vowel sound.
      a. True
      b. False

74. _____ Identify the word with the R-controlled vowel sound.
      a. bear
      b. soda
      c. brought
      d. all of the above

75. _____ Which of the following words has a silent consonant?
      a. snake
      b. gist
      c. wrap
      d. mass

Prefixes, Suffixs, and Spelling Rules

76. _____ A prefix is a group of letters that is added on _____.
    a. at the end of the word
    b. in the middle of the word
    c. at the beginning of the word
    d. at both ends of the word

77. _____ A suffix is a group of letters that is added on _____.
    a. at the end of the word
    b. in the middle of the word
    c. at the beginning of the word
    d. at both ends of the word

78. _____ One- and two-word numbers are usually _____ in a sentence.
    a. added together
    b. spelled out
    c. disregarded
    d. underlined

79. _____ Which of the following words is spelled incorrectly?
    a. seize
    b. field
    c. anchent
    d. neighbor

80. _____ Identify the prefixes below.
    a. hypo, para, trans, tri, ultra
    b. able, ful, ly
    c. ive, ize, less
    d. ine, ward, tude

Word Roots

81. _____ Word roots carry the _____ meaning of the word.
    a. secondary
    b. primary
    c. initial
    d. complementary

82. _____ The meaning of the root *thermo* is_____.
    a. water
    b. fire
    c. earth
    d. heat

83. _____ The root meaning of which of the following words is vocation/vocal?
    a. whisper
    b. scream
    c. call
    d. animal

84. _____ Words that begin with the root *zoo* have something to do with_____.
    a. fish
    b. planets
    c. carpet
    d. animals

85. _____ *Cardiac* and *cardinal* have a root word that means_____.
    a. satisfy
    b. heart
    c. feet
    d. card playing

Homonyms, Synonyms, Antonyms

86. _____ A homonym is a word that _____.
    a. has the same or similar meaning
    b. means the opposite
    c. sounds the same but has a different meaning
    d. all of the above

87. _____ Identify the synonyms below.
    a. giant/enormous
    b. black/white
    c. spend/save
    d. patients/patience

88. _____ Identify the homonyms below.
    a. giant/enormous
    b. black/white
    c. spend/save
    d. patients/patience

89. _____ The following words are _____: none/nun
    a. synonyms
    b. antonyms
    c. homonyms
    d. confusing words

90. _____ True or False? *A lot* is two words, not one word.
    a. True
    b. False

Idioms

91. _____ Idioms are _____ .
   a. figures of speech
   b. confusing
   c. not to be taken literally
   d. all of the above

92. _____ *As the crow flies* means_____
   a. the longest distance between two points
   b. the shortest distance between two points
   c. where the crow flies
   d. the path of a bird

93. _____ Identify the definition of *it's Greek to me.*
   a. a skilled gardener
   b. to pay an equal share
   c. someone who talks a lot
   d. something you do not understand

94. _____ To take on responsibility or a new challenge is to_____ .
   a. *ruffle a few feathers*
   b. *spill the beans*
   c. *step up to the plate*
   d. *rise from the ashes*

95. _____ When you cannot have things both ways, _____ .
   a. you *can't have your cake and eat it too*
   b. you can *sleep like a dog*
   c. you can *rest on your laurels*
   d. you will be *scraping the barrel*

Allusions

96. _____ Allusions are references to _____ .
   a. historical events
   b. mythology
   c. public figures
   d. all of the above

97. _____ The God of the west wind is _____ .
   a. Zeus
   b. Zephyr
   c. Venus
   d. Jupiter

98. _____ The man who was forced to a roll a giant boulder up a hill only to have it roll back down is _____.
   a. Snow White
   b. Sphinx
   c. Sisyphus
   d. Styx

99. _____ Lucifer is another name for _____.
   a. Medusa
   b. Little Red Riding Hood
   c. Satan
   d. Mercury

100. _____ The novel about a boy who runs away and rafts down the Mississippi River with a slave named Jim is titled_____.
   a. *The Adventures of Huckleberry Finn*
   b. *Finnegans Wake*
   c. *Portrait of a Lady*
   d. *The Legend of Sleepy Hollow*

Chapter 2

NOUNS

Nouns are words that name a person, place, thing, or idea. This is a simple enough idea to understand. However, what make nouns more complicated is the fact that there are many different types of nouns and many ways to use them. There are classes of nouns such as common, proper, concrete, abstract, and collective. Nouns are also grouped by number, gender, and case categories. Number nouns are singular, plural, compound, and collective. Gender nouns are feminine, masculine, neuter, or indefinite. To add to the confusion, nouns can be used as subjects, predicates, possessives, and objectives. Oddly enough, some nouns are verbs (action words). However, when an -ing is added to the end of the verb, these words can be used as nouns—and they are called gerunds. Never fear, all of this will be explained thoroughly. In fact, by the end of this chapter, you will probably be dreaming of nouns.

Vocabulary Development

1. **knight** (nít) A man of noble birth and military status in the Middle Ages (about A.D. 1000–1400)

2. **chaperone** (sha per own) An older person accompanying and responsible for a person (or persons) who is younger

3. **ideology** (i dee ol o jee) The main beliefs or ideas that represent a group of people or a movement.

4. **water polo** (wah ter po lo) A team sport that is played with a ball in a swimming pool.

5. **conservatory** (kunn serv a tor ee). A school for training musicians and composers.

6. **laboratory** (lab ra tor ee) A room or a building that is equipped for scientific research.

7. **tiara** (tee ar ah) An ornamental and crescent-shaped headdress that is worn by women for celebrations and other formal occasions.

8. **element** (el e ment) A part of something that makes up a whole.

9. **pride** (príd) A feeling of pleasure or satisfaction in one's deeds or characteristics. NOTE: Do not confuse this with a pride of lions.

10. **childhood** (child huud) The period or condition of being a child.

Classes of Nouns

There are several classes or types of nouns. These include abstract, concrete, collective, common, and proper nouns.

Abstract Nouns

Abstract nouns refer to feelings, a condition, concepts, ideas, and emotions. In other words, they are things that are not tangible—or literally cannot be touched.

- meeting
- Hinduism
- bravery
- justice
- freedom
- happiness
- love
- hope
- greed

Concrete Nouns

Concrete nouns can literally be seen, touched, heard, smelled, or tasted. In fact, the majority of nouns are concrete nouns. These nouns can be either common or proper nouns.

- apple
- bottle
- Seiko watch
- bus
- telephone
- Captain Smith
- stench
- television

Practice I

Directions: On the line next to the noun, classify each as either a concrete or abstract noun. Write *C* on the line if it is a **concrete** noun, and write *A* on the line if it is **abstract** noun.

1. poverty   _____
2. conservatory   _____

3. Mahatma Gandhi _____

4. jungle _____

5. pride _____

6. peace _____

7. generosity _____

8. Dr. Chang _____

9. envelopes _____

10. kindness _____

11. ideology _____

12. Jill _____

13. cousin _____

14. mayor _____

15. Marxism _____

16. Danube River _____

17. beauty _____

18. success _____

19. knight _____

20. childhood _____

Collective Nouns

Collective nouns name a group or a unit—a collection of things, people, places, or animals.

- swarm (of bees)
- pride (of lions)
- flock (of sheep)
- gaggle (of geese)
- herd (of cows)
- team
- crowds
- tribe
- congregation
- United States
- batch
- cluster
- Seattle Supersonics
- orchestra
- United Nations

Practice II

Directions: Read the following incomplete sentences. Use a word from the list of **collective** nouns above that best completes the sentence, and write it on the line provided.

EXAMPLE:

The <u>United States</u> includes 48 states that are connected and two that are not (Alaska and Hawaii).

1. The _____ of candied apples that my mother made last night look tasty.
2. The organization that was established to enable countries to work together toward peace and mutual development is called the _____.
3. Over the past week, there have been enormous _____ at the malls shopping for the holidays.
4. The Los Angeles Symphony _____ is a well-respected and admired group of musicians.
5. The _____ of bees attacked me when I tried to retrieve the baseball.
6. Seattle's basketball team, the _____, is looking for a new arena.
7. The _____ at Joshua's church look forward to their missionary work in Thailand.
8. Vicki, John, and Jake saw a _____ of lions on their trip to Kenya last year.
9. Ireland and Scotland are filled with sheep; there are _____ of sheep almost everywhere you drive outside the cities.
10. Our science _____ won a national competition in Washington, D.C.

Common Nouns

Common nouns are any nouns that do not name a specific person, place, thing, or idea. They are something that you cannot actually touch but come from your mind or heart. Common nouns are not capitalized or formal. They are common and ordinary.

- person nouns: man, girl, woman, nurse, teacher, salesperson, chef
- place nouns: kitchen, laboratory, office, zoo, beach, river, building
- thing nouns: toy, compact disc, spoon, taxes, paper, pencil, clock
- idea nouns: happiness, love, generosity, kindness, hate, selfishness

Practice III

Directions: Below is a list of **common** nouns. On the line next to the noun, write whether it is a person, place, thing, or idea noun.

EXAMPLE:

generosity <u>idea</u>

1. friend   _____
2. religion   _____
3. baseball   _____
4. government   _____
5. cousin   _____
6. element   _____
7. city   _____
8. sympathy   _____
9. mountain   _____
10. beach   _____

Proper Nouns

Proper nouns name a particular person, place, thing, or idea. Proper nouns are capitalized.

- person nouns: Mrs. Smith, Dr. Wilson, Samuel Clemens, Charles Dickens
- place nouns: France, Mt. Whitney, Connecticut, London, England
- thing nouns: Oakland Raiders, Empire State Building, U.S. Post Office
- idea nouns: Christianity, Judaism, Buddhism

Practice IV

Directions: Read the brief paragraph below and <u>*underline all of the proper nouns*</u>.

EXAMPLE:

The <u>Knights of the Garter</u> were founded at the end of the <u>Middle Ages</u>.

In medieval Europe, a knight was a man of some noble status. King Arthur led a group of knights of the highest order called the Knights of the Round Table. As knights, these men were admired for their battle skills, honesty, and bravery. Each year, King Arthur asked the knights to return to Camelot (the site of King Arthur's court) on Pentecost (a religious festival celebrated in May or June). There were twenty-five knights whose names are inscribed on the Winchester Round Table; Sir Galahad, Sir Gawain, and Sir Lancelot du Lac are three of the twenty-five knights.

Number of Nouns

The number of nouns determines whether the noun is singular (only one) or plural (two or more). Compare the singular noun list to the plural nouns directly below it. Compound nouns are those that combine two or more nouns to form one word.

Singular Nouns

Singular nouns simply refer to one single person, place, thing, or idea.

- boy
- chaperone
- ideology
- Canadian
- prisoner
- orca

Plural Nouns

Plural nouns name more than one person, place, thing, or idea. They end with an *s*. The spelling of a singular noun that ends with a *y* has to be changed to make it plural; notice the word *ideologies* below.

- boys
- chaperones
- ideologies
- Canadians
- prisoners
- orcas

Pratice V

Directions: The nouns listed below are either singular or plural. If the noun is singular, write its plural form on the line. If the noun is plural, write its singular form on the line. Hint: to make the word *melody* a plural, the ending must be changed similar to the word *ideology* above.

EXAMPLE:

leaf   <u>leaves</u>
men   <u>man</u>

1. stage   _____
2. concerts   _____

3. melody   _____

4. necklace   _____

5. dinners   _____

6. New York Knick _____

7. counselors   _____

8. assistant   _____

9. litter   _____

10. calendars   _____

Compound Nouns

Compound nouns are nouns made up of two or more words that together name a person, place, thing, or idea. Compound nouns are written as one word (sunset), separate words (high school), or hyphenated words (mother-in-law).

- snowshoe
- full moon
- West Virginia
- nondenominational
- football
- baseball
- no-hitter
- antihero
- civil rights
- South America

Practice VI

Directions: Turn each noun listed below into a compound noun by adding another word either before or after the word. Write the compound noun on the line.

EXAMPLE:

photo <u>photosynthesis</u>

1. French   _____

2. onion   _____

3. book   _____

4. father   _____

5. news   _____

6. ocean   _____

7. North   _____

    8. Mexican   _____

    9. university   _____

   10. Buddhist   _____

Gender of Nouns

The gender establishes the sex of the noun. English differs from many other languages in identifying word gender. English nouns are identified as feminine, masculine, neuter, or indefinite.

- Feminine nouns are female: mother, woman, hostess, countess, mistress, hen
- Masculine nouns are male: father, man, host, count, mister, rooster
- Neuter nouns are neither male nor female: education, window, convention
- Indefinite nouns can be either female or male: doctor, parent, chef, chaperone

Practice VII

Directions: Determine the gender of the noun being used in each sentence below, and write its gender (feminine, masculine, neuter, or indefinite) on the line at the end of the sentence.

EXAMPLE:

    Jean Piaget was a Swiss <u>psychologist</u> who developed a theory of intellectual growth in children. <u>indefinite</u>

1. The <u>crew</u> managed to restore electricity to most of the homes and businesses within twenty-four hours. _____

2. <u>Uncle Bill</u> drove to Kentucky to see the famous horse race, the Kentucky Derby. _____

3. During the course of the meal, our <u>waitress</u> was extremely attentive and help-ful._____

4. The <u>closet</u> was jammed full of clothes and shoes. _____

5. The <u>queen</u> dressed in stunning apparel for the coronation. _____

6. After landing safely at the air force base, the <u>astronaut</u> breathed a sigh of relief. _____

7. The chipped <u>vase</u> held a dozen wilted roses. _____

8. The <u>water polo team</u> won the state championship and is now headed to the national competition. _____

9. Benjamin's <u>parent</u> was unable to attend his show last night. _____

10. The crucial element was identified by the <u>scientist</u> in the laboratory of a well-known research institution. _____

Usage of Nouns

Noun usage explains exactly how nouns relate to the words that are used with them in sentences.

Subject Nouns (Nominative Case)

When a noun is the subject or primary focus of a sentence, it is the noun that does something or is being talked about. Again, if the noun is the subject of the sentence, it is in the nominative case.

- The <u>conservatory</u> has trained many of the most successful conductors.
- The <u>chaperone</u> participated in a training session before the trip.
- The <u>senator</u> seems passionate about the aid package to Africa.

Predicate Nouns (Predicate Nominative)

These are nouns that repeat or rename the subject. They always follow a form of the verb (an action word) *be,* such as *is, are, was, were, been.*

- The conservatory is a <u>place</u> that trains successful conductors.
- The chaperone is a <u>person</u> who watches over younger people.
- The senator was a <u>man </u>of great passion.

Possessive Nouns (Possessive Case)

The possessive noun demonstrates ownership or possession. To indicate possession, an apostrophe (') is added followed by an *s* unless it is plural. When the noun is plural and already has an *s,* add an apostrophe (') to the word to make it a possessive plural.

- The <u>conservatory's</u> reputation for training world-class conductors is stellar.
- The <u>chaperone's</u> calm and reassuring personality is what the school wanted.
- The <u>senator's</u> passion for the African cause helped the bill pass.

Object Nouns (Objective Case)

When a noun is used as a direct object, the noun receives the action from the subject of the sentence.

- The conservatory's training program produces fine <u>conductors</u>.
- The chaperone has a pleasant <u>personality</u>.
- The senator demonstrated great <u>passion</u>.

Practice VIII

Directions: Read the following sentences carefully and decide if the underlined noun is a **subject** noun, a **predicate** noun, a **possessive** noun, or an **object** noun. Then write the specific identification on the line.

EXAMPLE:

subject noun A gadfly is a type of fly that bites cattle.

1. _____ The queen's tiara sparkled in the sunlight.
2. _____ The chivalrous knight is a brave young man who saved the beautiful girl from a fire-breathing dragon.
3. _____ Buddhist ideologies are practiced in many countries around the world.
4. _____ The pride shown at school during the festival was admirable.
5. _____ Water polo is a sport for strong athletes and not for the weak at heart.
6. _____ An element in mathematics can be many things, including a part of a set, a point, a line, or an angle of a triangle.
7. _____ The laboratory's fame arrived from its discovery of a cure for infectious skin diseases.
8. _____ Meredith's childhood was a fantasy world made of candy and sweets.
9. _____ While longing for peace and solitude, the elderly woman left home for a far and distant land.
10. _____ The coyote is a wild dog that is native to North America.

Gerunds

A noun that is derived from a verb and ends with an *-ing* is a gerund.

- Singing made him cheerful and happy.
- He chose singing as a career in his early childhood.
- The success of his singing brings him wealth and fame.

Practice IX

Directions: Write a sentence for each of the gerunds listed below.

EXAMPLE:

  singing <u>Singing in the chorus is one of my favorite activities.</u>

1. winning _____

2. traveling _____

3. writing _____

4. whispering _____

5. swimming _____

6. snoring _____

7. canning _____

8. spelling _____

9. sleeping _____

10. walking _____

Chapter 2 Review Quizzes

Vocabulary Review Quiz

Directions: Write the letter of the correct definition on the line next to the noun that it defines.

1. _____ water polo

2. _____ chaperone

3. _____ element

4. _____ knight

5. _____ pride

6. _____ tiara

7. _____ childhood

8. _____ conservatory

9. _____ laboratory

10. _____ ideology

A. A man of noble birth and military status in the Middle Ages

B. An older person accompanying and responsible for a person who is younger

C. The main beliefs or ideas that represent a group of people or a movement

D. A team sport that is played with a ball in a swimming pool

E. A school for training musicians and composers

F. A room or a building that is equipped for scientific research

G. An ornamental and crescent-shaped headdress that is worn by women for celebrations and other formal occasions

H. A part of something that makes up a whole

I. A feeling of pleasure or satisfaction in one's deeds or characteristics

J. The period or condition of being a child

Noun Definitions

Directions: Select the correct definition and write the letter of the answer on the line to the right of the number.

1. _____ A *gerund* is a noun that is derived from
   a. pronouns
   b. verbs
   c. adjectives
   d. none of the above

2. _____ Proper nouns are always
   a. ordinary
   b. common
   c. capitalized
   d. used as verbs

3. _____ Which of the following is NOT an abstract noun?
   a. telephone
   b. freedom
   c. love
   d. hope

4. _____ Which of the following words is NOT a collective noun?
   a. orchestra
   b. swarm
   c. chaperone
   d. crowd

5. _____ Identify the sentence below that uses a plural noun.
   a. The prisoners are becoming restless and need to get some exercise.
   b. The boy went to school earlier than usual.
   c. The chaperone escorted the young girl to the restroom.
   d. The orca will give birth soon.

6. _____ Identify the compound noun in the list below.
   a. litter
   b. baseball
   c. dinners
   d. book

7. _____ Which of the following groups of words are considered indefinite nouns?
   a. mother, woman, hostess, countess, hen
   b. doctor, parent, chef, chaperone
   c. father, man, host, count, rooster
   d. education, window, convention

8. _____ Identify the possessive noun below.
   a. Xavier
   b. men
   c. duck's
   d. harbor

9. _____ A noun names a person, place, thing, and _____.
   a. verb
   b. carriage
   c. bolt
   d. idea

10. _____ Predicate nouns repeat or rename the subject and use a form of _____
    a. the verb *be*
    b. the possessive noun
    c. a common noun
    d. a gerund

Common and Proper Nouns

Directions: In the paragraph below, underline all common nouns and draw a box around all of the proper nouns.

EXAMPLE:

Galileo Galilei was an Italian astronomer, mathematician, and physicist.

The Dominican Republic is an independent nation that is located in the West Indies. The small country occupies the eastern two-thirds of the island called Hispaniola. The western third of the island is Haiti. The island was visited by Christopher Columbus in 1492. At that time, a Spanish settlement was established in Santo Domingo, which is the Dominican Republic's present-day capital. In 1697, the western third of the country was ceded to France. In 1795, the entire island was ruled by the French, but the eastern side was returned to Spain in 1809. The Dominican Republic won its independence a second time in 1844 after being annexed to Haiti in 1821.

Abstract and Concrete Nouns

Directions: Read the paragraph, and select a concrete or an abstract noun from the word bank below that best completes the meaning of the sentence. Write the noun on the line within the paragraph. Each word will be used only once.

EXAMPLE:

Oxygen is a colorless, odorless, tasteless, and nonmetallic gaseous element.

Transcendental _____ is a form of relaxation. This _____ is partly based on ancient Hindu ideology, and it was rediscovered in the twentieth _____ by an Indian spiritual teacher. Those who practice meditation concentrate on a _____, a word or phrase that they repeat over and over to achieve a state of relaxation. Physiologically, meditation decreases _____ consumption and _____ rate.

| **Word Bank:** | oxygen | technique | mantra | century | heart | meditation |

Singular and Plural Nouns

Directions: For each underlined noun in the following sentences, change the plural nouns to singular nouns and change the singular nouns to plural nouns. Write the new noun forms on the line beneath the sentence.

EXAMPLE:

A <u>firefly</u> is a winged nocturnal beetle that emits <u>light</u> through the bioluminescence process. <u>fireflies</u>   <u>lights</u>

1. The <u>flies</u> enjoyed our <u>picnic</u> as much as we did.

_____

2. Swimming in the <u>ocean</u> off the <u>coast</u> of Florida is dangerous because of a record number of <u>shark</u> attacks.

_____

3. A <u>neuron</u> is a basic structural <u>element</u> of the nervous system.

_____

4. The <u>Masai</u> are characteristically tall and slender <u>Africans</u> from Kenya and Tanzania.

_____

5. A <u>clock</u> is an <u>instrument</u> for measuring time.

_____

6. The little <u>pig</u> squealed when it was taken from its <u>mother</u>.

_____

7. Tiny Tim is the handicapped <u>son</u> of Bob Cratchit in Charles Dickens's *A Christmas Carol*.

_____

8. Kitsch, pronounced *kich*, is any <u>work</u> of art or other <u>objects</u> such as furniture that are intended to look expensive but are actually ugly or in bad taste.

_____

9. One of the most famous movie <u>monsters</u> is named King Kong, a giant <u>ape</u> that terrorizes New York City.

_____

10. Chicken pox is a mild but contagious <u>disease</u> that causes <u>blisters</u> on the skin.

_____

Feminine, Masculine, Neuter, and Indefinite Nouns

Directions: In the paragraph below, identify the gender of the underlined noun by writing the letter "F" for feminine, "M" for masculine, "N" for neuter, and "I" for indefinite noun on the line next to the noun.

EXAMPLE:

The <u>pterodactyl</u> ____N____ is an extinct flying <u>reptile</u> ____N____ from the Mesozoic age.

<u>Michel Foucault</u> _____ was a French <u>philosopher</u> _____ and <u>historian</u> _____. He studied the historical and social <u>contexts</u> _____ of <u>ideas</u> _____ and <u>institutions</u> _____ such as <u>prison</u> _____, <u>school</u> _____, <u>asylum</u> _____, and the <u>police force</u> _____. His basic <u>premise</u> was that <u>systems</u> _____ of knowledge, like <u>psychology</u> _____, have changed <u>humans</u> into <u>subjects</u> _____.

Noun Usage

Directions: Identify the usage of each of the underlined nouns in the following sentences by writing "subject noun," "predicate noun," and "possessive noun," or "object noun" on the blank at the beginning of the sentence.

EXAMPLE:

___object noun_____ The method of joining metal plates with a hot metal pin is called <u>riveting</u>.

1. _____ The <u>man's</u> face turned beet red when he heard the news about winning the prize.

2. _____ The young girl left her <u>surfboard</u> at the beach.

3. _____ <u>Jaundice</u> is the yellowing of the skin and the whites of the eyes that is caused by an excess of bile pigment in the blood.

4. _____ <u>Papyrus</u> is a perennial water plant that is native to southern Europe and was used by the ancient Egyptians to make writing material.

5. _____ The Eiffel Tower is a 985-foot Parisian <u>landmark</u> that was built for the Paris Exposition of 1889 and designed by Alexandre Gustave Eiffel.

6. _____ "Nukes" is a <u>slang term</u> for nuclear reactor or nuclear weapons.

7. _____ Dropping chemicals or a variety of small objects into clouds to produce rain is called <u>cloud seeding</u>.

8. _____ The Black Hills located in southwestern South Dakota and northeastern Wyoming are sacred mountains to the Sioux, a Native-American tribe.

9. _____ Passive resistance, which demonstrates opposition simply by not cooperating, is associated with Mahatma Gandhi, who opposed violence.

10. _____ Jack the Ripper, a nineteenth-century criminal responsible for several ghastly murders in London, was never caught.

Gerunds

Directions: Fill in the blanks with a gerund that best completes the thought of the sentence. Use the words in the Word Bank only once.

EXAMPLE:

Cheering loudly at a football game is part of the fun of going with your friends.

1. _____ is one of Fred Astaire's most notable talents. He and Ginger Rogers danced their way into the hearts of America in the early 1930s.

2. _____ across the English Channel would be a challenge for most people. Many people have difficulty getting from one end of a pool to the other.

3. _____ and marching in front of governmental buildings are effective ways for a group of people to draw attention to their beliefs and ideologies.

4. _____ is not one of the things that the Australian emu bird is capable of doing. With its powerful legs, though, it is a strong runner.

5. _____ is what happens at night when the old man sleeps on his back.

6. _____ can be beneficial to one's health and also makes others happy as well.

7. _____ is boring to those who dislike tedious tasks and being quiet for long periods of time.

8. _____ the piano will only improve your skills.

9. _____ in fresh snow is exhilarating and exhausting, especially when the slopes are steep and not crowded.

10. _____ new clothes and accessories at the mall is her favorite pastime.

Word Bank: laughing, dancing, fishing, swimming, protesting, buying, flying, practicing, snoring, skiing

Real-World Practice Activities

Reading

Directions: Read an article in a newspaper or a magazine. After you have completed reading the article, go back and find twenty (20) nouns that you find interesting and list them below. If you do not understand what the noun means, look for its definition in a dictionary.

1. _____
2. _____
3. _____
4. _____
5. _____
6. _____
7. _____
8. _____
9. _____
10. _____

11. _____
12. _____
13. _____
14. _____
15. _____
16. _____
17. _____
18. _____
19. _____
20. _____

Writing

Directions: Using some of the nouns that you found in the newspaper or magazine article, write a paragraph on the lines below that summarizes what you read.

_____

_____

_____

_____

_____

_____

_____

_____

_____

_____

_____

_____

Listening

Directions: Listen carefully to a news program on the radio, on television, or on the Internet. Write down a list of ten (10) nouns that you hear during the course of the show. Write them in the spaces provided below. When the show is over, write a sentence using each noun in its proper context according to the news story. NOTE: You will have to listen *carefully*—particularly in the beginning. However, the more you practice this skill of recognizing nouns while remembering the context of a story, the easier this skill will become.

1. (Noun)_____

_____

2. (Noun)_____

_____

3. (Noun)_____

_____

4. (Noun)_____

_____

5. (Noun)_____

_____

6. (Noun)_____

_____

7. (Noun)_____

_____

8. (Noun)_____

_____

9. (Noun)_____

_____

10. (Noun)_____

_____

Chapter 3

PRONOUNS

Pronouns are words that are used in place of nouns. *He, she, it, they, themselves, who,* and *what* are examples of pronouns. Basically, when we say that pronouns are used in sentences to replace a noun (here, the word *noun* is called the antecedent), the use of pronouns allow the sentences to be more interesting and less repetitious. Look at the sample sentences below. The first sentence uses the proper noun *Mary* (the antecedent) repeatedly. As you read it, you will probably understand why we should really be thankful for pronouns and whoever invented them. (Pronouns actually come from Old English, an early form of English dating from the mid-fifth century to the mid-twelfth century England.) However, back to the sentences: the first sentence is boring and repetitious to say the least. In the second sentence, two of the proper nouns are replaced with pronouns (*her* and *she*). Doing that drastically improves the sound of the sentence.

1. Mary went to see Mary's doctor to see if Mary had an infection.
2. Mary went to see *her* doctor to see if *she* had an infection.

Like nouns, pronouns are grouped into various categories according to their type (simple, compound, or phrasal), class (personal, relative, indefinite, interrogative, or demonstrative), number (singular or plural), gender (masculine, feminine, or neuter), person (first, second, or third), and case (nominative, possessive, or objective). There are also reflexive, intensive, and relative pronouns. The confusion that surrounds all of this will be clarified as we move through the chapter.

Vocabulary Development

1. **she** (shee) The girl, woman, or female animal that was previously named. Example: *She* bought tickets to see a play at the Globe Theatre in London.
2. **they** (thay) The group of people, animals, or things that were named previously. Example: Cape Canaveral is the site where *they* launch space flights and missiles.
3. **he** (hee) The boy, man, or male animal previously named. Example: Michel de Nostredame, better known as Nostradamus, was at one time an apothecary or pharmicist. However, *he* began making astrological predictions in 1547 and published them in rhyming quatrains.

4. **we** (wee) Referring to more than one person or to one person and one or more people who are associated with that person. Example: Sharks have well-developed jaws, and bony teeth. At least ten species of sharks attack humans. If *we* believe everything we read about sharks, it is a wonder how any human would have the courage to swim in tropical waters where sharks live.

5. **its** (its) The thing or object (occasionally an animal or small child) referred to or previously named. Example: Geology is the study of the Earth and *its* matter, origins, classifications, arrangements, changes, and history.

6. **us** (uhs) The objective form of *we* that refers to more than one person. Example: Jazz is a unique style of music that developed in the southern region of the United States and has captivated *us* for years.

7. **your** (yoor) Of or belonging to you. Example: *Your* collection of Terra-Cotta Warrior figures copied from those found in the tomb of Qin Shihuangdi in Xian, China, is remarkable.

8. **ours** (owrz) Referring to something, the one or ones that belong to us. Example: *Our* English class will be studying the works of Samuel Beckett, an influential writer of the twentieth century.

9. **whom** (hoom) What or which person or persons; the objective case of *who*. Example: The tennis player to *whom* you are referring is Arthur Ashe. He died of AIDS, which he contracted through a blood transfusion during heart surgery.

10. **theirs** (thairz) The one or the ones belonging to them or themselves. Example: The murals are *theirs*; they belong to the citizens of Mexico.

MASTER LIST OF PRONOUNS
(IN ALPHABETICAL ORDER)

all	him	other	they
another	himself	others	this
any	his	our	those
anybody	I	ours	us
anyone	it	ourselves	we
anything	its	several	what
both	itself	she	which
each	many	some	who
either	me	somebody	whom
everyone	mine	someone	whose
everything	my	something	you
few	neither	that	your
he	nobody	their	yours
her	no one	theirs	yourself
hers	nothing	them	yourselves
herself	one	these	

Antecedents

What are antecedents? The proper definition of the word in the broadest of terms is a preceding (something that comes before) thing or circumstance. However, in the grammatical sense that we are using it here, an antecedent is a word to which another word (particularly pronouns) refers. Example: The _author_ chooses to read from one of _his_ favorite books, *Waiting for Godot*. In this sentence, *author* is the antecedent and *his* is the word (a pronoun) to which it refers.

Practice I

Directions: Underline the antecedent in each of the sentences below and draw a box around the pronouns that refer to the antecedent.

EXAMPLE:

Jose thought the flowers he bought for his mother would make her happy.

1. The shark is determined to capture its next victim, the sea lion.
2. The volunteers worked day and night to meet their goals for the opening of the New Globe Theatre.
3. Geology is a broad field of science; it incorporates many areas of study, from rock to ice.
4. In a mural painted by Mexican muralist Diego Rivera, the woman seemed captivated by her surroundings.
5. Samuel Beckett was born in Ireland in 1906, but he emigrated to Paris in the 1920s.
6. Tennis is a game played by either two or four players, and it is sometimes known as lawn tennis.
7. The Theater of the Absurd developed from the philosophy of Albert Camus. However, it was applied to modern drama in 1961, which demonstrated the irrationality of life.
8. Terra-cotta is absorbent but rigid earthenware. It is used in building, sculpture, and pottery.
9. Shakespeare wrote plays that were performed in the Globe Theatre and he was part owner as well.
10. Although jazz trumpeter Miles Davis played with Charlie Parker, he formed a new band in 1955 that included saxophonist John Coltrane.

Pronoun Types

There are three different types of pronouns: simple, compound, and phrasal.

Simple

Simple pronouns are simply basic, everyday pronouns. Nothing complicated is involved. *I, he, she, it, its, you, we, they, who,* and *what* (among many others) are examples of simple pronouns.

Compound

A compound pronoun combines one (or more) words with a pronoun. Examples include *myself, himself, herself, yourself, itself, ourselves,* and *whatsoever.*

Phrasal

When two pronouns are placed together to form a phrase (a group of words that form a unit), they become phrasal pronouns. For example, *each other, one another, any others,* and *something that* are typical phrasal pronouns. The total list of all combined pronouns used to form phrasal pronouns would be lengthy.

Practice II

Directions: In the paragraph below, identify each of the italicized pronouns. If it is a simple pronoun, mark an "S" next to the pronoun. If it is a compound pronoun, mark a "C." If it is a phrasal pronoun, mark it with a "P."

EXAMPLE:

They compete against *each other* ___P___ only to improve their running times.

The continent of Asia is the home of the famous Terra-Cotta Warriors, *which* _____are found in China. Asia is the largest continent in the world. *It*____ extends in the north from a part of Russia that is in the area of the Arctic Circle to south of the equator in Indonesia. However, *its* _____western boundary with Europe follows a line that runs through the Ural Mountains, west of the Caspian Sea, and along the Caucasus. Asia's eastern border includes the islands of Japan. Although Europe and Asia form one large continent, *they* _____have always been considered two continents. The people *who*____ inhabit Asia make up half the world's total population. Mandarin Chinese has more speakers than *any other* _____ language of the continent. Economically, agriculture is important to Asia. Although less than 10 percent of the continent is cultivated, *it* _____ produces more than 90 percent of the world's rice, rubber, cotton, and tobacco.

Miscellaneous Pronouns

Personal, reflexive, relative, indefinite, interrogative, and demonstrative pronouns are unique. They are not categorized by type or form.

Personal

Personal pronouns are used in place of nouns and represent people, places, things, and ideas. *I, me, my, mine, you, your, yours, he, him, his, she, her, hers, they, them, their, theirs, we, us, our, ours,* and *it* are personal pronouns. However, a separate group of pronouns is included with the personal pronouns—the reflexive pronouns.

Reflexive

Reflexive pronouns are formed by adding the suffix *-self* or *-selves* to a personal pronoun. These are reflexive personal pronouns: *myself, himself, herself, itself, yourself, themselves,* and *ourselves*.

Practice III

Directions: Write a brief paragraph using ten (10) of the personal and reflexive pronouns listed: *I, me, mine, you, yours, he, him, his, she, her, hers, they, them, their, theirs, we, us, our, ours, it, myself, himself, herself, itself, yourself, themselves,* or *ourselves*. Choose sports, cooking, traveling, shopping, or animals as the subject of your paragraph. <u>Underline</u> each of the pronouns that you use.

_____

_____

_____

_____

_____

_____

_____

_____

_____

_____

_____

_____

Relative

A relative pronoun can be thought of just as you might consider a cousin, a brother or sister, or any other person that is related to you: a relative. This type of pronoun relates or links one part of a sentence to a word or phrase in another part of the sentence. The following words are relative pronouns: *who, whose, whom, which, what, that,* and *those.*

Practice IV

Directions: Identify the relative pronouns in the following sentences by <u>underlining</u> them. Reminder: *who, whose, whom, which, what, that,* and *those* are relative pronouns.

EXAMPLE:

The onion is a plant <u>that</u> belongs to the lily family and <u>whose</u> strong distinctive odor and taste are offensive to some.

1. It was Nostradamus, the French prophet and astrologer, who was afraid of being persecuted during the Inquisition for heresy.
2. Jazz music consists of syncopated rhythms that are based on improvisation or creative, spur-of-the-moment interpretations.
3. Mao Zedong is the Chinese statesman to whom credit is given for helping to establish the People's Republic of China.
4. The novella is a highly structured, short narrative that is longer than a short story but shorter than a novel.
5. Artists Diego Rivera and José Clemente Orozco, whose murals are known internationally, are both from Mexico.
6. The U.S. Open is now played at Arthur Ashe Stadium, which was named after the respected African-American tennis player.
7. Terra-cotta is known as "baked earth," which is fired in a kiln at fairly low temperatures.
8. The name *Canaveral* is Spanish for "canebreak" and is derived from those explorers who discovered the area.
9. The theory of continental drift and the concept of seafloor spreading that were replaced by the theory of plate tectonics are fairly new to the field of geology.
10. The original Globe Theatre was built in an area known as Southwark on the bank of the Thames (pronounced "tems") River, which is now known as Bankside.

Problems with "Who" and "Whom"

Using the two relative pronouns *who* and *whom* can be tricky and confusing. The word *who* is used commonly and informally in conversations and casual writing. It is used as the subject or noun part of the sentence. The word *whom* is more appropriately used in formal situations and is used as the object of the sentence. Review the following example sentences:

1. *Who* is singing that beautiful song? (*Who* is the subject of the sentence.)
2. You will be touring the museum with the guide to *whom* your group is assigned. (*Whom* is used here as part of the <u>object</u> of the sentence.)

Dreaded English Rules to Remember:

- If the *who* pronoun can be replaced with *he/his* or *she/her*, then it is the <u>subject</u> of the sentence. By applying this rule to the first sentence above, the word *who* can actually be replaced with either *he* or *she*. Therefore, the pronoun is the subject of the sentence and *who* should be used.

- When these prepositions (*in, of, on, without, at, from*, and *to*) precede (come before) the pronoun, use *whom*. Apply this rule to the second sentence above. The word *to* precedes the pronoun *whom*; therefore the use of *whom* is correct.

Practice V

Directions: Use the two rules listed above for the use of *who* and *whom*, and write the correct form of the pronoun on the line.

EXAMPLE:

To __whom__ are you speaking?

1. _____ became the only African-American tennis player to win the singles tournament at Wimbledon?

2. Louis Armstrong, without _____ the jazz world would be minus an influential and charismatic musician, was known for his flashy trumpet playing and gravelly voiced singing.

3. Sharks, _____ have a keen sense of smell, are able to detect an incredibly small amount of blood in seawater.

4. The original Globe Theatre was owned by actors _____ were shareholders and part of a group known as Lord Chamberlain's Men.

5. It is believed that the faces of the 8,099 Terra-Cotta Warriors in the archeological site, all of _____ were molded individually, are unique.

6. _____ was the first man in space?

7. Despite being plagued with controversy, Nostradamus, _____ allegedly wrote hundreds of quatrains, continues to fascinate many followers today.

8. John Glenn, _____ was the first man to orbit Earth in 1962, became a U.S. senator.

9. Professional tennis players are athletes _____ most would consider to be focused and competitive.

10. Billie Jean King, the U.S. tennis player on _____ many young players modeled their skills, dominated women's singles division tennis in the late 1960s and through the 1970s.

Problems with "Which" and "That"

The use of the relative pronouns *which* and *that* can also be tricky and confusing. In fact, most often *which* is used when *that* should be.

The pronoun *which* introduces a relative clause. Relative clauses provide additional information about something in a sentence. However, these relative clauses can be removed without changing the meaning of the statement in the main clause (the main part of the sentence).

EXAMPLE:

The launch pad, <u>which had recently undergone renovations</u>, was readied for the next rocket to be launched into space.

Look at the underlined portion of the sentence. If this section is removed, it does not affect the meaning of the sentence. This section simply adds detail. It is related but not vital to the sentence. Without the relative clause, the sentence reads, "The launch pad was readied for the next rocket to be launched into space." It still makes sense.

The word *that* introduces a clause and specifically identifies the thing to which the clause is attached.

EXAMPLE:

The launch pad that had recently undergone renovations was readied for the next rocket to be launched into space.

Here, the reader is told which launch pad it is. Because clauses beginning with *that* identify something specific, they cannot be removed without affecting the meaning of the sentence. Notice that there is no comma (,) preceding *that* as opposed to the comma that precedes the clause beginning with *which*. Clauses starting with *that* help form an entire unit of meaning.

Practice VI

Directions: In the sentences below, write either the word *that* or the word *which* on the line as needed to complete the sentence.

EXAMPLE:

Staccato is a term used in music <u>that</u> indicates <u>that</u> the notes should be performed in a sharp, abrupt, and clear-cut manner.

1. The Globe Theatre, _____ is located in London, was burned down in 1613 and rebuilt in 1614.

2. The sharks _____ swim off the coast of Florida are particularly dangerous to humans.

3. Glaciers, _____ are large masses of ice, are one area of geology that is of great concern considering the recent escalation of global warming.

4. Cape Canaveral was chosen for rocket launches to take advantage of the centrifugal force of Earth's rotation _____ is the greatest close to the equator.

5. Some of Diego Rivera's best murals, _____ express many of his political and social beliefs, can be found in the National Palace in Mexico City.

6. Modern tennis, _____ is a game played with a ball and racket, originated in England in the 1860s.

7. Teotihuacán is an ancient pre-Columbian city about thirty miles north of Mexico City _____ flourished between 100 B.C. and A.D. 700.

8. The name Teotihuacán, _____ was given by the Aztecs after the fall of the city, means "where man becomes god."

9. The Pyramid of the Sun and the Pyramid of the Moon are two archeological sites _____ still exist in the area of Teotihuacán.

10. Most of what is known about the ancient city was discovered from the murals _____ are found on the site.

Indefinite

Indefinite pronouns are those that refer to an unknown or unnamed person or thing. Compare the following list of indefinite pronouns to other pronouns that we have encountered. Indefinite pronouns definitely do not refer to anyone or anything specifically. They are representative of nonspecific people or things. *All, another, any, anybody, anyone, anything, both, each, each one, each other, either, everybody, everyone, everything, few, many, neither, nobody, none, no one, nothing, one, one another, ones, other, others, several, some, somebody, someone,* and *something* are indefinite pronouns.

Practice VII

Directions: Underline each **indefinite** pronoun in the list that follows.

you	him	that	your
her	no one	theirs	his
hers	nothing	them	yourselves
one	these	other	they
another	himself	others	this
any	many	our	those
both	he	nobody	their
itself	she	which	yours
each	neither	some	who
either	anybody	I	ours
anyone	it	ourselves	we
anything	its	several	what
me	somebody	whom	herself
everyone	mine	someone	whose
everything	my	something	yourself
few	such	all	us

Interrogative

Like the name implies, an interrogative pronoun asks a question or interrogates (like a detective). *Who, whose, whom, which,* and *what* are interrogative pronouns. NOTE: Interrogative sentences are punctuated with a question mark (?).

Practice VIII

Directions: Write one sentence for each of the following interrogative pronouns and underline the pronoun in each sentence that you write.

EXAMPLE:

<u>Who</u> is going to practice tennis in the morning?

who	1.	
whose	2.	
whom	3.	
which	4.	
what	5.	
which	6.	
what	7.	
who	8.	
whom	9.	
whose	10.	

Demonstrative

These pronouns demonstrate, show, or point out specific people, places, or things without naming them. *This, that, these,* and *those* are demonstrative pronouns.

Practice IX

Directions: Rewrite the following sentences by replacing the underlined words with one of the demonstrative pronouns listed below. NOTE: You may need to add, subtract, or change words from the sentence to make it grammatically correct. Demonstrative pronouns: *this, that, these, those*

EXAMPLE:

<u>The Puritans</u> closed the Globe Theatre in London in 1642.
<u>That</u> religious group closed the Globe Theatre in London in 1642.

1. After being demolished in 1644, <u>the Globe Theatre</u> was rebuilt and then reopened in 1995.

   _____

   _____

2. <u>The sample of fossilized</u> remains will be sent to the museum's laboratory for further study.

   _____

   _____

3. In 1980, Arthur Ashe became the nonplaying captain of the <u>United States' Davis Cup</u> team.

   _____

   _____

4. <u>Miles Davis, Charlie Parker, B. B. King</u>, and many others are legendary in the field of jazz and blues.

   _____

   _____

5. <u>Samuel Beckett's</u> plays, *Waiting for Godot, Endgame,* and *Happy Days,* explore ideas of survival, paralysis, and suffering.

   _____

   _____

6. <u>The main</u> street in the ancient city of Teotihuacán is called Avenue of the Dead.

   _____

   _____

7. *<u>Waiting for Godot</u>* the absurdist play by Samuel Beckett, was first performed in French at a theater in Paris.

   _____

   _____

8. <u>The uneventful and repetitive</u> plot of *<u>Waiting for Godot</u>* symbolizes the meaninglessness of human life and connects the play to the themes of existentialist philosophy.

   _____

   _____

9. <u>Dostoevsky and Kafka</u> are considered literary existentialists and wrote about characters who struggle with hopelessness and absurdity.

   _____

   _____

10. <u>The new Globe</u> Theatre in London is the first building with a thatched roof since the Great Fire of London in 1666.

    _____

    _____

Forms of Personal Pronouns

The form of a pronoun tells whether the personal pronoun is singular or plural and whether it is first person, second person, or third person. It also determines the pronoun's case, which could be nominative, possessive, or objective. Finally, the form of the personal pronoun indicates the pronoun's gender: masculine, feminine, or neuter. That sounds like a lot to take in at once, but it is easier to understand by taking it step by step.

Number of a Pronoun

The number simply indicates whether the pronoun is singular (one) or plural (more than one).

- Singular pronouns include *I, my, mine, me, you, your, yours, he, his, him, she, hers, her, its,* and *it*.
- Plural pronouns include *we, our, ours, us, you, your, yours, they, their, theirs,* and *them*.

Practice X

Directions: In the sentences that follow, choose the correct form of pronoun that best fits the sentence. Write the correct pronoun on the line provided.

EXAMPLE:

> she/her The Statue of Liberty in New York Harbor depicts a woman who represents liberty by raising a torch in ____her____ right hand and holding a tablet in ____her____ left.

1. your/I Yesterday _____ went to the theater to watch a play that was written by Samuel Beckett.

2. I/his It was _____ idea to listen to jazz music during our lunch break.

3. They/Mine _____ have achieved a strong following of admirers in the area of muralist painting.

4. she/our Like the groundlings who stood on the ground in front of the stage at the Globe Theatre hundreds of years ago, _____ family experienced the same.

5. it/they The sheer number of Terra-Cotta Warriors in the archeological dig as well as the manner in which _____ are lined up is a spectacular sight to see.

6. it/their Trompe L'oeil is a French term; _____means "trick the eye" and is a type of mural.

7. we/my In studying Hawaiian mythology, _____come to understand that sharks figure prominently in the stories that have been passed down for generations.

8. they/we Very few sharks are able to survive in public aquariums, but _____ are living longer now because of improved knowledge in feeding habits and habitat maintenance.

9. he/his   Tommy Johnson, a delta blues musician, is known for the story of selling _____ soul to the devil in exchange for musical talent.

10. Hers/Her   _____ voice is similar to Bessie Smith's, a blues singer of the 1920s and 1930s.

Person of a Pronoun

The person of a pronoun indicates whether the pronoun (person) is speaking, is spoken to, or is spoken about. An easy way to remember this is by looking at various novels. When the novel is written in first person, the word *I* is used because that is who is speaking and the narration is being told by someone specific. If a novel is written in second person (which is rare), the words *you* and *yours* would be used. Likewise, a novel written in third person would use *he, she,* or *it* because that is who is being discussed or observed. See the chart on page 50 to visualize person and case.

- First-person pronouns include *I, my, mine, me, we, our, ours,* and *us.*
- Second-person pronouns are *you, your,* and *yours*
- Third-person pronouns include *he, she, it, his, her, hers, its, him, her, it, they, their, theirs,* and *them.* Notice that third-person pronouns include masculine, feminine, and neuter pronouns.

Practice XI

Directions: Read the sentences below, and indicate what person they are written in by writing *first, second,* or *third* on the line that precedes the sentence.

EXAMPLE:

___*Third*___ Alexander Calder is an American sculptor who is well-known for his mobiles, a sculpture made up of suspended shapes that move.

_____ 1. When he left for France, Nostradamus was intent upon finishing his doctorate, but the university had other plans.

_____ 2. You know that if you study long enough, you will be able to finish your degree and work at the career of your choosing.

_____ 3. I did not understand the lecture topic; I thought the professor was going to discuss anatomy and not physiology.

_____ 4. That was all it needed, a little lubrication and the student's bicycle was ready for use.

_____ 5. Our knowledge in the field of pharmacology is limited, and we will have to take a course on it next semester.

_____ 6. I did not know that Mexico is officially known as Estados Unidos Mexicanos.

_____ 7. Your research on the history of jazz and blues music turned out to be quite interesting.

_____ 8. They began their journey to the Lascaux Caves after catching up on sleep from a long flight to Paris.

_____ 9. I discovered that the paintings in the Lascaux Caves date back to 13,000–15,000 B.C.

_____ 10. They told us that the caves were discovered in 1940 by four teenagers and a dog.

Pronoun Cases

The case of the pronoun is the form that it takes to show its relationship to the other words in a sentence. There are three cases of pronouns in the English language: nominative, possessive, and objective. See the chart on page 50.

Nominative Case

Pronouns in the nominative case describe a pronoun that is used as the subject of a clause. *I, you, he, she, it, we,* and *they* are pronouns in the nominative case.

EXAMPLE:

I went to the market this morning to get some milk. The pronoun *I* is used as the subject of the sentence. *I* is what the sentence is referring to or about.

Practice XII

Directions: Write a sentence for each of the nominative case pronouns listed below. Remember, in the nominative case, each pronoun is the subject of the sentence and should be placed at or near the beginning of the sentence.

EXAMPLE:

I am the leader of the discussion topic today in class.

1. you _____

2. he _____

3. she _____

4. it _____

5. we _____

6. they _____

7. we _____

8. they _____

9. she _____

10. you _____

Possessive Case

The possessive case describes a pronoun that shows ownership or possession. Unlike nouns, however, apostrophes (') are not used to show possession in pronouns. *Her, hers, his, its, my, mine, our, ours, their, theirs, your,* and *yours* are possessive case pronouns.

Practice XIII

Directions: Underline the possessive case pronouns in the following sentences. NOTE: There may be more than one pronoun in the sentences.

EXAMPLE:

My Fair Lady is a stage musical that is based on the play *Pygmalion* by George Bernard Shaw.

1. It was my understanding that your area of expertise would be the subject of a debate on ancient Mexico.

2. Her record for writing absurdist plays surpasses any that have preceded her.

3. That is not yours! Give it back! It belongs in his grandfather's ancient artifacts collection.

4. Mexico is proud of its historic achievements that date back to pre-Columbian times.

5. His newest piece of art is definitely more outlandish than yours.

6. Your wish to become the first to research the life expectancy of sharks may be a dream come true.

7. Their music originates not only in the southern regions of the United States but from Africa as well.

8. Its name is Spanish for "canebreak."

9. Much to her surprise, the award for best new artist was given to a young woman who was inspired by blues music.

10. His works are often linked to the Theater of the Absurd.

Objective Case

When a pronoun is used as the direct object, indirect object, or the object of a preposition, it is known as the objective case. *Me, you, him, her, it, us, you,* and *them* are examples of pronouns in the objective case.

Practice XIV

Directions: Using one of the following objective case pronouns, write in the word that best completes the following sentences. NOTE: There may be more than one pronoun that can be used to complete the sentence. However, read the sentences carefully; often there is a clue that indicates which pronoun to use. Use each word only once.

EXAMPLE:

> Yesterday when you gave ____me____ the article on the history of the War on Poverty, I did not realize the extent of the program. (Clue: The pronoun *I* indicates the need for using *me* in the early part of the sentence.)

> **Word Bank:** me, you, him, her, it, us, them

1. When was the last time that you gave _____ the directions? They should be here by now.
2. This discussion is all about _____. She is exaggerating everything that she is saying about herself.
3. The strange dream that I had last night did not scare _____ at all; it was simply weird and like science fiction.
4. Perhaps the next time you need a partner you could ask _____.
5. Judging the final contest will be up to _____, and we need to cooperate and think logically.
6. I refuse to say anything about _____. There really is no need to discuss it.
7. We do not want to know what he thinks; we want to know what _____ think.

Personal Pronouns: Number, Person, and Case

The following chart visually demonstrates the breakdown of pronouns in number (singular or plural), person (first, second, or third), and case (nominative, possessive, or objective). Review the chart and the sections above on number, person, and case. Then complete the exercise that follows.

NUMBER, PERSON, AND CASE OF PERSONAL PRONOUNS			
	Nominative Case	**Possessive Case**	**Objective Case**
First-Person Singular	I	my, mine	me
Second-Person Singular	you	your, yours	you
Third-Person Singular	he	his	him
	she	her, hers	her
	it	its	it
	Nominative Case	**Possessive Case**	**Objective Case**
First-Person Plural	we	our, ours	us
Second-Person Plural	you	your, yours	you
Third-Person Plural	they	their, theirs	them

Practice XV

Directions: On the lines below, write a sentence using the pronoun from the correct area of the chart above and then underline the pronoun that you used.

EXAMPLE:

Second-person singular—nominative case (that pronoun is <u>you</u>)
If <u>you</u> do not go to bed early tonight, *you* will never get up in time to get to the airport.

1. First-person singular—objective case

_____

_____

2. Third-person plural—possessive case

_____

_____

3. Second-person plural—objective case

_____

_____

4. Third-person singular—nominative case

_____

_____

5. First-person singular—possessive case

_____

_____

6. First-person plural—nominative case

_____

_____

7. Third-person plural—objective case

_____

_____

8. First-person singular—possessive case

_____

_____

9. Second-person singular—nominative case

_____

_____

10. Second-person plural—possessive case

_____

_____

Pronoun Genders

In the English language, nouns and pronouns are feminine, masculine, or neuter.

- Feminine pronouns are _she, her,_ and _hers._
- Masculine pronouns are _he, his,_ and _him._
- Neuter pronouns are _it, its, they, their, theirs, them, you, your,_ and _yours._

Practice XVI

Directions: Identify the gender of each of the underlined pronouns used in the sentences below. Write _F_ on the line for feminine pronouns, _M_ on the line for masculine pronouns, and _N_ on the line for neuter pronouns.

EXAMPLE:

   _M_   Although <u>he</u> was born in Ireland, Samuel Beckett is considered a French writer.

1. _____ The coat belonged to Mr. Beckett; <u>he</u> left it in the theater.
2. _____ <u>Their</u> reaction to the play _Endgame_ was mixed.
3. _____ The Nobel Prize Committee awarded <u>him</u> the coveted prize in 1969.
4. _____ Samuel Beckett wrote in both English and French; <u>he</u> was unique in that respect.

5. _____ <u>Your</u> understanding of the Theater of the Absurd is important in understanding Beckett's literary works.

6. _____ The Theater of the Absurd has <u>its</u> origins in Dadaism, nonsense poetry and avant-garde art that date back to the 1910s and 1920s.

7. _____ Meaningless plots and both repetitious and nonsensical dialogue are characteristic of <u>its</u> genre.

8. _____ <u>She</u> did not realize at the time that the play would be so unique.

9. _____ <u>Her</u> critique of *Waiting for Godot* was applauded by the editors of the entertainment section of the newspaper.

10. _____ After realizing that the stack of books was <u>theirs</u>, she boxed them up and shipped them to the school.

Chapter 3 Review Quizzes

Vocabulary Review Quiz

Directions: Write the letter of the correct definition on the line next to the pronoun that it defines.

1. _____ she   A. The one or ones belonging to them or themselves

2. _____ us   B. The female that was previously named

3. _____ your   C. The objective case of *we*, more than one person

4. _____ whom   D. Of or belonging to you

5. _____ ours   E. Referring to more than one person

6. _____ theirs   F. What or which person, the objective case of *who*

7. _____ they   G. The group that was named previously

8. _____ its   H. The male previously named

9. _____ we   I. The thing or object previously named

10. _____ he   J. Referring to something that belongs to us

Pronoun Definitions

Directions: Select the correct definition and write the letter of the answer on the line to the right of the number.

1. _____ There are three different types of pronouns. Which is not a type of pronoun?
   a. simple
   b. phrasal
   c. global
   d. compound

2. _____ A pronoun that shows possessive case does not use _____ to show possession.
   a. a comma
   b. an apostrophe
   c. a period
   d. a question mark

3. _____ The person of a pronoun indicates whether the pronoun (person) is speaking, is spoken to, or is spoken about. The three persons or voices of a pronoun are:
   a. first, third, sixth
   b. first, second, fourth
   c. first, fourth, third
   d. first, second, third

4. _____ Reflexive pronouns are formed by adding the suffix _____ .
   a. *-ed* or *-es*
   b. *-ate* or *-ite*
   c. *-self* or *-selves*
   d. *-tion* or *-ger*

5. _____ When a pronoun is used as the direct object, indirect object, or the object of a preposition, it is known as a pronoun in the _____ case.
   a. objective
   b. possessive
   c. relative
   d. interrogative

6. _____ *Who, whose, whom, which,* and *what* are _____ pronouns.
   a. objective
   b. possessive
   c. relative
   d. interrogative

7. _____ The type of pronoun that relates or links one part of a sentence to a word or phrase in another part of the sentence is known as a _____ pronoun.
   a. objective
   b. possessive
   c. relative
   d. interrogative

8. _____ Pronoun genders include_____ .
   a. masculine
   b. feminine
   c. neuter
   d. all of the above

9. _____ A pronoun is used to replace a _____ .
   a. noun
   b. verb
   c. adjective
   d. adverb

10. _____ *Yourselves* is a _____ pronoun.
   a. relative
   b. compound
   c. reclusive
   d. demonstrative

Pronoun Antecedents

Directions: In the paragraph below, underline all <u>of the antecedents</u> and draw a box around all of the pronouns.

<u>The Bogside Artists</u> are mural painters who live and work in Northern Ireland. Their names are Tom Kelly, William Kelly, and Kevin Hasson. After working together since 1993, they finally completed what is known as the *People's Gallery* in 2004. It is a tribute to the local residents and the struggles they have endured in the name of human rights. The ten large murals are located in the area of Bogside, which is a neighborhood outside the city of Derry in Northern Ireland. They span the entire length of Rossville Street. This area was the site of intense political unrest between the British Army and the Irish Republican Army, including the Battle of the Bogside and Bloody Sunday. Thousands of people visit the murals each year and pay tribute to lives lost in the name of human rights.

Pronoun Types: Simple, Compound, Phrasal

Directions: Read the paragraph below, and select a **simple**, **compound**, or **phrasal** pronoun from the Word Bank below that best completes the meaning of the sentence. Write the pronoun on the line within the paragraph. NOTE: You may use the words in the Word Bank more than once.

EXAMPLE:

The brothers Grimm were two German authors known for __their__ often frightening fairy tales such as *Little Red Riding Hood, Hansel and Gretel,* and *Rumpelstiltskin* among many others.

The other day while Tim and _____ were hanging out at home, and mostly because _____ had nothing better to do, _____ started a discussion about sharks of all things. _____ told Tim that there are more than 360 different species of sharks. Then _____ told _____ that sharks normally swim at about 5 miles (8 km) per hour, but when _____ attack _____ reach speeds up to about 30 miles (48 km) per hour. _____was interesting to discover that _____of us knew facts about sharks that the _____ _____ did not. So by the end of the discussion, _____were quite proud of _____. That was not only because _____ both managed to learn a great deal more about sharks but because the subject is _____ _____ neither one of us would ever bring up in a normal day-to-day conversation.

> **Word Bank:** I, he, she, each, it, its, me, they, us, we, who, what, myself, himself, herself, yourself, itself, ourselves, each other, one another, any others, other one, something that

Pronoun Classes: Personal/Reflexive, Relative, Indefinite, Interrogative, Demonstrative

Directions: For each sentence below, indicate whether the underlined pronoun in the sentence is used as a personal, reflexive, relative, indefinite, interrogative, or demonstrative pronoun. Write *P* for personal, *RX* for reflexive, *RL* for relative, *ID* for indefinite, *IT* for interrogative, and *D* for demonstrative.

EXAMPLE:

__*IT*__ What did <u>you</u> say about the film *The Illusionist?*

1. _____ Dominic should take better care of <u>himself</u> if he wants to succeed in politics.

2. _____ <u>I</u> believe that the Terra-Cotta Warriors that are located in China should be considered one of the wonders of the world.

3. _____ The song <u>that</u> just played on the radio sounded like a song that jazz great and one of the world's best saxophonists, Charlie Parker, used to play.

4. _____ To <u>whom</u> are you speaking?

5. _____ The New Globe Theatre, <u>which</u> is located in London, holds about 1,500 people as opposed to the 3,000 that the original Globe Theatre held.

6. _____ <u>All</u> of the officers will attend the initiation meeting on Monday.

7. _____ <u>This</u> is it? This is all there is to the show?

8. _____ <u>Whose</u> side are you on?

9. _____ <u>That</u> last tennis match will go down in history as one of the best played at Wimbledon.

10. _____ <u>Both</u> of you need to finish your dinner and then get your homework done.

Forms of Personal Pronouns: Number and Person

Directions: On the line at the beginning of each sentence below, identify whether the underlined pronouns are *FPS* for first person singular, *SPS* for second-person singular, *TPS* for third-person singular, *FPP* for first-person plural, *SPP* for second-person plural, or *TPP* for third-person plural.

EXAMPLE:

__*TPS*__ Although <u>he</u> is known for developing the hydrogen bomb, Andrei Sakharov, the Nobel Peace Prize winner, was an outspoken campaigner for human rights.

1. _____ <u>I</u> refuse to believe that the shuttle launch will be delayed another day.

2. _____ When the news of the crash hit the media, <u>they</u> handled it professionally and thoroughly.

3. _____ <u>She</u> said it was going to be a difficult lesson to learn.

4. _____ <u>You</u> told me that B. B. King was going to be playing at Birdland tonight.

5. _____ Since I know the history of Earth's icebergs, <u>it</u> does not make any sense to explore the glacier theory any further.

6. _____ When <u>they</u> mentioned that a film about Diego Rivera was going to be released, the citizens of Guanajuato, his birthplace, were excited.

7. _____ <u>It</u> has come to my attention that my edition of *Waiting for Godot* is in my suitcase at home.

8. _____ <u>We</u> do not know the true reason for the recent climate changes, although many scientists suspect global warming is the cause.

9. _____ After spending most of the day at the beach, <u>she</u> went home to study and prepare for her final exam.

10. _____ Considering the extent of damage that was suffered in the collapse of the scaffolding at the archeological site, <u>I</u> now understand why the results are taking so long.

Pronoun Cases: Nominative, Possessive, Objective

Directions: Identify the usage of each of the following pronoun cases by writing *N* for nominative, *P* for possessive, or *O* for objective on the line before the sentence.

EXAMPLE:

_*N*_ <u>He</u> said that he was going to Venice for the summer.

1. _____ <u>My</u> situation has changed since the last time you saw me.

2. _____ When was the last time that you called <u>her</u>? She seems to have lost her way.

3. _____ <u>Their</u> job is to complete the research and then to move on to the next exploration site.

4. _____ Knowing that our vacation will soon be over, it will be up to <u>you</u> to finish the painting when we return.

5. _____ That is <u>mine</u>.

6. _____ <u>We</u> will be going to Ireland soon to see the murals of the *People's Gallery*.

7. _____ Simply speaking, the legality of the matter is up to <u>him</u>.

8. _____ <u>Their</u> boat was attacked by a great white shark off the coast of California.

9. _____ Will you give <u>us</u> directions to the studio?

10. _____ <u>I</u> will be sending Benjamin the information as soon as it arrives from New York.

Pronoun Genders: Feminine, Masculine, Neuter

Directions: Identify each of the pronouns listed below—*F* for feminine, *M* for masculine, and *N* for neuter.

EXAMPLE:

  N   theirs

1. _____ hers
2. _____ his
3. _____ its
4. _____ they
5. _____ your
6. _____ she
7. _____ them
8. _____ he
9. _____ yours
10. _____ it

Real-World Practice Activities

Reading

Directions: Read the article below. When you have finished reading it, go back and underline at least twenty (20) pronouns.

Nostradamus, who was born in 1503, is considered one of the most well-known authors of prophecies. The first edition of his most famous work, *Les Propheties,* was published in approximately 1555. This book is internationally popular and has been rarely out of print since his death in 1566.

Nostradamus is known for predicting various world events, and the controversy that surrounds his writings continues today. What is interesting about his writings is the fact that Nostradamus wrote all of his predictions in rhyming quatrains. Because of his concern for the criticism of religious fanatics, he intentionally obscured the meanings of his prophecies by using a mixture of languages such as Greek, Italian, Latin, and French. He also included various word games and syntax that he imitated from the works of Virgil. The majority of his quatrains deal with various disasters such as plagues, earthquakes, floods, wars, invasions, battles, murders, and droughts, among many other traumatic events. However, these prophesies are approached by both supporters and skeptics alike, and the extent of the writings on Nostradamus is extensive.

In addition to his prophecies, Nostradamus wrote a series of almanacs beginning in the year 1550. Because of their popularity, he decided to write one each year and sometimes more than one per year. All totaled, the almanacs contain at least 6,338 prophecies. He became well-known for his almanacs and was sought out by prominent people from all over Europe who requested advice and horoscopes from him.

Near the end of his life, Nostradamus suffered from gout. He left an extensive amount of money and property to his wife and six children upon his death. Nostradamus is interred in the Collegiale St. Laurent in France.

Writing

Directions: Use an Internet search, an encyclopedia, or a book from a library to locate information about the life and prophecies of Nostradamus. After doing the research, write a paragraph on what you have discovered. What are your thoughts about this man's works? Are you a supporter or a skeptic of Nostradamus?

Listening

Directions: Listen carefully to a news program on the radio, on television, or on the Internet. Write down a list of ten (10) pronouns and their antecedents that you hear during the course of the show in the spaces provided below. NOTE: You will have to listen *carefully*—particularly in the beginning. However, the more you practice listening for specific items, the easier this skill will become.

Program Title: _____

Date: _____

1. Pronoun _____

   Antecedent _____

2. Pronoun _____

   Antecedent_____

3. Pronoun _____

   Antecedent _____

4. Pronoun _____

   Antecedent _____

5. Pronoun _____

   Antecedent _____

6. Pronoun _____

   Antecedent _____

7. Pronoun_____

   Antecedent_____

8. Pronoun_____

   Antecedent_____

9. Pronoun _____

   Antecedent_____

10. Pronoun_____

    Antecedent_____

Chapter 4

VERBS

Verbs are words that express action (read, fly), occurrence (shrink, flash), or a state of being (live, exist). Without verbs, a sentence would not be a sentence. Verbs are needed to complete a thought or statement. As we discovered with our studies of nouns and pronouns, there is a great deal to know about the various parts of speech; verbs are no different. In this chapter, we will explore the many types of verbs and their uses. The manner in which verbs are used varies according to many factors such as number, person, tense, mood, and voice. We will look at action verbs, irregular verbs, linking and helping verbs, auxiliary verbs, gerunds, infinitives, transitive verbs, intransitive verbs, participles, and the conjugation of verbs. Fasten your seat belt, because this is going to be one exciting ride through the world of verbs.

Vocabulary Development

1. **heed** (heed) Take notice of; attend to.
2. **operate** (op er ate) To manage, work, control; to put or keep in a functional state; to perform a surgical procedure.
3. **raft** (raft) To transport as or on a floating structure; to cross water.
4. **admonish** (ad mon ish) To reprove or give earnest advice.
5. **fortify** (for ti fy) To strengthen physically, morally, or mentally; to provide or equip with defensive works.
6. **juxtapose** (jux ta pose) To place things side by side or by another.
7. **unite** (u nite) To join together; to become one; to combine.
8. **shrink** (shrink) To make or become smaller.
9. **erode** (e rode) To wear away; to destroy or be destroyed gradually.
10. **minimize** (min i mize) To reduce to or estimate at the smallest possible amount or degree; to represent as less than the true value or importance.

Action Verbs

Action verbs are words that demonstrate what a person or a thing can actually do physically or mentally. Examples include: *run, swim, buzz, hope, giggle, watch, think, reach, eat, write, type,* and *sniff.*

Practice I

Directions: Write the action verb from each sentence on the line provided at the beginning of the sentence. On the line at the end of the sentence, write *Physical* if the verb is an action word that a person or thing can do physically, or write *Mental* if the verb is mental activity.

EXAMPLE:

_____*hope*_____ Member countries at the G8 conference hope to unite regarding matters of foreign policy. __*mental*__

1. _____ Bears kill their prey with blows from their powerful forepaws.
   _____

2. _____ Deep-sea divers ascend slowly to the surface to avoid the bends.
   _____

3. _____ Dorothea Dix inspired legislation for improved treatment of mentally ill patients in state mental hospitals. _____

4. _____ The Orinoco River flows from the Sierra Parima Mountains in southern Venezuela, northwest to Columbia, and then east to the Atlantic Ocean. _____

5. _____ Danish writer Isak Dinesen hoped to convey her life on an African coffee plantation through writing *Out of Africa*. _____

6. _____ Michelangelo believed that his statue *David* symbolized the newfound confidence of the Florentine Republic in the early 1500s.
   _____

7. _____ King Richard III's death at the Battle of Bosworth ended the Wars of the Roses in England in 1485. _____

8. _____ Ayers Rock, the largest single rock in the world, is known to Native Australians as Uluru. _____

9. _____ André Le Nôtre, the French landscape gardener, established a grandiose and geometric style in his gardens in Versailles, Chantilly, and the Tuileries in Paris. _____

10. _____ The pirates planned to attack unsuspecting ships on the high seas off Africa. _____

Linking Verbs

A linking verb connects or links the noun or pronoun of a sentence with another word or group of words in the sentence. These verbs are also known as subject complements or helping verbs. It is easier to remember that these verbs are helpers. Many linking verbs are forms of the verb "to be." The following chart illustrates the various forms of the linking verb "to be" as well as other linking verbs.

Linking Verb Forms of "To Be"		
am	may be	must be
are	could be	would be
be	had been	should be
being	has been	shall have been
is	have been	will have been
was	shall be	could have been
were	will be	should have been
can be	might be	would have been
Other Commonly Used Linking Verbs		
appear	feel	sound
become	look	taste
turn	stay	remain
grow	seem	stand

- The Pilgrims _were_ a group of English Puritans who immigrated to North America in 1620 seeking religious freedom. ("Were" is the linking verb. It links the phrase "a group of English Puritans" to the noun "Pilgrims.")
- The pineapple _is_ a tropical plant cultivated in many areas of the world. ("Is" is the linking verb. It connects the phrase "a tropical plant" to the noun "pineapple.")

NOTE: Some verbs (those that are listed on the chart under the heading "Other Commonly Used Linking Verbs" have a dual role in the verb world—and can be either action verbs or linking verbs.

- Pineapples _grow_ in tropical climates. (Action verb)
- Pineapples _grow_ best in tropical climates. (Linking verb)

Practice II

Directions: Read the following sentences, underline the <u>action verbs</u>, and draw a box around the |linking verbs|.

EXAMPLE:

1) Ray Bradbury <u>writes</u> science fiction pieces.
2) Novelist and short story writer Ray Bradbury |is| best known for his science fiction writings.

1. Lech Walesa, a Polish statesman and labor leader, organized an independent, self-governing labour union known as Solidarity in 1980.
2. In Greek mythology, dryads are nymphs of the woodland and guardian spirits of trees.
3. Scarlet fever, an acute infectious disease affecting children, is caused by bacteria.
4. Parvati, the wife of the Hindu god Shiva, is also the mother of the elephant-headed god Ganesh.
5. Lyme disease causes pain in the muscles and joints, a red rash, fever, and headache.
6. Paul McCartney cowrote most of the Beatles' hit songs with John Lennon.
7. The various forms of energy include: kinetic, potential, electrical, nuclear, thermal, light, and chemical.
8. The Lumière brothers, Louis and Auguste, are considered pioneers of cinematography with their invention of a combined motion picture camera and projector.
9. Salicylic acid, the colorless, crystalline ingredient used in aspirin, occurs naturally in plants such as willow bark and wintergreen oil.
10. The United States government financed the completion of the Panama Canal to use as a passage for war ships.

Verb Numbers

Verb numbers demonstrate whether the verb is singular or plural. Singular verbs, as you already know from the earlier chapters on nouns and pronouns, indicate or refer to one person or thing. Plural verbs demonstrate that there is more than one person or thing. Notice in the sample sentences below that the verbs must match the singular or plural number of the noun or pronoun. This is called subject/verb agreement, and we will spend an entire chapter focusing on this concept.

Singular Verbs

Some examples of singular verbs are *works, builds, spends, highlights,* and *heeds.*

- He *works* in Panama City.
- She *builds* teak dining furniture.
- My grandmother *spends* her summers in Copenhagen.
- Imelda *highlights* the important points in her speech.
- Franz *heeds* his father's warnings about life beyond Berlin.

Plural Verbs

Some examples of plural verbs are *work, build, spend, highlight,* and *heed.*

- <u>We</u> *work* in Panama City.
- <u>They</u> *build* teak dining furniture.
- <u>Our</u> grandmothers *spend* <u>their</u> summers in Copenhagen.
- <u>We</u> *highlight* the important points in <u>our</u> speeches.
- <u>They</u> will *heed* <u>their</u> father's warnings about life beyond Berlin.

Practice III

Directions: Write the correct verb, in the space provided, for each of the following sentences.

EXAMPLE:

unite/unites The president ___unites___ the two opposition candidates with optimism.

1. operate/operates The pilots _____ the navigational controls of the jet.
2. erode/erodes The sandy beach _____ with years and years of wave action.
3. rafts/raft The teams _____ down the Green River during early spring.
4. speed/speeds The hydroplane _____ toward the finish line.
5. shout/shouts After being patient all day, the teacher _____ at her sixth-period class, "Be quiet!"
6. collide/collides The ships are more likely to _____ in thick fog.
7. trust/trusts Greta _____ Hans with her life.
8. fly/flies Those large black flies that _____ and buzz everywhere are disgusting to me.
9. map/maps Victor _____ the route he will take from Kingston to Washugal.
10. wave/waves The Pasadena Rose Queen and her royal court _____ at the audience.

Person of a Verb

Like pronouns, the person of a verb demonstrates whether the subject of the verb is first, second, or third person. As an added bonus, it indicates whether the subject is singular or plural. For instance, *I shrink, you shrink,* and *he shrinks* are first-, second-, and third-person singular, respectively. *We shrink, you shrink,* and *they shrink* are first-, second-, and third-person plural, respectively. The form of the verb changes only in the third-person singular of the present tense. Sound confusing? Look at the following chart for additional clarification of the person of a verb. NOTE: Verbs in the chart are preceded by a pronoun to indicate person and number (singular/plural). However, there will be times when the pronoun will be implied and not actually spelled out. For example, The papaya <u>produces</u> an enzyme that is used to break down proteins. The verb *produces* is third-person singular. A papaya is an "it," and therefore the pronoun "it" is implied and not stated.

PERSON OF A VERB		
	Singular	**Plural**
First person	I act I sit I operate	we act we sit we operate
Second person	you act you sit you operate	you act you sit you operate
Third person	she acts he sits it operates	they act they sit they operate

Practice IV

Directions: Read the sentences below, and identify the person of the verb and whether it is singular or plural.

EXAMPLE:

   third person/plural They <u>operate</u> the cranes only during the early morning hours.

1. _____/_____ The Panama Canal <u>connects</u> the Pacific Ocean and the Atlantic Ocean across the Isthmus of Panama.

2. _____/_____ It <u>reduces</u> the sea voyage from New York to San Francisco by 7,800 miles (12,500 km).

3. _____/_____ Without the canal, ships <u>sailed</u> around Cape Horn at the tip of South America.

4. _____/_____ We <u>know</u> that more than 27,000 workers were killed while building the canal.

5. _____/_____ Landslides, malaria, and yellow fever <u>plagued</u> the efforts to build the canal.

6. _____/_____ Ferdinand de Lesseps <u>began building</u> the canal in 1882.

7. _____/_____ He <u>abandoned</u> the construction because of bankruptcy.

8. _____/_____ It <u>was completed</u> by the United States in 1914 when the first ship passed through.

9. _____/_____ It <u>is</u> 51 miles (82 km) long.

10. _____/_____ They <u>celebrated</u> the convenience and the time saved in transporting goods and products.

Voice of a Verb

The voice of the verb indicates that the subject of the verb is either doing something or being acted upon. Review the examples below. The <u>verbs</u> are underlined and the subjects of the verbs are boxed.

Active Voice

The subjects of these <u>verbs</u> are actually doing something.

- The silkworms <u>eat</u> mulberry leaves.
- Male newts <u>develop</u> ornamental fins during breeding season.
- Grass pollens <u>induce</u> many allergy symptoms.

Passive Voice

The subjects of these <u>verbs</u> are being acted upon. In other words, something or someone is doing something to them.

- The mulberry leaves <u>are eaten</u> by the silkworms.
- During breeding season, ornamental fins <u>are developed</u> by male newts.
- Many allergy symptoms <u>are induced</u> by grass pollens.

Practice V

Directions: On the line provided write *active* if the sentence is written in active voice or write *passive* if the sentence is written in passive voice.

EXAMPLE:

___active___ A cow shark is over 16 feet long and has six or seven gill openings.

1. _____ Cold deserts are covered with ice and snow most of the year.

2. _____ Hot deserts have little or no vegetation.

3. _____ The bugle, a simple brass instrument, produces a limited range of sound.

4. _____ The twenty-two members of the Vienna Boys' Choir, initially founded in 1498, tour regularly.

5. _____ The suspended liquid or solid particles of a gas in an aerosol are used in deodorants, cosmetics, paints, and other household products.

6. _____ Pollen is fine, dustlike grains discharged from the male part of a flower.

7. _____ The fibers from the raffia palm that is native to Madagascar are used to make hats and baskets.

8. _____ Huskies, a powerful breed of dog, are being used in the Arctic for pulling sleds.

9. _____ The fandango is not only a Spanish dance for two, but it is also a term that means "tomfoolery."

10. _____ When a submarine dives, valves are opened in each side of the hull to take on water that will cause the craft to submerge.

Tenses of a Verb

The tense indicates the time of the action or the state of being. English verbs have six tenses: past, present, future, past perfect, present perfect, and future perfect. Sound confusing? Read through the explanations, and then study the examples for clarification. The list of all forms of a verb is called verb conjugation. The chart on page 69 is a visual of that process and should help clarify any questions.

Present Tense

The present tense describes actions that are occurring now or continually.

- The intense waves are bashing the coast of North Carolina.
- Tom Hanks is admired for his acting and directing talents.
- It is represented by the well-known calculation of $E = mc^2$.

Past Tense

Past tense actions existed or happened in the past—they are completed actions.

- The intense waves destructively bashed the coast of North Carolina.
- Tom Hanks won an Oscar for the part he played in the film *Forrest Gump*.
- The theory of relativity was proposed by Albert Einstein.

Future Tense

Actions that will occur or happen in the future involve verbs in the future tense.

- The intense waves will continue to bash the coast for several days.
- He will continue to demonstrate his talents in future acting projects.
- Albert Einstein will continue to be admired for his intelligence.

Present Perfect Tense

Actions that began in the past but continue now or perhaps are completed now involve present perfect tense verbs.

- The people living on the coast have weathered worse storms than this and were well prepared.
- Although Tom Hanks has proven that his talents are varied and superior, he will continue to broaden his scope of abilities by choosing unique acting parts.
- His theory that the speed of light is the maximum velocity attainable in the universe has not been disproved.

Past Perfect Tense

The past perfect tense describes actions that began in the past and were completed at a specific time in the past.

- The meteorologist had predicted that the storm would last for only one day.
- By 1996, Hanks's directorial debut had met moderate success.
- Einstein had published four papers in 1905 that revolutionized physical science at the time.

Future Perfect Tense

The future perfect tense is used for actions that will occur or happen at a specific time in the future and be completed by a specific time in the future.

- Fortunately, by this time Monday, the intensity of the storm will have diminished.
- By the time Hanks is in his eighties, he most likely will have covered the entire range of acting and directing.
- Physicists will have continued to base further studies on the work that Einstein completed over eighty years ago.

Verb Conjugation

A listing of all forms of a verb according to its tense and number is shown in the following table.

CONJUGATION OF THE VERB *SQUEEZE*	
Singular	**Plural**
Present Tense	
I squeeze you squeeze he/she/it squeezes	we squeeze you squeeze they squeeze
Past Tense	
I squeezed you squeezed he/she/it squeezed	we squeezed you squeezed they squeezed
Future Tense	
I will squeeze you will squeeze he/she/it will squeeze	we will squeeze you will squeeze they will squeeze
Present Perfect Tense	
I have squeezed you have squeezed he/she/it has squeezed	we have squeezed you have squeezed they have squeezed
Past Perfect Tense	
I had squeezed you had squeezed he/she/it had squeezed	we had squeezed you had squeezed they had squeezed
Future Perfect Tense	
I will have squeezed you will have squeezed he/she/it will have squeezed	we will have squeezed you will have squeezed they will have squeezed

Practice VI

Directions: After reviewing the conjugated verb chart above, complete the chart below by conjugating the verb *talk*.

CONJUGATION OF THE VERB *TALK*	
Singular	**Plural**
Present Tense	
• I talk • •	• we talk • •
Past Tense	
• • •	• • •
Future Tense	
• • •	• • •
Present Perfect Tense	
• • •	• • •
Past Perfect Tense	
• • •	• • •
Future Perfect Tense	
• • •	• • •

Practice VII

Directions: Rewrite the following sentences below by changing the tense of the verb according to the direction given.

EXAMPLES:

- **change to past perfect tense singular** When disturbed, the moray eel bites severely.

  When disturbed, the moray eel had bitten severely.

- **change to present tense plural** They saw the moon with their telescopes.

  They see the moon with their telescopes.

1. **change to future perfect tense singular** The effects of global warming are attributed to human activities.

   _____

2. **change to present perfect tense plural** He has discovered that increased amounts of carbon dioxide and other greenhouse gasses are the leading cause.

   _____

   _____

3. **change to past perfect tense singular** The chemist Arrhenius first speculated about the greenhouse effect in 1887.

   _____

   _____

4. **change to past tense singular** Carbon dioxide and other greenhouse gasses are released by burning fossil fuels, agriculture, and land clearing.

   _____

   _____

5. **change to future perfect tense singular** The results of global warming can cause rising sea levels and changes in the amounts and patterns of precipitation.

   _____

   _____

6. **change to past perfect tense plural** Scientists believe that these changes will increase the frequency and intensity of extreme weather events such as flooding, droughts, hurricanes, and tornadoes.

   _____

   _____

7. **change to future perfect tense singular** They discussed the possibility of the destruction of ecosystems and the decline of various species due to global warming.

_____

_____

8. **change to past tense plural** Negative glacier mass or glacier retreat from 1900 to 1980 is seen in 142 of the 144 mountain glaciers with records.

_____

_____

9. **change to present tense singular** Global glacier retreat has been a significant concern since 1980.

_____

_____

10. **change to present perfect tense singular** Global warming will increase the reproduction rate of mosquitoes and the number of blood meals that they take; it will prolong their breeding season and shorten their maturation period.

_____

_____

Mood Forms of a Verb

The mood indicates the attitude, manner, or tone in which the verb expresses the action. There are three moods in English: indicative, imperative, and subjunctive.

Indicative Mood

The indicative is used to state a fact or an opinion or to ask questions.

- Cubism is an art movement originated by Picasso and Braque.
- Is Cubism partly inspired by African sculpture?

Imperative Mood

The imperative is used to give a command or a request. The subject of the sentence is always "you," but it is not usually expressed. Instead, it is understood or implied. This means the word _you_ is not literally spelled out. The reader should understand that _you_ is implied.

- Do not compare cubism to minimalism.
- Compare cubism to any other art movement.

When rewritten, the two sentences would look like this with the *you* added.

- Do not [you] compare cubism to minimalism.
- [You] compare cubism to any other art movement.

Subjunctive Mood

The subjunctive is used to express something that is contrary to fact (or not true) or to express a wish, a suggestion, a necessity, a doubt, or an uncertainty. Verbs in the subjunctive mood are not often used any more. However when this mood is used, the verb is often introduced with the word *if*. The word *were* is often used as well.

- *If* I *were* you, I would not compare cubism to realism. This just will not work.
- I wish I *were* more knowledgeable about Picasso and cubism.

Practice VIII

Directions: Read the following paragraph, and indicate whether the underlined verbs are used in the indicative, imperative, or subjunctive mood. Write the type of mood on the lines below.

EXAMPLE:

Cubism is a movement in modern art that emphasized the depiction of natural forms in a geometric manner.

Indicative Mood

As an art movement, cubism (1) <u>was</u> one of the most influential of the twentieth century. Lasting from about 1907–1914, cubism (2) <u>united</u> two artists: the Spanish artist Pablo Picasso and the French artist Georges Braque. It (3) <u>is essential</u> to recognize that their inspiration came from African sculpture, painters Paul Cézanne and George Seurat, and from the fauves (an art movement that translates from French to mean "wild beast" and included the works of Henri Matisse). The movement's name (4) <u>came</u> from the words of an art critic who wrote about an exhibition of Braque's work, "M. Braque scorns form and reduces everything, sites, figures and house, to geometric schemas and cubes."

Picasso and Braque (5) <u>heeded</u> the advice of Paul Cézanne, who said that artists should treat nature "in terms of the cylinder, the sphere and the cone." Therefore, in cubism, the subject matter (6) <u>is broken</u> up, analyzed, and then reassembled in an abstract form. Braque's and Picasso's compositions are broken into planes with open edges. They (7) <u>used</u> small brushstrokes and united letters, word fragments, musical notes, and sand or sawdust to create relief or dimension to the work. Later in the movement, the art (8) <u>juxtaposed</u> a variety of found items such as musical scores, playing cards, tobacco packets with trompe l'oeil patterns that imitate wood, marble, and newsprint.

World War I (1914–1918) (9) <u>ended</u> the joint collaboration of Picasso and Braque, but the core of artists that explored Cubism remained active until the 1920s. That group included Braque, Matisse, Laurens, Lipchitz, and Fernand Léger. Please (10) <u>read</u> more about these artists and the cubism movement on your own.

1. _____

2. _____

3. _____

4. _____

5. _____

6. _____

7. _____

8. _____

9. _____

10. _____

Classes of Verbs

Verbs are divided into three classes: auxiliary or helping verbs, transitive verbs, and intransitive verbs.

Auxiliary or Helping Verbs

These help the main verb express an action or state of being. They appear with action verbs to help form a verb phrase. Some helping verbs can be linking verbs if they are used alone in a sentence. In the following sentences, the ***helping verbs are in boldface and italicized*** and the <u>main verbs are underlined</u>.

- Clothes made of cotton ***do*** <u>shrink</u> in hot water.
- They ***might*** <u>raft</u> across the Mississippi River next week.
- The soldiers ***shall*** <u>fortify</u> their positions at daybreak.

COMMON HELPING OR AUXILIARY VERBS					
Forms of *be*	is be	am been	are being	was	were
Forms of *do*	do	does	did		
Forms of *have*	have	has	had		
Other helping verbs	can could	may might	must shall	should will	would

Transitive Verbs

A transitive verb is an action verb that expresses action toward a person or thing and is always followed by an object that receives the action. In essence, the action of the verb passes from the doer to the receiver. In the sentences below, the ***transitive verbs are in boldface and italicized*** and the <u>object that receives the action is underlined.</u>

- They ***minimized*** <u>the damage</u> because of careful preparations.
- He ***admonished*** <u>his peers</u> for slacking off on the assignment.
- She ***operates*** <u>a radar station</u> for the navy.

Intransitive Verbs

The intransitive verb expresses action without passing the action to a receiver. The action of the verb is complete by itself. The ***intransitive verbs are in boldface and italicized.***

- The family ***reunites*** in one month.
- Meredith ***plays*** well with other children.
- Chloe ***runs*** like lightning.

Practice IX

Directions: Read the sentences and determine whether the underlined verbs are used as auxiliary verbs, transitive verbs, or intransitive verbs. Write the class of verb *(auxiliary/transitive/intransitive)* on the line at the beginning of the sentence.

EXAMPLE:

auxiliary Anne Boleyn, the mother of Queen Elizabeth I, <u>was</u> convicted of adultery and beheaded; she <u>was</u> the second wife of King Henry VIII of England.

1. _____ In medieval times, gallows, the structures used to hang people, <u>would be built</u> in the center of town so everyone could witness the event.

2. _____ She <u>uses</u> shorthand, a method of rapid writing that uses abbreviations and symbols, to finish quickly.

3. _____ A hard, dense, and bony tissue called dentin <u>forms</u> the bulk of a tooth.

4. _____ A taste bud <u>consists</u> of receptor cells and supporting cells in the epithelium of the tongue.

5. _____ The aging and disheveled vagabond <u>wanders</u>.

6. _____ The large-headed right whale <u>is easily</u> caught.

7. _____ Little League, an international organization, <u>promotes</u> baseball and softball for youth.

8. _____ A devastating catastrophe <u>was diverted</u>.

9. _____ The penguin's flipper-like wings <u>make</u> them excellent swimmers.

10. _____ The Rolling Stones <u>entertained</u> wildly and energetically last night at the stadium.

Irregular Verbs

Irregular verbs form their past and past participle in some way other than by adding -d or -ed to the present tense form. For instance, look at the regular verbs below. Notice that -d or -ed is added to them. They do not change other than that. Now, compare them with the examples of irregular verbs. Notice how different each word is in the various tenses. There are many irregular verbs, and the chart will help clarify the irregularity of these verbs.

	Present tense	**Past tense**	**Past participle**
Regular Verbs:	call	called	called
	activate	activated	activated
	debate	debated	debated
Irregular Verbs:	fall	fell	fallen
	know	knew	known
	strive	strove	striven

\multicolumn{1}{c}{}			\multicolumn{1}{c}{IRREGULAR VERB FORMS}					
Present Tense	Past Tense	Past Participle	Present Tense	Past Tense	Past Participle	Present Tense	Past Tense	Past Participle
am, be	was, were	been	awake	awoke	awoke	beat	beat	beaten
become	became	become	begin	began	begun	bite	bit	bitten
blow	blew	blown	break	broke	broken	bring	brought	brought
burst	burst	burst	catch	caught	caught	choose	chose	chosen
climb	climbed	climbed	come	came	come	cut	cut	cut
dive	dived	dived	do	did	done	drag	dragged	dragged
draw	drew	drawn	drink	drank	drunk	drive	drove	driven
drown	drowned	drowned	eat	ate	eaten	fall	fell	fallen
flow	flowed	flowed	fly	flew	flown	forget	forgot	forgotten
freeze	froze	frozen	get	got	got/gotten	give	gave	given
go	went	gone	hang (picture)	hung	hung	hang (criminal)	hanged	hanged
know	knew	known	lay (to place)	laid	laid	lead	led	led
leave	left	left	lend	lent	lent	let	let	let
lie (to recline)	lay	lain	lie (to tell a falsehood)	lied	lied	lose	lost	lost
ride	rode	ridden	ring	rang	rung	rise	rose	risen
run	ran	run	say	said	said	see	saw	seen
send	sent	sent	shake	shook	shaken	shine (give light)	shone	shone
shine (polish)	shined	shined	shrink	shrank	shrunk	sing	sang	sung
sink	sank	sunk	sit	sat	sat	spring	sprang	sprung
steal	stole	stolen	swear	swore	sworn	swim	swam	swum
swing	swung	swung	take	took	taken	teach	taught	taught
tear	tore	torn	tell	told	told	thing	thought	thought
throw	threw	thrown	try	tried	tried	understand	understood	understood
wake	waked/ woke	waked	wear	wore	worn	weave	wove	woven
weep	wept	wept	wind	wound	wound	wring	wrung	wrung
write	wrote	written						

Practice X

Directions: In the chart that follows, some of the verb forms are removed. Replace the words by writing in the correct form of the verb in each box.

IRREGULAR VERB FORMS								
Present Tense	Past Tense	Past Participle	Present Tense	Past Tense	Past Participle	Present Tense	Past Tense	Past Participle
am, be		been	awake		awoke	beat	beat	
become		become	begin	began		bite		bitten
blow	blew	blown	break	broke	broken			brought
burst		burst		caught	caught	choose	chose	chosen
	climbed	climbed	come	came		cut	cut	cut
dive	dived	dived	do	did	done	drag		dragged
draw	drew		drink	drank	drunk		drove	driven
	drowned	drowned	eat	ate	eaten	fall	fell	
flow	flowed	flowed	fly		flown	forget	forgot	
freeze	froze	frozen	get	got	got/gotten	give		given
go	went	gone	hang (picture)	hung	hung	hang (criminal)	hanged	hanged
know		known	lay (to place)	laid	laid	lead	led	led
leave	left	left	lend	lent	lent	let	let	let
lie (to recline)	lay	lain	lie (to tell a falsehood)	lied	lied	lose	lost	lost
ride	rode		ring	rang	rung			risen
	ran	run	say	said	said	see	saw	seen
send	sent	sent	shake	shook	shaken	shine (give light)	shone	shone
shine (polish)	shined	shined	shrink		shrunk	sing	sang	sung
sink		sunk	sit	sat	sat	spring	sprang	sprung
steal		stolen	swear		sworn	swim		swum
	swung	swung	take	took		teach	taught	taught
tear	tore	torn		told	told	think		thought
throw		thrown	try	tried		understand	understood	
	waked/woke	waked	wear		worn	weave	wove	woven
weep	wept		wind	wound		wring		wrung
write	wrote	written						

The Verbal or Special Verb Forms

A verbal is a word that comes from a verb and has the power of a verb but acts as another part of speech, such as a noun, an adjective, or an adverb. There are three types of verbals: gerunds, infinitives, and participles.

Gerund

A gerund is a verbal that ends in an *-ing* and is used as a noun. It may also be used as a direct object or the object of the preposition

- *Swimming* the English Channel would be challenging.
- Before she knew it, *singing* became her ultimate passion.
- *Cleaning* the debris after a disastrous hurricane is disheartening.

Infinitive

An infinitive is a verbal that is most often introduced by the word *to*. It can be used as a noun, an adjective, or an adverb.

- Everyone wanted <u>to</u> *party*.
- Her passion was <u>to</u> *teach*.
- <u>To</u> *draw* in the wind seemed pointless.

Participle

A participle is a verbal that functions as an adjective. Present participles end in *-ing* or *-ed* and past participles end with *-ed, -en, -d, -t,* or *-n*.

- The *soaring* gas prices discouraged us from the road trip.
- *Shaken*, he was determined to reach shore once his boat capsized.
- The *murmuring* pines swayed in the evening breeze.

Practice XI

Directions: Using the verbal suggested, write a sentence using the verb form correctly.

EXAMPLE:

Gerund: skiing
<u>Skiing is a popular sport in the Scandinavian countries: Norway, Sweden, Denmark, and Finland.</u>

1. Infinitive: to wait

_____

_____

2. Gerund: smoking

_____

_____

3. Infinitive: to smell

_____

_____

4. Participle: whistling

_____

_____

5. Gerund: sleeping

_____

_____

6. Gerund: traveling

_____

_____

7. Infinitive: to learn

_____

_____

8. Participle: crying

_____

_____

9. Gerund: studying

_____

_____

10. Infinitive: to fly

_____

_____

Chapter 4 Review Quizzes

Vocabulary Review Quiz

Directions: Write the letter of the definition on the line next to the verb that it defines.

1. _____ raft
2. _____ minimize
3. _____ operate
4. _____ admonish
5. _____ unite
6. _____ shrink
7. _____ heed
8. _____ juxtapose
9. _____ erode
10. _____ fortify

A. to join together, to become one, to combine
B. to take notice of, to attend to
C. to make or become smaller
D. to wear away, destroy, or be destroyed gradually
E. to reduce to or to estimate at the smallest possible amount or degree
F. to place things side by side or by another
G. to strengthen physically, morally, or mentally
H. to transport as or on a floating structure
I. to manage, to work or control, to perform a surgical procedure
J. to reprove or give earnest advice

Verb Definitions

Directions: Select the correct definition and write the letter of the answer on the line to the right of the number.

1. _____ Tenses of a verb indicate _____.
   a. the time of action or the state of being
   b. whether the verb is singular or plural
   c. that the verb is a gerund
   d. how the verb functions in a sentence

2. _____ These words are considered to be _____: *swimming, dancing, singing,* and *cleaning.*
   a. infinitives
   b. pronouns
   c. gerunds
   d. participles

3. _____ Which of the following are singular verbs?
   a. operate, swim, unite
   b. fly, kick, push, tear
   c. work, build, spend, highlight
   d. works, builds, spends, highlights

4. _____ *You act, you sit,* and *you admonish* are in _____ person.
   a. first
   b. second
   c. third
   d. all of the above

5. _____ This sentence is written in _____ voice: *The mosquitoes buzz in our ears.*
   a. active
   b. passive
   c. aggressive
   d. interrogative

6. _____ Action verbs are words that demonstrate what a person or thing _____.
   a. can actually do physically or mentally
   b. will watch on television
   c. is in first, second, or third person
   d. is doing or is being acted upon

7. _____ *I will squeeze* is written in _____ tense.
   a. present
   b. future
   c. past perfect
   d. past

8. _____ Imperative mood is used to _____.
   a. compare past with present tense
   b. express something that is not true
   c. give a command or a request
   d. to state a fact or an opinion

9. _____ *Is, should, will, could, be, been,* and *was* are_____ verbs.
   a. transitive
   b. auxiliary
   c. gerunds
   d. irregular

10. _____ The correct conjugation of the irregular verb *freeze* is _____.
    a. froze, freeze, have frozen
    b. freeze, frozen, frozen
    c. freezen, frozen, have frozed
    d. freeze, froze, frozen

Action Verbs and Linking Verbs

Directions: In the paragraph below, underline all of the <u>action verbs</u> and draw a box around all of the | linking verbs | .

EXAMPLE:

The female emu <u>emits</u> a loud booming sound from the odd pouch that | is | on her wind-pipe.

The emu (pronounced "ee myoo") is the largest bird that is native to Australia. After its relative the ostrich, the emu is the second-largest bird in the world. It is a soft-feathered brown bird that reaches a height of up to 6 feet 6 inches (200 cm). Although the birds cannot fly, they can travel great distances at speeds over 30 miles (50 km) per hour. Emu feed on plants and insects, and they are farmed for their meat, oil, and leather. Considered the unofficial national bird of Australia, the emu appears on the coat of arms of Australia, on a 50-cent coin, and on various postage stamps. However, equally as important, the emu holds a prominent place in the myths of the Australian indigenous peoples, the Aborigines. They say that the Sun was made when an emu's egg was thrown into the sky. The emu is an important bird in Australia both culturally and as a national treasure.

Verb Numbers

Directions: For each sentence below, indicate whether the underlined <u>verb</u> in the sentence is a singular or plural verb. Write *S* on the line if it is singular and write *P* on the line if it is plural.

EXAMPLE:

___*P*___ Oil or gas-fired kilns <u>are used</u> to bake pottery and can reach temperatures up to 3,200°F.

1. _____ They <u>mash</u> the boiled grain before distilling it into alcohol.

2. _____ The senator <u>will attempt</u> to unite her party on the issue of health care.

3. _____ I <u>board</u> the train that leaves for Sorrento at noon.

4. _____ Locusts, a type of African or Asian grasshopper, <u>migrate</u> in swarms.

5. _____ They <u>practice</u> headhunting, collecting the heads of dead enemies for trophies.

6. _____ Advection fog <u>occurs</u> at sea when warm, moist air flows over cold sea water.

7. _____ Radiation fog <u>transpires</u> on land as the ground loses heat. It cools the air nearby and creates fog.

8. _____ People employed to tend sheep <u>are called</u> shepherds.

9. _____ A windsurfer <u>rides</u> on a sailboard that uses the wind's energy as a driving force.

10. _____ The dark volcanic rock obsidian <u>forms</u> from rapidly chilled hardened lava.

Person of a Verb

Directions: On the line at the beginning of each sentence below, identify whether the <u>underlined verbs</u> used are in *FP* for first person, *SP* for second person, or *TP* for third person.

EXAMPLE:

___*TP*___ The Rhine River in western Europe is 820 miles long.

1. _____ I <u>speak</u> Mandarin Chinese, not Cantonese.

2. _____ We <u>hear</u> sound via a complex organ known as the ear.

3. _____ She <u>spent</u> the better half of the month preparing for her trip to Laos.

4. _____ You <u>will</u> never believe that modern gymnastics dates from only the early nineteenth century.

5. _____ They <u>fish</u> for freshwater trout with expensive equipment.

6. _____ You <u>can never be certain</u> of the future. However, do not fall into the habit of becoming an advocate of doom.

7. _____ His compound fracture <u>will heal</u> well as long as it is in a cast.

8. _____ We <u>will condemn</u> the first person who violates the treaty.

9. _____ She <u>plays</u> the French horn for the Los Angeles Philharmonic.

10. _____ They <u>are</u> Hispanic students from Guatamala.

Voice of a Verb

Directions: Identify the voice of each of the following underlined <u>verbs</u>. Write *active* if the verb is being used with an active voice, and write *passive* if it is being used passively.

EXAMPLE:

*Active* A whale's skull is made up of 30 bones, compared with a human skull with 22 bones.

1. _____ Snakes and humans <u>hiss</u> to express disapproval.

2. _____ The women <u>are hired</u> to knit shawls for war veterans.

3. _____ Microorganisms <u>include</u> algae, bacteria, fungi, protozoa, and viruses.

4. _____ Semaphore, a system of sending messages by waving flags with specific arm positions, <u>may have originated</u> with the ancient Greeks and Romans.

5. _____ A smithy <u>is</u> a blacksmith's workshop.

6. _____ Most organized religions <u>have</u> monasteries where monks devote their lives to their religion.

7. _____ Golf <u>was established</u> in sixteenth-century Scotland.

8. _____ The acronym BBC <u>stands</u> for the British Broadcasting Corporation.

9. _____ To be ubiquitous means to be everywhere or present in several places at the same time. We could say that McDonald's fast food restaurants <u>are</u> somewhat ubiquitous.

10. _____ The Beatles <u>are considered</u> one of the most influential popular music groups of all time.

Tenses of a Verb and Verb Conjugation

Directions: Conjugate the verb *exist* by completing the chart below.

CONJUGATION OF THE VERB EXIST	
Singular	**Plural**
Present Tense	
I you he/she/it	we you they
Past Tense	
I you he/she/it	we you they
Future Tense	
I will you will he/she/it will	we will you will they will
Present Perfect Tense	
I have you have he/she/it has	we have you have they have
Past Perfect Tense	
I had you had he/she/it had	we had you had they had
Future Perfect Tense	
I will have you will have he/she/it will have	we will have you will have they will have

Mood Forms of a Verb

Directions: Write sentences using verbs with the mood form indicated at the beginning of the sentence.

EXAMPLE:

Indicative (state a fact) Paris is a romantic city.

1. Indicative (state a fact)

   _____

   _____

2. Imperative (give a command)

   _____

   _____

3. Imperative (offer a request)

   _____

   _____

4. Subjunctive (express a wish)

   _____

   _____

5. Subjunctive (express a suggestion)

   _____

   _____

6. Indicative (ask a question)

   _____

   _____

7. Imperative (ask a question)

   _____

   _____

8. Subjunctive (express a doubt or uncertainty)

   _____

   _____

9. Imperative (give a command)

   _____

   _____

10. Subjunctive (express something contrary to fact)

   _____

   _____

Classes of Verbs

Directions: Write the definition of each of the following classes of verbs and write an example sentence for each.

Auxiliary or helping verbs are _____

_____

Example sentence: _____

_____

Transitive verbs are _____

_____

Example sentence: _____

_____

Intransitive verbs are _____

_____

Example sentence: _____

_____

Irregular Verbs

Directions: Complete the conjugation of the following irregular verbs in the present tense, past tense, and past participle.

Present Tense	Past Tense	Past Participle
1. send	_____	_____
2. _____	swung	_____
3. break	_____	_____
4. _____	_____	blown
5. _____	wrung	_____
6. _____	_____	rung
7. draw	_____	_____
8. forget	_____	_____
9. _____	wove	_____
10. _____	_____	forsaken

Verbals—Gerunds, Infinitives, and Participles

Directions: Identify the verbs used in the sentences below as *gerunds, infinitives,* or *participles* by writing the form at the beginning of the sentence.

EXAMPLE:

gerund Sketching is fun.

1. _____ The teaching university was closed because of the flu.

2. _____ The pelting rain managed to destroy our crops.

3. _____ Drawing seemed to make Benjamin happy as a child.

4. _____ Everyone was ready to fly.

5. _____ Weaving wild tales of sorcery kept him busy.

6. _____ To flee the devastation seemed logical.

7. _____ Wounded, they were able to crawl from the mineshaft to safety.

8. _____ Swinging in the fresh spring air is exhilarating.

9. _____ The singing game, which was intended to keep us entertained, managed to bore us to death after the last verse of "99 bottles of beer on the wall" had been sung.

10. _____ "To be, or not to be" says Hamlet.

Real-World Practice Activities

Reading

Directions: On your way to school, work, shopping, or wherever you might be headed, look around you and pay attention to road signs, advertising, and various notices that you may find posted. Look for verbs. When you read one, write it down. Complete the chart below. Fill it in with various verbs that you saw/read on the road or while you were out.

1. _____	6. _____	11. _____	16. _____
2. _____	7. _____	12. _____	17. _____
3. _____	8. _____	13. _____	18. _____
4. _____	9. _____	14. _____	19. _____
5. _____	10. _____	15. _____	20. _____

Writing

Directions: Use the following verbs from the vocabulary list at the beginning of the chapter to write a brief story—an adventure, a mystery, or a story about a natural disaster—using all of the words. You may be creative and use your imagination. Have fun with it.

> **Word Bank:** heed, raft, fortify, juxtapose, unite, erode, minimize

_____

_____

_____

_____

_____

_____

_____

_____

_____

_____

_____

_____

_____

_____

_____

_____

_____

_____

_____

_____

Listening

Directions: Listen carefully while you are talking to a friend, a family member, a school-mate, or anyone that you might have a conversation with. Note the verbs that are being used. Identify ten action verbs and ten helping verbs during the conversation(s). It might take more than one conversation to complete the assignment. Reminder: action verbs = run, hope, spell, taste, and ski. Helping or auxiliary verbs = is, be, do, might, and shall. It might help to review the chart of auxiliary verbs earlier in the chapter.

Action Verbs	Helping/Auxiliary Verbs
1. _____	_____
2. _____	_____
3. _____	_____
4. _____	_____
5. _____	_____
6. _____	_____
7. _____	_____
8. _____	_____
9. _____	_____
10. _____	_____

Chapter 5

SUBJECT + PREDICATE = SIMPLE SENTENCES

The subject of the sentence is the noun or pronoun part of the sentence. In other words, the subject is the main part of the sentence—who or what is doing the action. Every sentence has a subject, although sometimes it is implied and not spelled out literally. For instance in the sentence "Go to the market," the pronoun *you* is implied. If it were literal, the sentence would include the word *you*. "You go to the market." Everything that is not a part of the subject is the predicate. It is the verb or action part of the sentence. When adding the two together, the subject plus the predicate, the end result is your everyday basic sentence: a complete thought. In this chapter, we will look at the parts separately and then combine them to understand fully what a simple but complete thought is, the simple sentence.

Vocabulary Development

1. **animation** (an i may shin) The technique of filming successive drawings to create an illusion of movement.
2. **cnidarian** (ni dair ee an) An aquatic invertebrate (without vertebrae) with a simple cup or tube-shaped body and tentacles, including jellyfish, corals, and sea anemones.
3. **column** (kol em) An upright, cylindrical pillar used as an architectural support.
4. **griffin** (grif en) A mythical creature with an eagle's head and wings but with a lion's body.
5. **limerick** (lim er ik or lim rik) A humorous form of a five-line stanza with a rhyme scheme of *aabba*.
6. **opus** (o pes) A separate musical composition or a set of compositions of any kind.
7. **orchestra** (or kes tra) A large group of instrumentalists that combines strings, woodwinds, brass, and percussion instruments.
8. **quixotic** (kwik so tik). Extravagantly and romantically chivalrous; visionary; pursuing lofty but unattainable ideals; ridiculously impractical.
9. **autonomous** (aw ton o mus) Having self-government.
10. **Uranus** (yoo ray nus) A planet, seventh in order from the Sun, discovered by Herschel in 1781.

The Subject

The subject is at all times a noun or other word or phrase that functions as a noun. The subject could be a pronoun, an infinitive, a gerund, or a noun clause (we will look at clauses later). In the subject family, there are simple, complete, and compound subjects.

Simple Subjects

Simple subjects are subjects without modifying words. The simple subject is not attached to a phrase or any adjectives that are used to describe it. Although there may be modifying words in the sentence, the simple subject is simply the noun or pronoun. The simple subjects in the sentences below are underlined.

- Cel <u>animation</u> was developed in the early 1910s.
- Computer <u>animation</u> has improved dramatically in recent years.
- Twenty-four different <u>drawings</u> are needed for one second of traditional animation.

Practice I

Directions: Identify the simple subjects in the sentences below by underlining them.

EXAMPLE:

<u>Mickey Mouse</u> is an animated character.

1. Animation is time-consuming and therefore expensive to produce.
2. Walt Disney was a pioneer in the field of animation.
3. Animation is not only used for entertainment, but it is used for educational purposes as well.
4. A storyboard, which looks similar to a comic strip, is the early production stage of traditional animation.
5. Because the cels have to be synchronized with the drawings, the dialogue is recorded first.
6. For every second of film, there are twenty-four drawings.
7. In one minute of animation, there are 1440 drawings.
8. The cartoon backgrounds are painted on cardboard or celluloid.
9. Rotoscoping is a method of animation that traces the movement of actors and scenery from actual film footage.
10. Some films use a combination of live-action footage and animation: actors appear to interact with cartoon characters.

Complete Subjects

The entire subject, the noun/pronoun part of the sentence, and all of the words that modify or describe it is called the complete subject. The subject of a sentence may be a single word, but it is nonetheless considered the complete subject. In other words, a simple subject as we learned above may also be a complete subject. The complete subjects are underlined in the examples below.

- Coral, found in reefs all over the world, are considered Cnidaria.
- Over 11,000 different species are found in the Cnidaria phylum.
- Cnidarians have radial symmetry, which means that no matter which way it is cut in half, both sides will be exactly the same.
- The cnidarian's stomach is only not used to ingest food but to excrete waste as well.

Practice II

Directions: Read the brief paragraph below and underline the complete subjects in each of the sentences.

EXAMPLE:

Jellyfish have an umbrella-shaped body made of a jellylike substance.

The Portuguese man-of-war is a member of the Cnidaria phylum. It is a part of the class of hydrozoa within this phylum. The Portuguese man-of-war looks like a blue jellyfish-like bubble or bottle and is often called a blue bubble or blue bottle. The hydrozoa's name comes from its air bladder, which looks like a "man of war"—a sailing vessel with cannons. Its long tentacles are used to hunt for prey and are dangerous to humans. The sting from the tentacles causes excruciating pain. Stings from the Portuguese man-of-war have been linked to several deaths. They are particularly dangerous to children, the elderly, asthmatics, and those with allergies. The tentacles are capable of stinging even if they are detached from the blue bottle's body. The best treatment for the sting is first of all to remove the barb with tweezers and then to apply ice or hot water.

Compound Subjects

Compound subjects are those with two or more simple subjects. The simple subjects are joined or connected by either one of two coordinating conjunctions, *and* or *or*. The compound subjects that use an *and* are plural, and those connected with an *or* are singular. The compound subjects are underlined in the examples below.

- Doric, Ionic, and Corinthian are three types of Greek architectural columns.
- Doric or Tuscan columns were incorporated into the architectural structures of the Romans.
- The Roman Doric and Tuscan columns have simple lines.

Practice III

Directions: Identify the coordinating conjunction used in the compound subjects in the following sentences. Write the coordinating conjunction on the line at the beginning of the sentence.

EXAMPLE:

___*and*___ Classical orders of Greek and Roman architecture are characterized by the columns used.

1. _____ Ionic and Corinthian columns are more elaborate than Doric columns.

2. _____ A shaft, base, and capital are the parts of a column; the capital is the decorative part of the column.

3. _____ The shaft or column is cylindrical in shape.

4. _____ Doric, Ionic, and Corinthian are orders, ancient styles of building designs, particularly in Greece and Rome.

5. _____ A plain round capital or top characterizes the simple Doric column.

6. _____ The volutes or scrolls that decorate the Ionic column sit upon a fluted pillar or shaft.

7. _____ The fluted pillar or shaft of the column adds vertical dimension to the design.

8. _____ Ornately carved acanthus leaves and scrolls decorate the top of a Corinthian column or order.

9. _____ The simple base, the unfluted shaft, and the unadorned capital describe the Tuscan column.

10. _____ Ionic scrolls and Corinthian leaves combine to form what is known as the composite order.

The Predicate

The predicate is the part of the sentence that is not the subject. It tells something about the subject and includes the verb or action part of the sentence and everything else that follows. The predicate may include phrases (which we will visit later), direct objects, and indirect objects. Normally in English, the subject comes first. For variety, though, writers often change the order of the sentence. Sometimes the predicate is first, and sometimes part of the predicate is before and part after the subject. Within the family of predicates are simple, complete, and compound predicates similar to the subject part of the sentence.

Simple Predicate

The simple predicate refers to the verb without any of the words that modify or describe it. The simple predicate in each sentence below is underlined.

- The tail of the griffin <u>looks</u> like a serpent.
- Many coats of arms <u>include</u> the griffin in their designs.
- The griffin <u>represents</u> wisdom and fortitude.

Practice IV

Directions: Write the simple predicate on the line at the beginning of each sentence.

EXAMPLE:

____*are*____ Griffins are mythological creatures.

1. _____ In the novel *The Chronicles of Narnia*, griffins are among the creatures in Aslan's army.

2. _____ Gryffindor is the name of Harry Potter's house at Hogwarts School of Witchcraft and Wizardry.

3. _____ The mascot of Sarah Lawrence College is a griffin.

4. _____ Griffins are often shown facing left and standing on one hind leg.

5. _____ Some say that only the female griffins have wings.

6. _____ The griffins were ordered to watch over gold mines and other treasures.

7. _____ Instead of laying eggs, these creatures lay agates.

8. _____ It is said that griffins had a strong dislike of horses.

9. _____ There is a breed of dog called griffons.

10. _____ The chariot of the Sun in ancient mythology was drawn by griffins.

Complete Predicate

The complete predicate is the verb or the simple predicate and all of the words that explain or modify it. It is everything except the subject.

- The mythological griffin <u>has the body of a lion and the head and wings of an eagle</u>.
- The griffins <u>were thought to be powerful creatures</u>.
- <u>Represented with four legs, wings, a beak, and the talons of an eagle instead of forelegs</u>, the griffin <u>also had feathered but horselike ears</u>.
- <u>It is said that</u> the griffin <u>built a nest like an eagle</u>.
- The griffin, <u>also spelled *gryphon*, *gryphen*, or *griffen*, is represented in literature through the ages</u>.

Practice V

Directions: Make complete sentences by adding a complete predicate to the subjects provided below.

EXAMPLE:

The hungry goblin <u>went haunting around the neighborhood</u>.

1. A soldier _____

2. The librarian's book _____

3. His daughter Nan _____

4. A maiden from Wales _____

5. Forrest's music _____

6. After Natalie _____

7. A mathematician _____

8. Baseball season _____

9. Candy wrappers _____

10. Permanent ink _____

Compound Predicates

These have two or more simple predicates.

- The term *opus* <u>is used</u> in architecture, and it <u>is used</u> in music also.

- Opus numbers <u>are given</u> or <u>assigned</u> to pieces of music written by composers in order of publication.

- In architecture, opus <u>describes</u> a technique or <u>discerns</u> a method or style of connecting various building elements.

Practice VI

Directions: Write ten sentences—five of them with compound predicates and five of them with compound subjects and predicates.

EXAMPLE:

Both baroque composers' and classical composers' works were at first written and then performed for an audience.

1. _____

_____

2. _____

_____

3. _____

_____

4. _____

_____

5. _____

_____

6. _____

_____

7. _____

_____

8. _____

_____

9. _____

_____

10. _____

_____

Direct Object

A direct object receives the action of the predicate and completes the meaning expressed by the verb. The direct object usually answers the questions *what?* or *whom?* and is usually a noun or a pronoun.

        noun   verb   direct object

- A full <u>orchestra</u> <u>has</u> about 104 <u>musicians</u>. (The orchestra has *what*? It has musicians—musicians is the direct object.)

        noun   verb   direct object

- An <u>orchestra</u> <u>is</u> often <u>called</u> a <u>symphony or philharmonic</u>. (The orchestra is called *what*? It is called a symphony or philharmonic—these are both the direct object, a compound direct object.)

        noun   verb   direct object

- Most <u>orchestras</u> <u>have</u> four groups of similar <u>instruments</u>. (Orchestras have *what*? They have instruments—instruments is the direct object.)

Practice VII

Directions: Underline the direct object in the sentences below.

EXAMPLE:

Johann Sebastian Bach is a well-known <u>composer</u>.

1. The woodwinds include flutes, piccolos, oboes, clarinets, and bassoons.
2. The brass section consists of horns, saxophones, trumpets, trombones, and tubas.
3. Timpani, snare drums, and bass drums are percussion instruments in an orchestra.
4. The string section includes harps, violins, violas, cellos, double bass, and pianos.
5. Beethoven's symphonic works were influential to orchestration.
6. All instrumental sections have one soloist except for the violin section, which has two.
7. The first violinist is considered the concertmaster and is ranked next to the conductor.
8. In the fifteenth and sixteenth centuries, most nobles had court musicians.
9. Monteverdi, Pachelbel, Vivaldi, Handel, Scarlatti, Bach, and Telemann are considered composers of the baroque period.
10. Johann Sebastian Bach composed music for choirs, orchestras, and solo instruments.

Indirect Object

Verbs that express action often take two objects, a direct object and an indirect object. The indirect object tells *to whom* the action is directed or *for whom* the action is directed. It always comes before the direct object. To determine the indirect object, first determine the direct object and then find the indirect object. The examples below have the <u>direct object</u> underlined and the indirect object in a box.

- Jackson's mother managed to buy him a new <u>cello</u>.
- Beethoven's music continues to inspire many composers <u>to write</u>.
- Esa-Pekka Salonen conducts Los Angeles's well-respected <u>orchestra</u>.

Practice VIII

Directions: Determine the <u>direct object</u> by underlining it, and then determine the indirect object by drawing a box around it.

EXAMPLE:

Mozart gave the world hundreds of <u>songs</u>.

1. Mozart wrote the king an opera.
2. Bach left the world a legacy of music.
3. He gave us over 300 cantatas.
4. Handel bought his son a new clavichord.

5. She practically fed her daughter music morning, noon, and night.

6. Monteverdi gave his friend music lessons.

7. His son returned Jason's guitar.

8. Stradivari built his sons the finest violins in the entire world.

9. Beethoven influenced composers the world over.

10. Frederic Chopin devoted his life to composing piano music.

Simple Sentences

A sentence must have a subject and a predicate. Add a subject and a predicate together to get a simple sentence. A sentence ALWAYS begins with a capital letter and ends with a period, question mark, or exclamation point. Note the examples below:

Subject	+ Predicate = Simple Sentence
• *Don Quixote*	+ is often considered the greatest work of fiction
	= *Don Quixote* is often considered the greatest work of fiction.
• The story	+ takes place in Spain
	= The story takes place in Spain.
• Quixote's adventures	+ get him into a great deal of trouble
	= Quixote's adventures get him into a great deal of trouble.

Practice IX

Directions: Using the part of the sentence provided, add either a predicate or a subject to make it a complete sentence.

EXAMPLE:

Sancho Panza ___is Don Quixote's friend and partner___.

1. _____ sent a letter to Dominic.

2. The letter _____.

3. When we _____?

4. _____ is going to Ireland next spring.

5. I _____.

6. England _____.

7. _____ loves to play football in Mexico.

8. Benjamin_____.

9. _____ challenges her neighbors to a wrestling match.

10. Meredith _____.

Chapter 5 Review Quizzes

Vocabulary Review Quiz

Directions: Write the letter of the definition on the line next to the noun that it defines.

1. _____ animation

2. _____ cnidarian

3. _____ column

4. _____ griffin

5. _____ limerick

6. _____ opus

7. _____ orchestra

8. _____ quixotic

9. _____ autonomous

10. _____ Uranus

A. Having self-government.

B. A mythical creature with an eagle's head and wings but with a lion's body.

C. A planet, seventh in order from the Sun, discovered by Herschel in 1781.

D. Extravagantly and romantically chivalrous; visionary; pursuing lofty but unattainable ideals; ridiculously impractical.

E. A humorous form of a five-line stanza with a rhyme scheme of *aabba*.

F. A separate musical composition or a set of compositions of any kind.

G. The technique of filming successive drawings to create an illusion of movement.

H. An aquatic invertebrate (without vertebrae) with a simple cup or tube-shaped body and tentacles, including jellyfish, corals, and sea anemones.

I. An upright cylindrical pillar used as an architectural support.

J. A large group of instrumentalists that combine strings, woodwinds, brass, and percussion instruments.

Subject, Predicate, and Simple Sentence Definitions

Directions: Select the correct definition, and write the letter of the answer on the line to the right of the number.

1. _____ A predicate is the _____ part of the sentence.
   a. pronoun
   b. verb
   c. first
   d. noun

2. _____ Simple subjects are subjects without _____ words.
   a. ordinary
   b. common
   c. modifying
   d. noun

3. _____ Which of the following does NOT have a compound subject?
    a. Doric and Ionic columns are less detailed.
    b. Beethoven, Bach, and Mozart are famous composers.
    c. Griffins are mythological creatures.
    d. Storyboarding and rotoscoping are parts of the animation process.

4. _____ Which of the following does NOT have a single subject?
    a. Chopin and Mendelssohn were friends.
    b. Doric columns are simple in detail and decoration.
    c. Corinthian columns are elaborately decorated.
    d. Franz Liszt performed in Paris.

5. _____ Identify the sentence with a direct object that is underlined.
    a. <u>Tibet</u> is located on the Tibetan Plateau.
    b. <u>Raising livestock</u> is a primary occupation in Tibet.
    c. Tibetan Buddhism is <u>the predominant religion</u>.
    d. The Yangtze, Yellow, Indus, Mekong, and Ganges Rivers <u>are among</u> those whose sources are in the Tibetan Plateau.

6. _____ Identify the sentence with the indirect object underlined.
    a. Chopin performed <u>his</u> music in Paris.
    b. <u>Chopin</u> performed his music in Paris.
    c. Chopin performed his <u>music</u> in Paris.
    d. Chopin <u>performed his music in Paris</u>.

7. _____ Which of the following is considered a simple sentence?
    a. Uranus is the seventh planet from the sun.
    b. It was named after the Greek god of the sky.
    c. It is the fourth-largest planet by mass.
    d. All of the above.

8. _____ The subject is the _____ part of the sentence.
    a. verb
    b. action
    c. indirect object
    d. noun or pronoun

9. _____ Which of the following has its subject underlined?
    a. Rembrandt <u>was a Dutch painter</u>.
    b. He settled in <u>Amsterdam</u>.
    c. His style <u>is considered </u>the Baroque style.
    d. <u>Rembrandt </u>withdrew from society because he was deeply in debt.

10. _____ Identify the simple predicate below.
    a. The Zulu wars
    b. was a conflict in South Africa.
    c. The British
    d. The Zulu attacked the British and killed 800 men.

Subjects

Directions: Underline all of the complete subjects in the paragraph below.

<u>Uranus</u> is the seventh planet from the Sun and the fourth largest in mass. It was the first planet that was discovered in modern times. Although it was seen by astronomers as early as 1690, it was always mistakenly documented as a star. Sir William Herschel discovered the planet in 1781, but he initially reported it to be a comet. It was first named Georgium Sidus, which means "Georgian star" after King George III of England. When Herschel was told that sidus means "star," he renamed it the Georgian Planet. However, that name was not accepted outside of England. It was suggested that the newly discovered planet be named after Herschel, the discoverer. There were as many as nine additional names suggested by astronomers all over the world, but finally the name Uranus was settled upon.

Simple, Complete, and Compound Subjects

Directions: Read the sentences below and decide if the underlined subject is *simple, complete,* or *compound*. Write the subject type on the line.

EXAMPLE:

     simple   *E pluribus unum* is a Latin motto for the United States that means, "Out of many, one."

1. _____ <u>Don Quixote</u> is a middle-aged man obsessed with the chivalrous ideas that he has read about in books.

2. _____ <u>Don Quixote and Sancho Panza</u> set out on another adventure after his first failed.

3. _____ On his old horse named Rocinante, <u>Don Quixote</u> seeks glory and adventure to win the hand of Dulcinea del Toboso, a peasant woman whom Don sees as a princess.

4. _____ <u>Don Quixote</u> is the tragicomic hero of the novel by Miguel de Cervantes Saavedra.

5. _____ <u>Rocinante and Dapple</u>, Quixote's horse and Sancho's donkey, are stories within themselves.

6. _____ <u>Dulcinea del Toboso</u> is a character that is constantly mentioned in the novel, but she never actually appears physically.

7. _____ <u>Books and manuscripts, horses, and inns</u> are symbols that are used to represent abstract ideas in the novel *Don Quixote*.

8. _____ <u>The novel</u> is narrated mostly in third person, but Cervantes, the author, changes to first person off and on.

9. _____ <u>The priest character in the novel</u> attempts to bring Quixote home to cure him of what he believes to be insanity.

10. _____ <u>The novel</u> was written in the late sixteenth and early seventeenth centuries.

Predicates

Directions: Underline the predicates in the following sentences.

EXAMPLE:

Ghenghis Khan <u>is known for his military leadership and cruelty</u>.

1. Tibet is an autonomous region in southwest China.
2. Surrounded by mountains, Tibet is historically inaccessible.
3. It is rich in mineral resources such as gold, copper, and uranium.
4. The principal religion of Tibet is Tibetan Buddhism.
5. The country flourished in the seventh century.
6. Early in the thirteenth century, Genghis Khan conquered the region. It remained under Mongol rule until 1720.
7. The Chinese Qing Dynasty claimed sovereignty in 1720. By 1912 and with the fall of the Qing Dynasty, Tibet reasserted its independence.
8. In 1950, China sent its new communist forces to invade Tibet.
9. The country was declared an autonomous region in 1951 and was governed by the Dalai Lama.
10. China launched a full-scale invasion in 1959, but the Dalai Lama managed to flee the country.

Simple, Complete, and Compound Predicates

Directions: Fill in the blanks with either a simple, complete, or compound predicate.

EXAMPLE:

Hieroglyphics <u>is a system of writing with pictures</u>.

1. The orchestra _____

_____

2. Uranus _____

_____

3. An animated cartoon _____

_____

4. Limericks _____

_____

5. An opus _____

_____

6. A Doric column _____

_____

7. Cnidarians _____

_____

8. A mythological griffin _____

_____

9. An autonomous country _____

_____

10. A quixotic person or character _____

_____

Direct and Indirect Objects

Directions: Read the following paragraph. Underline the <u>direct objects</u> and draw a box around the indirect objects .

    In 1965, China formally annexed <u>Tibet</u> as an autonomous region . During this time, the Cultural Revolution was occurring in China. Because of the new laws and regulations dictated by the revolution regarding religion, over 4,000 monasteries in Tibet were destroyed. Thousand of Tibetans were forced into exile. Rallies for proindependence in 1987–1989 were suppressed by the Chinese army. Human violations continue in the region despite restoration of some of the monasteries and a return of Tibetan as the official language.

Real-World Practice Activities

Reading

Directions: Find an article on Tibet in a newspaper, magazine, or online. Copy or print out the article, and underline the complete subject of each sentence. Write the first twenty simple subjects on the lines below.

1. _____ 6. _____ 11. _____ 16. _____

2. _____ 7. _____ 12. _____ 17. _____

3. _____ 8. _____ 13. _____ 18. _____

4. _____ 9. _____ 14. _____ 19. _____

5. _____ 10. _____ 15. _____ 20. _____

Writing

Directions: Write about freedom and basic human rights. How does this issue vary around the world? Underline or highlight the predicates in each of your sentences.

_____

_____

_____

_____

_____

_____

_____

_____

_____

_____

_____

_____

_____

_____

_____

_____

_____

_____

_____

_____

_____

Listening

Directions: Either tune into a classical music station on the radio or borrow a CD from the library or other source. Any works by Mozart, Beethoven, or Bach would be fine choices or you can choose any classical music. Listen carefully to one of the selections. Concentrate on it. Listen to it two to three times or more. What does the music do to your senses? Write down a few thoughts in complete sentences on the lines below, and underline or highlight the simple subject of each of your sentences.

1. _____

2. _____

3. _____

4. _____

5. _____

6. _____

7. _____

8. _____

9. _____

10. _____

Chapter 6

SUBJECT-VERB AGREEMENT

he first thing to remember about subject-verb agreement is that the subject rules the verb. Do not be confused by any other word or phrase in the sentence. A verb should always agree with its subject in number. For instance, a single noun (albatross) should have a single verb (flies) tagging along. A plural noun (switch-hitters) will take a plural verb (hit). Again, the subject and verb in any sentence or clause should agree in both person and number. What may seem a little confusing is that we are taught that in order for something to be plural, we add an *s* to the word. However, you will notice as you work through this chapter that singular subjects have verbs that end with an *s* and plural subjects have verbs that do not have an *s*. Do not worry. You will get used to it. The more English you read, the more you will understand the sound of agreement: singular subjects with singular verbs and plural subjects with plural verbs just sound better.

Vocabulary Development

1. **albatross** (al be traws) Any long-winged bird that inhabits the Pacific Ocean.
2. **bleak** (bleek) Bare, exposed, windswept; unpromising, dreary.
3. **disturbance** (dis ter benc) The act or an instance of unrest; an interruption of calm and quiet.
4. **frailty** (fray il tee) The condition of being fragile or delicate; liability to err or yield to temptation; a fault or weakness.
5. **fusion** (fyoo zhen) The act or instance of melting with intense heat; the blending of different things into one.
6. **magnifying** (mag ni fy ing) The act or an instance of making an object appear larger than it is with a lens or increasing the depth of a problem.
7. **persecute** (per si kyoot) To subject a person to hostility or ill-treatment, especially on the grounds of political or religious belief; harass.
8. **Pre-Raphaelite** (pree raf ay el ite) A member of a group of nineteenth-century English artists united for their distaste of formal academic art and the neoclassical style who looked to the past for inspiration, including William Holman Hunt, John Everett Millais, and Dante Gabriel Rossetti.

9. **stream-of-consciousness** (streem of konsh shus ness) A person's thoughts and conscious reactions to events perceived as a continuous flow; a literary style depicting events in such a flow in a character's mind.

10. **vertigo** (vir ti go) A condition that causes a sensation of whirling and a tendency to lose balance; dizziness.

Agreement in Number

Singular and Plural Subjects

Subjects that are singular are loners so to speak and do not have a plural ending (*s*, *es*, and so on). Subjects that are plural will have a plural ending such as *s* or *es*. Note the change in spelling in some of the examples below. It is often necessary to drop the *y* and add an *-ies*. Sometimes you just need to know the plural version of the word, for example, mouse = mice. Then again, sometimes the plural and the singular versions are the same.

Singular Subjects	Plural Subjects
mouse	mice
French fry	French fries
scissor	scissors
freak	freaks
doughnut	doughnuts

Practice I

Directions: Identify the subjects/nouns listed below as singular or plural. Write *S* on the line if it is singular and write *P* on the line if it is plural.

EXAMPLE:

hobby _____S_____

1. disturbances _____
2. artist _____
3. albatross _____
4. bats _____
5. writers _____
6. element _____
7. abilities _____
8. whisper _____
9. mountain _____
10. beaches _____

Singular and Plural Verbs

These are verbs that are used with singular and plural subjects.

Singular Verbs	**Plural Verbs**
(it) eats	(they) eat
(I) swim	(we) swim
(he) disturbs	(they) disturb
(she) persecutes	(we) persecute
(I) enable	(we) enable

Practice II

Directions: Underline the correct verb form for the subjects listed below.

EXAMPLE:

The peridot *are/is* a gemstone that has a transparent olive greenish color.

1. The albatross *has/have* the largest wingspan, which extends over eleven feet.
2. There *is/are* many different species of albatross.
3. These birds *is/are* efficient in the air.
4. The albatross can *soars/soar* with little exertion.
5. The bill of the albatross *is/are* hooked on the end.
6. They *has/have* an acute sense of smell.
7. Their feet *has/have* no hind toe, and the three front toes *is/are* webbed.
8. The albatross diet *consists/consist* of fish, crustaceans, and plankton.
9. Albatrosses *is/are* considered legendary and are often used as metaphors in literature.
10. Albatrosses *lives/live* as long as fifty years.

Collective Nouns and Agreement

These are nouns that name a group of people, animals, or things. *Army, herd, committee, team, gaggle, flock, troop, swarm, crowd,* and *squad* are examples of collective nouns. A collective noun takes a singular verb if it refers to the group as a unit. If the collective noun refers to a part of the group, it will use a plural verb.

- The *squad* is preparing for the next competition.
- The *squad members* are preparing for the next competition.
- The frail but determined *squad member* prepares for the next competition.

Practice III

Directions: Correct the sentences below by writing the correct form of the verb on the line at the beginning of the sentence. If the form of the verb used is correct, write a *C* on the line.

EXAMPLE:

_____*is*_____ The flock *are* flying south for the winter.

1. _____ The troop *were* sent to Germany.

2. _____ A member of the colony *are* investigating the events that led to the tragic incident.

3. _____ The bevy of quail *seem* exhausted from their migration.

4. _____ The entire fleet *are* being sent to the Middle East.

5. _____ Yesterday, the team captain *broke* his leg.

6. _____ A swarm *surround* the beekeeper.

7. _____ The pride *search* for prey.

8. _____ An avant-garde group of authors *takes* pride in writing in a stream-of-consciousness style.

9. _____ Twenty members of the gaggle *is* captured and relocated.

10. _____ An urban gang *destroy* the park with graffiti, magnifying the sense of decay in the neighborhood.

Compound Subjects

When there are two or more subjects and they are connected with an *and,* they usually take a plural verb.

Compound Subjects	Plural Verbs
Hunt and Rossetti	are
Hunt and Rossetti	paint
Woolner and Collinson	sculpt and paint

Practice IV

Directions: Read the brief paragraph below, and draw a box around the correct form of the verb needed for the subject.

EXAMPLE:

Raphael, an Italian painter of the sixteenth century, $\boxed{is}$ /*are* known for his paintings of the Madonna.

The Pre-Raphaelites *was/were* a group of English artists and poets who joined together in London in 1848. John Everett Millais, Dante Gabriel Rossetti, and William Holman Hunt *was/were* the founders of the group. These artists *wants/wanted* to reform art to the pre-Raphael period because they felt that the techniques used in art after Raphael and Michelangelo *was/were* mechanical and formulaic. They *wants/wanted* to return to the complex compositions, intense colors, and detailed works of Italian and Flemish art of the fifteenth century. The pre-Raphaelites *has been/have been* considered both avante-garde and controversial. Some *finds/found* their work to be blasphemous and disturbing, but others admired and were influenced by it.

Delayed Subjects

These subjects appear after the verb. These sentences are said to be inverted (or switched around) by moving the verb before the subject. Despite this change, the subject must agree with the verb in number. NOTE: The word *there* is never the subject of a sentence. Look for the subject after the verb. The true subjects of these sentences are underlined.

- There *are* many <u>reasons</u> for the novel *Bleak House* by Charles Dickens.
- There *appear to be* <u>dual-narrators</u> in the novel: an unnamed third-person narrator and orphan Esther.
- Present among the many characters in the novel *is* an orphaned <u>hero</u> named Esther.

Practice V

Directions: Write five sentences that have delayed subjects. Make sure that the subjects and verbs agree.

EXAMPLE:

There *is* a <u>ripe apple</u> in the refrigerator.

1. _____

   _____

2. _____

   _____

3. _____

_____

4. _____

_____

5. _____

_____

Pronoun Agreement

The word (usually a noun) that a pronoun refers to is called its antecedent, as we learned in Chapter 3. Just like nouns, pronouns must agree in number (singular/plural) with the verb. However, in addition to agreeing in number, pronouns must agree in gender. The pronoun and its antecedent are *italicized*. The verb is <u>underlined</u>.

- *Grandmother's* episodes of vertigo <u>bother</u> *her* more in the afternoon.
- The *judge* <u>decided</u> to persecute himself by postponing *his* vacation until after the trial.
- The science *classes* <u>were punished</u> because *they* misbehaved during the experiment in chemical fusion.

Practice VI

Directions: Choose from the Word Bank on the next page, and write in the correct form of the verb that agrees with the pronoun and its antecedent. Use each verb form only once.

EXAMPLE:

Braille ___is___ a unique form of communication for the blind.

1. The system of reading and writing known as Braille _____ by Louis Braille, who lost his sight at the age of three.
2. Braille _____ in 1809 near Paris, France.
3. Louis Braille was a bright student, and he _____ a scholarship to the National Institute of Blind Youth in Paris, although generally the life of the blind person was rather bleak at this time.
4. At first Braille _____ a student, and later he became a teacher at the National Institute of Blind Youth in Paris.
5. Braille _____ a talented musician during his time at the school.
6. In inventing his system of reading, Braille _____only six raised dots that corresponded to letters instead of corresponding to sounds as a previous system invented by Barbier did.
7. Braille also_____ his system of writing for music and mathematics.

8. The system of reading that Braille invented _____ at the school during his lifetime but was rediscovered and used later.

9. Braille and his friend Pierre Foucault _____ a machine that made the process of printing the six-dot system easier.

10. Louis Braille _____ of a disease called tuberculosis at the age of forty-two.

> **Word Bank:** was born, adapted, died, invented, became, was invented, was, won, used, was not used

Indefinite Pronouns (Singular)

The indefinite pronouns *another, anybody, each, either, everybody, everyone, neither, nobody, one, somebody,* and *someone* are singular and require a singular verb. The *indefinite pronoun* is italicized, and the <u>singular verb</u> is underlined in the examples below.

- *Everyone* <u>is</u> going to homecoming.
- *Someone* <u>needs</u> to explain that to you.
- *Each* person <u>contributes</u> to the fundraising event.

Indefinite Pronouns (Singular or Plural)

The indefinite pronouns *all, any, half, most, none,* and *some* can be either singular or plural. There is usually a phrase in the sentence that spells out the number (singular or plural). The *indefinite pronoun* is italicized, the <u>verb</u> is <u>underlined</u>, and the ⬚phrase that indicates the number of the noun⬚ is ⬚boxed⬚.

- *All* ⬚of the participants⬚ <u>will receive</u> a certificate of completion.
- *Most* ⬚of the food⬚ <u>is stored</u> in the pantry.
- *Half* ⬚of the students⬚ <u>do not want</u> homework.

Practice VII

Directions: Draw a box around the correct form (singular or plural) of the verb that is appropriate for the subject in each of the following sentences.

EXAMPLE:

Most of the electrical circuits ⬚are⬚/*is* down because of the tremendous storm.

1. Most of the dogs that *is/are* kenneled need baths.
2. Another one *bites/bite* the dust.
3. Neither of the two candidates *is/are* qualified for the position.

4. Somebody please *tells/tell* me where I can find my backpack!

5. Some of the events *is/are* canceled.

6. Each of us *need/needs* to practice our roles for the play.

7. Everything *have/has* to be shipped before Friday.

8. Half of the Halloween candy *is/was* eaten before the thirty-first.

9. All of the cans *is/are* donated to the homeless shelter.

10. Another fly *is/are* on the barbequed beef.

Chapter 6 Review Quizzes

Vocabulary Review Quiz

Directions: Write the letter of the definition on the line next to the noun that it defines.

1. _____ albatross

2. _____ bleak

3. _____ disturbance

4. _____ frailty

5. _____ fusion

6. _____ magnify

7. _____ persecute

8. _____ Pre-Raphaelite

9. _____ stream-of-consciousness

10. _____ vertigo

A. A member of a group of nineteenth-century English artists united for their distaste of formal academic art and the neoclassical style.

B. Blending of different things into one; the act or instance of melting with intense heat.

C. Bare, exposed, windswept; unpromising, dreary.

D. The act or an instance of unrest; an interruption of calm and quiet.

E. A person's thoughts and conscious reactions to events perceived as a continuous flow; a literary style depicting events in such a flow in a character's mind.

F. Any long-winged bird that inhabits the Pacific Ocean.

G. The act or an instance of making an object appear larger than it is with a lens or increasing the depth of a problem.

H. A condition that causes a sensation of whirling and a tendency to lose balance; dizziness.

I. To subject a person to hostility or ill-treatment, especially on the grounds of political or religious belief; harass.

J. The condition of being fragile or delicate; liability to err or yield to temptation; a fault or weakness

Subject-Verb Agreement Definition Review

Directions: Select the correct definition and write the letter of the answer on the line to the right of the number.

1. _____ Delayed subjects appear _____ the verb.
   a. with
   b. after
   c. before
   d. none of the above

2. _____ The indefinite pronouns *another, anybody, each, either, everybody, everyone, neither, nobody, one, somebody,* and *someone* are _____ and require a _____ verb.
   a. singular . . . singular
   b. plural . . . plural
   c. plural . . . singular
   d. singular . . . plural

3. _____ The word that a pronoun refers to is called its _____.
   a. adjective
   b. friend
   c. verb
   d. antecedent

4. _____ Compound subjects connected with an *and* usually take a _____ verb.
   a. French
   b. singular
   c. plural
   d. crowded

5. _____ Collective nouns that name a group of people, animals, or things such as *army, herd,* and *committee* take a _____ verb if they refer to the group as a unit.
   a. singular
   b. double
   c. plural
   d. compound

6. _____ Collective nouns that refer to a part of the group will take a _____ verb.
   a. singular
   b. double
   c. plural
   d. compound

7. _____ A subject and verb should always agree in _____.
   a. size
   b. color
   c. gender
   d. number

8. _____ True or False? Singular subjects take plural verbs.
   a. True
   b. False

9. _____ Identify the sentence with the correct subject/verb agreement.
   a. They wants to eat ice cream.
   b. We will spends the day walking.
   c. Hannah like to eat bananas.
   d. Monserrat loves to count butterflies.

10. _____ Which sentence does NOT have correct subject/verb agreement?
    a. Nicky and Mariah laugh too much.
    b. David and Ryan are conscientious students.
    c. Annia have a pretty smile.
    d. Marcello studies all the time.

Singular and Plural Subjects

Directions: In the paragraph below, underline all <u>singular subjects</u>, and draw a box around all of the plural subjects .

EXAMPLE:

<u>Langston Hughes</u> is an American author who is known for his poems about the African-American experience in the United States.

The Harlem Renaissance was a movement or period of creativity in literature, art, and music among African Americans in the 1920s. The movement centered in the Harlem area of New York City. The participants of the movement were children of parents who, for the most part, had endured the injustices of slavery. Many of them were a part of what was known as the "Great Migration" out of the South and into the less divisive regions of the North after the Civil War. The Harlem Renaissance represented a "new negro" and served to negate stereotypes often held. It allowed a new sense of self-worth and intellectualism to develop and evolve. Countee Cullen, Zora Neale Hurston, Langston Hughes, and Claude McKay were exemplary writers of the movement. Louis Armstrong, Duke Ellington, Ethel Waters, and Paul Robeson were well-known entertainers of the era.

Singular and Plural Verbs

Directions: On the line before each of the following verbs, write *S* if the verb is singular and write *P* if the verb is plural.

EXAMPLE:

A Portrait of the Artist as a Young Man and *Ulysses* ___*P*___ are two of James Joyce's novels that ___*P*___ are written in stream-of-consciousness.

Stream-of-consciousness _____ is a literary technique in which the thought processes of a character _____ are presented in a chaotic, disconnected, and illogical manner by the author. Also called interior monologue, stream-of-consciousness writings ____are challenging for the reader to follow. The character's thoughts ____appear to be quite random and disconnected. Although the technique _____ gained prominence in the twentieth century, prominent writers such as Leo Tolstoy and Edgar Allan Poe used similar techniques in their works in the 1800s. James Joyce, Virginia Woolf, and William Faulkner _____ are best known for their works using stream-of-consciousness.

Collective Nouns and Compound Subjects

Directions: Identify the following words as either collective nouns or compound subjects. Write *CN* on the line before the word(s) if it is a collective noun and write *CS* on the line if the word(s) is a compound subject.

EXAMPLE:

_____*CN*_____ team

1. _____ species
2. _____ music and lyrics
3. _____ sheep and shepherd
4. _____ crew
5. _____ gaggle
6. _____ flock
7. _____ clams and oysters
8. _____ Shakespeare and Chaucer
9. _____ assembly
10. _____ committee

Pronoun Agreement

Directions: Identify the pronouns and the antecedents in the following sentences. Draw a box around the pronouns, and underline the antecedents.

EXAMPLE:

Dostoevsky is one of the greatest Russian authors of his time.

1. Raskolnikov, the protagonist in the novel *Crime and Punishment,* plans to murder the pawnbroker to solve his money problems.

2. The Russian author Fyodor Dostoevsky began writing his famous novel in 1864.

3. St. Petersburg is where the novel is set; it is a city in Russia.

4. Raskolnikov believes that he is above the law and is doing everyone a favor by murdering the old woman.

5. In addition to murdering the old pawnbroker, Raskolnikov murders her sister, who innocently stumbles onto the murder scene.

6. Marmeladov is a friendly drunkard, and he has a daughter named Sonya.

7. Sonya is forced into prostitution to help support her father's young family, but she is extremely religious.

8. Dunya is Raskolnikov's sister, who agrees to marry Luzhin to save her family from financial ruin.

9. Razumihkin is a friend of Raskolnikov's who falls in love with Dunya.

10. Porfiry is a clever police detective who investigates the murders of the two women.

Indefinite Pronouns

Directions: Underline the **indefinite pronoun** in each of the sentences below. On the line at the beginning of the sentence, write *S* if it is singular and write *P* if it is plural. **Indefinite pronouns** include: *all, another, any, anyone, each, either, everyone, everything, most, neither, some,* and *someone.*

EXAMPLE:

    S   Everything is going wrong at work today.

1. _____ Each of the students is going to give a presentation.

2. _____ Most of the neighbors are in agreement with the proposal for new sidewalks.

3. _____ Someone needs to take responsibility for the mistake.

4. _____ Everything is going to be okay.

5. _____ All of the titles are misspelled and need to be corrected.

6. _____ Neither of the women likes the food at the newly opened restaurant.

7. _____ Another beautiful place to visit is Prague in the Czech Republic.

8. _____ Anyone with any common sense knows not to shout out answers like that.

9. _____ Some shall be banished, and some shall be punished.

10. _____ Any laptop computer will do at this point.

Real-World Practice Activities

Reading and Writing

Directions: Find an article or an encyclopedia entry on one of the following authors: Gabriel Garcia Marquez, Fyodor Dostoevsky, Chinua Achebe, or James Joyce. Write down ten facts about his life using complete sentences. Make sure that you pay attention to subject-verb agreement in writing the sentences.

1. _____
2. _____
3. _____
4. _____
5. _____
6. _____
7. _____
8. _____
9. _____
10. _____

Listening

Directions: Plan to conduct an interview with a friend or relative. Before the interview, write down a few questions that you might want to ask. For instance, you might ask about hobbies, a job, family, friends, travel, or pets. Once you have the questions planned, sit down with the person you are interviewing and ask. Listen carefully to the answers, and write down what the person is saying using complete sentences. Again, watch for subject-verb agreement as you write. Write five of the answers below.

1. _____
2. _____
3. _____
4. _____
5. _____

Chapter 7

ADJECTIVES

Adjectives are words that describe or modify nouns or pronouns. For instance, *ugly, spotted,* and *smelly* are adjectives that could modify or describe the noun *dog*: *ugly dog, spotted dog, smelly dog*. Adjectives add personality and color to sentences that would otherwise be boring or drab without them. Read the following sentences, one without adjectives the other with adjectives.

- The dog ate food.
- The black-spotted dog ate crunchy, dried dog food.

Notice the difference? Adjectives allow the reader to paint a picture in his/her mind about what is going on in a sentence. An adjective also tells what kind, how many, how much, and which one. The list of adjectives is almost infinite. The articles *a, an,* and *the* are probably the most frequently used adjectives. However, there are proper adjectives, pronouns used as adjectives, predicate adjectives, absolute adjectives, and positive form, comparative form, and superlative forms of adjectives.

Vocabulary Development

1. **civilian** (siv il yen) Of or for a person who is not in the armed services or a police force.
2. **roomy** (roo mee) Having much room; spacious.
3. **tart** (taart) Sharp or acidic taste; cutting or bitter.
4. **auburn** (aw bern) Reddish brown (usually a person's hair).
5. **audacious** (aw day shush) Daring, bold.
6. **bogus** (bo gess) Sham, spurious.
7. **Bohemian** (bo hee mee en) A person who is socially unconventional or different.
8. **diplomatic** (dip le ma tic) Skilled in diplomacy or dealing with relationships (personal or international).
9. **malignant** (ma ligg nent) Harmful, infectious, cancerous disease.
10. **malnourished** (mal ner isht) Suffering from malnourishment or lack of food.

Articles

Articles are simple and straightforward. There are three articles that are considered adjectives. They are by far the most used of all adjectives: *a, an,* and *the*. There are two indefinite articles and one definite article.

Indefinite Articles

A and *an* are indefinite articles. Each of them refers to someone or something, but not to someone or something specific. The article *a* is used before a word beginning with a consonant sound (b, c, d, f, g, and so on). The article *an* is used before words beginning with a vowel sound (a, e, i, o, u).

- <u>A</u> roomy office was exactly what the young executive needed.
- <u>A</u> malnourished African child was given food and water by the charitable organization.
- <u>An</u> audacious young woman attempted and succeeded at impressing her new employers.

Definite Article

The is the only definite article in English and is used to refer to a particular someone or something. It is <u>the</u> person, place, thing, or idea, not merely *a* random selection.

- <u>The</u> tart plum caused him to cringe when he bit into it.
- <u>The</u> civilian volunteer wanted desperately to join the police force.
- <u>The</u> bogus currency was passed from bank to bank until an alert teller noticed it.

Practice I

Directions: Note the underlined article in each of the sentences below. On the line, write either *definite* or *indefinite* to identify the article.

EXAMPLE:

_____*indefinite*_____ Africa is <u>a</u> large continent.

1. _____ Darfur is in <u>the</u> western region of Sudan, a country in Africa.

2. _____ There has been <u>an</u> ongoing conflict in the area since 2003.

3. _____ The conflict is between <u>a</u> militia group known as Janjaweed and the civilian, mostly land-tilling tribes of the area.

4. _____ <u>The</u> Sudanese government denies supporting Janjaweed, but it supplied weapons and participated in attacks on several ethnic groups.

5. _____ <u>A</u> United Nations–approved resolution was passed in August 2006 after the conflict had escalated.

6. _____ Resolution 1706 called for over 17,000 peacekeeping troops to join <u>the</u> poorly equipped African peacekeeping force.

7. _____ Estimates of between 9,000 and 400,000 citizens were killed or died from starvation and malnourishment during <u>the</u> conflict.

8. _____ It is believed that as many as 2.5 million people were displaced in <u>the</u> region during an eighteen-month period.

9. _____ <u>The</u> conflict has many causes, ranging from environmental issues to political opportunism.

10. _____ In <u>an</u> attempt to raise awareness of the severity of the civilian problems in the region, several television shows, including *West Wing* and *ER*, have used Darfur for a subject of one or more episodes.

Common and Proper Adjectives

Common adjectives are basically all adjectives that are not capitalized: *dusty, yellow, auburn, tart,* and *audacious.* Proper adjectives modify nouns or pronouns, but the difference between a common adjective and a proper adjective is that a proper adjective is ALWAYS capitalized. *French, Roman, Japanese*, and *Swiss* cheese are examples of proper adjectives.

Practice II

Directions: On the lines below, write ten common adjectives and ten proper adjectives. Make certain that all proper adjectives are capitalized.

Common Adjectives	Proper Adjectives
Example: _____*grand*_____	_____*Spanish*_____
1. _____	_____
2. _____	_____
3. _____	_____
4. _____	_____
5. _____	_____
6. _____	_____
7. _____	_____
8. _____	_____
9. _____	_____
10. _____	_____

Demonstrative Adjectives or Pronouns Used as Adjectives

That, these, this, and *those* are words that can be used as both pronouns and adjectives. These words are considered demonstrative adjectives when they modify a noun or a pronoun. *That, these, this,* and *those* point out a specific person, place, thing, or idea.

- *That* box seems to be mislabeled.
- *These* dogs will be shipped to their new owners in one week.
- According to my records, *this* shipment was delivered yesterday.
- If you will please take *those* boxes to the shipping company, that will be it for the day.

Practice III

Directions: Read the following paragraph and fill in the blanks with the demonstrative adjective that best fits the meaning of the sentence *(that, these, this, those).*

EXAMPLE:

   These   are the most unusual people that I have ever met. They are truly Bohemian.

The word Bohemian can be used in either of _____ two ways. First of all, it can be used to describe the people who live in the Bohemia region or area now known as the Czech Republic. The term for _____ area comes from a Latin term for the original Celtic tribe that once lived there. Secondly, the term bohemian in modern-day usage represents any person who lives an unconventional and artistic life. _____ subscribing to a bohemian lifestyle believe that self-expression is vital to their existence and _____art (dancing, painting, writing, singing, and so on) is the primary focus of _____ lifestyle. _____ term was originally applied to a group of "bohemians" known as the Bloomsbury group in London and a group of writers in Carmel-by-the-Sea, California, in the early 1900s.

Nouns Used as Adjectives

These are words that can actually stand alone as nouns, but when they are used to modify a noun or a pronoun, they become adjectives. The following groups of words are both nouns, but the word that modifies (the first of the two words) becomes an adjective.

fleece coat	*snow* country	*ring* finger
rubber boots	*mountain* bike	*household* goods
freshman class	*snack* food	*Washington* coast
country club	*India* ink	*pecan* pie
human nature	*bedtime* story	*Chagall* painting

Practice IV

Directions: Read the following incomplete sentences. Choose a noun (used as an adjective) from the Word Bank that best completes the sentence, and write it on the line provided. Use each word only once.

EXAMPLE:

The *chili* cook-off contest was a great success.

1. Smokers often suffer from _____ disease.
2. The _____ doughnut looked and smelled delicious.
3. Those who study _____ science become geologists.
4. The _____ meow seems to be coming from up in that tree.
5. _____ work entails typing, filing, organizing, and answering the phone.
6. The antique _____ cabinet was large enough to hold all of my clothes.
7. As a _____ maid, she had to take care of the three children.
8. Last night's episode of *Ugly Betty,* her favorite _____ show, was one that she had seen earlier in the year.
9. The _____ commercial looked romantic with the beautiful young woman smiling at a young man and the city of Paris in the background.
10. Our group _____ ticket to the museum cost over three hundred dollars.

Word Bank: entry, nurse, cat, lung, earth, television, perfume, office, wardrobe, cream

---

Forms of Adjectives

There are three forms of adjectives: positive, comparative, and superlative.

Positive Form

The positive form simply describes a noun or pronoun without comparing it to anyone or anything.

- The ocean is calm.
- The sun is bright.
- The sand feels warm.

Comparative Form

The comparative form compares two persons, places, things, or ideas. The comparative form usually takes an -*er* ending. Longer, multisyllabic adjectives do not take an -*er* ending. Instead, the word *more* precedes the adjective.

- The river flows faster than the stream.
- The sun is brighter than the moon.
- The sand at the beach is more malleable than the sand at the river.

Superlative Form

The superlative form compares three or more persons, places, things, or ides. The superlative form usually takes an -*est* ending. Similar to the comparative form, adjectives with two or more syllables do not take the -*est* ending. These words require the word *most* to make them superlative forms.

- The ocean is the largest body of water.
- The sun is the brightest star in the sky.
- Sand is one of the roughest textures.

Practice V

Directions: Complete the chart below by filling in the blanks with the proper form of the word listed.

Positive	Comparative	Superlative
Example: *low*	*lower*	*lowest*
1. _____	louder	loudest
2. _____	higher	highest
3. tart	_____	most tart
4. _____	more grand	most grand
5. easy	easier	_____
6. gloomy	gloomier	_____
7. expensive	_____	most expensive
8. _____	_____	happiest
9. late	later	_____
10. _____	roomier	_____

Chapter 7 Review Quizzes

Vocabulary Review Quiz

Directions: Write the letter of the definition on the line next to the adjective that it defines.

1. _____ malnourished

2. _____ civilian

3. _____ audacious

4. _____ tart

5. _____ bogus

6. _____ auburn

7. _____ roomy

8. _____ Bohemian

9. _____ diplomatic

10. _____ malignant

A. Having much room; spacious.

B. Sharp or acidic taste; cutting or bitter.

C. Reddish brown (usually a person's hair).

D. Daring, bold.

E. Of or for a person who is not in the armed services or a police force.

F. Sham; spurious.

G. A person who is socially unconventional or different.

H. Skilled in diplomacy or dealing with relationships (personal or international).

I. Harmful, infectious, cancerous disease.

J. Suffering from malnourishment or lack of food.

Adjective Definitions Review Quiz

Directions: Select the correct definition, and write the letter of the answer on the line to the right of the number.

1. _____ Which of the following is a common adjective?
   a. French
   b. Swiss
   c. Spanish
   d. none of the above

2. _____ Proper adjectives are always _____.
   a. ordinary
   b. common
   c. capitalized
   d. used as nouns

3. _____ Which of the following is NOT an article?
   a. their
   b. a
   c. an
   d. the

4. _____ Which of the following words IS a definite article?
   a. their
   b. a
   c. an
   d. the

5. _____ Identify the group of demonstrative adjectives below.
   a. they, their, take
   b. the, an, a
   c. that, those, these, this
   d. easy, fast, smooth, rough

6. _____ True or False? Some nouns are used as adjectives.
   a. True
   b. False

7. _____ Which of the following uses the positive form of an adjective?
   a. The boy is the most intelligent in his class.
   b. The boy is more intelligent than his brother.
   c. The boy is intelligent.
   d. None of the above.

8. _____ Which of the following uses the superlative form of an adjective?
   a. China has a large population.
   b. China has the largest population in the world.
   c. China's population is larger than India's population.
   d. India is large.

9. _____ True or False? This sentence uses the comparative form of an adjective, "Disneyland is the happiest place on Earth."
   a. True
   b. False

10. _____ Identify the positive form of the word *expensive*.
    a. expensive
    b. more expensive
    c. expensiver
    d. most expensive

Articles: Definite and Indefinite

Directions: In the paragraph below, underline indefinite articles and draw a box around the definite articles.

Rolling Stone Magazine published an article in 2004 that listed the top 500 greatest songs of all time. Over 170 musicians, music critics, and other officials in the music industry voted for the songs. The list caused a reasonable amount of controversy because the only song that is not sung in English is a song called *La Bamba* by Ritchie Valens. Of the 500 songs listed, 357 are from the United States, 117 are from the United Kingdom, 10 are from Canada, and 8 are from Ireland. The list includes 202 songs from the 1960s and 144 are from the 1970s. Although there are 24 songs from the 1980s, there is an extremely limited number from the twenty-first century (one by Outkast and two by Eminem). The oldest song is from 1948, which is a song titled "Rollin'Stone" by Muddy Waters. The Beatles have the most songs on the list, 23. The Rolling Stones, Bob Dylan, and Elvis Presley each have more than 10 songs listed. The top song is by Bob Dylan, "Like a Rolling Stone." The remainder of the top 10 songs are "(I Can't Get No) Satisfaction" by the Rolling Stones, "Imagine" by John Lennon, "What's Going On" by Marvin Gaye, "Respect" by Aretha Franklin, "Good Vibrations" by the Beach Boys, "Johnny B. Goode" by Chuck Berry, "Hey Jude" by the Beatles, "Smells Like Teen Spirit" by Nirvana, and the last of the top ten is "What'd I Say" by Ray Charles.

Common and Proper Adjectives

Directions: Read the paragraph. Select a common or proper adjective from the Word Bank below that best completes the meaning of the sentence, and write it on the line within the paragraph. Use each word only once.

The largest _____ known in the world weighs just over 14 pounds (6 kg) and has a 10-inch (25-cm) diameter. The pearl, called the Pearl of Lao Tzu, was the subject of a Chinese _____ that was passed down for generations. The Pearl of Lao Tzu was cultivated in 600 B.C. Also called the Pearl of Allah, the giant pearl was rediscovered inside a giant _____ by a _____ diver off the coast of Palawa, which is in the Philippines, in 1934. As the _____ is told, a man named Cobb offered to buy the pearl, but his offer was rejected. Later, when Cobb returned to the village, the chief's son was dying and Cobb helped save his _____. The chief gave the pearl to Mr. Cobb as a _____ of his appreciation. Although Cobb was offered as much as $10 million for the pearl, he refused to sell it. After his death however, Mr. Cobb's _____ sold the pearl for $200,000. At present, the pearl is thought to be priceless, but a $75,000,000 price is associated with it.

Word Bank: clam, pearl, story, legend, token, Filipino, family, life

Demonstrative Adjectives or Pronouns Used as Adjectives and Nouns Used as Adjectives

Directions: Write four sentences using the demonstrative adjectives listed on the lines, and then write six sentences using nouns that are used for adjectives. Underline the demonstrative adjectives and the adjectival nouns.

EXAMPLES:

Take <u>this</u> loaf of bread to your grandmother.
The <u>P. Diddy concert</u> was packed with fans.

1. (this)_____

2. (that)_____

3. (these)_____

4. (those)_____

5. _____

6. _____

7. _____

8. _____

9. _____

10. _____

Forms of Adjectives: Positive, Comparative, Superlative

Directions: Fill in the blanks with the correct form of the adjective that best completes the meaning of the sentence. If the word is correct in form, write a *C* on the line.

EXAMPLE:

Coral reefs provide an (immense) ___*C*___ habitat for nearly 100,000 different species of living organisms.

1. The (large)_____ coral reef in the world is the Great Barrier Reef off the coast of Australia.

2. The reef is (large)_____ enough to be seen from outer space.

3. It has a (great) _____ number of reefs and islands that stretch over 1,600 miles (2,575 km), more than any other in the world.

4. The reef is one of the (popular)_____ tourist destinations because of its biodiversity.

5. The crown of thorns starfish is the (threatening)_____predator of coral reefs.

6. Many scientists believe that the (great)_____ threat to the Great Barrier Reef is climate change.

7. Poor water quality is also considered an (ominous)_____ threat, particularly from industrial runoff.

8. In 2005 Australia experienced its (warm) _____ year ever.

9. Unusually (high) _____ temperatures cause coral bleaching.

10. Coral bleaching causes the corals to lose their photosynthesizing zooxanthellae, which causes them to lose color with continued (warm)_____ temperatures.

Real-World Practice Activities

Reading

Directions: Locate and read an article in a newspaper, magazine, or encyclopedia about the Great Barrier Reef. After you have completed reading the article, go back and find twenty (20) adjectives that you find interesting. List them below. If you do not understand what the adjective means, look for its definition in a dictionary.

1._____	6._____	11._____	16._____
2._____	7._____	12._____	17._____
3._____	8._____	13._____	18._____
4._____	9._____	14._____	19._____
5._____	10._____	15._____	20._____

Writing

Directions: Using some of the adjectives that you found in the article on the Great Barrier Reef, write a one-paragraph summary of what you read on the lines below.

_____

_____

_____

_____

_____

_____

_____

_____
_____
_____
_____
_____
_____
_____
_____

Listening

Directions: Listen carefully to a news program on the radio, on television, or on the Internet. Write down a list of ten (10) adjectives that you hear during the course of the show. Write them in the spaces provided below. When the program is over, write a sentence using the adjective in its proper context according to the news story. NOTE: You will have to listen **carefully**—particularly in the beginning. The more you practice this skill of recognizing adjectives while remembering the context of story, the easier it will become.

1. (Adjective)_____

_____

2. (Adjective)_____

_____

3. (Adjective)_____

_____

4. (Adjective)_____

_____

5. (Adjective)_____

_____

6. (Adjective)_____

_____

7. (Adjective)_____

_____

8. (Adjective)_____

_____

9. (Adjective)_____

_____

10. (Adjective)_____

_____

Chapter 8

ADVERBS

Adverbs are words that describe or modify verbs for the most part. For instance, the dog barked <u>viciously</u> at the intruder. However, adverbs also modify adjectives or other adverbs. Most adverbs end in -ly, but not always. Be cautious when making that call—make certain that the "adverb" in question is modifying a verb. Words such as *never, too, far, fast,* and *often* are adverbs. Adverbs tell how, when, where, why, how much, and how often. The three forms of adverbs are positive, comparative, and superlative. (Does that sound familiar? Hint: think adjectives.)

Vocabulary Development

1. **artistically** (ar tis tick lee) Showing or prepared with good skill and taste.
2. **boastfully** (boste ful lee) Boasting or speaking freely with great pride to impress people.
3. **dramatically** (dra mat tick lee) Exciting, impressive.
4. **extravagantly** (ex trav a gant lee) Spending more than is necessary.
5. **meticulously** (me tick u lus lee) Giving or showing great attention to detail, very careful, exact.
6. **offensively** (of fens iv lee) Causing offense, insulting.
7. **poetically** (po e tick lee) Of or like poetry, written in verse.
8. **serpentinely** (ser pen tin lee) Twisting and curving like a snake.
9. **tranquilly** (tran qwil lee) Quiet, peaceful, calm.
10. **whimsically** (wim sick lee) Impulsive, playful.

The Position of the Adverb

The adverb may appear in various positions in the sentence. Adverbs may appear next to or between, before, or after the word or words they modify. In the examples below, the adverbs are ***italicized and boldface*** and the verbs they modify are <u>underlined</u>.

- The students ***boastfully*** <u>announced</u> their science fair victories. (next to verb)
- ***Boastfully***, the students <u>announced</u> their science fair victories. (before verb)
- The students <u>announced</u> their science fair victories ***boastfully***. (after verb)

Practice I

Directions: Using the adverbs listed at the beginning of each of the lines below, write a sentence using the adverb and place it in the sentence in the position that is indicated, next to, before, after, and so on.

EXAMPLE:

quickly (before the verb) <u>The rabbit *quickly* burrowed back into its hole when it heard the train approach</u>.

1. warmly (next to verb) _____

_____

2. religiously (before the verb) _____

_____

3. tranquilly (next to the verb) _____

_____

4. dramatically (after the verb) _____

_____

5. artistically (next to the verb) _____

_____

6. weakly (after the verb) _____

_____

7. mysteriously (before the verb) _____

_____

8. less (next to the verb) _____

_____

9. faster (after the verb) _____

_____

10. gracefully (before the verb) _____

_____

Adverbs That Modify Verbs

The primary job of an adverb is to modify or describe the verb in the sentence. In the examples below, the adverbs are ***italicized and boldface*** and the verbs they modify are <u>underlined</u>.

- *Angrily*, the clerk <u>emptied</u> his drawer.
- The young boy's headache was *easily* <u>relieved</u> with medicine.
- Because the day was hot and humid, we *lazily* <u>completed</u> our tasks.

Practice II

Directions: Fill in the blanks in the following paragraph with **adverbs that modify verbs.**

EXAMPLE:

According to Louis Pasteur, germs are more **easily** *transmitted* in a handshake than in kissing. He refused to shake hands with acquaintances for fear of infection. (I wonder if he kissed them instead?)

Pasteurization is a heat treatment of food that is <u>used</u> _____ to kill bacteria and other microorganisms. The treatment was _____ <u>discovered</u> by a French chemist named Louis Pasteur in the 1860s, for whom the process is named. He is known as one of the founders of microbiology. Pasteur also discovered that he could _____ <u>weaken</u> certain disease-causing microorganisms and then use the weakened culture to vaccinate against the disease. Milk is _____ <u>pasteurized</u> by heating it to 161.6°F (72°C) for 16 seconds. Today a process known as ultrapasteurization is used to produce milk that is called UHT (ultra-heat-treated) milk. It is heated to 270°F (132°C) for one second to _____ <u>add</u> a shelf life of several months to the product.

Adverbs That Modify Adjectives

Adverbs also have the job of modifying adjectives. In the examples below, the adverbs are *boldface and italicized* and the adjectives that they modify are <u>underlined</u>.

- The ants, *meticulously* <u>fast</u> workers, build what seem to be miles of trails.
- The comic, who is a *whimsically* <u>funny</u> woman, had the audience in tears.
- The *dramatically* <u>modern</u> production of the ancient play won several awards.

Practice III

Directions: On the line next to the adjective listed, write an **adverb** that modifies it.

EXAMPLE:

_____luxuriously_____ gorgeous

1. _____ narrow
2. _____ ordinary
3. _____ scrawny
4. _____ roasted
5. _____ tall

6. _____ green
7. _____ nutritious
8. _____ ugly
9. _____ frail
10. _____ nasty

Adverbs That Modify Other Adverbs

As confusing as it may seem, adverbs can modify other adverbs in the same sentence. The adverb that modifies another adverb is **boldface and italicized** in the examples below. The modified adverb is underlined.

- The writing, **almost** poetically tragic, became a best seller.
- The heiress used money **too** extravagantly.
- The pianist's **often** frantically fast playing impressed the audience.

Practice IV

Directions: Read the sentences below and add an adverb from the Word Bank that best modifies the adverb that is underlined in the sentence. You will **NOT** use all of the words in the Word Bank.

EXAMPLE:

The hot summer day seemed to almost lazily disappear into a steamy night.

1. The river _____ meanderingly wound its way through the canyon.
2. Because of their vows of silence, the monks _____ loudly complete their daily tasks.
3. _____ unexpectedly, the candidate changed his mind and dropped out of the race.
4. The officer arrived _____ punctually.
5. The _____ joyously content mother was the one whose baby was sleeping.
6. All _____ rarely did our local team win any football games this season.
7. _____ offensively, the home team audience chanted against the winning team.
8. _____ vivaciously, the introverted child completes his speech.
9. Being _____ cautiously optimistic, the doctor continued the patient's treatments.
10. The Arctic explorers traveled courageously _____ through the region.

> **Word Bank:** well, almost, even, only, very, too, more, less, soon, far, so, really, most, never, seldom

Other Adverbs

Adverbs can describe time, place, manner, or degree.

Adverbs of Time

These tell *when, how often*, and *how long*. They include *yesterday, tomorrow, afterward, today, recently, frequently, annually, daily, seldom, yearly, quarterly, eternally, briefly, quickly, speedily*, and *swiftly*.

Adverbs of Place

These tell *where, to where*, and *from where*. They include *here, there, abroad, anywhere, outside, somewhere, underground*, and *upstairs*.

Adverbs of Manner

These tell *how* something is done and often end in *-ly*. They include *anxiously, badly, kindly, gentlemanly, weakly, luckily*, and *meticulously*.

Adverbs of Degree

These tell *how much* or *how little*. They include *adequately, almost, entirely, extremely, greatly, highly, hugely, immensely, moderately, partially, perfectly, practically, profoundly, strongly, totally, tremendously, very*, and *virtually*.

Practice V

Directions: Identify the following adverbs as adverbs of *time, place, manner*, or *degree*.

EXAMPLE:

_____manner_____ gentlemanly

1. _____ today		6. _____ outside
2. _____ very		7. _____ strongly
3. _____ greatly		8. _____ yearly
4. _____ weakly		9. _____ meticulously
5. _____ here		10. _____ daily

Forms of Adverbs

There are three forms of adverbs: positive, comparative, and superlative. NOTE: Many adjectives can be changed from adjectives to adverbs by adding an -ly ending.

Positive Form

The positive form of adverbs describes a verb, an adjective, or another adverb without comparing it with anything or anyone else.

Comparative Form

This form compares two persons, places, things, or ideas.

Superlative Form

The superlative compares three or more persons, places, things, or ideas.

Positive	Comparative	Superlative
happily	more happily	most happily
inquisitively	more inquisitively	most inquisitively
well	better	best
far	farther	farthest
tranquilly	less tranquilly	least tranquilly

Practice VI

Directions: In the sentences below, use the correct form of the adverb (positive, comparative, or superlative) for the word in parentheses by writing it on the line that is provided.

EXAMPLE:

Jupiter is the (large) ___*largest*___ planet.

1. The young woman is the (artistic) _____ talented in her class and loves to paint.
2. The animated cartoon was (whimsical) _____ created.
3. During the drought, their village was (far) _____from the water source.
4. They will live (happy) _____ ever after.
5. He is the (inquisitive) _____ student ever.
6. They are doing quite (well) _____.

7. Taking Interstate 5 is the (fast) _____ route to Seattle.

8. That is the (badly) _____ interpretation that I have ever seen.

9. People tend to behave (aggressive) _____ in crowds.

10. Her hiking boots are (well) _____than her cousin's.

Chapter 8 Review Quizzes

Vocabulary Review Quiz

Directions: Write the letter of the definition on the line next to the noun that it defines.

1. _____ artistically

2. _____ boastfully

3. _____ dramatically

4. _____ extravagantly

5. _____ meticulously

6. _____ offensively

7. _____ poetically

8. _____ serpentinely

9. _____ tranquilly

10. _____ whimsically

A. Of or like poetry, written in verse.

B. Exciting, impressive.

C. Showing or completed with good skill and taste.

D. Impulsive, playful.

E. Boasting or speaking freely with great pride to impress people.

F. Spending more than is necessary.

G. Causing offense, insulting.

H. Twisting and curving like a snake.

I. Giving or showing great attention to detail, very careful, exact.

J. Quiet, peaceful, calm.

Adverb Definitions

Directions: Select the correct definition and write the letter of the answer on the line to the right of the number.

1. _____ An adverb may be positioned _____ the word that it modifies.
   a. before
   b. next to
   c. after
   d. all of the above

2. _____ True or False? Adverbs do not modify verbs.
   a. True
   b. False

3. _____ Which of the following sentences includes an adverb that modifies an adjective?
   a. The meticulously dressed woman flies first class.
   b. The unusually fast response was unexpected
   c. Suddenly, the fire enveloped the entire neighborhood.
   d. None of the above.

4. _____ Which of the following is an example of an adverb modifying another adverb?
   a. extremely
   b. really
   c. loudly
   d. too recklessly

5. _____ Adverbs of time tell _____ .
   a. how much or how little
   b. where, to where, and from where
   c. when, how often, and how long
   d. how something is done

6. _____ Adverbs of place tell_____ .
   a. how much or how little
   b. where, to where, and from where
   c. when, how often, and how long
   d. how something is done

7. _____ Adverbs of manner tell _____ .
   a. how much or how little
   b. where, to where, and from where
   c. when, how often, and how long
   d. how something is done

8. _____ Adverbs of degree tell _____ .
   a. how much or how little
   b. where, to where, and from where
   c. when, how often, and how long
   d. how something is done

9. _____ *Fastest, most respectfully,* and *worst* are examples of _____ .
   a. positive forms of adverbs
   b. comparative forms of adverbs
   c. superlative forms of adverbs
   d. all of the above

10. _____ The adverb form that compares three or more is _____
   a. superlative
   b. comparative
   c. positive
   d. redundant

Adverbs that Modify Verbs, Adjectives, or Other Adverbs

Directions: In the following sentences, identify whether the adverb that is underlined modifies the verb, an adjective, or another adverb. Write *verb, adjective,* or *adverb* on the line accordingly.

EXAMPLE:

_____*verb*_____ The word *helium* comes from the <u>commonly</u> referred to Greek word "helios," meaning *Sun.*

1. _____ Helium is a nonmetallic element <u>clearly</u> discovered in 1868.

2. _____ It was first found in the mineral cleveite, a <u>radioactively</u> impure variety of uraninite.

3. _____ William Ramsay <u>cleverly</u> discovered the gas in 1895.

4. _____ <u>Truthfully</u>, the chief source of helium today is natural gas.

5. _____ <u>Oddly</u> enough, the gas is found in Earth's atmosphere as well (0.0005% by volume).

6. _____ It <u>honestly</u> has the lowest melting and boiling points of any element.

7. _____ Helium is <u>always</u> colorless, odorless, and nonflammable.

8. _____ The gas is <u>regularly</u> used to float light-air balloons that are frequently decorations for parties.

9. _____ It is <u>deliberately</u> combined with oxygen to make artificial air for deep sea divers.

10. _____ A member of the noble gases, helium <u>rarely</u> reacts with any other chemical. Its atomic number is 2, and its symbol on the periodic table of chemical elements is He.

Adverbs of Time, Place, Manner, and Degree

Directions: Complete the chart below with adverbs of time, place, manner, and degree.

Adverbs of Time	Adverbs of Place	Adverbs of Manner	Adverbs of Degree
Example: *yesterday*	*here*	*kindly*	*perfectly*

Forms of Adverbs: Positive, Comparative, Superlative

Directions: Complete the chart below by writing in the correct form of the adverb.

Positive	Comparative	Superlative
Example: lazy	*lazier*	*laziest*
fast		fastest
quietly	more quietly	
seriously		most seriously
	later	latest
well	better	
	more tranquilly	most tranquilly
	more artistically	most artistically
little	less	
far		farthest
stately		most stately

Real-World Practice Activities

Reading

Directions: Find an article on the South American country of Brazil. After you have completed reading the article, go back and find twenty (20) adverbs that you find interesting and list them below. If you do not understand what one of the adverbs means, look for its definition in a dictionary.

1. _____
2. _____
3. _____
4. _____
5. _____

6. _____
7. _____
8. _____
9. _____
10. _____

11. _____
12. _____
13. _____
14. _____
15. _____

16. _____
17. _____
18. _____
19. _____
20. _____

Writing

Directions: Using some of the adverbs that you found in the article on Brazil, write a one-paragraph summary of what you read on the lines below.

_____

_____

_____

_____
_____
_____
_____
_____
_____
_____
_____
_____
_____
_____

Listening

Directions: Listen carefully to a news program on the radio, on television, or on the Internet. Write down a list of ten (10) adverbs that you hear during the course of the show. Write them in the spaces provided below. When the show is over, write a sentence using the adverb in its proper context according to the news story.

1. (Adverb)_____
_____

2. (Adverb)_____
_____

3. (Adverb)_____
_____

4. (Adverb)_____
_____

5. (Adverb)_____
_____

6. (Adverb)_____
_____

7. (Adverb)_____
_____

8. (Adverb)_____
_____

9. (Adverb)_____
_____

10. (Adverb)_____
_____

Chapter 9

PREPOSITIONS, CONJUNCTIONS, AND INTERJECTIONS

Vocabulary Development

1. **aboard** (a bohred) On board of, in, on.
2. **against** (a genst) In opposition to; in contact with.
3. **concerning** (cun sir ning) Relating to, regarding, about.
4. **despite** (des spyt) In spite of, notwithstanding.
5. **excepting** (x sepp ting) Excluding, barring.
6. **notwithstanding** (not with stan ding) In spite of.
7. **regarding** (ree gar ding) Concerning, with reference to.
8. **underneath** (unn dir neeth) Below or beneath something.
9. **via** (vee ah) By way of, through.
10. **within** (with inn) Inside, enclosed by.

Prepositions

A preposition is a word that shows the relationship between a noun or a pronoun and another word, such as *after, against, unto, until,* and *within*. There are three types of prepositions: simple, compound, and phrasal. The best way to get to know prepositions is to memorize or study thoroughly the list of prepositions that is presented in the table. They are simple to understand once you know what they are. Each of the examples below contains a preposition. Note how the preposition demonstrates position and the relationship between two words (noun and noun or noun and pronoun).

- The cold wind blew strongly *against* the tree and toppled it.
- *Below* the box is a paper that I need to copy.
- He will accept the award *on behalf of* the winner, who cannot attend the ceremony.

Simple Prepositions

These are one-word words, such as *under, over, about, above, up,* and *back.*

Compound Prepositions

These are two words that are combined into one word. Examples include *alongside, within, without,* and *underneath.*

Phrasal Prepositions

These are a collection of two or three words (mini phrases in a sense) made of prepositions. Examples include *in place of, together with, in spite of,* and *by means of.*

PREPOSITIONS—SIMPLE, COMPOUND, AND PHRASAL					
aboard	about	above	according to	across	across from
after	against	along	alongside	alongside of	along with
amid	among	apart from	around	aside from	at
before	behind	below	beneath	beside	besides
between	beyond	but	by	by means of	concerning
considering	despite	down	down from	during	except
except for	excepting	for	from	in	in addition to
in behalf of	in front of	in place of	in regard to	inside	inside of
into	like	near	near to	notwithstanding	of
off	on	on account of	on behalf of	onto	on top of
opposite	out	out of	outside	outside of	over
past	regarding	round	round about	save	since
subsequent to	together with	through	throughout	till	to
toward	under	underneath	until	unto	up
upon	via	with	within	without	

Practice I

Directions: Identify each of the following prepositions as simple, compound, or phrasal by writing *S* on the line if it is simple, *C* on the line if it is compound, and *P* on the line if it is phrasal.

EXAMPLE:

up   *S*

1. regarding	_____	6. underneath	_____
2. alongside	_____	7. on behalf of	_____
3. of	_____	8. over	_____
4. on top of	_____	9. into	_____
5. opposite	_____	10. near	_____

Practice II

Directions: Read the sentences below, and ⟨circle⟩ the correct preposition for the context of the sentence.

EXAMPLE:

Michelangelo is considered one of the greatest artists ⟨*of*⟩/*after* all time.

1. The Sistine Chapel is a private chapel *of/over* the popes.
2. It is located *in/on behalf of* the Vatican City, a sovereign state within the city of Rome, Italy.
3. It was built *into/between* 1473 and 1481 for Pope Sixtus IV.
4. The building is 134 feet (40 m) long, 44 feet (13 m) wide, and *about/opposite* 68 feet (21 m) high.
5. The side walls were painted with frescoes *toward/by* the artists Perugino, Pinturicchio, Botticelli, Ghirlandaio, and Signorelli.
6. Frescoes are paintings that are completed *past/on* wet plaster.
7. *Without/Through* question, the chapel's most celebrated feature is its ceiling.
8. The ceiling, window lunettes, and altar wall were all painted *inside/by* Michelangelo from 1508 until 1541.
9. Despite the fact that Michelangelo considered himself a sculptor and not a painter, he accepted the commission *near/from* the pope to paint the ceiling.
10. He lay *out/on* his back on top of wooden scaffolding to paint.

Conjunctions

A conjunction is a word that connects individual words or a group of words. There are three types of conjunctions: coordinate, correlative, and subordinate.

Coordinate Conjunctions

These connect words or phrases that are used the same way or are the same type. Coordinating conjunctions include *and, so, but, nor, yet, or,* and *for.*

- Juan *and* Jose volunteered for the job.
- Take whatever you need, *but* do not leave a mess.
- It is quite possible, *yet* it is not completely probable.

Correlative Conjunctions

These are words that are used in pairs to connect words or groups of words: *either/or, neither/nor, not only/but also, both/and, whether/or, just/as, just/so,* and *as/so.*

- *Not only* did Juan and Jose volunteer, *but* Frida and Maria volunteered as well.
- *Neither* David *nor* Joey completed their assignments.
- *Whether* it was Michael *or* Joe who hacked into the school computers, I do not think we will ever know.

Subordinate Conjunctions

These connect two clauses—a dependent clause to an independent clause. Examples include *after, although, as, as if, as long as, as though, because, before, if, in order that, provided that, since, so, so that, that, though, till, unless, until, when, where, whereas,* and *while.*

- *Although* we are anxious to solve the problem (dependent clause), we will need more evidence (independent clause).
- *Until* you understand the importance of the assignment (dependent clause), the class will continue to work on Chapter 4 (independent clause).
- *In order that* we continue on our trip (dependent clause), our car will have to be repaired at an authorized dealership (independent clause).

Practice III

Directions: Underline each of the conjunctions used in the sentences below.

EXAMPLE:

Unless we become more market savvy, our new line of products will never succeed.

1. Since the ancient Greek Olympics, running competitions have been part of history.
2. The effects of running are felt not only in the body but in the mind as well.
3. Running is a complex physical activity that requires the use of many muscles.
4. Although walking is less stressful to the body, running can burn 50 percent more calories than walking.
5. Because it is a high-impact sport, there are many injuries associated with running.
6. Jogging is a slow type of running that used to be called roadwork.
7. There are many different running events, and they are ranked according to distance.
8. Sprints are short but very fast events when the runner runs his or her fastest for the entire race.
9. Marathons are long-distance events and measure 26 miles (42 km) and 385 yards (352 m) long.
10. Although running is a competitive sport itself, it is also an important part of other team sports such as soccer (football), American football, basketball, lacrosse, and rugby.

Practice IV

Directions: Identify each of the conjunctions below as either coordinate, correlative, or subordinate.

EXAMPLE:

   Correlative   just/as

1. _____ in order that
2. _____ and
3. _____ neither/nor
4. _____ either/or
5. _____ so

6. _____ since
7. _____ while
8. _____ as though
9. _____ as if
10. _____ but

Interjections

These are words or phrases used to exclaim, protest, or command, such as *ah, alas, ouch, oh no, well,* and *yikes.* Most interjections have an exclamation point (!) after them—or are set off by a comma. They are used to grab the reader's attention.

Practice V

Directions: Read the paragraph below, and underline the interjections in the sentences.

EXAMPLE:

The duck screamed, *"Quack! Quack! Quack!"*

There once was a sailor named Naylor, who sat on a tack and said "Quack!" Not knowing the meaning he started repeating, five hundred and fifty one "Quacks!" His commander named Ander heard the commotion on board and hurriedly went to discover. "Oh my!" said Ander, "What's got into your dander, and when are you going to stop?" "I don't know what's wrong," said Naylor the sailor as he continued to bellow the word. But drawing a crowd by shouting out loud caused a ruckus that definitely turned into a fruckus. The last that we heard, Naylor was swimming the sea, shouting "Quack!" at the top of his lungs. His only friends now are the ducks that scream "Wow!" And that is the end of our sailor.

Chapter 9 Review Quizzes

Vocabulary Review Quiz

Directions: Write the letter of the definition on the line next to the noun that it defines.

1. _____ aboard		A.	Below or beneath something.
2. _____ against		B.	Inside, enclosed by.
3. _____ concerning		C.	In spite of, notwithstanding.
4. _____ despite		D.	Relating to, regarding, about.
5. _____ excepting		E.	On board of, in, on.
6. _____ notwithstanding		F.	By way of, through.
7. _____ regarding		G.	Concerning, with reference to.
8. _____ underneath		H.	In opposition to; in contact with.
9. _____ via		I.	Excluding, barring.
10. _____ within		J.	In spite of.

Preposition, Conjunction, and Interjection Definitions

Directions: Select the correct definition, and write the letter of the answer on the line to the right of the number.

1. _____ An interjection is a word that _____.
   a. connects a word
   b. is the object of a preposition
   c. communicates strong emotion or surprise
   d. none of the above

2. _____ Which of the following are interjections?
   a. Oh no! Grhhhh! Hey!
   b. over, under, above, beyond
   c. just as, smelly, French
   d. after, although, so that

3. _____ Which of the following is NOT a preposition?
   a. out
   b. from
   c. toward
   d. hope

4. _____ Which of the following words is NOT a coordinating conjunction?
   a. smelly
   b. and
   c. but
   d. so

5. _____ Identify the sentence below that uses a subordinating conjunction.
    a. As long as he had his blanket, the toddler seemed happy.
    b. Either the dog goes or I go.
    c. She waited by the phone for over a month.
    d. None of the above.

6. _____ Identify the correlative conjunction(s) in the list below.
    a. but
    b. not only, but also
    c. so
    d. after

7. _____ Which of the following groups of words is considered prepositions?
    a. sheep, flocks, ewes, lambs
    b. doctor, nurse, surgeon, anesthesiologist
    c. along, around, beyond, near
    d. education, teacher, school, principal

8. _____ A preposition shows the relationship between _____ to another word.
    a. a verb and an adverb
    b. a noun and a pronoun
    c. a preposition and a verb
    d. a verb and an adjective

9. _____ Identify the sentence that begins with a preposition.
    a. Jaundice causes yellowing of the skin and the whites of the eyes.
    b. Mild jaundice is common in newborns.
    c. In adults, jaundice may occur with diseases such as gallstones.
    d. Cirrhosis, hepatitis, and anemia are other diseases that cause jaundice.

10. _____ Which of the sentences below contains an interjection?
    a. Wow! Will you look at that kingbird!
    b. B. B. King is one of America's best blues guitarists.
    c. Stephen King is a successful American novelist.
    d. Martin Luther King, Jr. was a minister and civil rights leader.

Prepositions

Directions: In the paragraph below, underline all of the <u>prepositions</u>.

EXAMPLE:

Bob Dylan's style <u>of</u> music has changed many times <u>over</u> the years.

Bob Dylan is a popular singer and composer from the United States. He was born in 1941, and his real name is Robert Allen Zimmerman. Dylan changed his name to Bob Dylan when he began his music career and originally was going to call himself Robert Allen. However, he decided upon Bob Dylan after reading the works of poet Dylan Thomas. Although Dylan is known for rock and roll, gospel, hard rock, folk music, blues, jazz, and rockabilly, some of his most memorable works are the protest/social commentary songs such as "Blowin' in the Wind" and "The Times They Are a-Changin'." He has won many awards, including the Grammy, Academy Award, and Golden Globe. Dylan is listed not only as one of *Time Magazine's* one hundred most influential people of the twentieth-century but also as one of *Rolling Stone Magazine's* one hundred greatest artists of all time.

Conjunctions

Directions: Write a sentence using each of the conjunctions that are listed below.

EXAMPLE:

Whether we visit Santa Catalina or San Quentin, neither the train nor the bus makes a stop there.

1. and _____

2. while   _____

3. not only, but also _____

   _____

4. although _____

5. yet _____

6. when _____

7. but _____

8. neither, nor _____

9. in order that _____

   _____

10. since _____

Interjections

Directions: List ten interjections on the lines below.

EXAMPLE:

Stop! Look! Listen!

1. _____   6. _____

2. _____   7. _____

3. _____   8. _____

4. _____   9. _____

5. _____   10. _____

Real-World Practice Activities

Reading

Directions: Find a comic book, a newspaper's comics page, or a graphic novel either at the library or at a book store. Write down a list of twenty (20) interjections that you find. They usually stand out because they are followed by an exclamation point.

1. _____   6. _____   11. _____   16. _____

2. _____   7. _____   12. _____   17. _____

3. _____   8. _____   13. _____   18. _____

4. _____   9. _____   14. _____   19. _____

5. _____   10. _____   15. _____   20. _____

Writing

Directions: Using some of the prepositions and conjunctions from the lists that you read earlier in this chapter, write a funny story about your family or some of your relatives. Have fun with it! Try to use comedy to explain some of their antics.

_____

_____

_____

_____

_____

_____

_____

_____

_____

_____

_____

_____

_____

_____

Listening

Directions: Listen carefully to a soap opera or telenovela on television. Write down a list of ten (10) interjections that you hear during the course of the program. Write them in the spaces provided below. When the show is over, write a sentence using the interjection as you remember it in the show.

1. (Interjection)_____

_____

2. (Interjection)_____

_____

3. (Interjection)_____

_____

4. (Interjection)_____

_____

5. (Interjection)_____

_____

6. (Interjection)_____

_____

7. (Interjection)_____

_____

8. (Interjection)_____

_____

9. (Interjection)_____

_____

10. (Interjection)_____

_____

Chapter 10

PHRASES AND CLAUSES

A phrase is a group of related words that do not contain both a subject and a verb. In contrast, a clause is a group of words with a subject and a predicate. It is something like a sentence within a sentence.

Vocabulary Development

1. **crater** (kra ter) A bowl-shaped cavity or hole.
2. **diverge** (di verg) To go in different directions.
3. **homily** (hom i lee) A sermon or moralizing speech or lecture.
4. **informant** (in for mant) A person who gives information.
5. **kabuki** (kah boo kee) A traditional Japanese drama with song and dance that is acted out by males only.
6. **pang** (pang) A sharp feeling of pain.
7. **pantomime** (pan toe mime) To express a story by movements and without verbal expressions.
8. **redundant** (ree dun dunt) Not necessary, superfluous.
9. **superfluous** (soo per floo us) More than needed or required.
10. **unravel** (un rav il) To disentangle or untangle.

Phrases

A phrase is used as a single part of speech. Note in the following examples of phrases that none of them form a complete thought on their own and may have a subject but no predicate, or a predicate and no subject, or simply a group of related words: *The old woman and the shoe; flying through space; from the lake.* There are adjective, adverb, appositive, gerund, infinitive, noun, participial, prepositional, and verb phrases.

Appositive Phrases

An appositive phrase is a group of words with a noun or a pronoun that is situated next to another noun or pronoun in order to identify or explain it.

- Ariadne, <u>the Cretan princess of Greek mythology</u>, fell in love with Theseus, but he abandoned her.
- <u>Fifty heroes of Greek legend</u>, the Argonauts, were led by Jason, the husband of Medea.
- Ares, <u>the Greek god of war</u>, was the son of Zeus and Hera and the lover of Aphrodite.

Practice I

Directions: Underline the <u>appositive phrases</u> in the following sentences.

EXAMPLE:

Central America, an <u>area located north of South America and south of North America</u>, is an historic part of the world

1. Belize, a Republic in Central America, is located on the Caribbean Sea.
2. Between 300 B.C. and A.D. 1000, Belize was a part of the Mayan empire, an outstanding and highly skilled culture.
3. Shipwrecked sailors from Britain, who eventually took control of the country, founded the first European settlement in 1638.
4. Belize, previously known as British Honduras, achieved independence in 1981.
5. Guatemala, a neighboring country to the east, claimed Belize at that time, but British troops remained in Belize to discourage an invasion.
6. Belmopan, the capital of Belize, is the site of its government, a constitutional monarchy.
7. The economy of Belize, a lower-middle-income developing country, is based on agriculture.
8. Agriculture, particularly sugar cane, is the chief commercial crop of Belize.
9. Mestizos, a mix of Spanish-Indian ethnicities, make up 44 percent of the population.
10. Creoles, those who are primarily African American, represent about one-third of the population.

Noun Phrases

These function as would a simple noun and consist of a noun or a pronoun and the words that modify it. A noun phrase can be one word, or it can consist of many words. The noun phrases in the examples below are underlined.

- <u>I</u> have many goals in life.
- <u>The crowd that I noticed hovering around the door of the theater</u> has finally left.
- <u>The witty Mr. T. Han</u> will spend the rest of his life at the zoo.

Verb Phrases

A verb phrase begins with a verb and is usually followed by various modifiers. A verb phrase can be a one-word phrase, but most often it is not.

- Pantomime <u>originated in ancient Greece with one masked performer who was called Pantomimus.</u>

- The definition of pantomime <u>is different now than its original meaning</u>.

- It <u>is often performed at Christmas and New Year in Great Britain, Ireland, Australia, and New Zealand.</u>

Practice II

Directions: <u>Underline the noun phrases</u> in the sentences below and draw a | box around | | verb phrases |.

EXAMPLE:

The moon | has more than 300,000 craters that are over six miles in diameter |.

1. An impact crater is a depression or hole found in the surface of a planet.

2. It is caused by two bodies hitting each other, such as a meteorite, asteroid, or a comet hitting the moon's surface.

3. The moon has about one-half-million craters on its surface.

4. The largest-known crater in the solar system is on the moon.

5. This crater is called the South Pole-Aitken basin and is 1,388 miles (2,240 km) in diameter and 8 miles (13 km) deep.

6. A crater generally has a circular shape with steep sides.

7. A volcanic crater is also called a caldera.

8. It is caused when a vent of lava is expelled explosively.

9. Craters can also be caused by human-made explosives.

10. An example of a human-made explosive is underground nuclear tests.

Prepositional Phrases

Revisit the chart of prepositions that follows. A prepositional phrase begins with a preposition and includes the object of the preposition and its modifiers. The object of the preposition is the noun or pronoun in the prepositional phrase. The <u>prepositional phrases</u> in the following examples are underlined, and the | object | of the preposition is boxed. All other words in the phrase are modifiers of the object.

PREPOSITIONS—SIMPLE, COMPOUND, AND PHRASAL					
aboard	about	above	according to	across	across from
after	against	along	alongside	alongside of	along with
amid	among	apart from	around	aside from	at
before	behind	below	beneath	beside	besides
between	beyond	but	by	by means of	concerning
considering	despite	down	down from	during	except
except for	excepting	for	from	in	in addition to
in behalf of	in front of	in place of	in regard to	inside	inside of
into	like	near	near to	notwithstanding	of
off	on	on account of	on behalf of	onto	on top of
opposite	out	out of	outside	outside of	over
past	regarding	round	round about	save	since
subsequent to	together with	through	throughout	till	to
toward	under	underneath	until	unto	up
upon	via	with	within	without	

- During the Great Depression, life was filled with economic hardships.
- The Great Depression began with the stock market crash of 1929.
- Although the Depression started in the United States, it quickly spread to Europe and the rest of the world.

Adjective Phrases

These are prepositional phrases that modify a noun or a pronoun. The adjective phrases are boxed, and the prepositional phrases are underlined in the examples.

- In the first week of the stock market crash, stock values declined by $30 billion.
- At the depth of the Depression from 1932–1933, unemployment left about 33 percent of the population without jobs.
- The gross national product (GNP) fell by almost 50 percent according to historical accounts of the time.

Adverb Phrases

The adverb phrase is a prepositional phrase that modifies a verb, an adjective, or another adverb.

- With the passing of the Hawley-Smoot Tariff Act, tariffs (taxes charged on goods entering the U.S.) were raised on imported goods by 60 percent.

- The depression, according to many economic historians, deepened because <u>of the act.</u>
- Many countries retaliated <u>against these tariffs</u> and caused exports and imports to drop more than 50 percent.

Practice III

Directions: Write a paragraph using five adjective phrases and five adverb phrases. Underline the phrases that you use. Choose any topic that you are interested in: friends, hobbies, sports, politics, and so on.

EXAMPLE:

Forensic science is a unique field <u>of science</u>. It involves using special techniques <u>in solving criminal cases</u>. Forensic science incorporates many other areas <u>of science</u> as well. <u>Among these areas</u> are chemistry, physics, botany, zoology, and medicine. Identifying human bodies or traces of humans is just a part <u>of the growing field</u>. <u>In addition to identifying human remains</u>, ballistics, or the study <u>of the projectile</u> of bullets, is another area <u>of forensics</u>. <u>At the core</u> of forensics is the use of fingerprinting, blood analysis, forensic dentistry, voice and speech spectrograms, analysis of drugs and chemicals, and many other areas <u>of solving crimes</u>. This is what forensic science is all about.

_____

_____

_____

_____

_____

_____

_____

_____

_____

_____

_____

_____

Verbal Phrases

There are three types of verbal phrases: gerund, infinitive, and participial. Each phrase is used in a different way. The gerund phrase is used as a noun. The infinitive phrase is used as a noun, an adjective, or an adverb. Finally, the participial phrase is used as an adjective.

Gerund Phrases

A gerund is a verb form ending in *-ing* that is used as a noun. The gerund phrase includes the gerund and its modifiers or complements. It is used as a noun.

- <u>Confronting a problem</u> honestly is the best way to deal with it.
- <u>Pursuing knowledge</u> can be one of the most rewarding experiences in life.
- <u>Exaggerating the benefits</u> of education is impossible.

Infinitive Phrases

An infinitive is a verb form that can be used as a noun, an adjective, or an adverb. An infinitive phrase consists of an infinitive and any of its modifiers or complements. It is also used as a noun, an adjective, or an adverb. Most infinitives and infinitive phrases begin with the word *to*.

- <u>To creative chefs</u>, sage is an herb that is used for seasoning.
- A sage man is a wise and judicious man <u>to respect and admire</u>.
- <u>To those living in the Western U.S.</u>, sagebrush is a low-growing shrub found in the plains.

Participial Phrases

These are phrases that include a participle, which is a verb form that can be used as an adjective. Present participles have *-ing* endings, and past participles usually end in *-d* or *-ed*. Participial phrases are used as adjectives.

- <u>By standing at the front of the line</u>, she was the first to buy a ticket to the concert.
- <u>Shocked at the behavior of the crowd at the concert</u>, many of us enjoyed the show despite the disruptions.
- <u>After praising the experience of live music</u>, Nick will continue to seek out and appreciate the opportunities to attend concerts.

Practice IV

Directions: In the sentences below, underline the gerund, infinitive, and participial phrases. Write *G* on the line if it is a gerund phrase, *I* on the line for an infinitive phrase, and *P* for participial phrases.

EXAMPLE:

   I   To many who have never seen a real desert, it is a place that is seen only in films or on television.

1. _____ By covering nearly one-third of Africa's land area, the Sahara Desert is the world's largest desert.

2. _____ To understand the desert's expanse, it has an area of about 3,500,000 square miles (9,065,000 sq km).

3. _____ Extending west to east for 3,000 miles (4,800 km), the Sahara reaches from the Atlantic Ocean in the west to the Red Sea in the east.

4. _____ Being less than 4 inches (10 cm), the annual rainfall of the Sahara makes it one of the driest areas in the world.

5. _____ Covered with sand and stone, there is little natural vegetation in the desert.

6. _____ To be exact, two-thirds of the Sahara is stony desert.

7. _____ Tibesti Massif, rising to 11,000 feet (3,350 m), is the highest point in the Sahara.

8. _____ Qattara Depression, the lowest point of the desert, is located at 436 feet (133 m) below sea level.

9. _____ Nurturing civilizations for thousands of years, oases are important centers for water, crop farming, and transportation.

10. _____ Two main ethnic groups, including the Tuareg and the Tibu, inhabit the Sahara, but Nomads continue to herd goats and sheep.

Clauses

A clause is a group of words that has both a subject and a predicate. Clauses can often stand alone as simple sentences. However, not all of them express a complete thought and, therefore, cannot stand alone. Independent (or main) clauses are much like a simple sentence and can stand alone: *The dog barked yesterday.* Dependent (or subordinate) clauses cannot stand alone as a sentence, hence the name dependent: *eating hamburgers in the cafe.* These clauses are dependent upon other words or phrases to make a complete sentence. Dependent clauses can be identified as to their function in the sentence: noun, adjective, or adverbial clauses. The various clauses include independent subordinate or dependent clauses, adjective, adverb, and noun clauses.

Independent Clauses

These are main clauses that express a complete thought and can stand alone as a sentence. An independent clause has a subject and a predicate.

- <u>Weaving is a process of making fabric</u> by intertwining two sets of threads.
- <u>The warp threads are threaded on a loom.</u>
- <u>The weft thread is wound around a shuttle</u> and then passed between the warp threads.

Dependent or Subordinate Clauses

These do not express a complete thought and therefore cannot stand alone as a sentence. The words *when, whom, because, which, that, if,* and *until* indicate that the clauses that follow will be dependent clauses.

- Samuel Taylor Coleridge, an English poet, critic, and philosopher, was born in 1772 and lived <u>until 1834</u>.
- Coleridge and William Wordsworth collaborated and published *Lyrical Ballads,* <u>which was a fundamental work of English Romanticism.</u>
- Coleridge's most noted poems include *The Rime of the Ancient Mariner, Christabel,* and *Kubla Khan* <u>which were published early in his career.</u>

Practice V

Directions: Identify the underlined clauses in the following paragraph as either independent or subordinate. Write *I* on the line before the clause if it is independent and *D* on the line if it is a dependent clause.

EXAMPLE:

_*I*_ <u>An explorer is someone who travels into unknown territory</u> and wants to learn more about it.

_____ <u>Hernando De Soto was a Spanish explorer.</u> After taking part in the conquest of Central America under Francisco Pizarro, he was appointed the governor of Cuba in 1537. Given permission to conquer the North American mainland, _____ <u>his expedition landed in Florida in 1539.</u> De Soto advanced north _____ <u>until he reached the Carolinas.</u> _____ <u>Later the expedition traveled as far west as the Mississippi River.</u> _____ <u>Because his ruthless search for treasure</u> proved to be nonsuccessful, coupled with his extremely brutal treatment of the native inhabitants, a battle was fought in 1540 at Maubila. _____ <u>Thousands of native inhabitants were killed</u> either through fighting, fire, or suicide. De Soto lived until 1542, _____ <u>when he died of a fever.</u>

Adjective Clauses

An adjective clause is used to modify a noun or a pronoun, just like an adjective. It directly follows the word or words that it modifies. The adjective clause tells *what kind* and *which one*.

- Frostbite, <u>which causes a burning or tingling sensation</u>, is the freezing of living body tissue in subzero temperature.
- The body's defense mechanism to preserve the core body temperature <u>is when the blood vessels shut down in the areas farthest from the heart.</u>
- Skin destroyed by frostbite <u>is where the skin is colored black and is loose, almost as if burned.</u>

Adverb Clauses

Adverb clauses are used like an adverb: to modify a verb, an adjective, or another adverb. However, the uniqueness of adverb clauses is that they all begin with a subordinating conjunction. As a reminder, a list of subordinating conjunctions follows.

> after, although, as, as if, as long as, as though, because, before, if, in order that, provided that, since, so, so that, that, though, till, unless, until, when, where, whereas, while

- We will have to spend two boring hours listening to the minister's homily <u>unless we hurry out now.</u>
- The informant told the entire story truthfully <u>in order that he be released from custody.</u>
- <u>If you wander down that path,</u> you will eventually end up at the cabin.

Noun Clauses

The noun clause is a subordinate or dependent clause that is used as a noun. Subordinate clauses, as you remember, have a subject and predicate but cannot stand alone because they do not express a complete thought. Many noun clauses are introduced with the words in the following box.

> that, when, whether, whom, what, whenever, who, whomever, whatever, where, whoever, why.

- <u>Whenever you hear the emergency bell ring,</u> stop what you are doing immediately and take cover.
- In an emergency, <u>whether you are prepared or not,</u> help young children and the elderly first.
- <u>Whoever arrives at the station first</u> will ring the alarm.

Practice VI

Directions: List five words that introduce adverb clauses, list five words that introduce noun clauses, and then write five sentences using an adjective clause that tells what kind or which one.

Adverb Clauses	**Noun Clauses**
EXAMPLE:	
though	whom
1. _____	1. _____
2. _____	2. _____
3. _____	3. _____
4. _____	4. _____
5. _____	5. _____

Adjective Clauses that Tell *What Kind* or *Which One*

EXAMPLE:

The first group to go to the park is the group that has finished its homework.

1. _____
2. _____
3. _____
4. _____
5. _____

Chapter 10 Review Quizzes

Vocabulary Review Quiz

Directions: Write the letter of the definition on the line next to the word that it defines.

1. _____ crater
2. _____ diverge
3. _____ homily
4. _____ informant
5. _____ kabuki
6. _____ pang
7. _____ pantomime
8. _____ redundant
9. _____ superfluous
10. _____ unravel

A. More than needed or required.

B. A traditional Japanese drama with song and dance acted by males only.

C. A sharp feeling of pain.

D. To disentangle or untangle.

E. To express a story by movements and without verbal expressions.

F. A sermon or moralizing speech or lecture.

G. A bowl-shaped cavity or hole.

H. Not necessary, superfluous.

I. To go in different directions.

J. A person who gives information.

Phrase and Clause Definitions

Directions: Select the correct definition, and write the letter of the answer on the line to the right of the number.

1. _____ A phrase is a group of related words that _____.
    a. lacks either a subject or a predicate
    b. lacks punctuation
    c. contains only adjectives
    d. contains only the subject

2. _____ An independent clause _____.
    a. is dependent on another clause
    b. can stand on its own
    c. spends weekends in the Hamptons
    d. all of the above

3. _____ Which of the following is NOT a dependent clause?
   a. a French fry flew out of the sky
   b. beyond the moon
   c. when the sun
   d. spelling the word

4. _____ An appositive phrase is used to _____.
   a. add new information or explain
   b. tell the difference between a noun and verb
   c. create atmosphere in a poem
   d. encourage others

5. _____ Which of the following sentences has a noun phrase underlined?
   a. The trails <u>diverge at the river; one goes up the mountain and the other down</u>.
   b. She <u>had a sudden pang in her stomach that caused her to double over in agony</u>.
   c. <u>We</u> will unravel the mystery if it's the last thing we do.
   d. The information <u>that we received at the convention was redundant</u>.

6. _____ An adjective phrase is a prepositional phrase that modifies a _____.
   a. verb or adverb
   b. preposition
   c. noun or a pronoun
   d. phrase

7. _____ An adverb phrase is a prepositional phrase that modifies a _____.
   a. verb, an adjective, or another adverb
   b. noun or a pronoun
   c. participle
   d. all of the above

8. _____ True or False? Independent clauses express a complete thought.
   a. True
   b. False

9. _____ True or False? Dependent clauses express a complete thought.
   a. True
   b. False

10. _____ The three basic types of clauses are _____.
    a. French, Spanish, and German
    b. noun, adjective, and adverb
    c. verb, conjunctive, and interjection
    d. none of the above

Appositive Phrases

Directions: In the paragraph below, underline all of the appositive phrases.

Genghis Khan, the word *Khan* means ruler, was born about 1165. He was a political and military leader, who united the Mongol tribes in 1206. Later he demonstrated his military genius by conquering Peking, now known as Beijing, in 1215 and continuing to annex Iran and invading Russia as far as Moscow. Although he is often thought to be a bloodthirsty and ruthless ruler because of his many military successes, he is also appreciated and respected for establishing the Mongol nation, the largest empire ever known. After his death in 1227, his sons and grandsons continued to rule the empire, which endured for another 150 years.

Noun and Verb Phrases

Directions: Write ten sentences. Underline the noun phrases and draw a box around the verb phrases.

EXAMPLE:

An exuberant person is one who is lively and high-spirited.

1. _____
2. _____
3. _____
4. _____
5. _____
6. _____
7. _____
8. _____
9. _____
10. _____

Prepositional Phrases

Directions: In the paragraph below, underline the prepositional phrases.

Wales is a constituent member of the United Kingdom. It is located on the southwest side of Great Britain and is bordered by England on the east. The capital of Wales is Cardiff, and it is located in the south. During the eleventh century, the Celtic-speaking Welsh were conquered by the English Norman King Edward I. In 1301, Prince Edward (later King Edward II) became the Prince of Wales. Today, Prince Charles is the Prince of Wales. North Wales has the greatest density of sheep in the world. The economy relies on agriculture now, although in the past, it was the leading producer of coal. With the decline of its traditional heavy industries of coal and steel, lighter industries such as electronics are partially offsetting the loss.

Gerund, Infinitive, and Participial Phrases

Directions: Underline each of the phrases in the following sentences. Look for gerund, infinitive, and participial phrases.

EXAMPLE:

They are anxious <u>to finish the reading project</u>.

1. Winning the lottery is the only excitement that remains constant in my life.
2. To write down those five little numbers makes me want to shout, "This is it! The winning ticket!"
3. To walk up to the counter with my numbers and my money sends chills down my spine.
4. After wishing me luck, the clerk calls me by name. He has seen me many times before.
5. Carefully, I place my ticket in my wallet and I wait; waiting can be torture.
6. My hands tremble with anticipation to turn the pages of the newspaper where the winning numbers are printed.
7. While holding my breath, I compare the numbers, one by one.
8. After reading the numbers, I slowly reread, recheck, and compare the numbers to my ticket.
9. Quickly, disappointment hangs heavy in my heart when the numbers do not match.
10. Then soon enough the excitement begins welling up again the following week with one little dollar and the hope that someday it will turn into millions.

Independent and Dependent Clauses

Directions: Complete the following sentences by either adding an independent clause or a dependent clause. Remember that independent and subordinate clauses have a subject and predicate and that subordinate clauses are signaled by the words *when, whom, because, which, that, if,* and *until.*

1. _____ because you seem exhausted.
2. Going to the market yesterday was entertaining _____.
3. When you make fresh noodles, _____.
4. Monty works in a bakery _____.
5. _____ because the message was superfluous.
6. Gardening can be relaxing and useful _____.
7. If I speak French with my neighbors, _____.
8. _____ when I heard my favorite song on the radio.
9. _____ which is really not funny because it hurts.
10. _____ until you finish washing the dishes.

Adjective, Adverb, and Noun Clauses

Directions: Review the definitions and rules for adjective, adverb, and noun clauses. Write ten sentences using the specific type of clause listed at the beginning of the sentence. Underline the clause.

EXAMPLE:

Noun Clause <u>Whatever you do</u>, do not forget the milk.

1. Adjective Clause _____
2. Noun Clause

    _____
3. Adverb Clause _____
4. Adverb Clause _____
5. Adjective Clause _____
6. Noun Clause _____
7. Adjective Clause _____
8. Noun Clause _____
9. Adverb Clause _____
10. Noun Clause _____

Real-World Practice Activities

Reading

Directions: Find an article on Ivan IV of Russia, also known as Ivan the Terrible. While you read and discover why he was so terrible, find twenty prepositional phrases in the article and write them on the lines below.

1. _____   11. _____
2. _____   12. _____
3. _____   13. _____
4. _____   14. _____
5. _____   15. _____
6. _____   16. _____
7. _____   17. _____
8. _____   18. _____
9. _____   19. _____
10. _____   20. _____

Writing

Directions: By using some of the prepositional phrases that you found in the article about Ivan the Terrible, write a synopsis or review of the article below.

_____

_____

_____

_____

_____

_____

_____

_____

_____

_____

_____

_____

Listening

Directions: Listen to a favorite CD (that has lyrics) or your favorite radio station. Write down ten of your favorite phrases or clauses from any of the songs that you hear.

1. _____

2. _____

3. _____

4. _____

5. _____

6. _____

7. _____

8. _____

9. _____

10. _____

Chapter 11

SENTENCE STRUCTURE AND CLASSIFICATION

Sentences are classified according to purpose and structure. Chapter 13 will focus on purpose, but we will look at sentence structure now. Sentences can be classified into four different categories according to structure: simple sentences, compound sentences, complex sentences, and compound-complex sentences. We have reviewed simple sentences in Chapter 5, so we will focus on the more complex combinations here. If you notice, the structures of sentences are similar to simple math problems. Just as adding a subject and a predicate together equals a simple sentence, similar equations using clauses and phrases, add up to making more complex sentence structures.

Vocabulary Development

1. **chameleon** (kam eel eon) A small lizard that can change color according to its surroundings.
2. **dank** (dank) Unpleasantly damp or moist and cold.
3. **legato** (la go to) In music, a smooth and easy manner.
4. **mestizo** (mes teez o) A person of mixed ancestry such as Spanish and Native American.
5. **mocha** (mo ka) A coffee with chocolate flavoring added.
6. **descent** (dee cent) The climb down or lowering.
7. **oration** (or a shun) A long speech.
8. **plebian** (plee bee en) Of the lower social classes, vulgar, uncultured.
9. **racketeer** (rak e teer) Someone who owns or runs a dishonest business.
10. **sabotage** (sab e tahz) Intentional damage of materials or machinery.

Compound Sentences

Remember that all clauses have a subject and a predicate. Combine two clauses together to make a compound sentence. There are no subordinate or dependent clauses in a compound sentence. Compound sentences are usually joined by a coordinating conjunction (*and, but, or, nor, for, yet, so*), by punctuation, or by both. <u>All clauses are underlined</u> and (numbered) in the following examples.

Equation for a Compound Sentence:

1 Independent Clause
+ 1 Independent Clause (or more)
= Compound Sentence

- <u>The Equal Rights Amendment to the U.S. Constitution was passed by Congress in 1972,</u> (1) <u>but it provoked great controversy</u> (2) <u>and by the 1982 deadline only 35 of the necessary 38 states had ratified it.</u> (3)
- <u>Antonio Gaudi is a Spanish architect who employs bizarre sculptural forms and details in his work,</u> (1) <u>and he is often associated with the art nouveau movement.</u> (2)
- <u>Memphis is a major transportation center and livestock market located in Southwest Tennessee on the Mississippi River,</u> (1) <u>yet it was used as a fort for the French in 1682 and later for the Spanish.</u> (2)

Practice I

Directions: Underline and number the clauses in the following compound sentences.

EXAMPLE:

<u>Lightning begins inside a thundercloud,</u> (1) yet <u>when water and ice particles are tossed together by air currents, static electricity is created</u> (2).

1. Although today's popular musicals are a genre of light entertainment that embodies a plot, strong songs, and energetic dance numbers, they developed in the late nineteenth century combining elements of light opera, revue, and burlesque.
2. A chameleon is an arboreal lizard found primarily in Madagascar, Africa, or Asia, but it is known for its ability to change color.
3. Cafe mocha is a combination of espresso, steamed milk, and chocolate, and although it is a popular beverage served in the U.S., it is not as popular in Europe.
4. A guitar is a plucked string instrument first associated with the Moors, a group of medieval Muslim inhabitants of the western Mediterranean area, and the people who first introduced it to Spain as early as the twelfth century.
5. Baja California means "Lower California," and it is a peninsula located in Northwest Mexico and it consists of two states, Baja California Norte and Baja California Sur.

6. Agronomy is the science of soil management and improvement, but it also includes the studies of the interrelationships of plants and soils.

7. Click language is any of several southern African languages belonging primarily to the Khoisan group and characterized by the use of suction speech sounds known as clicks.

8. Goldfish are freshwater carp that were originally found in China but were domesticated about 1,000 years ago and have become one of the most popular aquarium fish.

9. Jimi Hendrix was an influential and innovative guitarist and rock musician and is renowned for his colorful and improvisational live performances.

10. Today, Osaka, Japan, is the third largest city in Japan as well as a major transportation hub and principal industrial port, but it was heavily bombed during World War II.

Complex Sentences

These are sentences that contain one independent clause and at least one dependent clause. Remember that clauses have a subject and a verb. Independent clauses can stand alone and have a complete thought. However, dependent or subordinate clauses cannot. Dependent clauses add additional information. The independent clauses are <u>underlined</u> and the dependent clauses are *italicized* in the examples below.

> Equation for a Complex Sentence:
>
> 1 Independent Clause
> + 1 Dependent/Subordinate Clause (or more)
> = Complex Sentence

- <u>Aten is an Ancient Egyptian god</u>, *known as the sun god.*

- <u>Aswan is a city in Southeast Egypt,</u> *benefiting greatly from the Aswan High Dam.*

- *Creating over 10 billion kilowatt-hours of power,* <u>the Aswan High Dam can generate power that helps millions.</u>

Practice II

Directions: Identify the complex sentences in the following paragraph. Underline the <u>independent clauses,</u> and draw a box around the subordinate clauses. NOTE: Not all of the sentences are complex. Look for sentences with one independent clause and one or more dependent clauses.

EXAMPLE:

Officially called Mount Rushmore National Memorial, <u>Mount Rushmore is located in the Black Hills of South Dakota.</u>

Mount Rushmore is a giant granite sculpture of four U.S. presidents located in South Dakota. Known as a presidential memorial, it represents 150 years of American presidential history. The four presidents included in the monument are George Washington, Thomas Jefferson, Theodore Roosevelt, and Abraham Lincoln. Each of the sculptures is 60 feet (18 m) high and rises 5,725 feet (1,745 m) above sea level. Historian Doane Robinson, who convinced sculptor Guntzor Borglum to visit the site to be certain that the project could be accomplished, conceived the idea for the sculpture. Congress authorized the project in 1925. Calvin Coolidge, the sitting president at the time, insisted that in addition to George Washington, two Republicans and one Democrat be included in the memorial. Borglum and 400 assistants worked on the sculpture from October 4, 1927 until October 31, 1941. Borglum died of an embolism in 1941, and his son Lincoln Borglum continued the project, but funding was exhausted and the project halted. Originally, the sculptures were going to continue to the waist of each man, but that did not come to fruition. The total cost of the sculpture was nearly $990,000. Although there were a few injuries, no deaths occurred with the work.

Compound-Complex Sentences

A compound-complex sentence is the most complicated of the four types of sentences. It has two or more independent clauses and at least one subordinate clause. The clauses are underlined and labeled (IC for independent clause and SC for subordinate clause) in the following examples. Note, upon occasion, the pronoun subject (such as *you*) is implied and not always stated.

Equation for a Compound-Complex Sentence:

1 Independent Clause
+ 1 Independent Clause (or more)
+ 1 Subordinate Clause (or more)
= Compound-Complex Sentence

- A muckraker is a term first used by Theodore Roosevelt (IC) and was given to journalists and other writers in the U.S. (IC) who exposed corruption in politics and business in the early twentieth century. (SC)

- The air grew steadily more polluted because of heavy industries in the area, (IC) and health officials cited it as the cause of more and more pulmonary illnesses, (IC) particularly noticeable in the elderly and the young. (SC)

- Inside the musty and damp room, (SC) which was filled with dusty trunks and old furniture, (IC) we found some valuable antiques. (IC)

Practice III

Directions: Write clauses as directed on the lines below. Once combined, they should make a compound-complex sentence. *IC* is an independent clause, and *SC* is a subordinate clause.

EXAMPLE:

(SC) Important in the development of many civilizations, *(IC)* the Euphrates River flows through eastern Turkey, Syria, and Iraq, *(IC)* and it extends over 1,740 miles (2,800 km) in length.

1. (SC)_____
   (IC) _____
   (IC) _____

2. (IC) _____
   (IC) _____
   (SC)_____

3. (IC) _____
   (SC)_____
   (IC) _____

4. (SC)_____
   (IC) _____
   (IC) _____

5. (SC)_____
   (IC) _____
   (IC) _____

6. (IC) _____
   (IC) _____
   (SC)_____

7. (SC)_____
   (IC) _____
   (IC) _____

8. (IC) _____

(IC) _____

(SC)_____

9. (IC) _____

(SC)_____

(IC) _____

10. (IC) _____

(IC) _____

(SC)_____

Chapter 11 Review Quizzes

Vocabulary Review Quiz

Directions: Write the letter of the definition on the line next to the noun that it defines.

1. _____ mocha

2. _____ oration

3. _____ plebian

4. _____ mestizo

5. _____ dank

6. _____ sabotage

7. _____ racketeer

8. _____ descent

9. _____ chameleon

10. _____ legato

A. Intentional damage of materials or machinery.

B. A long speech.

C. A person of mixed ancestry such as Spanish and Native American.

D. Someone who owns or runs a dishonest business.

E. Of the lower social classes, vulgar, uncultured.

F. In music, a smooth and easy manner.

G. A coffee with chocolate flavoring added.

H. A small lizard that can change color according to its surroundings.

I. Unpleasantly damp or moist and cold.

J. To lower, to go down.

Sentence Definitions

Directions: Select the correct definition, and write the letter of the answer on the line to the right of the number.

1. _____ A simple sentence contains _____ .

   a. two or more independent clauses and one or more subordinate clauses

   b. two or more independent clauses and no subordinate clauses

   c. one independent clause and one or more subordinate clauses

   d. one independent clause and no subordinate clauses

2. _____ A compound sentence contains _____ .
   a. two or more independent clauses and one or more subordinate clauses
   b. two or more independent clauses and no subordinate clauses
   c. one independent clause and one or more subordinate clauses
   d. one independent clause and no subordinate clauses

3. _____ A complex sentence contains _____.
   a. two or more independent clauses and one or more subordinate clauses
   b. two or more independent clauses and no subordinate clauses
   c. one independent clause and one or more subordinate clauses
   d. one independent clause and no subordinate clauses

4. _____ A compound-complex sentence contains _____ .
   a. two or more independent clauses and one or more subordinate clauses
   b. two or more independent clauses and no subordinate clauses
   c. one independent clause and one or more subordinate clauses
   d. one independent clause and no subordinate clauses

5. _____ The following sentence is an example of a_____.
   The mouse is a common rodent.
   a. compound sentence
   b. simple sentence
   c. complex sentence
   d. compound-complex sentence.

6. _____ Identify the compound sentence below.
   a. The plebeians were happy to see Caesar.
   b. The basement is dark and dank, but it has some interesting treasures.
   c. Pneumonia is the inflammation of the lung tissue and most often caused by bacterial infection.
   d. The test will cover the entire chapter.

7. _____ The following sentence is an example of a _____.
   Because Ben wanted to take his guitar, they decided to drive.
   a. compound sentence
   b. simple sentence
   c. complex sentence
   d. compound-complex sentence

8. _____ There are _____ different types of sentences.
   a. two
   b. three
   c. four
   d. five

9. _____ True or False? A simple sentence has a subject and a predicate.
   a. True
   b. False

10. _____ Two independent clauses equal a _____ sentence.
    a. compound-complex sentence
    b. simple sentence
    c. compound sentence
    d. complex sentence

Compound, Complex, and Compound-Complex Sentences

Directions: Classify each of the following sentences according to its structure. Write *CD* on the line if it is a compound sentence, *CX* on the line if it is a complex sentence, and *CD-CX* if it is a compound-complex sentence.

EXAMPLE:

<u>*CD-CX*</u>   The air grew more polluted in modern-day China because of the heavy industries in and around Beijing, which health officials cited as the cause of more and more pulmonary illnesses, noticeable more frequently in the elderly and the young.

1. _____ A chain reaction is a self-sustaining reaction in which one reaction is the cause of a second; the second is responsible for the third reaction and so on.

2. _____ Diving is a water sport in which acrobatic maneuvers are performed from a springboard or platform.

3. _____ Dominic announced that getting tickets to the Dodger game was the best idea.

4. _____ Meredith interrupted and argued her case for getting tickets to see the Lakers in the playoffs.

5. _____ While they argued about which tickets to buy, Ben went ahead and managed to get great seats to a Stones concert.

6. _____ Ralph Waldo Emerson was an American essayist, philosopher, and poet as well as being a minister in the Unitarian Church, which he became disillusioned with and resigned from.

7. _____ Harmony in music is the structure of chords and the relationships between them and includes the diatonic scale, which ranges from one C to the next.

8. _____ Rose likes Jude Law, but Cheri loves him.

9. _____ A harp is an ancient musical instrument with 47 strings that are stretched over a triangular frame.

10. _____ Antiseptics, which were pioneered by the English surgeon Joseph Lister in 1867, are chemicals that destroy or stop the growth of microorganisms.

Real-World Practice Activities

Reading

Directions: Find an article or book on the Russian-French painter Marc Chagall. While reading the article or book, notice the structure of the sentences. Write down five compound sentences, five complex sentences, and five compound-complex sentences.

Compound Sentences

1. _____
2. _____
3. _____
4. _____
5. _____

Complex Sentences

1. _____
2. _____
3. _____
4. _____
5. _____

Compound-Complex Sentences

1. _____
2. _____
3. _____
4. _____
5. _____

Writing

Directions: Write a journal entry about how your day is going. Write without worrying about sentence structure at first. When you have finished the paragraph, go back over your writing and try to identify sentence structure. Underline any of the compound, complex, or compound-complex sentences that you might have included naturally without thinking about it.

_____

_____

_____

_____

_____

_____

_____

_____

_____

_____

_____

_____

_____

_____

Listening

Directions: Listen carefully to any kind of program that you are interested in—radio, television, and so on. Listen for sentence structure, as difficult as that may seem. Notice the pauses in the conversation. Are the speakers sentences complex or are they simple and to the point? You might try to write down a few sentences to see what they look like in writing.

1. _____

2. _____

3. _____

4. _____

5. _____

Chapter 12

PUNCTUATION

Without punctuation, any kind of writing would be chaotic. Not knowing where one sentence ends and another begins would make reading and writing beyond difficult. Sentences are ended with a variety of little marks to indicate the purpose of the sentence. We will look at sentence purpose in the next chapter because you need to know what the marks are before you can figure out what purpose they are suppose to serve. Periods (.), ellipses (. . .), exclamation points (!), and question marks (?) are end marks. Commas (,), semicolons (;), colons (:), hyphens (-), dashes (—), quotations marks (" "), *italics* or <u>underlining</u>, parentheses ( ), apostrophe ('), brackets ([ ]), and a diagonal (/) are all punctuation marks.

Vocabulary Development

1. **disband** (diss band) To break up or separate.
2. **fizz** (fizz) To make a hissing or sputtering sound as from a carbonated soda pop.
3. **glorify** (glor e fi) To praise or complement highly.
4. **honeycomb** (hun ee kohm) The six-sided cell and wax structure used by bees for holding honey and eggs.
5. **nepotism** (nep o tiz em) Favoritism shown to relatives by appointing them to jobs.
6. **orbit** (or bit) The curved path of a planet or a satellite.
7. **patriarch** (pate tree ark) The male head of a family or tribe.
8. **pathos** (pay thos) A quality or personality trait that arouses pity or sadness.
9. **proximity** (prox sim i tee) Nearness, closeness.
10. **wig** (wigg) A covering made of hair to wear on the head.

Periods

Periods (**.**) are used for many reasons. However, their primary use is to end a sentence that makes a statement. Periods are also used after mild commands and simple requests, initials, abbreviations, and as decimal points.

- A patriarch is a male head of a family or a tribe.
- Please read the pages in your book about patriarchal societies.
- Note that the word patriarch comes from the Latin words *pater familias*.

After an Initial or an Abbreviation

- Mr.
- Mrs.
- Ms.
- M.D.
- Jr.
- U.S.
- T.V.

- B.C.
- A.D.
- A.M.
- P.M.
- Sen. H. Clinton
- Dr. D. Yoon

- Prof. J. Liu
- E. E. Cummings
- etc.
- in.
- ft.
- yds.

As decimal points

- 1.25
- 2.7
- 1.033333

- 100.00
- 56.79

Ellipsis

The ellipsis is a series of three periods (. . .). It is used to show that one or more words have been omitted from a quote. When you type an ellipsis, leave one space before the three periods and one space after. Note the ellipses in the following quotes from Shakespeare's play *Othello*.

- "He takes her by the palm. Ay, well said, whisper! With . . . this will I ensnare as great a fly as Cassio. Ay, smile upon her, do!"
- "Lechery, by this hand! An index and obscure prologue to the history of lust and foul thoughts. They met so near . . . that their breaths embraced together."
- "By heaven, he echoes me, as if there were some monster in his thought too hideous to be shown. Thou dost mean something. I heard . . . thou lik'st not that when Cassio left my wife."

Question Marks

The question mark (**?**) is obviously used to indicate a question. In reading, sentences marked with a question mark are read differently. The reader's voice usually changes—by sounding a bit higher pitched at the end of a question. The Spanish language begins (and ends) its sentences with question marks and exclamation points, making it easier on the reader to know what is ahead. However, we do not have that luxury in English.

- Did you know that the Danish writer Isak Dinesen's real name is Karen Blixen?
- Were you aware that her book *Out of Africa* was made into a film?
- How did you like the descriptions that she uses in *Out of Africa?*

Exclamation Points

Exclamation points are used at the end of a word or group of words that express strong feelings. The exclamation point (!) attracts the reader's attention.

- Do not shake that! The can will explode!
- Use your head!
- Stop!

Practice I

Directions: Punctuate the following sentences as needed. Use a period, a question mark, an exclamation point, or an ellipsis.

EXAMPLE:

> Disneyland is a park that is well taken care of and always busy
> Disneyland is a park that is well taken care of and always busy.

1. Have you ever been to Disneyland
2. It is supposed to be the happiest place on Earth
3. My favorite ride is the Pirates of the Caribbean
4. I could go on that ride all day hey, watch it
5. Ouch
6. You stepped on my toe
7. What is your favorite ride
8. I have never been on that, and I am afraid of roller-coaster rides
9. For some reason they make me well, let us just say nauseous
10. When shall we go

Commas

Commas (,) are used for many reasons. They separate independent clauses that are joined by coordinating conjunctions (*but, or, nor, for, yet, and, so*). They separate individual words, phrases, or clauses in a series. Commas set off an expression that interrupts a sentence. They appear after an introductory prepositional phrase. They separate items in dates and addresses and also adjectives that modify a noun or pronoun equally. NOTE: If you change the order of the adjectives and it does not sound correct, the adjectives do not modify equally. *He has many fine examples of Russian art.* OR *He has fine many examples of Russian art.* The first sentence sounds correct, but the second does not. Therefore, the adjectives do not modify equally.

- No, I have not been to Russia before, but I am planning a trip for next fall.
- Moscow, St. Petersburg, Kazan, and Omsk are a few of the cities that I plan to visit.

- During the trip, I plan to see a great deal of the countryside as well as learn about the culture of Russia by visiting famous museums and seeing the well-known Bolshoi ballet.

Practice II

Directions: Insert commas in the appropriate places in the following paragraph.

EXAMPLE:

Sir Isaac Newton whose three laws are known as the Clockwork Universe provided a general view of nature.

Sir Isaac Newton, whose three laws are known as the Clockwork Universe, provided a general view of nature.

Sir Isaac Newton was an English physicist mathematician astronomer natural philosopher and alchemist. Born in 1643 he is well regarded as one of the most influential figures in the history of science. Newton is most noted for his treatise *Philosophiae Naturalis Principia Mathematica* which was published in 1687. In it he describes universal gravitation and the three laws of motion both of which laid the groundwork for classical mechanics. Newton was the first to demonstrate that the motion of objects on Earth and of celestial bodies is governed by the same set of natural laws. Newton is also credited with the advancement of heliocentrism and the principles of conservation of momentum and angular momentum. He invented the reflecting telescope and developed a theory of color. He based his observations on a prism that he discovered decomposes white light into a visible spectrum. Calculus the speed of sound the origin of stars and many other areas were advanced because of Newton's work.

Semicolon

A semicolon (;) looks like a comma with a period on top of it. Semicolons are used to separate independent clauses that are long or not connected by a coordinating conjunction (*and, but or, not for, so, yet*). Use semicolons sparingly—sometimes it is better to turn one long sentence into two shorter sentences.

- Henri Matisse was a French designer, sculptor, graphic artist, and painter; he developed a style of painting that became known as fauvism.
- Fauvism was a short-lived movement that lasted from 1905–1907; its artists simplified lines, exaggerated perspective, and used bright and arbitrary colors.
- The leaders of the movement were Henri Matisse and Andre Derain; they were somewhat friendly rivals, each having their own followers.

Colon

A colon (:) looks like one period on top of anther period. A colon is easily confused with semicolons, but if you look at the word colon you see two o's—and the colon has two dots (:). The semicolon, on the other hand, is not quite a full colon. It is semi—with one dot and a comma. The job of the colon is much different than that of a semicolon. A colon is used before a list of items. Most notably, a colon is often used after the word *follows*. A colon is also utilized before long formal statements or quotations, in telling time, and after a salutation in a formal business letter.

- The following groups have disbanded over the years: The Beatles, Herman's Hermits, The Turtles, The Monkees, and The Mamas and the Papas.
- Dear Senator Clinton: Dear Mr. Xingchen Liu: Dear Dr. N. Auricchio:
- 8:55   10:35   23:10

Practice III

Directions: Correct the following sentences by adding either a colon or a semicolon.

EXAMPLE:

Hiking as a hobby provides the following exercise, relaxation, and peace.
Hiking as a hobby provides the following: exercise, relaxation, and peace.

1. There are many reasons for hiking enjoying the scenery, exercise, exploring unfamiliar territory, and silence.
2. Yesterday we hiked the 5-mile (8-km) loop up into the Olympics in the rain getting soaked and muddy was worth the view.
3. Hiking supplies that should always be carried include the following compass, water, snacks, warm clothes, and first aid supplies.
4. When hiking alone, take precautions it can be very dangerous.
5. She has hiked in British Columbia, Canada Northern Cascades, Washington and Mt. McKinley, California.
6. Hiking in Tibet and Nepal is known as trekking it is often strenuous and steep.
7. The Pacific Crest Trail is 2,650 miles (4,260 km) long it extends from Canada to Mexico and parallels the Pacific Ocean.
8. Distress signals used in the mountains include three blasts on a whistle with a one-minute pause, three fires, or piles of stone in a triangle.
9. In open air, the most heat is lost through the head hypothermia can be prevented by covering the head.
10. "Leave No Trace" is a list of principles that hikers should follow carry out all trash, respect nature and wildlife, plan ahead, be prepared, and be considerate of other visitors.

Apostrophes

Apostrophes (') are used with nouns to form the possessive case. The possessive case means that something belongs to someone or something—it demonstrates ownership. Apostrophes are also used for contractions and to form plurals.

Apostrophes and Possessive Case

The possessive case shows ownership. To do that, an apostrophe is used. There are a few rules to follow when adding an apostrophe to show ownership, including rules for singular and plural nouns.

- For singular nouns (book, boy, patriarch) as well as plural nouns that do not end in an *s* (geese, men, deer), add an apostrophe and an *s* to the word. The same rule applies to form plurals of letters and numbers
    - the book's table of contents; the boy's childhood friend; the patriarch's extended family
    - the geese's feathers; the men's department; the deer's mating habits
    - A's not B's; 7's not 9's
    - 1950's, 1960's, '70's
- For plural nouns ending in *s* (snakes, wigs, honeycombs) as well as proper nouns ending in *s* (Ms. Torres, Los Angeles, Tyra Banks), add only an apostrophe after the *s*.
    - the snakes' eggs; the wigs' owner; the honeycombs' texture
    - Ms. Torres' application; Los Angeles' museums; Tyra Banks' show
- Apostrophes are NOT used with possessive personal pronouns (hers, mine, its, his, yours, ours, theirs) but they are used with some indefinite pronouns.
    - anybody's, everyone's, anyone's, somebody's, something's, nobody's

Apostrophes and Contractions

Contractions are shortened forms of words, dates, and time. Letters that are removed from a word to shorten it are replaced by an apostrophe. In general, avoid contractions in writing. They are used for informal writing and speaking.

- I am = I'm   can not = can't   has not = hasn't   she would = she'd
- 2007 = '07   1978 = '78   1999 = '99   2000 = '00
- of the clock = o'clock   ten o'clock   12 o'clock
- will not = won't   it is = it's   it has = it's

Practice IV

Directions: Add an apostrophe to the sentences as needed below.

EXAMPLE:

She cant seem to get over the flu.
She can't seem to get over the flu.

1. The disbanding of the 1960s rock group caused great turmoil.
2. The orbits path appeared to curve.
3. The wigs color did not blend well with the original.
4. The honeycombs texture disintegrated in the extreme heat.
5. A deacon is an ordained minister who serves as a priests assistant.
6. Samuel Goldwyns commercially successful films included *Wuthering Heights, Guys and Dolls,* and *Porgy and Bess.*
7. Plato was a the Greek philosopher. The writers greatest work was *The Republic.*
8. New Yorks state capital is Albany.
9. One of Marvin Gayes most famous single recordings was "I Heard It Through the Grapevine."
10. King Henry VIIIs court imprisoned Sir Thomas Wyatt because he was allegedly the former lover of Anne Boleyn and a friend of Thomas Cromwell.

Quotation Marks

Quotation marks (" ") are used before and after a person's exact words in what is known as a direct quotation. Direct quotations begin with a capital letter. When a quoted sentence is interrupted by identifying the speaker, the second part of the quote is not capitalized. Punctuation marks (periods, commas, exclamation points, and question marks) are placed inside the quotation marks unless the quote is not an exclamation or a question used originally but, instead, added to a statement to make a point. Quotation marks are also used to punctuate song titles, poems, short stories, courses, lectures, chapters of books, episodes of a radio or television program, and articles found in a periodical, newspaper, or encyclopedia.

- "The mind is a dangerous weapon, even to the possessor, if he knows not discreetly how to use it." (Montaigne)
- "Look at the deer," whispered Elaine, "it is nursing its fawn."
- What did Franklin Roosevelt mean when he said, "Men are not prisoners of fate, but only prisoners of their own minds"? (note punctuation outside of quotation marks)
- "Ode on a Grecian Urn" "The Most Dangerous Game" "India and Pakistan: Unfriendly Neighbors" (titles of poems/stories/articles)

Practice V

Directions: Use quotation marks to punctuate the following quotes correctly.

EXAMPLE:

A Scottish folk song repeats in its refrain, Oh, you'll take the high road, and I'll take the low road, and I'll be in Scotland before you; But me and my true love will never meet again, On the bonnie, bonnie banks of Loch Lomond.

A Scottish folk song repeats in its refrain, "Oh, you'll take the high road, and I'll take the low road, and I'll be in Scotland before you; But me and my true love will never meet again, On the bonnie, bonnie banks of Loch Lomond."

1. Ten persons who speak make more noise than ten thousand who are silent. (Napoleon)
2. What did Kahlil Gibran mean when he wrote, Even as love crowns you so shall he crucify you. Even as he is for your growth so is he for your pruning ?
3. John Keats wrote Ode on a Grecian Urn and Ode to a Nightingale.
4. Love built on beauty, soon as beauty, dies. (John Donne)
5. The meaning of William Blake's Expect Poison from Standing Water escapes me.
6. A man may die, said John F. Kennedy, nations may rise and fall, but an idea lives on. Ideas have endurance without death.
7. The song she sang was titled Concrete Angel.
8. Friends show their love in times of trouble, not in happiness. (Euripides)
9. Rudeness writes Eric Hoffer, is the weak man's imitation of strength.
10. The youth of a nation are the trustees of posterity. (Benjamin Disraeli)

Parentheses and Brackets

Parentheses ( ) are used to enclose additional or explanatory information within a sentence. Brackets [ ] are used when words are added to a quote that are not the author's original words.

• Xylem, the transport tissue of a plant (which conducts water and minerals from the roots) provides support.

• Thyroxine (a hormone secreted by the thyroid gland) contains iodine and aids in regulating the body's metabolism.

• "Pain [ouch] will force even the truthful to speak falsely." (Publilius Syrus)

Practice VI

Directions: Use parentheses and brackets as needed in the following sentences.

EXAMPLE:

George Eliot the nom de plume for Mary Ann Evans is the author best known for *Middlemarch, The Mill on the Floss,* and *Silas Marner.*

George Eliot (the nom de plume for Mary Ann Evans) is the author best known for *Middlemarch, The Mill on the Floss,* and *Silas Marner.*

1. "Let us not burden groan our remembrance with a heaviness that's gone." (Shakespeare)
2. Toxicology is the study of poisonous substances and their effects on living things.
3. Computer software as opposed to computer hardware or equipment is the coded programs and their associated files.
4. The osprey or hawk lives in coastal regions or around lakes.
5. Daniel Ortega a Nicaraguan president and statesman joined the Sandanistas and was then exiled to Cuba.
6. The Battle of Hastings fought in Southeast England in 1066 brought an end to the Anglo-Saxon monarchy.
7. "Trees are the earth's endless effort to speak to the listening heaven sigh." (Rabindranath Tagore)
8. Sorghum the most widely cultivated grain in Africa is far more tolerant of hot climates than corn or other grains.
9. The ant a social insect belongs to a family that also includes bees and wasps.
10. "There is no harbor of peace from the changing waves of joy hee hee and despair." (Euripides)

Hyphens

A hyphen (-) is used for the following reasons: to make a compound word, to join a capital letter to a noun, between elements of a fraction, to connect numbers that indicate a life span, to form new words that have the prefixes *self-, ex-, all-, great-, half-,* to connect two or more words that are used as adjectives, and to separate a word at the end of a written line (do not separate one-syllable words).

- seventeen-year-olds, brother-in-law, meat-eating
- D-Day, U-turn, V-shaped
- second-half, two-thirds, fifty-five men, 1930-2006, 1800-1865

- self-cleaning, ex-wife, all-knowing, great-great-grandmother, half-cooked
- long-haired dog, French-speaking students, oval-shaped face
- During the Berlin Airlift (1948-1949), U.S. and British air-craft flew more than 270,000 flights to deliver food and sup-plies to the people of Berlin after the Soviet Union closed all roads and rail links to the city.

Dashes

Dashes are two hyphens together (—) and are used to show a sudden break, interruption, or change in a sentence or dialogue. They are also used to emphasize a word, a clause, or a phrase.

- Friends, Romans, Countrymen—lend me your ears.
- We were driving down the freeway yesterday—when all of a sudden—the car in front of us swerved over into the left lane, hit the barrier, and flipped over—that was frightening to say the least.
- All roads lead to France—Michael states—with a devilish grin and an evil look in his eye.

Diagonal, Forward Slash, or Virgule

The diagonal, forward slash (/), or virgule is used for fractions, to show where one line of poetry ends and a new line begins (when quoting poetry), and to demonstrate that either one option or another is suitable (an either/or option).

- 10½ feet, 11¼ inches, 12½ miles
- Wealth I ask not, hope nor love, / Nor a friend to know me; / All I seek, the heaven above / And the road below me. (Robert Louis Stevenson—"The Vagabond")
- The commuter jet/aircraft eases travel time exponentially.

Practice VII

Directions: Use hyphens, dashes, or slashes to punctuate the following sentences.

EXAMPLE:

Count Dracula is the title character a bloodthirsty nobleman from the Middle Ages of the novel written by Bram Stoker.

Count Dracula is the title character—a bloodthirsty nobleman from the Middle Ages—of the novel written by Bram Stoker.

1. Irving Berlin (1888 1989), a songwriter and composer, wrote nearly 1,000 songs.
2. The proximity of the pollution spewing factory is unacceptable.
3. That loud crackle fizz sound is coming from the soda pop can.
4. Aunts, uncles, cousins, grandparents it does not matter who just get some volunteers to help.
5. Rain or shine the show will go on.
6. Roses are red Violets are blue Sugar is sweet And so are you.
7. They will have to dig 10 1 2 feet to find the pipe.
8. The Spanish speaking woman tried to find her way through the maze of traffic.
9. Whatever you do, always buy a self cleaning oven. They are the best!
10. My mother in law makes the best casseroles.

Italics or Underlining

Italics are printed letters *that lean to the right*. However, when you write by hand, <u>underlining</u> serves the same purpose, which is to indicate the titles of books, plays, periodicals, newspapers, works of art, films, radio and television programs, recordings, long musical compositions, trains, ships, aircraft, and spacecraft.

Crime and Punishment   Metamorphosis   Waiting for Godot
Bridget Jones' Diary   Notting Hill   Four Weddings and a Funeral
The Spirit of St. Louis   Enola Gay   Queen Elizabeth 2   Orient Express

Practice VIII

Directions: Punctuate the following paragraph by underlining the words of all titles.

EXAMPLE:

> <u>The Strange Case of Dr. Jekyll and Mr. Hyde</u> is a novel by Robert Louis Stevenson that offers the reader a classic view of a person with a split personality.

Englishman Charles Dickens was a prolific writer who lived from 1812–1870. He began his writing career as a parliamentary reporter for the Morning Chronicle. Dickens's earliest success was a satirical piece titled Sketches by Boz, but The Pickwick Papers launched his early literary career. All of Dickens's novels appeared in serial form before being published in their entirety. His early novels include Oliver Twist, Nicholas Nickleby, and Barnaby Rudge. After a trip to America, he completed Martin Chuzzlewit and then wrote A Christmas Carol. Dickens's more sophisticated novels include David Copperfield, Bleak House, Hard Times, Little Dorrit, and A Tale of Two Cities. Great Expectations, Our Mutual Friend, and the incomplete The Mystery of Edwin Drood are his last novels. He provided literature with some of its most memorable characters and was able to capture the mood of Victorian England very descriptively.

Chapter 12 Review Quizzes

Vocabulary Review Quiz

Directions: Write the letter of the definition on the line next to the noun that it defines.

1. _____ disband

2. _____ fizz

3. _____ glorify

4. _____ honeycomb

5. _____ nepotism

6. _____ orbit

7. _____ patriarch

8. _____ pathos

9. _____ proximity

10. _____ wig

A. A quality or personality trait that arouses pity or sadness.

B. The curved path of a planet or a satellite.

C. A covering made of hair to wear on the head.

D. To make a hissing or sputtering sound as from a carbonated soda pop.

E. To break up or separate.

F. The six-sided cell and wax structure used by bees for holding honey and eggs.

G. To praise or complement highly.

H. Nearness, closeness.

I. Favoritism shown to relatives by appointing them to jobs.

J. The male head of a family or tribe.

Punctuation Definitions

Directions: Select the correct definition, and write the letter of the answer on the line to the right of the number.

1. _____ Periods, question marks, and exclamation points are _____ .
    a. punctuation marks that separate two exclamations
    b. hieroglyphics from Egypt
    c. punctuation that are end marks
    d. two or more independent clauses and one or more subordinate clauses

2. _____ A comma is used _____ .
    a. to separate independent clauses that connect with a coordinating conjunction
    b. after an introductory prepositional phrase
    c. to separate items in dates and addresses
    d. all of the above

3. _____ Which of the following is an example of adjectives that are NOT equally modifying?
    a. He has several fine works on display.
    b. He has three paintings, ten collages, and six sculptures on display
    c. He has unique, creative, and well-admired works on display.
    d. He has multicolored and more subtly colored works on display.

4. _____ A semicolon looks like _____ .
    a. two or more independent clauses and one or more subordinate clauses
    b. two periods stacked on top of each other
    c. a period on top of a comma
    d. none of the above

5. _____ A colon looks like _____ .
    a. two periods stacked on top of each other
    b. a simple sentence
    c. a period on top of a comma
    d. a bird on top of a worm

6. _____ True or False? Semicolons are used to indicate time.
    a. True
    b. False

7. _____ Apostrophes are used _____ .
    a. as a pause
    b. to indicate possession
    c. as a complex sentence
    d. all of the above

8. _____ Which of the following demonstrates the proper way to punctuate a song title?
    a. *God Bless America*
    b. God Bless America
    c. "God Bless America"
    d. all of the above

9. _____ Which of the following demonstrates the proper way to punctuate a book title?
    a. *Of Mice and Men*
    b. "Of Mice and Men"
    c. of mice and men
    d. all of the above

10. _____ Dashes are _____ .
    a. races during track season
    b. two hyphens together
    c. a pause during a test
    d. none of the above

Punctuation

Directions: Use the punctuation marks from the chart to correct the punctuation errors in the sentences.

PUNCTUATION MARKS		
Period .	Ellipsis . . .	Exclamation Point !
Question Mark ?	Comma ,	Semicolon ;
Colon :	Apostrophe '	Quotation Marks " "
Parentheses ( )	Brackets [ ]	Hyphen -
Dashes -- or —	Forward Slash /Diagonal /	*Italics* or Underlining

1. As a child one of my favorite song lyrics When the moon hits the sky like a bigga pizza pie thats amore was popular
2. Oh no
3. One of the best books that I have ever read is Crime and Punishment by Fyodor Dostoevsky
4. Where do you think you are going
5. Martin Scorsese a film director who recently won an Oscar for his film The Departed is passionate about his work
6. America Ferrera who plays Betty in the television program Ugly Betty is the daughter of Honduran immigrants
7. Garry Kasparov is a well respected chess player who grew up in the former Soviet Union but is opposed to the way things are going in Russia at present
8. Michael J. Fox famous for his acting in both television and film was diagnosed with a young onset of Parkinsons disease in 1991
9. Alas
10. Screenwriter Shonda Rhimes is a single mom whose Emmy winning show Grey's Anatomy has taken the world by surprise
11. The remarkable thing about Pepsis new boss is that she is a woman she is from India and she is concerned about communities, energy use, and health
12. Virgin Galactic is one of the first commercial airlines to envision space flight for everyone
13. Elizabeth Windsor is also known as Queen Elizabeth II Britains head of state
14. How many commonwealth countries does Britain oversee
15. Charles and Mary Lamb a brother and sister collaboration team are most remembered for their childrens books Tales from Shakespeare
16. Ennio Morricone an Italian film composer wrote scores for A Fistful of Dollars The Good the Bad and the Ugly Once Upon a Time in the West The Untouchables and the Mission

17. Robert Oppenheimer a theoretical physicist headed the Manhattan Project to develop the atomic bomb

18. Wernher von Braun a rocket engineer who was born in Germany is largely responsible for launching the first U.S. satellite *Explorer I* and later worked on the development of the Saturn rocket for the Apollo program

19. Nightshade is a deadly poisonous plant with purple leaves

20. Watch out

Real-World Practice Activities

Reading and Writing

Directions: Locate an article on the dread pirate Jean Lafitte. After reading the article, write a synopsis of what you discovered about his life. Be aware of your punctuation. Integrate three quotes from the article into your synopsis, and use quotation marks.

Quotations

1. _____

_____

2. _____

_____

3. _____

_____

_____

_____

_____

_____

_____

_____

_____

_____

_____

_____

_____

Listening

Directions: Sit in a public place somewhere: a park, subway, bus stop, shopping mall, and so on. Listen carefully to conversations around you. Write down five quotes that you overhear. Use proper punctuation and quotation marks.

1. _____

2. _____

3. _____

4. _____

5. _____

Chapter 13

SENTENCE PURPOSE

We have already looked at sentence structure with our study of phrases and clauses. Now that we know the difference between the various types of punctuation from the previous chapter, we can look at sentences that are classified according to purpose. There are four different purposes for sentences: declarative, exclamatory, imperative, and interrogative.

Vocabulary Development

1. **anopheles** (a nof e leez) A mosquito that carries malaria.
2. **beacon** (bee kun) A light used as a signal or warning.
3. **cosmopolitan** (kos mo pol i tan) Of or from many parts of the world, containing many people from various places in the world.
4. **egotism** (ee go tism) The practice of talking too much about oneself.
5. **gullible** (gull li bull) Easily tricked or deceived.
6. **learned** (ler ned) Having acquired much knowledge through study.
7. **pedigree** (ped i gree) A lineage or line of ancestors, especially of a distinguished or noble nature.
8. **radiate** (ray dee ate) To spread out from a central point.
9. **steppe** (step) A level grassy plain with few trees, such as those found in Southeast Europe and Siberia.
10. **trailblazer** (trayl blaze er) A person who pioneers new approaches or makes a new path to an unsettled area.

Declarative Sentences

A declarative sentence makes a statement about something—a person, place, thing, or idea. Declarative sentences end with a period and are the most common type of sentence.

* Brass is a yellow-colored alloy of mainly copper and zinc used primarily for pipe and electrical fittings, musical instruments, and ornamental metalwork.

- Brassica is a genus of plants with edible roots and leaves that include cabbages, cauliflowers, Brussels sprouts, turnips, and rutabagas.
- Brassäi was a Hungarian-born French painter and photographer who focused on taking photographs of Paris nightlife and portraiture.

Exclamatory Sentences

Exclamatory sentences demonstrate strong feelings or emotions and end with an exclamation point.

- Take the wheel Ahab, I am going to be sick!
- Watch out! Do not step on that snake!
- Mustard! Did I say that I wanted MUSTARD!

Imperative Sentences

Imperative sentences give commands or make requests. Most often these sentences end with a period. However, imperative sentences with stronger emotion end with an exclamation point.

- Please take out the trash.
- Do not forget to make your bed.
- Do your homework before dinner!

Interrogative Sentences

These sentences ask questions and end with a question mark.

- What is your middle name?
- How long did she spend in the concentration camp?
- Where were the Dead Sea Scrolls discovered?

Practice I

Directions: Identify each of the following sentences by writing *declarative, exclamatory, imperative,* or *interrogative* on the line at the beginning of the sentence.

EXAMPLE:

   interrogative Where are my keys?

1. _____ Take care of the leg.

2. _____ London is quite the cosmopolitan city.

3. _____ Do you know the history of Lewis and Clark?

4. _____ They were trailblazers looking for a water route from the Mississippi River to the Pacific Ocean.

5. _____ Which president initiated the two-year exploration?

6. _____ Sacajawea was the Shonshone woman who helped Lewis and Clark find their way to the Pacific Northwest.

7. _____ Yes! True beacons of light!

8. _____ Level grassy plains with limited trees are called steppes.

9. _____ You seriously are not THAT gullible!

10. _____ The sun radiates heat and light over Earth.

11. _____ Do not forget to use insect repellent; you do not need to come down with malaria caused by anopheles.

12. _____ I have never seen such egotism!

13. _____ My favorite dogs are not of any fancy pedigree; they are rescue mutts from the shelter.

14. _____ The learned professor was taken to the ceremony by his colleagues.

15. _____ Stay away!

16. _____ What are you talking about?

17. _____ Hold the phone!

18. _____ When you get to the store, give me a call.

19. _____ You have got to visit more often.

20. _____ During the parade, the drum majorette tossed her baton hundreds of times and never missed.

Chapter 13 Review Quizzes

Vocabulary Review Quiz

Directions: Write the letter of the definition on the line next to the word that it defines.

1. _____ anopheles

2. _____ beacon

3. _____ cosmopolitan

4. _____ egotism

5. _____ gullible

6. _____ learned

7. _____ pedigree

8. _____ radiate

9. _____ steppe

10. _____ trailblazer

A. To spread out from a central point.

B. Having acquired much knowledge through study.

C. A person who pioneers new approaches or makes a new path to an unsettled area.

D. The practice of talking too much about oneself.

E. A light used as a signal or warning.

F. A level grassy plain with few trees, such as those found in Southeast Europe and Siberia.

G. A mosquito that carries malaria.

H. Of or from many parts of the world, containing many people from various places in the world.

I. Easily tricked or deceived.

J. Lineage or line of ancestors, especially of a distinguished or noble nature.

Sentence Type Definitions

Directions: Select the correct definition, and write the letter of the answer on the line to the right of the number.

1. _____ There are _____ types of sentences used for various purposes.
   a. ten
   b. six
   c. five
   d. four

2. _____ Which of the following is an interrogative sentence?
   a. Do not bother me!
   b. Will you take me to the mall?
   c. *Spiderman 3* is playing at the theaters now.
   d. Eat your breakfast.

3. _____ Which of the following is NOT an imperative sentence?
   a. Use the money for something practical.
   b. Are you leaving so soon?
   c. Take your medicine with dinner.
   d. Watch the way you chew, please.

4. _____ An interrogative sentence ends with a _____ .
   a. question mark
   b. period
   c. dash
   d. exclamation point

5. _____ A declarative sentence _____ .
   a. asks a question
   b. makes a command
   c. makes a statement
   d. communicates strong emotion

6. _____ Identify the declarative sentence below.
   a. Litter is a nuisance to society.
   b. Will you please pick up your trash?
   c. Take out the trash now, please.
   d. Do you recycle?

7. _____ Exclamatory sentences end with a _____ .
   a. question mark
   b. period
   c. dash
   d. exclamation point

8. _____ Identify the interrogative sentence below.
   a. Don't!
   b. Franciso Franco ruled Spain for 36 years.
   c. Where are you going for vacation this year?
   d. I will not have any part of that.

9. _____ A declarative sentence ends with a _____ .
   a. question mark
   b. period
   c. dash
   d. exclamation point

10. _____ An exclamatory sentence uses _____ .
    a. melodies
    b. quotations
    c. emotion
    d. all of the above

Declarative, Exclamatory, Imperative, and Interrogative Sentences

Directions: In the paragraph below, identify each of the numbered sentences as *declarative, exclamatory, imperative,* or *interrogative* by writing the sentence type on the numbered line below the paragraph.

EXAMPLE:

Ecuador is a republic in western South America.
Declarative

1) Have you ever heard of a city named Quito? 2) Quito is the capital of Ecuador, a country in the northern part of South America. 3) Quito is situated almost exactly on the equator, and it is 9,260 feet (2,820 m) above sea level. 4) Ecuador/equator, is there a link? 5) It sounds like it. 6) When you think of the equator, what is your first thought? 7) Heat? 8) Consider, if you will, the equator is over 9,000 feet (2,740 m) above sea level. 9) What might the weather be like? 10) Originally, the site was settled by Native Americans and then captured by the Incas in 1487. 11) Spain invaded and settled in the area in 1534. 12) Antonio José de Sucre led the liberation from Spain and was successful in 1822. 13) Quito is a cultural and political center as well as the site of the Central University of Ecuador, which was established in 1787. 14) Now that is an established university! 15) Quito has a population of over 1,000,000 people, who are known for their textiles and handicrafts.

1. _____   6. _____   11. _____

2. _____   7. _____   12. _____

3. _____   8. _____   13. _____

4. _____   9. _____   14. _____

5. _____   10. _____   15. _____

Real-World Practice Activities

Reading and Writing

Directions: Find an article on Antonio José de Sucre. Read the article carefully, and then write ten interesting facts about him. Use each type of sentence at least once: declarative, exclamatory, imperative, and interrogative. You will need to be creative to include more than just declarative sentences.

1. _____

2. _____

3. _____

4. _____

5. _____

6. _____

7 _____

8. _____

9. _____

10. _____

Listening

Directions: Listen carefully to a dramatic program or show either on television or on the radio. As you listen, write down each of the types of sentences on the lines below: declarative, exclamatory, imperative, and interrogative.

1. Declarative:

_____

2. Declarative:

_____

3. Exclamatory:

_____

4. Exclamatory:

_____

5. Imperative:

_____

6. Imperative:

_____

7. Interrogative:

_____

8. Interrogative:

_____

9. Declarative:

_____

10. Declarative:

_____

Chapter 14

CAPITALIZATION RULES

The rules for capitalization seem long and complex. When you read more and more, though, capitalization soon becomes second nature. To make a long story short (that is a cliché), capitalize most things that are formal—titles, names, places, and so on. Review the capitalization rules several times to fix or log them in your brain.

Vocabulary Development

1. **barometer** (ba rom ee ter) An instrument used to measure atmospheric pressure.
2. **confederacy** (con fed er a cee) A union of states or a group of people.
3. **flamboyant** (flam boy ant) Dressed, colored, or decorated in a showy manner.
4. **heron** (har on) A long-legged and long-necked bird who lives in and around marshy areas.
5. **jinx** (jinkx) A person or thing that is believed to bring bad luck.
6. **lasagna** (la zan ya) A pasta that is formed into long, thin strips.
7. **premature** (pree ma toor) Occurring before the proper time, too early.
8. **seasonable** (see son a bull) Timely, suitable for the season.
9. **tintinnabulation** (tin tin abb yu lay shun) The sound of ringing bells.
10. **virgule** (vur gyool) a slanting line (/) that separates words or lines.

Capitalization Rules

- **The first word of every sentence**
  o The barometer is an instrument used to measure atmospheric pressure.
  o They are used primarily in weather forecasting.
  o A rising barometer indicates dry weather, and a falling barometer indicates wet weather.

- **Proper nouns, the names of people and animals**
  - Juli, Birgit, Ann, Vicki, Smith, Snodgrass, Castaldo, Schoenfeld
  - Chloe, Roxy, Ruka, Tippy, Maya, Nina, Katie
- **Proper adjectives**
  - French, Icelandic, Russian, Martian, Roman
- **Races, nationalities, languages**
  - African-American, Caucasian, Native American
  - African, South American, Mexican, Greek
  - Russian, Slavic, Danish, Gaelic
- **The pronoun *I***
- **All words in a title (books, magazines, newspaper, poems, short stories, historical documents, movies, TV programs, works of art, and musical compositions) except for articles *(a, an, the)* and the word *of***
  - *The Way of the Peaceful Warrior*
  - *Redbook Magazine*
  - *The Los Angeles Times*
  - "Ode On a Grecian Urn"
  - Bill of Rights
  - *Miss Congeniality*
  - *Grey's Anatomy*
  - *Mona Lisa*
  - "Let It Be"
- **Organization names, teams and their members, businesses, institutions, associations, and government bodies**
  - NAACP
  - San Diego Chargers
  - the Chargers
  - Target
  - Massachusetts Institute of Technology
  - Parent Teacher Association
  - Department of Social Services
- **Abbreviations of titles and organizations**
  - Dr. Ms. Mrs. Mr. PhD.
  - PTA, NRA, GOP
- **Letters that indicate form or shape**
  - U-turn, V-shape, T-bone, O-shaped
- **Words like uncle, aunt, mother, or father when they are part of a title or used in place of a name**
  - When is Uncle Walt going to arrive?
  - I cannot wait for Mom and Dad to see this.
- **Course titles such as language and those with a course number**
  - History 101, English, French, Spanish, Calculus CD

- **Nouns or pronouns that refer to a Supreme Being, religions, specific deities, sacred writings**
  - He, Him, You, Thou
  - Jewish, Muslim, Hindu, Buddhist, Catholic
  - Allah, God, Buddha, Jehovah, the Lord
  - the Bible, the Koran, the Talmud, Book of Genesis, Psalms
- **Buildings and structures**
  - Empire State Building, Sears Tower, Peace Arch
- **Days of the week and their abbreviations**
  - Sunday, Monday, Tuesday, Wednesday
  - Thur., Fri., Sat.
- **Months of the year and their abbreviations**
  - January, March, April, May, August
  - Feb., Jun., Dec.
- **Holidays and holy days**
  - Halloween, Memorial Day, Labor Day
  - Christmas, Purim, Good Friday
- **Events in history, historical periods**
  - Battle of Hastings, American Revolution, Civil War
  - the Renaissance, the Iron Age, Industrialization
- **Special Events**
  - Celebration of Wisdom, New Year's Celebration, Quinciñera
- **Awards**
  - Nobel Peace Prize, Newberry Medal, Pulitzer Prize, Academy Award
- **Names of ships, trains, spacecraft, and airplanes (the specific names are also italicized)**
  - *Titanic, Calypso, Queen Elizabeth II*
  - Orient Express, Santa Fe Railroad
  - *Apollo 13, Voyager 2*
  - *Enola Gay, Air Force One*
- **Political parties**
  - Democrats, Republicans, Independents, Green Party
- **Official documents**
  - Declaration of Independence, the Magna Carta, Articles of Confederation
- **Trade names**
  - Kellogg's, Ford, IBM, iPod, Hershey's
- **Formal epithets or titles**
  - King Henry the VIII, William the Conqueror, Alexander the Great
- **Official state nicknames**
  - the Evergreen State, the Sunshine State, the Cotton State
- **Geographical names**
  - **Planets, stars, and other heavenly bodies**
    - —Earth, Mars, Andromeda, the Sun, Halley's Comet, Comet Hale-Bopp, Taurus, the Moon

o **Continents**

—Asia, Africa, Australia, North America, South America

o **Countries**

—England, Romania, China, Mexico, Brazil

o **States, provinces, and their abbreviations**

—WA, MA, Maine, Ohio, Iowa, South Dakota

—BC, Quebec, Nova Scotia, Valpariso Region

o **Cities, towns, and villages**

—Taos, Boston, Chicago, Julian, Portland, Stratford-upon-Avon

o **Streets, roads, and highways**

—Hawthorne Blvd., Ridgecrest Rd., Interstate 5, San Diego Freeway, Pacific Coast Highway

o **Sections of a country or continent**

—the South, the Northwest, Canadian Arctic, Amazon Basin

o **Landforms**

—Cliffs of Moher, Ireland

—Trango Towers, Pakistan

—El Capitan, Yosemite Valley, California

—Mount Rainier, Washington

o **Bodies of Water**

—Lake Superior, Baltic Sea, Irish Sea, Pacific Ocean

o **Public areas such as parks and monuments**

—Yellowstone National Park, Montana

—Banff National Park, Alberta, Canada

—Bryce National Park, Utah

—Mount Rushmore

—Vietnam Memorial

—Washington Memorial

Practice I

Directions: Correct the capitalization errors in the sentences below by drawing a box around the letters that need to be capitalized.

EXAMPLE:

[o]ver there you will see the [t]ower of [p]isa.

1. on our vacation, we will be visiting the southeast, the great lakes area, and then on to yellowstone national park.
2. the naacp stands for the national association for the advancement of colored people.
3. the *nina,* the *pinta,* and the *santa maria* were the ships that columbus sailed.

4. The U.S. purple heart medal is awarded to those who have been injured or killed while serving in the military.

5. She was selling african goods in her shop on 331st st.

6. during the great depression, work and food were at a premium.

7. After church services, we will celebrate el dia de la virgin guadalupe with a grand feast.

8. the entries in the cannes film festival seem outstanding this year.

9. the nfl will reevaluate their decision.

10. my sister will fly to oahu first and then on to new zealand.

11. Take highway 101 until you get to highway 67 and then go east.

12. Next september and october, they are taking a trip to russia.

13. the nile river flows through egypt and other african countries.

14. Who do you think is going to win, the democratic party or the republican party?

15. name the men who signed the declaration of independence.

16. my jewish friends will fly to israel for chanukah next year.

17. we did not get to see the cliffs of moher on our trip to ireland.

18. cinco de mayo is on a saturday this year.

19. from san antonio, i plan on flying to chicago and then on to montreal.

20. if you will please read this passage from the koran, you will better understand what we are discussing.

Practice II

Directions: Write a sentence for each of the vocabulary words, using the words correctly and capitalizing as necessary.

1. (Barometer)
   The barometer fell dramatically just before Hurricane Katrina struck the South.

2. (Confederacy)
   _____

3. (Flamboyant)
   _____

4. (Heron)
   _____

5. (Jinx)
   _____

6. (Lasagna)
   _____

7. (Premature)

_____

8. (Seasonable)

_____

9. (Tintinnabulation)

_____

10. (Virgule)

_____

Chapter 14 Review Quizzes

Vocabulary Review Quiz

Directions: Write the letter of the definition on the line next to the word that it defines.

1. _____ barometer

2. _____ confederacy

3. _____ flamboyant

4. _____ heron

5. _____ jinx

6. _____ lasagna

7. _____ premature

8. _____ seasonable

9. _____ tintinnabulation

10. _____ virgule

A. Timely, suitable for the season.

B. An instrument used to measure atmospheric pressure.

C. Dressed, colored, or decorated in a showy manner.

D. A slanting line (/) that separates words or lines.

E. A pasta that is formed into long thin strips.

F. A long-legged and long-necked bird who lives in and around marshy areas.

G. A union of states or a group of people.

H. The sound of ringing bells.

I. A person or thing that is believed to bring bad luck.

J. Occurring before the proper time, too early.

Capitalization Rules

Directions: Select the correct definition, and write the letter of the answer on the line to the right of the number.

1. _____ Which of the following should NOT be capitalized?
   a. common nouns
   b. proper nouns
   c. proper adjectives
   d. titles

2. _____ Which of the following is properly capitalized?
   a. Lake Erie
   b. Pacific Ocean
   c. Baltic Sea
   d. all of the above

3. _____ Which of the following is NOT correctly capitalized?
   a. virgin atlantic airlines
   b. United Airlines
   c. American Airlines
   d. Alaska Airlines

4. _____ Which of the following words is NOT a building or structure?
   a. Empire State Building
   b. Sears Tower
   c. Windsor Castle
   d. New York Philharmonic Orchestra

5. _____ Identify the continents from the list below.
   a. Sudan, Asia, Nova Scotia
   b. Tennessee, Florida, Texas
   c. Australia, Africa, South America
   d. Australia, New Zealand, New Guinea

6. _____ True or False? The only pronoun that is capitalized all the time is *she*.
   a. True
   b. False

7. _____ Which of the following sentences is correctly capitalized?
   a. Will Aunt Jean be joining us for a picnic?
   b. take your mother to the zoo.
   c. In the middle ages, life was cruel and primitive.
   d. The democratic party hopes to win control of the senate.

8. _____ Which of the following should not be capitalized?
   a. French
   b. Friend
   c. Dr. Park
   d. Mrs. Horne

9. _____ True or False? Titles to movies are not capitalized.
   a. True
   b. False

10. _____ Which of the following should be capitalized?
   a. lake
   b. ocean
   c. river
   d. lake tahoe

Capitalization

Directions: In the paragraph below, correct all punctuation errors by drawing a box around the letters that need to be capitalized.

⬚lawrence ⬚ferlinghetti, an ⬚american poet, was born on march 24, 1919. he was born in yonkers, new york, where he attended high school and earned the rank of eagle scout. Later he attended the university of north carolina at chapel hill. ferlinghetti served as an officer in the navy during world war II and afterward earned a master's degree at columbia and a doctorate at the sorbonne in paris. While in paris, he met a man who convinced him to go to san francisco, where ferlinghetti taught french, painted, and wrote literary criticism. in 1953, he and peter d. martin opened city lights bookstore, which was named after the charlie chaplin film *city lights*. ferlinghetti opened a publishing company when martin left for new york and began to publish the early works of poets who are known as the beat generation. poets jack kerouac and allen ginsberg were among this group. ferlinghetti's *a coney island of the mind* is his best-known collection of poetry and has been translated into nine languages.

Real-World Practice Activities

Reading

Directions: Read an article on the nurse Clara Barton. List twenty (20) words that are capitalized in the article.

1. _____	11. _____
2. _____	12. _____
3. _____	13. _____
4. _____	14. _____
5. _____	15. _____
6. _____	16. _____
7. _____	17. _____
8. _____	18. _____
9. _____	19. _____
10. _____	20. _____

Writing

Directions: Write a paragraph about the city or town that you live in. Describe its buildings, streets, schools, hospitals, businesses, and so on. Use correct capitalization.

_____

_____

_____

_____

_____

_____

_____

_____

_____

_____

_____

_____

_____

Listening

Directions: Listen carefully to a news program on the radio, on television, or on the Internet. Write down a list of ten (10) words that you know should be capitalized. You may want to review the list of rules again before you listen to the program.

1. _____   6. _____

2. _____   7. _____

3. _____   8. _____

4. _____   9. _____

5. _____   10. _____

Chapter 15

WRITING PARAGRAPHS

Writing paragraphs is a skill that comes with practice just like almost everything else in life. Once the formulaic understanding of the types of sentences is mastered, joining these sentences together is the next major task in the writing process. A good paragraph has a beginning, middle, and end. A good paragraph is one that is well developed and organized. It has a main idea or topic sentence. It has supporting sentences that add clarification or detail to help the reader understand the topic. Finally, it has either a concluding sentence or a transitional sentence that ends the paragraph's idea completely or moves the reader smoothly to the next paragraph. Developing well-organized paragraphs is vital to writing good essays, which will be addressed later in this book. Remember—all paragraphs should be indented.

Vocabulary Development

1. **desperado** (des per a do) A desperate or reckless person; a criminal.
2. **facilitate** (fas sill i tait) To make easy or less difficult.
3. **governess** (guv er ness) A woman employed to teach children in a private household.
4. **ingrain** (in grain) To implant permanently a habit, belief, or attitude in a person.
5. **kaput** (ka put) Broken; ruined.
6. **nebulous** (neb u less) Cloudlike; hazy; indistinct; vague.
7. **omega** (o meg ga) The last letter of the Greek alphabet Ω or the last of a series; the final development.
8. **reciprocate** (ree cip pro kait) To return or requite emotion or a favor or action equally.
9. **ruminate** (roo mi nait) To ponder or meditate on.
10. **vagrant** (vay grent) A person without a settled home or regular work.

The Beginning: The Topic Sentence

A topic sentence reveals the writer's direction. It tells the reader where the idea of the paragraph is going. A topic sentence is the beginning, the jumping-off point of the paragraph. Think of each paragraph as a separate entity. Each has a beginning—the topic sentence. A topic sentence is usually the first sentence of the paragraph but not always. For what we are attempting to accomplish, which is a basic understanding of the structure of a paragraph, we will keep the topic sentence as the first sentence. Review the following rules for the topic sentence.

- One topic equals one main idea per paragraph.
- The support sentences that follow the topic sentence are closely related to the topic or main idea.
- The topic sentence forces the writer to control the writing of the paragraph by keeping it within the boundaries of the main idea or topic.
- The topic sentence should be neither too broad of an idea nor too narrow in scope.

Example Topic Sentences

The following topics will be developed into full paragraphs. These are the main ideas, the controlling topics of our soon-to-be written paragraphs.

- The pyramids in Egypt are huge monuments that were built as burial vaults or tombs for the pharaohs.
- Rock 'n' roll music is a combination of various music styles, including blues, gospel, and country and western.
- A bar or bat mitzvah is a ceremony in Judaism that marks the beginning of religious responsibility in the lives of Jewish boys and girls.
- Marie Antoinette was a young French queen who was born in Austria and who was beheaded on the guillotine during the French Revolution.
- Shangri-La is a fictional land of peace and everlasting youth.

Practice I

Directions: Practice writing topic sentences with the following broad suggestions. Make sure that you know enough about the topic to be able to write an entire paragraph.

EXAMPLE:

An extraordinary animal: <u>The hummingbird is the only bird that can fly backward</u>.

1. A recent film/movie

_____

_____

2. A favorite city

_____

_____

3. Television (show/concept)

_____

_____

4. Book(s)

_____

_____

5. Sport(s)

_____

_____

The Middle: Support Sentences

Support sentences do just that, support. These sentences provide the reader with more specific or concrete details about your topic sentence or main idea of the paragraph. Usually there are about three to five support sentences in a paragraph, depending on the topic. Support sentences help to explain the topic and provide interesting facts. NOTE: The following support sentences (**in bold print**) tie into the topic sentences that are listed above.

- The pyramids in Egypt are huge monuments that were built as burial vaults or tombs for the pharaohs. **The largest remaining pyramid is at Giza, which has a square base and four triangular faces and was finished in about 2590 B.C. Building the pyramid took 84,000 workers at least 20 years to build. Although the building of the structure itself was complicated, only the simplest of tools were used: levers, pulleys, rollers, and human muscle.**

- Rock 'n' roll music is a combination of various music styles, including blues, gospel, and country and western. **It is a popular music that is known for its strong beat and commanding lyrics. Rock 'n' roll has evolved over the years and has taken many different paths. Rap, punk rock, heavy metal, grunge, hip hop, and techno are among the genres that have evolved from rock 'n' roll.**

- A bar or bat mitzvah is a ceremony in Judaism that marks the beginning of religious responsibility in the lives of Jewish boys and girls. **Bar/bat Mitzvah means "son" or "daughter" "of the commandment." The ceremonies take place when the boys and girls are thirteen years old. Usually there is a symbolic reading in Hebrew of the Torah by the young person in the temple followed by a party for the young girl or boy being honored.**

- Marie Antoinette was a young French queen who was born in Austria and who was beheaded on the guillotine during the French Revolution. **She was born in 1755 to the Emperor Francis I and his wife Maria Theresa. Marie married the Dauphin, King Louis XVI, in 1770 when she was about fifteen years old. Extravagant by nature, the young queen made many enemies. When the**

French Revolution broke out, she and the royal family made a failed attempt to flee from France.

- Shangri-La is a fictional land of peace and everlasting youth. **This fictional land first had its beginning as the setting of the novel *Lost Horizon,* which was written by an English author named James Hilton. However, the concept of Shangri-La is better known from a film that was made based on the novel. Shangri-La, this land of peace and youthfulness, is allegedly to be found in the mountains of Tibet.**

Practice II

Directions: Write three support sentences linking information to the topic sentences that you wrote in Practice I. Make certain that these sentences focus on your topic and add detail and interest.

EXAMPLE:

The hummingbird is one of the best and most adroit at flying of all bird species. It can fly forward, sideways, and backward as well as hover in one place. Its long bill allows it to consume nectar from plants and flowers. The hummingbird name comes from the sound that its wings make because it flaps at such an astounding speed.

1. A recent film/movie

   _____
   _____
   _____
   _____
   _____
   _____

2. A favorite city

   _____
   _____
   _____
   _____
   _____
   _____

3. Television (show/concept)

   _____
   _____
   _____
   _____
   _____
   _____

4. Book(s)

_____
_____
_____
_____
_____
_____
_____

5. Sport(s)

_____
_____
_____
_____
_____
_____
_____

The End: Concluding and Transitional Sentences

These are used to complete a thought about the topic of the paragraph. A concluding or clincher sentence ends a stand-alone paragraph with a more thought-provoking statement. These are the grand finales so to speak; the paragraph is concluded, finished. Transitional sentences lead the reader via a link or transition to the next paragraph—leaving one idea behind but smoothly moving into the next idea without major turbulence.

Concluding Sentences

The **boldface** sentences that are added onto the support sentences are concluding sentences. These paragraphs are finished and are not leading to another paragraph.

- The pyramids in Egypt are huge monuments that were built as burial vaults or tombs for the pharaohs. The largest remaining pyramid is at Giza, which has a square base and four triangular faces and was finished in about 2590 B.C. Building the pyramid took 84,000 workers at least 20 years to build. Although the building of the structure itself was complicated, only the simplest of tools were used: levers, pulleys, rollers, and human muscle. **The pyramids of Egypt are structures that have been admired for centuries and are included on the list of the Seven Wonders of the Ancient World.**

- Rock 'n' roll music is a combination of various music styles, including blues, gospel, and country and western. It is a popular music that is known for its strong beat and commanding lyrics. Rock 'n' roll has evolved over the years and has taken many different paths. Rap, punk rock, heavy metal, grunge, hip hop, and techno are among the genres that have evolved from rock 'n' roll. **With musical talent that ranges from Chuck Berry, the Beatles, AC-DC, The Red Hot Chili Peppers, and Busta Rhymes to Christina Aguilera, Madonna, and Sheryl Crow, rock 'n' roll is here to stay.**

- A bar or bat mitzvah is a ceremony in Judaism that marks the beginning of religious responsibility in the lives of Jewish boys and girls. Bar/bat mitzvah means "son" or "daughter" "of the commandment." The ceremonies take place when the boys and girls are thirteen years old. Usually there is a symbolic reading in Hebrew of the Torah by the young person in the temple followed by a party for the young girl or boy being honored. **Bar and bat mitzvahs are important and often life-changing social events in Jewish families.**

- Marie Antoinette was a young French queen who was born in Austria and who was beheaded on the guillotine during the French Revolution. She was born in 1755 to the Emperor Francis I and his wife Maria Theresa. Marie married the Dauphin, King Louis XVI, in 1770 when she was about fifteen years old. Extravagant by nature, the young queen made many enemies. When the French Revolution broke out, she and the royal family made a failed attempt to flee from France. **While the poor of France were going hungry without even a piece of bread to eat, the insensitive and, as it seems, foolish young Marie Antoinette retorted, "Let them eat cake," which, as the story ends with her head in a basket, was not a wise thing to say.**

- Shangri-La is a fictional land of peace and everlasting youth. This fictional land first had its beginning as the setting of the novel *Lost Horizon,* which was written by an English author named James Hilton. However, the concept of Shangri-La is better known from a film that was made based on the novel. Shangri-La, this land of peace and youthfulness, is allegedly to be found in the mountains of Tibet. **Whether the concept of Shangri-La is true or not, the dream of eternal peace and an eternal youthful life is a vision that many in the world treasure and hold to dearly in their imaginations.**

Transitional Sentences

A paragraph that has a transitional ending ends one thought but slides into the topic of the next paragraph for a smooth transition. There are a number of ways to accomplish this transition—the use of any of the following words from the chart helps to link one paragraph to another depending on the purpose of the paragraph. These are just a sampling of transitional expressions or linking words to help move the writing from one idea to another.

TRANSITIONAL EXPRESSIONS AND LINKING WORDS				
Words That Express Time or Position				
about	above	across	against	along
afterward	around	among	at once	away from
at the present time	at	before	behind	below
beneath	beside	between	beyond	by
down	eventually	finally	first	in back of
in front of	inside	into	here	meanwhile
near	next	off	onto	on top of
outside	over	presently	thereafter	thereupon
throughout	to the right	under	until	first/second/and so on
Words That Link Similar Ideas				
again	also	as	and	another
besides	furthermore	for example	for instance	in the same way
likewise	like	moreover	similarly	too
Words That Link Dissimilar Ideas				
although	as if	but	conversely	even if/though
however	in spite of	instead	nevertheless	otherwise
on the other hand	provided that	still	yet	
Words That Indicate Cause, Purpose, Result				
as	as a result	all in one	because	consequently
for	for this reason	hence	in conclusion	in summary
finally	since	so	then	therefore
to sum up	in summary	thus		

We will once again revisit the topic and support sentences that we have developed earlier in the chapter. However, this time we are going to finish with a transitional sentence instead of a concluding sentence. By ending with a transitional sentence, the topic of the paragraph that we are ending is being linked to the next paragraph. When writing various types of essays, transitional sentences are connectors or links from one thought to the next, making the reading smooth from paragraph to paragraph. The **boldface** sentences are transitional sentences leading the reader to another paragraph while closing the thought on the previous idea.

- The pyramids in Egypt are huge monuments that were built as burial vaults or tombs for the pharaohs. The largest remaining pyramid is at Giza, which has a square base and four triangular faces and was finished in about 2590 B.C. Building the pyramid took 84,000 workers at least 20 years to build. Although the building of the structure itself was complicated, only the simplest of tools were used: levers, pulleys, rollers, and human muscle. **Besides these grand structures in Egypt that are included on the list of the Seven Wonders of the Ancient World is the Colossus at Rhodes, which was the giant statue of the sun god Helios.** (This transitions to the next paragraph on another ancient wonder.)

- Rock 'n' roll music is a combination of various music styles, including blues, gospel, and country and western. It is a popular music that is known for its strong beat and commanding lyrics. Rock 'n' roll has evolved over the years and has taken many different paths. Rap, punk rock, heavy metal, grunge, hip hop, and techno are among the genres that have evolved from rock 'n' roll. **However, in addition to the broad spectrum of music genres that have evolved over the years, so has the variety of artists**. (This transition leads to a paragraph that will address specific artists in music.)

- A bar or bat mitzvah is a ceremony in Judaism that marks the beginning of religious responsibility in the lives of Jewish boys and girls. Bar/bat Mitzvah means "son" or "daughter" "of the commandment." The ceremonies take place when the boys and girls are thirteen years old. Usually there is a symbolic reading in Hebrew of the Torah by the young person in the temple followed by a party for the young girl or boy being honored. **Not only is the bat or bar mitzvah an opportunity to demonstrate religious stability, it is an important social event in the lives of Jewish families.** (This transition links the religious aspect to the next paragraph, which will address the social aspect.)

- Marie Antoinette was a young French queen who was born in Austria and who was beheaded on the guillotine during the French Revolution. She was born in 1755 to the Emperor Francis I and his wife Maria Theresa. Marie married the Dauphin, King Louis XVI, in 1770 when she was about fifteen years old. Extravagant by nature, the young queen made many enemies. When the French Revolution broke out, she and the royal family made a failed attempt to flee from France. **Angry with the lavish and grandiose lifestyle of the royalty, the poor had spoken. As a consequence, the life that Marie Antoinette had once taken for granted was about to change drastically**. (This transitions to the next paragraph, which will explain this change in her life and that of the French.)

- Shangri-La is a fictional land of peace and everlasting youth. This fictional land first had its beginning as the setting of the novel *Lost Horizon*, which was written by an English author named James Hilton. However, the concept of Shangri-La is better known from a film that was made based on the novel. Shangri-La, this land of peace and youthfulness, is allegedly to be found in the mountains of Tibet. **Although the fictional concept of a Shangri-La is ever present in the minds of many, there are concrete ways to achieve peace and youth through exercise and meditation.** (This transition links to the next paragraph, which will address exercise and meditation.)

Practice III

Directions: Write two types of sentences in this exercise: a concluding sentence and a transitional sentence. The concluding sentence will end the paragraph with a strong or more dynamic statement or thought. The transitional sentence will lead the reader to another idea or point while closing the door on the current thought.

EXAMPLES:

Concluding Sentence: The hummingbird is the lightest, eats the most, and is considered the fastest bird of all, which is quite a reputation to live up to.

Transitional Sentence: In addition to the hummingbird's flying capabilities, its feeding habits are astounding as well.

1. A recent film/movie
   Concluding Sentence:

   _____

   _____

   Transitional Sentence:

   _____

   _____

2. A favorite city
   Concluding Sentence:

   _____

   _____

   Transitional Sentence:

   _____

   _____

3. Television (show/concept)
   Concluding Sentence:

   _____

   _____

   Transitional Sentence:

   _____

   _____

4. Book(s)
   Concluding Sentence:

   _____

   _____

   Transitional Sentence:

   _____

   _____

5. Sport(s)
   Concluding Sentence:

   _____

   _____

   Transitional Sentence:

   _____

   _____

Chapter 15 Review Quizzes

Vocabulary Review Quiz

Directions: Write the letter of the definition on the line next to the noun that it defines.

1. _____ desperado
2. _____ facilitate
3. _____ governess
4. _____ ingrain
5. _____ kaput
6. _____ nebulous
7. _____ omega
8. _____ reciprocate
9. _____ ruminate
10. _____ vagrant

A. A person without a settled home or regular work.

B. The last letter of the Greek alphabet Ω or the last of a series; the final development.

C. A woman employed to teach children in a private household.

D. To return or requite emotion or a favor or action equally.

E. To implant permanently a habit, belief, or attitude in a person.

F. Cloudlike; hazy; indistinct; vague.

G. To make easy or less difficult.

H. A desperate or reckless person; a criminal.

I. Broken; ruined.

J. To ponder or meditate on.

Paragraph Writing Definitions

Directions: Select the correct definition, and write the letter of the answer on the line to the right of the number.

1. _____ A paragraph contains a _____ .
   a. beginning
   b. middle
   c. end
   d. all of the above

2. _____ A _____ sentence introduces the idea or main topic.
   a. concluding
   b. transitional
   c. topic
   d. support

3. _____ A _____ sentence ends the thought of the paragraph completely.
   a. concluding
   b. transitional
   c. topic
   d. support

4. _____ A _____ sentence moves the reader from one idea and paragraph to the next idea and paragraph.
   a. concluding
   b. transitional
   c. topic
   d. support

5. _____ _____ sentences should add detail and interesting facts to the topic sentence.
   a. Concluding
   b. Transitional
   c. Topic
   d. Support

6. _____ There are roughly _____ support sentences in a paragraph, depending on the topic.
   a. three to five
   b. infinite
   c. one
   d. zero

7. _____ The topic sentence generally is the _____ sentence of the paragraph.
   a. last
   b. second
   c. first
   d. none of the above

8. _____ "Warfare played a significant role in gaining regional control during the Middle Ages" is an example of a _____ sentence.
   a. topic
   b. conclusion
   c. transitional
   d. none of the above

9. _____ True or False? Paragraphs should be well structured and organized.
   a. True
   b. False

10. _____ Support sentences are located in the _____ of the paragraph.
    a. beginning
    b. end
    c. middle
    d. all of the above

Writing Paragraphs

Directions: Identify the parts of the paragraph below by writing its title on the lines provided below the paragraph. Identify each as either a *topic, support,* or *concluding sentence.*

(1) Uganda is a landlocked nation in East-central Africa. (2) It is bordered by Tanzania and Rwanda to the south, Zaire to the west, Sudan to the north, and Kenya to the east. The capital of Uganda is Kampala, which is also its largest city. (3) From 1971 to 1979, Uganda was ruled by a military strongman named Idi Amin. (4) It is estimated that over 300,000 Ugandans were killed during his reign. (5) Amin is the subject of a film released in 2006 titled *The Last King of Scotland* and for which Forrest Whitaker, who plays Amin, won the Academy Award for best actor.

1. _____
2. _____
3. _____
4. _____
5. _____

Real-World Practice Activities

Reading and Writing

Directions: Find an article or book about the planet Venus. Look for details about the planet regarding its name, location, and scientific knowledge gathered about it. Write a well-structured paragraph with a topic sentence, supporting sentences, and a concluding sentence.

_____
_____
_____
_____
_____
_____
_____
_____
_____
_____
_____

_____

_____

_____

_____

_____

_____

Listening

Directions: Listen carefully to any kind of program that you are interested in—radio, television, and so on. Listen for topic sentences. Attempt to hear where one idea ends and another begins. Write down a few of these topic sentences.

1. _____

2. _____

3. _____

4. _____

5. _____

Chapter 16

PRONUNCIATION REVIEW

Before learning the ins and outs of spelling, knowing the ins and outs of pronunciation is important. Chances are that if a word is mispronounced, it will also likely be mis-spelled. A review of the basic rules of sounds and pronunciations should be helpful.

Vocabulary Development

1. **annotate** (an no tait) To add notes to explain or clarify.
2. **beguile** (bee gile) To win the attention or the interest of.
3. **carotene** (kare o teen) The orange or red substance occurring in carrots, tomatoes, and other vegetables that is a source of vitamin A.
4. **darn** (darn) To mend by weaving yarn across a hole.
5. **excerpt** (ex cerpt) A part or extract of a film, book, or song.
6. **point-blank** (point blank) Aimed or shot at a very close range.
7. **reservoir** (re ser voor) An artificial or natural lake that is used to store a water supply.
8. **ricochet** (ric o shea) To rebound or bounce off a surface.
9. **tsunami** (su naam ee) A series of giant waves caused by a disturbance in the ocean floor.
10. **turbid** (tur bid) Cloudy, muddy, not clear.

Diacritical marks are marks that have a specific function in deciphering the way to pronounce words.

- (¯) **macron**—placed over a vowel to indicate that it has a long sound
- (˜) **tilde**—placed over a letter to indicate a change in pronunciation, particularly in Spanish. Example: mañana (means "tomorrow" in Spanish, sounds like *mun yanna*)
- (˘) **breve**—placed over a vowel to indicate that it has a short sound
- (´) **acute accent**—placed over a vowel to indicate a stress or focus on a louder sound

---

Vowels

Vowels are a good place to begin for reviewing pronunciation rules. The vowels are *a, e, i, o, u* and *sometimes y and w*. There is a vowel in every word in the English language. We will also look at digraphs, diphthongs, and other situations in which we find vowels.

Long Vowel Sounds

- long $\bar{a}$: cape, tape, cane, lane, lake, make, take, main, sane, wane, plain
- long $\bar{e}$: flea, wee, feet, sweet, peas, tea, peach, leech, reach, bee
- long $\bar{i}$: bike, Mike, blight, white, fight, kite, might, pie, lie, sigh, bile
- long $\bar{o}$: goat, moan, bone, moat, boat, tote, load, toad, dough, so
- long $\bar{u}$: tube, glue, Sue, rule, fuel, mule, ridicule, tune (drool, tool)

Short Vowel Sounds

- short $\breve{a}$: fan, man, tan, land, and, ant, pant, sand, flan, Dan, clan, can
- short $\breve{e}$: bet, met, set, let, pet, threat, yet, whet, wet, rest, best, bed, wed
- short $\breve{i}$: gift, tiff, lift, big, lick, tick, film, fill, mill, sill, lid, build, killed, till
- short $\breve{o}$: cot, soft, sought, fought, thought, chop, mop, top, opt, plot
- short $\breve{u}$: jump, pump, fun, gun, suck, tuck, truck, ugly, jungle, bunk, sunk

Practice I

Directions: Below is a list of words with short and long vowel sounds. Write an *L* on the line if the word has a long vowel, and write *S* on the line if it has a short vowel.

EXAMPLE:

jump __*S*__

1. threat _____
2. tape _____
3. ball _____
4. tea _____
5. cat _____

6. seed _____
7. dough _____
8. woe _____
9. clan _____
10. beach _____

Vowel Digraphs

These are words with two vowels together that have one vowel sound. For instance, *threat* sounds like "thret." A vowel digraph usually has one long sound.

- *ai*—(long a) Spain, rain, plain, main, attain, contain, brain, domain
- *ay*—(long a) slay, way, day, stay, may, pay, stingray, hay, play, lay
- *oa*—(long o) moat, boat, petticoat, throat, ferryboat, towboat, oat
- *oe*—(long o) roe, toe, doe, foe, sloe, woe
- *ow*—(long o) snow, sow, crow, glow, below, blow, elbow, sideshow
- *ee*—(long e) bee, meet, greet, deed, birdseed, succeed, knee, feed, weed
- *ey*—(long e) key, turkey, passkey, off-key, low-key
- *ey*—(long a) they, prey, grey, whey, agley
- *ea*—(long e) eat, meat, treat, wheat, seat, bead, knead, plead, read
- *ea*—(long a) break, steak, beefsteak
- *ea*—(short e) head, read, spread
- *ie*—(long i) lie, pie, tie, belie, magpie, untie, underlie
- *ie*—(long e) piece, niece, Brie, curie, tier
- *ei*—(long a, silent gh) weight, weigh, neigh, freight, eight, aweigh
- *ei*—(long e) either, weird, seize

Practice II

Directions: On the lines next to the vowel digraph, list three words that include the digraph.

EXAMPLE:

ei	*either*	*neither*	*weirdly*
1. *eigh* (long a)			
2. *ea* (long e)			
3. *ow* (long o)			
4. *ee*			
5. *ey* (long e)			
6. *ai*			
7. *ie* (long i)			
8. *oa*			
9. *ea* (short e)			
10. *ay*			

Vowel Diphthongs

These are made of two vowels together that have a unique sound—neither long nor short. The diphthongs *oy, ow, ew, aw, y,* and *w* act as vowels. For example, *oil* sounds like "oyl."

- *au*—auditorium, autocratic, audience, audio, audit, audition, auction, audacious
- *aw*—draw, caw, saw, craw, straw, outdraw, redraw
- *eu*—milieu, sleuth, pas de deux
- *ew*—chew, crew, threw, stew, bestrew, askew
- *oo*—moon, soon, baboon, noon, goon, room, cocoon, spoon, raccoon, bloom
- *oo*—book, took, look, Chinook, hook, crook, cook, gobbledygook
- *oi*—oil, spoil, void, deltoid, steroid, asteroid, broil, foil, toil, embroil
- *ou*—group, soup, troupe, recoup, regroup, croup
- *ou*—louse, house, mouse, ground, hound, sound, bounce
- *ow*—plow, cow, sow, how, brow, chow, how, now, endow, bowwow, meow
- *oy*—toy, boy, coy, decoy, enjoy, convoy, bok choy, deploy, McCoy
- *ui*—juice, sluice
- *ue*—revue, blue, imbue, subdue, avenue, ensue, clue, due, true

Practice III

Directions: Read the (strange and nonsensical) paragraph below, and underline all of the words that include one of the vowel diphthongs from the list above.

Once there was a ___sow___, named Chow, who seemed to be able to plow. She toiled in the oil and ended up stewing in the house, and then her husband named McCoy brought home some bok choy. Not long in the soup, the room filled with straw, and then the raccoon started skipping until noon. Once he was subdued, the mouse threw a louse, and the Mr. and Mrs. finally subdued the coy boy.

R-Controlled Vowel Sounds

The sound of the letter *r* in a word varies according to what letters precede it and those letters that follow it.

- *ar*—car, card, star, mar, bar, tsar, par
- *ar*—(er sound) dollar, scholar, collar, nectar, standard, Oscar
- *er*—her, per, coffer, corer, defer, deter, were
- *ir*—fir, stir, sir, shirr
- *or*—store, more, form, chore, bore, lore, core, shore
- *ur*—fur, burr, cur, purr
- *air*—chair, pair, stair, lair, Claire
- *are*—care, share, fare, stare, mare, rare, ensnare

- *ear*—(long e sound) ear, hear, fear, clear
- *ear*—(er sound) learn, early, pearl, earl
- *ear*—(air sound) bear, tear, pear, swear
- *eer*—steer, beer, deer, cheer, jeer
- *oar*—boar, soar, board, roar
- *or*—(er sound) proctor, actor, factor, doctor, tractor, mentor, scissors
- *ore*—chore, bore, sore, tore, core, chore
- *oor*—poor, moor, boor
- *our*—sour, dour, hour
- *our*—(er sound) courage, journey
- *war*—(wor sound) warm, warden, war, warble, warp
- *wor*—(wer sound) worth, world, work, worry, worm, worse

R-Controlled Vowels Followed by Another Vowel

The sound of an *r*-controlled vowel can be affected when it is followed by another vowel.

- car + e = care
- fir + e = fire
- bar + e = bar
- mar + e = mare
- her + e = here

Practice IV

Directions: Complete the words by adding one of the following combinations of letters: *ar, er, ir, or, ur*.

EXAMPLE:

m__er__e

1. m_____ket
2. st_____k
3. t_____key
4. terr_____
5. _____ban

6. g_____den
7. s_____e
8. maj_____
9. m_____chant
10. c_____emony

The Letter Y

The letter *Y* is sometimes considered a vowel, and the function of a *y* in a word is a bit tricky. A *y* that appears at the beginning of a word sounds like a consonant (*you, your, yen*). When it appears at the end of a word, it sounds like a vowel. When *y* is the only vowel in the word and the word is a one-syllable word (*try, my, sky*), it is pronounced as a long *i* sound. When *y* appears at the end of a multisyllable word, it most always has a long *e* sound (*baby, lazy, lady*).

- beginning *y* = consonant sound—*you, young, yard, Yankee, yak*
- ending *y* = vowel sound—*party, evidently, weekly, meekly*
- one-syllable ending *y* = long *i* sound—*sly, ply, why*
- multisyllable ending *y* = long *e* sound—*evidently, concurrently, exclusively, determinedly*

Practice V

Directions: Complete the chart below with *y* words as directed.

Beginning Y Consonant Sound	Ending Y Vowel Sound	One-syllable Ending Y = Long I Sound	Multisyllable Ending Y = Long E Sound
yeast	*treaty*	*spy*	*duplicity*

Consonants

Consonants are all of the letters that are not vowels: *b, c, d, f, g, h, j, k, l, m, n, p, q, r, s, t, v, w, x, y,* and *z* . Many consonants can make more than one sound.

Consonant Sounds

The consonants *c, g, s,* and *x* are unusual cases in the world of consonants. Their sounds can be soft or harsh, an *s* sound or a *z* sound.

- c—*(soft s sound)* center, city, circuit, cent, cellar, grace, recess
- c—*(harsh k sound)* cat, corner, carry, cash, cave, candy
- g—*(soft j sound)* gym, giant, gist, general, generous, genius
- g—*(harsh g sound)* giggle, grass, gum, give, gouge, go, golf
- s—*(s sound)* see, snake, snuggle, sap, sarcastic, supper, moose, mass
- s—*(z sound)* abuse, choose, lose, says, lays, excuse
- x—*(k sound)* exit, exist, axis

Prctice VI

Directions: Complete the chart below with words as directed. You may want to use a dictionary for help.

C S Sound	*C* K Sound	*G* J Sound	*G* G Sound	*S* S Sound	*S* Z Sound
circus	couch	ginger	grate	side	muse

Silent Consonants

Some words have two consonant letters placed together. One of the two consonants is silent, not audible when the word is pronounced.

- *kn*—*(n sound, silent k)* knock, knuckle, knife, knight, knave, knapsack, knead
- *wr*—*(r sound, silent w)* wrap, wrong, written, wrath, wreath

- *rh—(r sound, silent h)* rhythm, rhapsody, rhyme, rhombus
- *mb—(m sound, silent b)* tomb, comb, thumb, bomb
- *mn—(m sound, silent n)* column, hymn, acronym, homonym, synonym
- *gh—(silent g and h)* high, sigh, thigh, dough, bright, sight, tight
- *gn—(n sound, silent g)* gnaw, gnat, gnarl, gnu, gnawing

Practice VII

Directions: Complete the following sentences with words that have a silent consonant. Use the list of words above to complete the sentences.

EXAMPLE:

She let out a giant *sigh* of relief once she finished the project.

1. After fighting for his true love's life, the _____ rode off on his white horse.
2. The _____ was dark and full of spider webs, but we continued our search for ancient relics.
3. The _____ of the Cuban music is exotic.
4. Please hang the _____ on the door.
5. The baker has to _____ the _____ for about ten minutes before he allows it to rise.
6. Tomorrow I am going to _____ all of the gifts for the party.
7. A _____ is a word that means the same or close to the same as another word.
8. I told Tina not to suck her _____ any more, but she will not listen.
9. _____ on the door to see if they are home.
10. The _____ Sun caused the fabric to fade.

Qu Sounds

The letter q in the English language is always followed by the letter *u*. There are exceptions. However, these exceptions are words that have been adopted, so to speak, from other languages such as Arabic, French, and Hebrew. The sounds of *qu* vary, however.

- *qu—(kw sound)* quick, quaint, quality, qualify, queen, question, squire
- *qu—(k sound)* antique, oblique, mosquito, technique
- *qu—(kwah sound)* quadrant, quantum, qualified, quality, squat, squad

Practice VIII

Directions: <u>Underline</u> the "*qu*" words that have a *kw* sound. Draw a box around the words that have a simple *k* sound. Highlight the "*qu*" words that have a *kwah* sound.

EXAMPLE:

<u>quick</u>   quadrant   opaque

oblique	croquet	quiz
quaint	clique	turquoise
quarter	unique	queasy
squint	antique	boutique
quill	mystique	pique

Consonant Blends

When two or more consonants are either at the beginning of the word or at the end, their sounds are unique.

Beginning Consonant Blends

When a word has two or more consonant letters at the beginning, the consonants are blended and all of the letters can be heard when the word is pronounced.

- *bl*—blend, bland, blonde
- *br*—bread, brat, brawl
- *cl*—clean, clan, claw
- *cr*—creek, crumb, crazy
- *dr*—drop, drone, drive
- *fl*—flank, flee, fly
- *fr*—friend, frenzy, fraternity
- *gl*—glee, glare, gloomy
- *gr*—graze, gravy, gravel
- *pl*—plural, place, plaza
- *pr*—practical, pretend, prance
- *tr*—trace, trade, trek
- *sc*—scab, scaffolding, scuff
- *scr*—scream, scrape, scrub
- *sk*—skunk, skin, skill
- *sl*—sleek, slant, slime
- *sm*—smell, small, smile
- *sn*—snail, snarl, snap
- *sp*—spell, space, spat
- *spl*—spleen, splice, splinter
- *spr*—spring, spry, sprawl
- *st*—stare, star, stipend
- *str*—straight, street, stream
- *sw*—sweat, swim, swear
- *tw*—twist, twirl, twinge

Practice IX

Directions: Write three words using the beginning consonant blends listed at the left.

EXAMPLE:

st	story	stare	stifled

1. sw   _____   _____   _____
2. br   _____   _____   _____
3. spr _____   _____   _____
4. gr   _____   _____   _____
5. cr   _____   _____   _____
6. dr   _____   _____   _____
7. tr   _____   _____   _____
8. tw   _____   _____   _____
9. sn   _____   _____   _____
10. gl _____   _____   _____

Ending Consonant Blends

When two or more consonants end a word, the consonants can be heard when pronounced.

- *-dge*—fudge, budge, judge
- *-ft*—sift, thrift, swift
- *-lk*—milk, silk, ilk
- *-nt*—aunt, taunt, jaunt
- *-nd*—round, sound, unbound
- *-ng*—wing, stung, long
- *-nk*—pink, drink, lank
- *-pt*—inept, swept, kept
- *-sp*—lisp, crisp, wisp
- *-st*—pest, Midwest, molest

Practice X

Directions: Write three words with the ending consonant blends listed at the left of the page.

EXAMPLE:

–st	best	quest	west

1. -sp   _____   _____   _____
2. -dge _____   _____   _____
3. -pt   _____   _____   _____
4. -lk   _____   _____   _____

5. -ng	_____	_____	_____
6. -nd	_____	_____	_____
7. -ft	_____	_____	_____
8. -nk	_____	_____	_____
9. -nt	_____	_____	_____
10. -st	_____	_____	_____

Consonant Digraphs

These are consonants that are clustered together. Unlike blends, digraphs do not sound exactly like the letters used.

- *ch*—*(ch sound)* church, chimes, choke
- *ch*—*(k sound)* choir, chemical, character
- *ch*—*(sh sound)* chef, charades, chivalry
- *ck*—chick, tack, rack
- *gh*—laugh, neigh, high
- *lk*—milk, silk, bilk
- *ph*—*(f sound)* phone, graph, phase
- *sh*—hush, brush, rush
- *th*—tenth, teeth, mouth

Practice XI

Directions: Write a sentence using a word that contains the consonant digraph at the left of the page.

EXAMPLE:

    lk   The <u>milk</u> was sour and curdled when we opened the carton.

1. lk _____
2. sh_____
3. th_____
4. ch—ch sound_____
5. ch—k sound _____
6. ph _____
7. gh_____
8. ck_____
9. ch—sh sound _____
10. th _____

Chapter 16 Review Quizzes

Vocabulary Review Quiz

Directions: Complete the sentence by writing the vocabulary word that best completes the thought of the sentence. Use the words from the Word Bank below.

1. If you eat too many carrots, the _____ begins to turn your skin a lovely shade of orange.

2. My mom used to _____ my socks, but now her time is more valuable than the time needed to get it done.

3. There was a _____ off the coast of Indonesia following the earthquake that centered just off shore.

4. If we do not get rain soon, the level of water in the _____ will continue to fall and the community will have to begin conservation efforts.

5. Read this _____ of the article, and that will clarify your confusion over the issue.

6. You will need to _____ your notes before you give them to me; otherwise I will never understand.

7. The victim was shot at a _____ range, and he was extremely lucky to survive the wound.

8. At the bottom of the canyon, our voices echoed and the sound_____ off the walls over and over again.

9. Puck in Shakespeare's play, *A Midsummer Night's Dream,* loves to play tricks and to _____ various creatures.

10. The _____ water was unsafe to dive into; we could not determine how deep it was.

Word Bank: annotate, beguile, carotene, darn, excerpt, point-blank, reservoir, ricochet, tsunami, turbid

---

Pronunciation Definitions

Directions: Select the correct definition, and write the letter of the answer on the line to the right of the number.

1. _____ Identify the word that has a long *a* sound.
   a. rat
   b. rate
   c. cat
   d. draw

2. _____ Which word below does NOT have a short *u* sound?
   a. punish
   b. luggage
   c. pumpkin
   d. music

3. _____ Two vowels together form a _____ , but they have one vowel sound.
   a. diphthong
   b. digraph
   c. blend
   d. consonant

4. _____ Two vowels that come together and have a unique sound are a _____ .
   a. diphthong
   b. digraph
   c. blend
   d. consonant

5. _____ When an R-controlled vowel is followed by another vowel, its sound is affected. Which of the following is an example of the above statement?
   a. world
   b. tractor
   c. scissors
   d. fire

6. _____ Which of the following words has a *y* with a long *e* sound?
   a. baby
   b. bay
   c. dry
   d. yard

7. _____ Which of the following words has a *c* with a *k* sound?
   a. cent
   b. censure
   c. couch
   d. cyst

8. _____ Identify the word that does NOT have a silent consonant.
   a. high
   b. wrist
   c. dough
   d. cash

9. _____ True or False? Both consonants of a consonant blend can be heard when the word is pronounced.
   a. True
   b. False

10. _____ Which of the following words changes drastically in sound when an *e* is added
to the end?
   a. fir
   b. rat
   c. mat
   d. all of the above

Long and Short Vowel Sounds

Directions: In the lists of words below, draw a box around the words with short vowel
sounds , and underline the words that have **long vowel sounds**.

1. mules	2. dock	3. life	4. deal
5. sunshine	6. mate	7. fifty	8. wayside
9. punish	10. ruler	11. throw	12. coach
13. rat	14. grow	15. peach	16. joy
17. bay	18. cut	19. slow	20. timid

Vowel Digraphs and Diphthongs

Directions: Identify each of the following words as either a vowel digraph or a vowel diphthong. Write the correct name on the line to the left of the word.

EXAMPLE:

___digraph___ throat

1. _____ prey

2. _____ auditorium

3. _____ succeed

4. _____ pray

5. _____ sail

6. _____ tier

7. _____ turkey

8. _____ deploy

9. _____ asteroid

10. _____ plain

R-Controlled Vowel Sounds

Directions: Add one of the following vowel combinations to make an R-controlled word.

EXAMPLE:

m <u>ir</u> ror

| ar, er, ir, or, ur |

1. terr____   6. st____dust
2. hamb____ger   7. sc____let
3. th____sty   8. conc____t
4. w____ned   9. f____mally
5. g____den   10. t____e

The Letter Y

Directions: Complete the following chart using *y* words. *Y*'s can be used as a vowel or a consonant. Remember, words that have the *y* at the beginning sound like consonants.

Y Consonant Words	Y Vowel—Long I Sound	Y Vowel—Long E Sound
EXAMPLE: *yearn*	*try*	*baby*

Consonants

Directions: Write a sentence using a word that contains the consonant listed at the beginning of the line. Draw a box around the consonant word that you used in the sentence.

EXAMPLE:

d   *There is a* |dog| *that loves to bark at the moon.*

1. c _____

2. f _____

3. g _____

4. h_____

5. l _____

6. p _____

7. q _____

8. s _____

9. w _____

10. z _____

Silent Consonants

Directions: Underline all of the words in the list below that have silent consonants.

kn, wr, rh, mb, mn, gh, gn

<u>gnaw</u>	ship	comb
<u>column</u>	left	silt
music	wrap	tell
bomb	swim	wreath
knapsack	mellow	forgive
elbow	tomb	hymn
homonym	dough	spaghetti
silent	mischief	sigh
star	gnu	swear
thumb	money	wheat

Consonant Blends and Digraphs

Directions: Identify the following words as either consonant blends or consonant digraphs. Write *CB* on the line if it is a blend, and write *CD* on the line if it is a digraph.

EXAMPLE:

___CD___ hush

1. _____ drawl

2. _____ clump

3. _____ chivalry

4. _____ gherkin

5. _____ skate

6. _____ twinge

7. _____ probe

8. _____ cough

9. _____ charade

10. _____ globe

Real-World Practice Activities

Reading

Directions: Read any article in a newspaper or a magazine. After you have completed reading the article, go back and find twenty (20) words that you find interesting and list them below. After listing them, look at the words carefully; circle any of the vowel or consonant digraphs that you find in the words.

1. _____

2. _____

3. _____

4. _____

5. _____

6. _____

7. _____

8. _____

9. _____

10. _____

11. _____

12. _____

13. _____

14. _____

15. _____

16. _____

17. _____

18. _____

19. _____

20. _____

Writing

Directions: Using the list of words with silent consonants below, write a story using the words. The story does not have to make complete sense—it can be nonsense. Have fun with it, and use your imagination.

hymn, knight, thumb, know, rhyme, night, bright, write, wrist, knock

_____

_____

_____

_____

_____

_____

_____

_____

_____

_____

_____

_____

_____

Listening

Directions: Listen carefully to a song (with lyrics) that you really like. Write down the refrain on the following lines. The refrain is the group of words/sentences that are repeated several times throughout the song. Look at the refrain, and then underline the words that begin with a vowel. Circle the words that begin with a consonant. Count the number of each in the refrain.

_____

_____

_____

_____

_____

_____

_____

_____

_____

_____

_____

_____

- Number of words that begin with a vowel _____
- Number of words that begin with a consonant _____

Chapter 17

PREFIXES, SUFFIXES, AND SPELLING IMPROVEMENT

One of the many challenges in learning or improving skills in a second or third language is learning the nuances of spelling. English is challenging in this respect because there are certain rules to follow in spelling, but there always seems to be an exception or two that causes confusion. Many words in the English language have evolved from Latin, Greek, French, and other languages. So we have quite a melting pot or conglomeration of exceptions to consider. Adding suffixes, or word endings, changes the way many words are spelled; so reviewing that procedure is valuable as well. The best way to learn to spell is to read as much as possible, especially nonfiction (newspapers, magazines, and articles in encyclopedias), keep a dictionary close at hand, and make certain that your pronunciation is correct. Some online dictionaries pronounce the words for you. Now let us jump into this crazy world of prefixes, suffixes, and spelling rules.

Vocabulary Development

1. **abrasive** (a brace iv) Causing angry feelings, harsh.
2. **asteroid** (as tir oid) Any of the small planets rotating around the Sun, particularly between the orbits of Mars and Jupiter.
3. **chanteuse** (shan tooz) A female singer of popular songs, particularly in nightclubs.
4. **fallow** (fal low) Land that is plowed but left unplanted to restore its fertility.
5. **kinetic** (ki net ik) Of or produced by movement.
6. **peccadillo** (pek a dill oh) A trivial offense.
7. **self-preservation** (self pres er va shun) The protection of oneself from harm or injury.
8. **summon** (sum un) To call together or to send for someone to appear in a law court.
9. **trance** (trans) A sleeplike state as that induced by hypnosis.
10. **vesicle** (vess i kel) A small, hollow structure in a plant or animal body.

Prefixes

Prefixes are word parts one to six letters long that are added to the beginning of a word to change its meaning or intent. Adding a prefix is a simple process that does not affect the way the word is spelled. Knowing what the prefixes mean, though, will allow you to understand the new meaning of the word once the prefix has been added. The following chart lists prefixes and their meanings.

Prefix	Meaning	Prefix	Meaning	Prefix	Meaning
a-, an-	without	**hypo-**	under	**poly-**	many
ab-, abs-, a-	away	**il- ir-, im-**	not	**post-**	after
anti-, ant-	against	**in-**	into	**pre-**	before
be-	on/away	**inter-**	between	**pro-**	in favor of
bi-, bin-	both, two	**intra-**	within	**pseudo-**	false
by-	near	**intro-**	into	**quad-**	four
circum-	around	**mal-**	badly	**quint-**	five
co-, con-	together	**meta-**	beyond	**re-**	back
contra-	against	**mis-**	incorrect	**retro-**	backward
de-	from/down	**miso-**	hate	**se-**	aside
dia-	through	**mono-**	one	**self-**	by oneself
dis-	apart/away	**multi-**	many	**semi-**	partly
dys-	badly/ill	**neo-**	new	**sex-, sest-**	six
em-, en-	in/into	**non-**	not	**sub-**	under
ex-	out	**oct-**	eight	**syn-**	with
extra-	beyond	**over-**	above	**trans-**	across
for-	away	**para-**	beside	**tri-**	three
fore-	before	**penta-**	five	**ultra-**	beyond
hemi-	half	**per-**	throughout	**un-**	not
hyper-	over/above	**peri-**	around	**vice-**	in place of

Practice I

Directions: On each of the lines below, write a word that includes the prefix that is listed to the left. You may use a dictionary to help you find the words.

EXAMPLE:

extra-   <u>extraordinary</u>   <u>extravagant</u>   <u>extracurricular</u>

1. hyper- _____ _____ _____
2. dys- _____ _____ _____
3. pro- _____ _____ _____
4. tri- _____ _____ _____
5. quad- _____ _____ _____
6. bi- _____ _____ _____
7. retro- _____ _____ _____
8. anti- _____ _____ _____
9. mal- _____ _____ _____
10. un- _____ _____ _____

Suffixes

Suffixes are the opposite of prefixes; they are added to the end of a word. Suffixes are two to six letters long. Believe it or not, with the addition of these groups of letters, identifying nouns, adjectives, and adverbs is easier. The challenging thing about suffixes is that when adding them, certain rules have to be followed. These rules will be addressed in the spelling section below.

Suffix	Meaning	Suffix	Meaning	Suffix	Meaning
-able	able, likely	**-esque**	in style of	**-ive**	causing
-ade	result of	**-et, -ette**	small one	**-ize**	make
-age	act of	**-fic**	making	**-less**	without
-ance	action	**-ful**	full of	**-ly**	like
-ant	performing	**-fy**	make	**-ment**	act of
-ate	cause	**-hood**	order/condition	**-ness**	state of
-cian	having skill	**-ibel**	able, likely	**-oid**	resembling
-cy	action	**-ic**	nature of	**-ology**	study
-dom	quality/realm	**-ice**	condition	**-ous**	full of
-ee	receives action	**-ile**	relating to	**-ship**	office
-en	made of	**-ine**	nature of	**-some**	like/apt
-ence	action	**-ish**	origin, nature	**-tude**	state of
-ese	a native of	**-ism**	system, manner	**-ure**	state of
-ess	female	**-ity**	state of	**-ward**	direction of

Practice II

Directions: Read the brief paragraphs below, and <u>underline</u> the words that have suffixes from the chart above.

Confucius, a revered <u>Chinese</u> philosopher and thinker, was born in 551 B.C. His philosophies, which emphasize morality in both governmental and personal areas as well his beliefs in justice and sincerity, have influenced many people for centuries. In fact, Confucius's philosophies have been developed into a system of thought known as Confucianism. A collection of his teachings titled *Analects of Confucius* were compiled many years after his death in 479 B.C.

Born into a poor family, Confucius's family at one time held a noble ranking. However, the family fled from the State of Song to the State of Lu, which is now a part of Shandong Province. According to records, his father was seventy and his mother eighteen when he was born. His father died when he was three. Confucius married Qi Quan at the age of nineteen, and his wife had their first child, Kong Li, one year later. Confucius worked at various jobs, including sheepherding, cow herding, clerking, and bookkeeping. Later he became an administrative manager and eventually the justice minister in the State of Lu. At the age of fifty-five, he quit the position because of philosophical and moral differences between himself and the politics of the duke.

Soon after Confucius's departure from his job in the State of Lu, he began a long journey of teaching his beliefs. He did not return home until he was sixty-eight, where he spent his last years teaching his disciples and transmitting old wisdoms into a set of books called the *Five Classics.* His beliefs and philosophies, known as Confucianism, dominated China until the early twentieth century and influenced the Japanese, Koreans, and Vietnamese.

Spelling Improvement

The following suggestions should help in learning to improve your spelling.

- Pronounce words correctly. If words are mispronounced, chances are they are going to be misspelled.

- Use a dictionary to help with pronunciation or an online dictionary that can be used to actually hear the pronunciation.

- Spell words by syllable. Breaking words down into smaller pieces (by syllables) will simplify the task and allow you to hear the sounds more clearly.

- Practice writing the words that are troublesome. Keep a notebook or journal of words that you need to review continuously.

Spelling Rules

The following rules will help to clarify the spelling confusion that English brings to the task.

- Rule 1: *i* before *e* except after *c*—or write *e* before *i* when the sound is long *e*—or—write *i* before *e* except after *c* or when it sounds like an *a* as in *neighbor* or *neigh*. To understand this spelling rule better, look at it when broken down into its parts.
  - o *i* before *e* except after *c*: *achieve, chief, field, believe, friend, mischief*
  - o *e* before *i*—long *e* sound: *ceiling, receive, deceit, conceited, seize, sheik, protein, neither, leisure, either*
  - o *e* before *i*—long *a* sound: *neighbor, weigh, sleigh, reign, veil, their, neigh*
  - o exceptions (*ie*): *ancient, conscience, deficient, efficient*

Practice III

Directions: Circle or draw a box around the word in each line that is spelled correctly.

EXAMPLE:

| fiend | feened | feined |

1. waigh	weigh	waygh
2. ceeling	ceiling	cealing
3. neibor	neighbor	naghbor
4. deseet	deciet	deceit
5. baige	beige	baje
6. chief	cheaf	cheif
7. anchent	ancient	anchint
8. beleeve	beleave	believe
9. seize	seeze	sieze
10. feald	fild	field

- Rule 2: Double a consonant and add a suffix.
  - o Double the ending consonant of one-syllable words with:
    - o A single final consonant
    - o A single final consonant that is preceded by a single vowel
    - o The suffix begins with a vowel
  - o *sit + t+ ing = sitting; sum + m+ ary = summary; tan +n+ ing = tanning*

Practice IV

Directions: Add an *-ing* or *-ed* suffix to the following words. Follow the rules that were outlined above.

EXAMPLE:

hop + -ing =   *hopping*

1. drag + -ed = _____   6. drop + -ing = _____
2. stop + -ing = _____   7. throb + -ed = _____
3. sag + -ing = _____   8. wrap + -ing = _____
4. brag + -ing = _____   9. strap + -ed = _____
5. shop + -ed = _____   10. pin + -ing = _____

- Rule 3: If a word ends with a silent *e*, drop the *e* before adding a suffix that begins with a vowel.
  - o   *stare + ing = staring; mope + ed = moped; smile + ing = smiling*
- Rule 4: Do NOT drop the *e* when the suffix begins with a consonant. Exceptions—judgment, truly, argument, ninth
  - o   *care + ful = careful; hope + less = hopeless; state + ment = statement*

Practice V

Directions: Circle or draw a box around the correct spelling of the words.

EXAMPLE:

frameing   fraiming   framing

1. skated   skatted   skated
2. fileing   filleing   filing
3. flameless   flaimless   flammless
4. timeing   timing   timeeing
5. priming   primeing   primming
6. hopefull   hoppful   hopeful
7. judgment   judgement   jugment
8. stated   statted   stateed
9. careing   caring   carring
10. placment   placeement   placement

- Rule 5: When *y* is the last letter of a word and is preceded by a consonant, change the *y* to *i* before adding any suffix, except those beginning with *i*.
  - o   *baby + i+ es = babies*; *lullaby + i + es = lullabies*; *wallaby + i + es = wallabies*
  - o   *fry + ing = frying*; *fry + i + ed = fried*; *try + ing = trying*

- Rule 6: Words that end with the suffixes *-cede, -ceed, -sede* are easier to understand than they look. Although they all have the same sound:
  - o   the ONLY word that has the *-sede* ending is *supersede*
  - o   the ONLY words that have the *-ceed* ending are *exceed, proceed,* and *succeed*
  - o   ALL the other words with this ending sound have the *-cede* ending: *secede, precede, intercede, accede*

Practice VI

Directions: Correct the spelling of each of the words listed below. Write the correct spelling on the line. If the word is spelled correctly, write *Correct* on the line.

EXAMPLE:

precceed   __precede__

1. triing	_____	11. plentyful	_____
2. varyous	_____	12. merryment	_____
3. fairries	_____	13. beautyful	_____
4. succeed	_____	14. marriage	_____
5. daisyies	_____	15. happyness	_____
6. prying	_____	16. interceed	_____
7. ladyies	_____	17. scaryiest	_____
8. candyied	_____	18. companion	_____
9. universitys	_____	19. acceede	_____
10. crying	_____	20. excede	_____

Plural Forms of Nouns

To make most nouns plural, just add *-s*. However, nouns that are abstract or noncount nouns (such as sugar, honesty, intelligence, cheese) generally take a singular verb. In some cases, they follow the rules for pluralizing based on their spelling. The rules for forming plurals of regular and irregular nouns are as follows:

- Rule 1: Nouns that end with *-s, -z, -x, -sh, -ch,* add *-es.*
  - o   *glass/glasses, buzz/buzzes, box/boxes, bush/bushes, switch/switches*

- Rule 2: Nouns that end in *-o*, add *-es*.
  - o *potato/potatoes, echo/echoes, hero/heroes*
    - EXCEPTIONS: *studio/studios, piano/pianos, kangaroo/kangaroos, zoo/zoos*
- Rule 3: Nouns that end in *-f or -fe* change the *-f* to *-v* and add *-es*
  - o *elf/elves, shelf/shelves, wolf/wolves, knife/knives, wife/wives*
- Rule 4: Nouns that have only a plural form take a plural verb, such as things that come in pairs. These words are left alone—without adding additional suffixes.
  - o *glasses, scissors, binoculars, forceps, tweezers, tongs, jeans, shorts, pants, pajamas, trousers*
- Rule 5: Nouns that are plural but do not end in *-s* are left as is.
  - o *people, cattle, police*

Irregular Nouns

The following is a list of irregular nouns and their plurals. They are irregular because the normal spelling rules do not apply to them. The best thing to do is to review this list once in a while to keep these oddball words in mind.

alumnus/alumni	analysis/analyses	antenna/antennae/antennas
appendix/appendices	axis/axes	bacterium/bacteria
basis/bases	beau/beaux	bureau/bureaus
child/children	crisis/crises	criterion/criteria
curriculum/curricula	datum/data	deer/deer
diagnosis/diagnoses	ellipsis/ellipses	fish/fish
focus/focuses/foci	foot/feet	formula/formulae/formulas
fungus/fungi/funguses	goose/geese	hypothesis/hypotheses
louse/lice	man/men	matrix/matrices
means/means	medium/media	mouse/mice
nucleus/nuclei	oasis/oases	ox/oxen
paralysis/paralyses	parenthesis/parentheses	phenomenon/phenomena
sheep/sheep	species/species	stimulus/stimuli
stratum/strata	synthesis/syntheses	synopsis/synopses
thesis/theses	tooth/teeth	vertebra/vertebrae
woman/women		

Practice VII:

Directions: Write the plural or singular form of the words on the lines.

EXAMPLE:

wife ___*wives*___

1. tooth	_____
2. glasses	_____
3. _____	synopses
4. potato	_____
5. _____	men

6. shelf	_____
7. box	_____
8. deer	_____
9. _____	geese
10. _____	scissors

Spelling Numbers

There are specific rules for spelling numbers.

- Rule 1: Spell out numbers that begin sentences.
  - o *Three hundred and fifty* seniors will be going on the field trip.
- Rule 2: Spell out numbers within a sentence that can be written in one or two words.
  - o There are only *three* weeks left of school.
  - o Tiffany wore *twenty-six* yellow ribbons in her hair.
- Rule 3: If you use a mixture of numbers (one- or two-word and larger numbers), use the numerals and not words to be consistent.
  - o There are *4* calling birds, *3* French hens, and *2* turtle doves, but there are *1,555* ants.

Commonly Misspelled Words

The following chart is for reference. These are words that are often misspelled. Review them frequently.

abbreviate	brochure	debt	harass	naïve	rhyme	vacuum
abscess	bruise	deceitful	hygiene	necessary	ridiculous	vague
absurd	budget	defendant	hymn	necessity	salary	vegetable
ache	bureau	defense	illegible	nuisance	Saturday	veil
a lot (two words)	bury	diamond	indictment	obey	scarcely	vengeance
aerial	business	discipline	intermittent	oblige	schedule	visitor
aisle	campaign	disease	iridescent	omitted	scissors	volume
amateur	carriage	doubt	janitor	outrageous	separate	warrant
annoyance	cemetery	drudgery	jealous	pageant	sergeant	Wednesday
anoint	cessation	dyeing	judgment	personnel	sincerely	weird
arctic	chauffeur	dying	label	plateau	sophomore	wholly
arithmetic	cocoa	eager	laboratory	playwright	sponsor	wreckage
ascend	collar	earnest	lieutenant	pneumonia	stomach	wrestler

assassin	concede	embarrass	liaison	possess	subtle	wrought
association	conceive	envelop	license	pursuit	suspicious	yield
assume	condescend	envelope	loneliness	rapport	syllable	
auxiliary	conscience	etiquette	maintenance	receive	terrestrial	
balloon	conscientious	fallacy	maneuver	recipe	thorough	
bankrupt	conscious	futile	medieval	reminisce	unique	
boundary	courtesy	gadget	miscellaneous	rendezvous	unnecessary	

Chapter 17 Review Quizzes

Vocabulary Review Quiz

Directions: Write the letter of the definition on the line next to the noun that it defines.

1. _____ abrasive

2. _____ asteroid

3. _____ chanteuse

4. _____ fallow

5. _____ kinetic

6. _____ peccadillo

7. _____ self-preservation

8. _____ summon

9. _____ trance

10. _____ vesicle

A. A sleeplike state as that induced by hypnosis.

B. Land that is plowed but left unplanted to restore its fertility.

C. The protection of oneself from harm or injury.

D. Any of the small planets rotating around the Sun, particularly between the orbits of Mars and Jupiter.

E. A trivial offence.

F. To call together or to send for someone to appear in a law court.

G. Causing angry feelings, harsh.

H. A female singer of popular songs, particularly in nightclubs.

I. Of or produced by movement.

J. A small hollow structure in a plant or animal body.

Suffixes, Prefixes, and Spelling Rules

Directions: Select the correct definition, and write the letter of the answer on the line to the right of the number.

1. _____ A _____ is a cluster of one to six letters that is added to the beginning of a word and changes its meaning.
   a. prefix
   b. suffix
   c. consonant
   d. vowel

2. _____ A _____ is a group of letters that is added to the end of a word.
   a. prefix
   b. suffix
   c. consonant
   d. vowel

3. _____ Which of the following words does NOT have a prefix?
   a. unnecessary
   b. immobile
   c. misspell
   d. playfully

4. _____ Which of the following words does NOT have a suffix?
   a. orchestration
   b. swarming
   c. unplanned
   d. crowding

5. _____ Identify the word that is correctly spelled.
   a. intercede
   b. preceede
   c. conceed
   d. receeve

6. _____ Identify the word that is incorrectly spelled.
   a. reign
   b. foreign
   c. peece
   d. chief

7. _____ Which of the following words is spelled correctly?
   a. senseible
   b. dining
   c. determineation
   d. surprisede

8. _____ Identify the misspelled word below.
   a. frend
   b. friend
   c. license
   d. balloon

9. _____ In spelling numbers, which of the following is true?
   a. Spell out numbers with one or two words.
   b. Spell out numbers that begin a sentence.
   c. Do not spell out numbers if there is a mix of one-word, two-word, or more-than-two-word numbers.
   d. all of the above

10. _____ True or False? Irregular words are called irregular because "normal" spelling rules do not apply.
   a. True
   b. False

Suffixes and Prefixes

Directions: Complete the chart below by filling in the rows with words using either the suffix or prefix listed at the left.

EXAMPLE:

ex	extra	excess	excellent
1. non-	_____	_____	_____
2. -ed	_____	_____	_____
3. -ment	_____	_____	_____
4. pre-	_____	_____	_____
5. para-	_____	_____	_____
6. -est	_____	_____	_____
7. -ing	_____	_____	_____
8. un-	_____	_____	_____
9. anti-	_____	_____	_____
10. -er	_____	_____	_____

Spelling Rules

Directions: Draw a box around the word that is correctly spelled in each of the lines below.

EXAMPLE:

shout	showt	shought
1. generashun	generation	generacion
2. takeing	takking	taking
3. possession	poscession	poccession
4. terifing	terrifying	tarrifying
5. preceed	precead	precede
6. presence	presense	presens
7. sweatting	sweating	sweeatting
8. flame	flaime	flayme
9. babyies	babees	babies
10. triangle	tryangle	triangyle
11. glasses	glases	glass
12. boxs	boxes	boxxes
13. trowsers	trousers	troussers
14. etiquette	etickette	etikette

15. ernest	earnest	errnest
16. subbtel	subtel	subtle
17. playwrite	playright	playwright
18. assassin	asassin	assassyn
19. vakume	vackum	vacuum
20. sponcer	sponsor	sponsir

Real-World Practice Activities

Reading

Directions: Find a resource that will help you identify all of the prefixes that have to do with numbers and shapes. For instance, *pent = five; pentagon = five-sided figure.* Complete the chart below by filling in the blanks with a prefix and the name of a shape or figure as indicated.

Number (for Prefix)	Prefix	Name of Item/Shape
One	*uni-*	*unicycle*
Two		
Three		
Four		
Five		
Six		
Seven		
Eight		
Nine		
Ten		

Writing

Directions: Write a paragraph about a process of any sort, such as making a cake, drawing a picture, sculpting a pot, selecting a prom dress, or how to teach salsa dancing—any sort of process that you can think of. Once the paragraph is written, go back and underline any of the prefixes and suffixes that you have used in any of the words of the paragraph. Feel free to review the charts provided earlier in the chapter.

_____
_____
_____
_____
_____
_____
_____
_____
_____
_____
_____
_____
_____
_____
_____
_____
_____
_____

Listening

Directions: Listen to a conversation between several groups of people. Write down twenty (20) random words that you overhear. Review the words that you have written down. Underline any of the words with prefixes, and circle any of the words with suffixes.

1. _____		11. _____	
2. _____		12. _____	
3. _____		13. _____	
4. _____		14. _____	
5. _____		15. _____	
6. _____		16. _____	
7. _____		17. _____	
8. _____		18. _____	
9. _____		19. _____	
10. _____		20. _____	

Chapter 18

WORD ROOTS AND VOCABULARY IMPROVEMENT

Word roots and vocabulary improvement will be the focus of this chapter. In strengthening our vocabularies, it is important to understand the bits and pieces that go together to make words whole. We are going to see how learning the roots of words will help decipher word meanings. The more vocabulary we learn, the more our language skills will improve in reading, writing, and speaking.

Vocabulary Development

1. **antebellum** (an ti bell um) Before the Civil War in the United States.
2. **bog** (bog) An area of ground that is permanently wet and spongy from decayed plants.
3. **cavern** (kav ern) A large cave.
4. **decapitate** (de kap i tait) To behead.
5. **detain** (dee tain) To keep in confinement or to cause delay.
6. **eclipse** (ee klips) The blocking of light of either the Sun or the Moon.
7. **humiliate** (hue mill ee ate) To cause a person to feel disgraced or embarrassed.
8. **oenophile** (ee no file) A connoisseur of wines.
9. **plutocracy** (ploo tock ra cee) A nation ruled by the wealthy.
10. **spindly** (spind lee) Long or tall and thin.

Word Roots

Word roots or root words are the part of the word that carries the primary meaning of the word. The root cannot stand alone. It is always combined with additional word parts such as the prefixes and suffixes that we reviewed in Chapter 17. Review the chart below of common root words and their meanings. There are too many to list—but this will give you an idea of how words are generated: root + prefix and/or suffix = word.

COMMON ROOTS		
Word Root	**Meaning**	**Examples**
agri	field	agronomy, agricultural
anthropo	study of man	anthropology, anthropod
astro	star	astronaut, astronomy
bio	life	biology, antibiotic
cardio	heart	cardiac, cardinal
cede	go	precede, cede
chromo	color	monochromatic
demos	people	democratic
dict	speak	dictation, dictionary
duc/duct	lead	educate, conduct
geo	earth	geology
graph	write, writing	biography, autograph
helio	sun	heliotrope
hydro	water	hydroponics
ject	throw	eject
liber	free	liberation
magni	great, big	magnify
mal	bad	malice
man (u)	hand	manuscript
mit/miss	send	omit, omission
mono	one	monoplane
ortho	straight	orthodox
pend	weigh, hang	pending, suspend
port	carry	portable, transport
psycho	mind	psychology
spec	look	spectacles, spectator
struct	build	construct
terra	earth	terrace
thermo	heat	thermometer
vid/vis	see	videotape, invisible
voc	call	vocation, vocal
zoo	animal	zoology

Practice I

Directions: Below is a list of **roots**. Write words that are formed from this root on the lines provided. You may want to use a dictionary.

EXAMPLE:

vid   vide   video   videogame

1. cardio
2. bio
3. liber
4. pend
5. agri
6. pyro
7. ject
8. helio
9. anthro
10. dem

Practice II

Directions: Write a sentence using each of the words listed below. Note that each of these words has a root that we have reviewed.

EXAMPLE:

zoology   My friend is going to study zoology at the university.

1. omit
2. biography
3. dictation
4. precede
5. cardiac
6. magnify
7. monochromatic
8. psychology
9. transport
10. manuscript

Vocabulary Improvement

Learning new words and improving vocabulary is a lifelong task. It is a good habit to get into, like eating healthy foods and exercising. There are millions of words in the English language if you consider each of their forms. For instance, the word *set* has forty-seven different variations—all of them separate words. As impossible a task as it may seem, there are many reasons to try to improve our vocabulary continually. The more expansive the vocabulary, the better we speak, the better we write, and the better we read. Follow these suggestions for improving your vocabulary:

- Read books, magazines, encyclopedias, and newspapers as often as possible. The more you read, the more language you are exposed to.
- Try to learn one new word each day.
- Keep a dictionary nearby, and use it frequently.
- Play word games like crossword puzzles, Scrabble, or Mad Libs.
- Develop a word bank—collect words.
  - o Write unfamiliar words in a journal or notebook, and look them up in a dictionary.
  - o Use the new word in a sentence—write the sentence.
  - o If possible, use the new word in your conversations.
  - o Memorize the word.
- Use flashcards to help memorize new words.
- Use knowledge and understanding of word parts to understand new words.
  - o Learn the meanings of root words, suffixes, and prefixes.
- Learn words from context—look for clues to the meaning of the unfamiliar word by looking at the words, phrases, and sentences around the word.
  - o Definitions or synonyms—occasionally an author will provide a definition or a synonym (a word with the same or similar meaning) for the unfamiliar word in the text.
    - —(Definition) Sahar will have to take three years of *zoology*, <u>the study of animals</u>, before she can apply to veterinary school.
    - —(Synonym) Jeff, the young Korean man, *desired* or <u>longed for</u> a brand-new sports car.
  - o Examples—writers will often provide examples of a difficult term to help clarify its meaning.
    - —A *sedimentary rock* <u>such as a conglomerate</u> is commonly found on beaches or riverbeds and consists of rounded pebbles embedded in a sandy matrix or silt.
  - o Contrast—by using words that are the opposite, the meaning is clarified.
    - —The *plebeians*, <u>unlike the patricians</u> of ancient Rome, had a far more difficult life.
  - o Cause and effect—word clues that may show that an unfamiliar word is related to a cause or the effect of an idea, action, or feeling.
    - —Because of the resulting angry *repercussions* of yesterday's campaign speech, he decided to <u>soften his message to appease the crowd</u>.

o   Description—a word may be described or clarified later in the text (perhaps in the next paragraph or two).

—Strychnine is a poisonous alkaloid found in the plant *Strychnos nux-vomica*. At one time, it was thought to have therapeutic value in small doses. However, strychnine poisoning causes death because of spasms of the breathing muscles, symptoms similar to those of *tetanus*. Similar to strychnine poisoning, <u>tetanus is a life-threatening disease</u> that causes lockjaw, muscular spasms, and rigidity that spreads to other parts of the body and culminates in death.

o   Repetition of words—the repetition or echoing of words allows the reader to construct meaning in a variety of ways. Repeating a word more than once ensures that the reader will more fully understand its importance. Echoing also attracts the reader's attention.

—*Primates are* an order of mammals that include monkeys, apes, and human beings. *Primates* have a good sense of hearing and acute binocular vision but a poor sense of smell. However, <u>the primate's strength</u> is a large, complex brain and high intelligence.

o   Conjunctions showing connecting ideas and word relationships—the words *and, but, or, nor, for,* and *yet* allow the reader to make connections between or link unknown ideas or thoughts.

—*Excavating deeply* into Earth's surface would eventually prove to be beneficial to the Dutch, <u>for</u> these excavations resulted in finding diamond mines that made them extremely wealthy.

o   Word modifiers—words such as adjectives and adverbs, or phrases and clauses often contain clues to a word's meaning.

—The novel is a *picaresque* story that tells the <u>tale of a low-class, almost fumbling man's travels</u> throughout the country.

o   Implied or unstated meanings is when the meaning becomes clear as the reader applies his/her own knowledge and experience to the situation in the reading.

—Caedmon, an *illiterate* herdsman from the seventh century, is considered the earliest-known English poet. Although Caedmon <u>could not read or write</u>, he was commanded in a vision to turn scriptures into poems.

Practice III

Directions: In the following exercise, write a sentence that uses a context clue to clarify or explain a word or term (we will use the vocabulary words for this exercise). The term is in the first column, the task is in the second column, and the blank line is for your sentence.

WORD	TASK
1. antebellum	Repeating words

EXAMPLE:

<u>The antebellum southern United States was not the kindest nor the friendliest place for African-American slaves. The antebellum South, though, was forced to change as a result of the Civil War.</u>

2. bog   Description clues

_____

_____

3. cavern   Definition

_____

_____

4. decapitate   Word modifiers

_____

_____

5. detain   Synonyms

_____

_____

6. eclipse   Contrast clues

_____

_____

7. humiliate   Conjunction showing link

_____

_____

8. oenophile   Definition

_____

_____

9. plutocracy Cause and effect

_____

_____

10. spindly   Description

_____

_____

Chapter 18 Review Quizzes

Vocabulary Review Quiz

Directions: Complete the sentences below with the vocabulary word (or one of its forms) from the word bank that best completes the meaning of the sentence.

1. Yesterday when Tiffany fell in front of the class, she was completely _____ .

2. The gentleman who writes the articles on wines is a real_____.

3. The _____ South slowly became more and more disordered as what would become the Civil War approached.

4. _____ of the Moon and Sun are rare occurrences.

5. At times, life does not seem fair and it appears as though we have become a _____ instead of a democracy.

6. King Henry was known for _____ his wives.

7. The _____ plant lacked sunlight and slowly lost its leaves.

8. The peat _____ provided fuel for the community's homes.

9. We were _____ at the border because Monserrat could not find her passport.

10. The _____ extended far into the depths of the cliff, and the air grew colder and damper as we followed it.

> **Word Bank:** antebellum, bog, cavern, decapitating, detained, eclipses, humiliated, oenophile, plutocracy, spindly

Root Words and Vocabulary Improvement Definitions

Directions: Select the correct definition, and write the letter of the answer on the line to the right of the number.

1. _____ A _____ is a part of the word that carries the primary meaning.
   a. prefix
   b. suffix
   c. root
   d. none of the above

2. _____ Which of the following is a set of roots?
   a. bio, ped, mal
   b. es, s, y
   c. hood, ment, ous
   d. anti, co, bi

3. _____ Which of the following is NOT a set of roots?
   a. voc, vis, struct
   b. mit, mis, mal
   c. y, ty, tion
   d. ject, liber, graph

4. _____ Which of the following uses a definition to clarify an unfamiliar term?
   a. The orchestra, a large group of people playing various instruments, is traveling throughout Europe this summer.
   b. The swarm of bees attacked the keeper.
   c. A chaperone will go with the group.
   d. The strict rules of the game will be followed.

5. _____ True or False? Clarification of unfamiliar terms can often be discovered within the context of the sentence or surrounding words, phrases, or clauses.
   a. True
   b. False

6. _____ Which of the following is NOT a way to clarify an unfamiliar term in context?
   a. definition
   b. synonyms
   c. concrete examples
   d. writing the word ten times

7. _____ Cause and effect is _____ in understanding unfamiliar terms in a reading.
   a. a relationship or link between a conjunction and an idea
   b. a clue that shows an unfamiliar term's opposite
   c. a clue showing that an unfamiliar word is the result of an action, feeling, or idea
   d. none of the above

8. _____ Identity the meaning of the root in the following words: *dictionary, dictate.*
   a. salsa
   b. mango
   c. speak
   d. listen

9. _____ The root *terra* means_____.
   a. water
   b. jungle
   c. earth
   d. fire

10. _____ The root *magni* means_____.
    a. small
    b. magnificent
    c. large
    d. tiny

Root Identification

Directions: In the list below, underline the roots of the words.

EXAMPLE:

<u>mal</u>ice

1. suspend
2. antibiotic
3. eject
4. pedestrian
5. videotape
6. democracy
7. genetic
8. educate
9. genuine
10. mission
11. portable
12. pending
13. liberate
14. autograph
15. dictionary
16. vocation
17. malice
18. omit
19. construct
20. reject

Vocabulary Improvement

Directions: Write ten (10) tips that will help you to improve your vocabulary.

1. *Read more nonfiction and other literature.* _____
2. _____
3. _____
4. _____
5. _____
6. _____
7. _____
8. _____
9. _____
10. _____

Real-World Practice Activities

Reading

Directions: Read a long article in a newspaper that is about a current event. Write ten (10) words that are unfamiliar to you on the lines below, and try to clarify their meanings through context clues in the writing or by looking up their definitions in a dictionary.

WORD   **DEFINITION**

1. _____   _____

2. _____   _____

3. _____   _____

4. _____   _____

5. _____   _____

6. _____   _____

7. _____   _____

8. _____   _____

9. _____   _____

10. _____   _____

Writing

Directions: Using some of the words that you discovered in the exercise above, write a summary of the article.

_____

_____

_____

_____

_____

_____

_____

_____

_____

_____

_____

Listening

Directions: Listen carefully to a news program on the radio, on television, or on the Internet. Write a list of ten (10) unfamiliar words that you hear during the course of the show and then find the definition of the words. Make certain that you write the correct definition of each word for the context of the story.

1. (Word) _____

_____

2. (Word) _____

_____

3. (Word) _____

_____

4. (Word) _____

_____

5. (Word) _____

_____

6. (Word) _____

_____

7. (Word) _____

_____

8. (Word) _____

_____

9. (Word) _____

_____

10. (Word) _____

_____

Chapter 19

HOMONYMS, SYNONYMS, ANTONYMS, AND CONFUSING WORDS

Homonyms are words that are spelled differently, mean different things, but sound similar when pronounced (to/two/too). Synonyms are words that have the same or similar meanings (hot/scorching). Antonyms, however, are words that mean the opposite (hot/cold). Finally, we have words that cause confusion no matter what. Those are the troublemakers—the confusing words upon which we hope to shed light.

Vocabulary Development

1. **anoint** (a noynt) To apply ointment or oil to.
2. **chariot** (cha ree ut) A two-wheeled horse-drawn carriage used in ancient times.
3. **dowdy** (dow dee) Unattractive, dull.
4. **glisten** (gliss en) To shine like something wet or polished.
5. **indigo** (inn di goh) A deep-blue dye or color between blue and violet in the color spectrum.
6. **lottery** (lot er ee) A system of selling numbered tickets for an opportunity to win money or prizes.
7. **mountainous** (moun tin us) Full of mountains.
8. **peer** (peer) One who is equal to another in rank, merit, or quality.
9. **usury** (yoo zhu ree) The lending of money at an extremely high rate of interest.
10. **voluminous** (vo loo min us) Having great volume or bulk.

Homonyms

The following list of words are homonyms. Homonyms are words that sound alike but are spelled differently and have different meanings. It is important to become familiar with these words, especially for writing. In speaking, the words sound the same. In writing, it is a different story. For instance, *Hannah is going **to** the store. To* is a direction—toward something or someone. If either of the other homonyms for *to* are used in writing, the sentence makes no sense at all. *Hannah is going **two** the store* or *Hannah is going **too** the store.*

COMMON HOMONYMS A–C			
Homonyms	**Meanings**	**Homonyms**	**Meanings**
acts	deed	**ad**	advertisement
ax	sharp tool	**add**	to increase
ail	pain/illness	**air**	atmosphere
ale	beer	**heir**	inheritor
aisle	passage way	**all**	everyone
isle	island	**awl**	tool
I'll	I will		
aloud	out loud	**altar**	for worship
allowed	permitted	**alter**	change
ant	insect	**ante**	before
aunt	relative	**anti**	against
arc	part of a circle	**ate**	to eat/devour
ark	boat/chest	**ait**	an island
		eight	a number
aye	yes, affirmative	**ball**	round body/dance
eye	organ of sight	**bawl**	to cry
I	me/myself		
bare	naked	**baron**	nobleman
bear	animal/to carry	**barren**	sterile/unfruitful
base	the mean	**beach**	shoreline
bass	musical instrument	**beech**	tree
beat	to hit/strike	**beau**	man of dress/boyfriend
beet	vegetable	**bow**	archery term
bee	insect	**berry**	fruit
be	to exist	**bury**	to inter underground

Homonyms	Meanings	Homonyms	Meanings
billed	to request payment	**bin**	container
build	to construct	**been**	of the verb 'to be'
birth	being born	**blew**	to blow wind
berth	place for ship/sleep	**blue**	color
boar	swine/pig	**bowled**	game with ball
bore	to drill a hole	**bold**	courageous
bore	uninterested		
bow	to salute/part of ship	**brake**	stop motion
bough	tree limb	**break**	shatter
		break	short rest period
bread	food	**brewed**	to ferment
bred	brought up	**brood**	offspring
		brood	to mope about
brews	to make liquor	**bridal**	for a wedding
bruise	to crush/injure	**bridle**	for a horse/to curb
burrow	hole for rabbit	**by**	near
borough	a town	**buy**	to purchase
cache	to store/collect	**canvas**	cloth
cash	money	**canvass**	to solicit
capital	assets	**carat**	weight
capitol	state house	**caret**	punctuation mark
		carrot	vegetable
cast	to throw/to mold	**cede**	to give up
caste	rank in society	**seed**	plant pit/germ
ceiling	top of a room	**cell**	small room
sealing	to close off	**sell**	to put up for sale
		sale	a transaction
cent	a penny/coin	**chance**	by accident
sent	to cause to go	**chants**	melodies
scent	an odor or smell		
cite	to summon	**coarse**	rough
site	a place or location	**course**	route
sight	a view		

Homonyms	Meanings	Homonyms	Meanings
colonel	officer	cord	string
kernel	seed in a nut	chord	musical sound
		cored	remove center of
council	assembly	creak	loud noise
counsel	to advise	creek	stream
cue	a hint	currant	fruit
queue	waiting line	current	flowing stream

Practice I

Directions: Draw a box around the correct form of the word that best fits the meaning of the sentence.

EXAMPLE:

Steve was going to repair the ***creek***/***creak*** in the floor because it annoyed the neighbors below him.

1. *Bread/Bred* is a staple food that is made by mixing flour, salt, yeast, and water.
2. They will be using the *altar/alter* for a special ceremony.
3. We will need to trim the *bows/boughs* before the next big storm.
4. They say that eating *carat/carrots* is good for your eyesight.
5. Our team *bold/bowled* their best game yet.
6. The *berry/bury* pie was delicious.
7. They were attacked by a *bare/bear* while hiking.
8. *Eye/I* really do not know what to say about your predicament.
9. The strange *cent/scent* coming from the closet was sickening.
10. She will be *air/heir* to an extremely large corporation.

COMMON HOMONYMS D–L			
Homonyms	Meanings	Homonyms	Meanings
dam	wall to hold water	days	more than one day
damn	to curse or doom	daze	to confuse
dear	beloved	dents	marks/indentations
deer	animal	dense	close/compact
descent	downward	desert	to abandon
dissent	disagreement	dessert	sweet course of meal

Homonyms	Meanings	Homonyms	Meanings
dew	mist/moisture	die	to expire/decease
do	to perform	dye	to color
due	owed to		
doe	female deer	draft	draw up/prepare
dough	unbaked bread	draught	to extract from container
earn	to gain by labor	ewe	female sheep
urn	a vase	yew	tree
		you	pronoun
fair	pleasingly beautiful/just	find	to discover
fare	price/food	fined	punishment
fir	tree	flea	insect
fur	animal hair	flee	to run away
flew	did fly	flour	ground grain
flue	chimney	flower	a blossom
flu	influenza		
for	because of	fort	fortified place
fore	preceding	forte	marked talent
four	number		
fourth	number	frays	quarrels
forth	forward	phrase	parts of a sentence
gage	a pledge	gait	manner of walking
gauge	a measure	gate	opening in fence
gild	overflow with gold	gilt	gold covering
guild	a corporation	guilt	at fault
gnu	animal	grate	iron frame
knew	understood	grate	annoy
new	not old	great	large
grisly	frightful	groan	loud sigh/moan
grizzly	bear	grown	to increase in size
guessed	conjectured	hail	icy rain/to salute
guest	a visitor	hale	healthy
hair	on head	hall	large room
hare	rabbit	haul	to pull or carry
hay	dried grass	heal	to cure
hey	an expression	heel	part of foot/scoundrel

Homonyms	Meanings	Homonyms	Meanings
herd	a group of animals	**here**	this place
heard	to hear	**hear**	to hearken/listen to
hew	to cut down	**higher**	more lofty
hue	a color	**hire**	to employ
him	that man	**hoard**	to store
hymn	sacred song	**horde**	a crowd
idol	worshipped image	**in**	within
idle	unemployed	**inn**	place to stay/tavern
idyll	peaceful scene		
intense	extreme	**jam**	fruit preserves
intents	purpose	**jamb**	side of doorway
key	to open a lock/answers	**knap**	depth of fabric
quay	wharf	**nap**	short sleep/rest
knave	a rogue	**knead**	to work dough
nave	center or hub	**need**	to want
		kneed	with knees
knight	title of honor	**knit**	to weave with yarn
night	darkness	**nit**	insect egg
knot	tied	**know**	to understand
not	word of refusal	**no**	not so
knows	understands	**lacks**	without, to need
nose	organ of smell	**lax**	loose, slack
leach	to filtrate	**lead**	metal
leech	an insect/worm	**led**	guided
leak	to seep out	**lean**	not fat, thin
leek	vegetable/plant	**lien**	mortgage
lee	shelter	**lesson**	a task to learn
lea	meadow	**lessen**	to ease, diminish
liar	one who tells falsehoods	**links**	connecting
lyre	musical instrument	**lynx**	animal, cat family
loan	lend money or item	**lye**	liquid
lone	alone, single	**lie**	falsehood

Practice II

Directions: Draw a box around the word that best completes the meaning of the sentence.

EXAMPLE:

If your dentist gives you an anesthesia before she fills a cavity, it will *lesson*/ *lessen* the pain.

1. Get plenty of sleep and eat healthy, thus avoiding the *flue/flu*.
2. The ship was made of *led/lead*.
3. Once the *jam/jamb* is built, the door can be hung.
4. *Hey/hay*, don't you think you should be doing your homework?
5. Be careful when you drive at night, the *dear/deer* seem to jump into the streets out of nowhere.
6. William *lacks/lax* motivation; he needs to improve his study habits.
7. There was no room at the *in/inn,* and they had to continue their travels.
8. The *links/lynx* slept peacefully in its cage.
9. Shannon injured her *heal/heel* and was unable to compete in the finals.
10. The *fir/fur* trees drop needles and cones most of the year.

COMMON HOMONYMS M–R			
Homonyms	**Meanings**	**Homonyms**	**Meanings**
made	created	**mail**	letters
maid	an unmarried woman	**male**	masculine
maid	housekeeper		
main	primary, foremost	**maize**	corn
mane	hair, esp. on lion	**maze**	labyrinth, web
mall	shopping area or walkway	**manner**	method
maul	mangle	**manor**	an estate
marshal	officer	**meat**	animal protein
martial	warlike, soldierly	**meet**	to encounter
meddle	to interfere	**mettle**	spirit or courage
medal	an award, token	**metal**	mineral
mews	cat cries	**might**	power
muse	inspiration, thought	**mite**	insect
moan	complain, lament	**morning**	early part of day
mown	to cut down	**mourning**	grieve for dead
naval	nautical	**nay**	no
navel	center of abdomen	**neigh**	whinny of horse

Homonyms	Meanings	Homonyms	Meanings
none nun	without any female devotee	oar or ore	rowing blade otherwise mineral
ode owed	poem under obligation	ought aught	should anything
our hour	belonging to us sixty minutes	paced paste	moved slowly sticky substance
packed pact	bound tightly a contract	pail pale	bucket whitish
pane pain	piece of glass agony	pair pare pear	two of a kind to peel skin off a fruit
patience patients	calmness sick persons	paws pause	animal feet a brief stop, rest
peace piece	quiet a part of	peal peel	loud sound to peel
peer peer pier	to gaze an equal wharf	pistil pistol	part of flower firearm
plain plane plane	clear, simple flat surface tool, flying machine	pleas please	to beg, argue to delight
pore pour	minute opening cause to flow	praise prays preys	to compliment to call upon feed upon, hunt
presence presents	being present gifts	pride pride pried	self-respect group of lions open with lever, meddle
principal principle	chief, head of school an element	profit prophet	to gain foreteller
quartz quarts	rock crystal measure	rain reign rein	falling water to rule leather strap for horse
raise rays raze	to lift up sunbeams to demolish	rap wrap	to strike to cover

Homonyms	Meanings	Homonyms	Meanings
read	to peruse	real	true
reed	plant	reel	to wind
		reel	to lurch or stagger
red	color	reek	to emit vapor
read	perused	wreak	to inflict
residents	citizens	rest	quiet
residence	place to live	wrest	to twist
retch	to vomit	right	correct
wretch	miserable person	write	to form letters
		rite	a ceremony
ring	a circular band	road	a street, highway
ring	a sound	rode	did ride
wring	to twist	rowed	did row with oars
rote	by memory	rout	rabble, disperse
wrote	did write	route	course
row	to move with oars	rye	grain
roe	a deer	wry	crooked

Practice III

Directions: Write a sentence using the word listed at the left of the line correctly within the context of the sentence.

EXAMPLE:

wry   Nathan has a wry sense of humor.

1. raze _____

2. wrap _____

3. pact _____

4. mail _____

5. wreak _____

6. principal _____

7. route _____

8. wry _____

9. quartz _____

10. prophet _____

COMMON HOMONYMS S–Y			
Homonyms	**Meanings**	**Homonyms**	**Meanings**
saver	one who saves	**scene**	a view
savor	taste, enjoy taste	**seen**	viewed
scull	oar, boat	**sea**	ocean
skull	bone of head	**see**	to perceive
seal	to close	**seam**	juncture, joint
seal	sea animal	**seem**	to appear
seas	oceans	**serf**	slave
sees	perceives	**surf**	ocean wave
seize	to take by force		
sew	to stitch	**shear**	to clip (as in sheep)
sow	to scatter seeds	**sheer**	steep
so	in this manner	**sheer**	utter, absolute
shoe	covering for foot	**shone**	did shine
shoo	be gone	**shown**	exhibited
shoot	to kill or let fly	**side**	edge, margin
chute	a ramp	**sighed**	did sigh
sighs	deep breaths	**slay**	to kill
size	bulk	**sleigh**	a horse-drawn vehicle
soar	to rise high	**sole**	part of foot
sore	painful	**sole**	only
		soul	spirit
some	a part	**stair**	steps
sum	total	**stare**	to gaze
stake	a post	**stationary**	motionless
stake	wager	**stationery**	paper
steak	meat		
straight	not crooked	**suite**	set of rooms
strait	narrow pass	**sweet**	pleasant taste
symbol	emblem	**tacks**	small nails
cymbal	musical instrument	**tax**	tariff
tale	story	**taught**	instructed
tail	hind part of animal	**taut**	tight
team	two or more	**tear**	moisture from eye
teem	full of	**tier**	a row or rank

Homonyms	Meanings	Homonyms	Meanings
teas	variety of tea	tense	rigid
tease	to torment	tents	canvas abodes
their	belonging to them	threw	to toss
they're	they are	through	from beginning to end
there	in that place		
throne	seat of a king or queen	thyme	herb
thrown	tossed or hurled	time	duration
toad	reptile	told	to relate information
toed	with toes	tolled	rang
towed	pulled		
too	also	tracked	followed
to	toward	tract	area or region
two	number		
vane	weathercock	vale	valley
vain	proud, conceited	veil	covering for face
vein	blood vessel	veil	to cover
vial	a bottle	vice	sin
vile	wicked	vise	a press
wade	to go into water, plow through	wail	to moan
weighed	to balance	whale	sea mammal
waist	mid part of body	wait	to stay, remain
waste	to use unwisely	weight	heaviness
waive	to relinquish	way	road or manner
wave	a hand gesture	whey	watery liquid from curdled milk
wave	surf	weigh	to balance
weak	not strong	wear	to use
week	seven days	ware	merchandise
whole	entire	wholly	completely
hole	cavity	holy	sacred
wood	from trees	yolk	yellow of egg
would	willing	yoke	collar for oxen
your	belonging to you		
you're	you are		

Practice IV

Directions: Draw a box around the correct form of the word that best suits the meaning of the sentence.

EXAMPLE:

The rabbit ran into its **whole**/|hole|.

1. David's long and mysterious *tale/tail* seemed far-fetched and untrue.
2. All *week/weak*, Loomee forced herself to study for the exam.
3. Valerie is going to *sew/sow* a project for art class.
4. *Would/wood* you please tell me where to find the museum?
5. "Oh no!" she *side/sighed*, "We missed the last train to Kilarney."
6. Avoid eating the *yoke/yolk* of the egg; it is full of cholesterol.
7. As a response to the story, there were *tears/tiers* falling from everyone in the audience.
8. The rescue team arrived on the *seen/scene* before the police.
9. Queen Elizabeth II continues on the *throne/thrown* of Great Britain.
10. The large *toad/towed* hopped from one lily pad to another.

Synonyms

Synonyms are words that have similar meanings. Synonyms can often be substituted for another word in the sentence without changing the meaning significantly. The best source to find synonyms is in a thesaurus. A thesaurus is a type of dictionary. However, instead of definitions, a thesaurus lists synonyms (and often antonyms).

generous	unselfish
smart	intelligent
deliberate	intentional
indigo	navy blue
peer	colleague

Practice V

Directions: Write a synonym for each of the words listed below.

EXAMPLE:

dark   dim

1. strong   _____
2. distant   _____

3. knave _____

4. clever _____

5. sharp _____

6. prey _____

7. glisten _____

8. assistant _____

9. boring _____

10. coarse _____

Antonyms

Antonyms are words that have opposite meanings. A thesaurus often lists antonyms.

black	white
vacant	full
rough	smooth
real	imaginary
subtract	add

Practice VI

Directions: Underline the pairs of words that are antonyms.

EXAMPLE:

<u>lazy/diligent</u>   <u>clear/hazy</u>   <u>vibrate/still</u>

1. fast/quick	11. far/close	21. dim/bright
2. buy/sell	12. harmless/harmful	22. pull/push
3. hate/love	13. hate/despise	23. dumb/stupid
4. sloppy/neat	14. beautiful/ugly	24. hot/cold
5. before/after	15. include/contain	25. outside/inside
6. narrow/thin	16. narrow/wide	26. today/present
7. decrease/add	17. powerful/strong	27. wave/ripple
8. tardy/late	18. tardy/early	28. rascal/knave
9. jabber/babble	19. lazy/ambitious	29. disagreement/agreement
10. clear/muddy	20. peaceful/calm	30. free/imprisoned

Confusing Words

In addition to understanding homonyms, which can cause a fair amount of confusion themselves, many other words in the English language can cause even more confusion. To de-confuse yourself, study the following chart of confusing or troublesome words.

Confusing Words	Description
a **an**	use before words that begin with consonants: a bug, a mouse use before words that begin with vowels: an elephant, an ox
accept **except**	to believe or recognize: *I will accept your offer.* not including: *We will read the entire chapter except for page 9.*
affect **effect**	to influence: *Vinit's lungs were affected by secondhand smoke.* to produce change: *Mixing oil and water has an interesting effect.*
allusion **illusion**	reference to: *There are many Biblical allusions in that novel.* false impression: *Her speech had the illusion of being antiwar.*
a lot (two words)	NEVER use these two words as one—they are always separate words: *If you use a lot as one word, you will get into a lot of trouble.*
among **between**	surrounded by: *We were among like-minded people in class.* sandwiched (two people): *Joe stood between Mike and Jackson.*
anyway NOT **anyways**	Do not use the word *anyway* with an *s* on the end: *Not knowing what to do, he continued to the meeting anyway.*
can **may**	suggests ability: *Can you ride a bicycle?* asks permission: *May I eat these plums?*
chose **choose**	past tense: *I chose to go to Harvard and not Stanford.* present tense: *I will choose one of the two schools.*
farther **further**	physical distance: *Rene ran farther than Ryan.* added time, quantity, degree: *We will need further studies to determine the cause of the disease.*
fewer **less**	number of units: *There are fewer math problems in this book.* quantity: *The less you study, the more chances you have to fail.*
good **well**	used as an adjective: *Sophia has good cooking skills.* used as an adverb: *She is doing well at culinary school.*
immigrate **emigrate**	to go to a new country: *Ms. Choi will immigrate to Hong Kong.* to leave one country for another: *She will emigrate from Taiwan to Hong Kong.*
imply **infer**	suggest indirectly: *Her boss implied that she might be fired.* draw a conclusion: *From what he was saying, she inferred that she was going to be fired.*

Confusing Words	Description
it's	it is—a contraction: *It's going to be a long day.*
its	pronoun: *Tim will take care of its needs.*
lay	to place: *Lay the carpet in this room, please.*
lie	to recline: *I am going to lie down for a short nap.*
like	similar to: *You do not always have to be like your friend.*
as	same/similar degree: *It will not be as rainy today as it was yesterday.*
loose	free, untied: *The ornaments were loose in the box.*
lose	lost: *Danielle will lose her book if she does not put it away.*
principal	chief/head of school: *The principal forbids cheating at school.*
principle	belief or standard: *According to our principles, you are out of order.*
set	to place something: *Set the plates onto the table.*
sit	to seat the body: *Trevor will sit in his teacher's chair.*
than	comparison: *Evelyn's scores are higher than William's.*
then	when: *After dinner, only then will we have dessert.*
who	refers to people: *Colin, who is going to work tonight?*
which	refers to nonliving things: *Which of these shirts do you like?*
that	refers to living or nonliving: *I will take that to Europe with me.*
who	subject of a verb: *Who will go with me?*
whom	object of a preposition: *To whom do I owe an apology?*
who's	who is (contraction): *Who's going to my house tonight?*
whose	possessive pronoun: *Do you know whose house this is?*
your	possessive pronoun: *That is your notebook.*
you're	you are (contraction): *You're going to get into trouble.*

Practice VII

Directions: Draw a box around the correct form of the word that best completes the meaning of the sentence.

EXAMPLE:

Do you know ⌐*whose*¬/*who's* jacket this is?

1. Will you *sit*/*set* the flower vase onto the kitchen table?
2. You have completely mistaken our true *principals*/*principles* in your response.
3. *Which* /*That*/*Who* of the chemical experiments will Mrs. Hescox demonstrate today?
4. Nick did *good*/*well* on the test today.

5. The *effect/affect* of the smog on his lungs was disturbing.

6. *Your/you're* going to spend the holidays with your grandmother in Guadalajara.

7. Jinny needs to fix the clasp on her necklace or else she will *loose/lose* the pendant.

8. Sara will investigate the meanings of the *illusions/allusions* in the novel *Crime and Punishment*.

9. Buddy has *a/an* pleasant personality.

10. There are a *lot/alot* of students who do not read their books.

Chapter 19 Review Quizzes

Vocabulary Review Quiz

Directions: Write the letter of the definition on the line next to the word that it defines.

1. _____ usury

2. _____ chariot

3. _____ voluminous

4. _____ indigo

5. _____ anoint

6. _____ dowdy

7. _____ mountainous

8. _____ glisten

9. _____ peer

10. _____ lottery

A. To apply ointment or oil to.

B. Unattractive, dull.

C. A two-wheeled horse-drawn carriage used in ancient times.

D. To shine like something wet or polished.

E. One who is equal to another in rank, merit, or quality.

F. A deep-blue dye or color between blue and violet in the color spectrum.

G. Having great volume or bulk.

H. Full of mountains.

I. The lending of money at an extremely high rate of interest.

J. A system of selling numbered tickets for an opportunity to win money or prizes.

Homonyms, Synonyms, Antonyms, and Confusing Words Definitions

Directions: Select the correct definition, and write the letter of the answer on the line to the right of the number.

1. _____ A homonym is a word that _____.
   a. has the same or similar meaning
   b. has the opposite meaning
   c. sounds the same but has different meanings and spelling
   d. none of the above

2. _____ Which of the following are homonyms?
   a. generous, unselfish
   b. yolk, yoke
   c. exit, enter
   d. throw, hurl

3. _____ Which of the following is the definition of a synonym?
   a. It has the same or similar meaning.
   b. It has the opposite meaning.
   c. It sounds the same but has different meanings and spelling.
   d. none of the above

4. _____ Which of the following words are NOT synonyms?
   a. late, tardy
   b. foremost, primary
   c. chaperone, escort
   d. crowd, loner

5. _____ Identify the definition of an antonym below.
   a. It has the same or similar meaning.
   b. It has the opposite meaning.
   c. It sounds the same but has different meanings and spelling.
   d. all of the above

6. _____ Which of the following words are antonyms?
   a. unique, common
   b. purchase, buy
   c. fast, quick
   d. stationary, motionless

7. _____ Identify the word that is a synonym for *harmless*.
   a. harmful
   b. safe
   c. crooked
   d. terrifying

8. _____ Identify the word below that is an antonym for *compliment*.
   a. dowdy
   b. praise
   c. criticism
   d. anoint

9. _____ The words *rough* and *smooth* are _____.
   a. synonyms
   b. confusing words
   c. antonyms
   d. homonyms

10. _____ The words *to, two,* and *too* are _____.
    a. synonyms
    b. confusing words
    c. antonyms
    d. homonyms

Homonyms

Directions: Correct the sentences below by <u>underlining</u> the incorrect homonym, and then write the correct homonym on the line at the end of the sentence.

EXAMPLE:

The too of us will go tomorrow. ____two____

1. The mane idea of the sentence is not always easy to find. _____

2. During the rush, the isle was blocked and no one could leave. _____

3. At the sound of a loud noise, the hair ran into its burrow. _____

4. The dents cloud formation is a certain sign of rain. _____

5. Anthony will become a night at the Queen's command. _____

6. Olivia was in morning for her dead brother for many years. _____

7. Nun of the waiters is paying any attention to us. _____

8. Going back home at this point does not make any scents. _____

9. James will urn a living by designing a unique computer program. _____

10. It is going to take me a month to rap all of those gifts. _____

Synonyms and Antonyms

Directions: Identify each of the following pairs of words as either synonyms or antonyms. Write *S* on the line if the pair is a synonym and *A* on the line if the pair is an antonym.

EXAMPLE:

____*S*____ smelly/stinky   ____*A*__ sweet/sour

1. _____ petite/large   11. _____ stare/glance

2. _____ repeat/duplicate   12. _____ minor/major

3. _____ drizzle/pour   13. _____ fasten/unlock

4. _____ avoid/encounter   14. _____ peaceful/warlike

5. _____ clever/intelligent   15. _____ gentle/harsh

6. _____ dull/shiny   16. _____ merry/happy

7. _____ error/mistake   17. _____ hasty/slowly

8. _____ distrust/trust   18. _____ vacant/empty

9. _____ total/sum   19. _____ friend/pal

10. _____ ponder/think   20. _____ adore/despise

Confusing Words

Directions: Identify the correct and incorrect use of confusing words in the sentences below. Write *C* on the line if the sentence is correct. Write *E* on the line if there is an error in word usage, and identify the error by underlining it.

EXAMPLE:

    E   There are <u>alot</u> of people at the beach today.

1. _____ Do not forget, your purse is under the table.

2. _____ The school principle was given an award for bravery.

3. _____ I am going to go to the post office anyways; I might as well stop at the dry cleaners too.

4. _____ Whether you approve or not, there is an new necklace in your jewelry box.

5. _____ Global warming is having a disturbing effect on the climate patterns around the world.

6. _____ Between thousands in the crowd watching the game, there were dozens of celebrities.

7. _____ They were cent to visit the museum.

8. _____ Your mother is waiting.

9. _____ Which animal in the zoo do you like best?

10. _____ To who shall we send the invitation?

Real-World Practice Activities

Reading and Writing

Directions: Read/review the following list of words, and choose ten (10) of the groups. Write a sentence for both words. Make certain that you use each word correctly in the sentence.

whether/weather	way/weigh	cite/sight
chord/cord	cache/cash	rain/reign
right/write	sees/seize	desert/dessert
brake/break	brews/bruise	whine/wine
who's/whose	tacks/tax	tail/tale
side/sighed	rote/wrote	rose/rows
prays/praise	pries/prize	pail/pale
oar/ore	one/won	lie/lye
hear/here	guessed/guest	forth/fourth
foul/fowl	freeze/frees	fairy/ferry
use/ewes	fair/fare	crews/cruise

1. _____

_____

2. _____

_____

3. _____

_____

4. _____

_____

5. _____

_____

6. _____

_____

7. _____

_____

8. _____

_____

9. _____

_____

10. _____

_____

Listening

Directions: Throughout your day, listen for words that you have reviewed in this chapter. Write the words on the lines below. Next to the words, write either a synonym or an antonym (or both if you feel inspired).

1. _____   Synonym:_____   Antonym: _____

2. _____   Synonym:_____   Antonym: _____

3. _____   Synonym:_____   Antonym: _____

4. _____   Synonym:_____   Antonym: _____

5. _____   Synonym:_____   Antonym: _____

6. _____   Synonym:_____   Antonym: _____

7. _____   Synonym:_____   Antonym: _____

8. _____   Synonym:_____   Antonym: _____

9. _____   Synonym:_____   Antonym: _____

10. _____   Synonym:_____   Antonym: _____

Chapter 20

IDIOMS

I dioms are unique and strange little figures of speech that are found scattered throughout the English language. When you look at an idiom literally such as, *it's raining cats and dogs,* the idiom does not make much sense. We can visualize the literal meaning of the sky pouring cats and dogs, but that would be a mess. After all, how can it rain cats and dogs. Come on—that just does not make any sense at all. However, the figurative meaning behind the idiom is where we actually find the meaning. Even then the figurative, metaphorical, or nonliteral meaning is a stretch to understand**.** *It's raining cats and dogs* means that the rain is pouring down hard. Idioms cause a great deal of confusion for those learning English because they are difficult to translate, if not impossible. Idioms, though, are interesting and can be fun to try to figure out. This chapter lists many of them, but there are hundreds of them. Study them so that if you hear one—(most people do not use them in writing)—you will not be completely confused.

Vocabulary Development

1. **bawl** (bawl) Loud weeping, to shout or cry loudly.
2. **civilize** (civ i lize) To cause an improvement in behavior from savage to a more developed society.
3. **effigy** (ef i gee) A sculpture or model of a person.
4. **flux** (flux) Constant or continuous succession of changes.
5. **horror** (hor or) Extreme feeling of fear or loathing.
6. **loathing** (lothe ing) Feeling of extreme dislike, hate.
7. **modus operandi** (mo dus op er an die) A person's way or method of working.
8. **posterior** (po steer e or) Situated in the back or behind.
9. **stomp (**stomp) To tread heavily or loudly.
10. **vagrant** (vay grant) A person who has no settled home or regular work.

Alphabetical List of Idioms

The idiom is *italicized,* and the figurative meaning is in parentheses ( ).

A:

- *A day late and a dollar short* (too little, too late)
- *A fool and his money are soon parted* (those who are not careful with money spend it quickly)
- *A little bird told me* (if the information that you were told is private and you do not want to say who told you)
- *A penny for your thoughts* (a way to ask what someone is thinking)
- *A rolling stone gathers no moss* (a person who is always moving does not acquire possessions)
- *Absence makes the heart grow fonder* (when people are separated, their love grows stronger)
- *Ace up your sleeve* (you have an advantage that others do not know about)
- *Achilles' heel* (a person's weak spot)
- *Actions speak louder than words* (what people do is more important than what they say)
- *Add fuel to the fire/add insult to injury* (make a bad situation worse)
- *Age before beauty* (allow older people to go first—usually used sarcastically)
- *All ears* (very interested in listening to you)
- *All fingers and thumbs* (someone who is clumsy)
- *All hell broke loose* (chaos and confusion)
- *All roads lead to Rome* (there are many ways to do something)
- *All that glitters is not gold* (appearances can be deceptive, it may look/sound valuable but, in fact, may be worthless)
- *All the tea in China (not for)* (would not do it no matter how much money is offered)
- *All your eggs in one basket* (spread the risk instead of risking everything at one time)
- *Ants in your pants* (someone excited or agitated)
- *Any Tom, Dick, or Harry* (anyone can do it)
- *Apple of your eye* (someone who is very special to you)
- *An arm and a leg* (very expensive item)
- *As cold as ice* (person who shows no emotion)
- *As cool as a cucumber* (a person who is calm and composed)
- *As the crow flies* (the shortest distance between two places)
- *Ax to grind* (anger or resentment that you want to confront someone with)

Practice I

Directions: Match the idioms to their meanings by writing the letter of the meaning on the line.

1. _____ As the crow flies	A. appearance can be deceptive
2. _____ Ants in your pants	B. calm and composed
3. _____ All ears	C. shows no emotion
4. _____ Apple of your eye	D. a person's weak spot
5. _____ As cold as ice	E. what are you thinking
6. _____ Achilles' heel	F. interested in listening to you
7. _____ A penny for your thoughts	G. shortest distance
8. _____ Ace up your sleeve	H. a secret advantage
9. _____ As cool as a cucumber	I. someone very special to you
10. _____ All that glitters is not gold	J. excited or agitated

B:

- *Bad egg* (someone not trustworthy)
- *Ball is in your court* (it is up to you to make the next decision)
- *Bark is worse than their bite* (a person who may scream or yell but does not act)
- *Barking up the wrong tree* (a complete misunderstanding and error in judgment)
- *Barrel of laughs* (someone or something who jokes and laughs a lot)
- *Beat about the bush* (not saying what you mean right away)
- *Beating a dead horse* (raising an issue about something that no one cares about)
- *Beauty is in the eye of the beholder* (different people find different things beautiful)
- *Beauty is only skin deep* (what may look beautiful may not be, appearances are deceptive)
- *Bells and whistles* (attractive features that are not always necessary)
- *Below the belt* (a cruel or unfair statement)
- *Best thing since sliced bread* (excellent invention or discovery)
- *Better late than never* (better to be late than not do it at all)
- *Between a rock and a hard place* (having to choose between two unpleasant alternatives)
- *Between the lines (read)* (find the real meaning through interpretation, not literally)
- *Big cheese* (the boss)
- *Big fish in a small pond* (an important or seemingly important person in a small organization)
- *Big picture* (the overall perspective, not the fine detail)
- *Bigger fish to fry* (more important things to do than what is being asked)
- *Bird in the hand is worth two in the bush* (to have something that is certain is better than taking a risk and losing everything)
- *Bird brain* (someone who is stupid)
- *Birds of a feather flock together* (people with similar interests stick together)

- *Birds and the bees* (talking about sex)
- *Birthday suit* (being naked)
- *Bite off more than you can chew* (take on more responsibilities than you can handle)
- *Bite the bullet* (accept what you have to do and do it)
- *Bite the dust* (to die)
- *Bite your tongue* (be careful of what you say)
- *Bitter pill to swallow* (something that is difficult to accept)
- *Black and white* (a situation is very clear if it is black and white—there are not other options)
- *Black sheep* (someone who does not fit into the group or family because he/she is different)
- *Bleeding heart* (someone who is excessively sympathetic to a cause or people)
- *Blessing in disguise* (misfortune can often turn out to be a positive thing)
- *Blood is thicker than water* (family relationships are stronger than others)
- *Blow off steam* (express anger or frustration)
- *Born with a silver spoon in your mouth* (born into a wealthy family)
- *Break a leg* (wishing someone good luck, especially actors and performers)
- *Break the ice* (getting over the awkwardness of meeting someone for the first time)
- *Bring home the bacon* (someone who earns the money in the family)
- *Brush under the carpet* (ignoring a problem or hiding it from others)
- *Bull in a china shop* (someone who is loud and clumsy when he/she should be careful)
- *Burn the candle at both ends* (hectic, chaotic life or pace, unhealthy)
- *Burn your bridges* (destroying something or a relationship in a way that makes it impossible for you to go back if you need to)
- *Bury the hatchet* (to make peace with someone, stop arguing)
- *Bury your head in the sand* (ignoring something instead of dealing with it)
- *Butterflies in your stomach* (feeling nervous or stressful about something)
- *By the book* (do something exactly as you are supposed to)
- *By word of mouth* (information is spread by people talking about it rather than by publicity or advertising)

Practice II

Directions: Write the **figurative** (not literal) meaning of the following idioms on the lines provided.

EXAMPLE:

By the book: <u>something done exactly as it is supposed to be done.</u>

1. Bury the hatchet: _____

2. Break the ice: _____

3. Beauty is in the eye of the beholder: _____

4. Break a leg: _____

5. Black sheep: _____

6. Blood is thicker than water: _____

7. Birthday suit: _____

8. Blessing in disguise: _____

9. Between the lines: _____

10. Black and white: _____

C:

- *Call a spade a spade* (someone who is honest and frank, does not hide feelings)
- *Can of worms* (an action may cause a serious problem)
- *Cat got your tongue?* (someone wants to know why you are not speaking)
- *Catnap* (short nap or rest during the day)
- *Catch someone red-handed* (catch someone doing something wrong or illegal)
- *Chip off the old block* (a person resembles one or both parents in character)
- *Chip on your shoulder* (someone who is resentful and has an attitude about it)
- *Clear as mud* (something that is confusing and unclear)
- *Cloud nine* (being extremely happy)
- *Cold feet* (lose courage to do something)
- *Cold shoulder* (deliberately unfriendly or uncooperative toward someone)
- *Could eat a horse* (someone who is very hungry)
- *Cry crocodile tears* (pretend to be upset or affected by something)
- *Cross to bear* (a heavy responsibility or burden to deal with)
- *Cry wolf* (to raise a false alarm or warning about something that does not exist)
- *Curiosity killed the cat* (being excessively curious may not be a good thing, especially if it is not his/her business to be concerned with)
- *Cut off your nose to spite your face* (doing something silly or rash when you are upset that ends up making things worse for you in the long run)
- *Cut the mustard* (someone who cannot do something or fails to reach the required standard)

Practice III

Directions: Match the meaning of the idiom by writing the letter on the line to the left.

1. _____ cry wolf	A. fails to reach the standard
2. _____ cross to bear	B. to lose courage to do something
3. _____ cold feet	C. very hungry
4. _____ cry crocodile tears	D. extremely happy
5. _____ chip on your shoulder	E. heavy burden to deal with
6. _____ clear as mud	F. a false alarm or warning
7. _____ catch someone red-handed	G. angry and with an attitude
8. _____ cloud nine	H. unclear and confusing
9. _____ cut the mustard	I. caught doing something wrong
10. _____ could eat a horse	J. pretending to cry and to be upset

D:

- *Dark horse* (a person who is mysterious, unknown)
- *Devil's advocate* (someone who argues for something that he/she does not believe in just to argue)
- *Diamond in the rough* (someone with potential but who is not refined or polished)
- *Die is cast* (an unalterable decision has been made and only fate will decide the consequences)
- *Discretion is the better part of valor* (better to think carefully and not act than to take a risk and do something that may be a mistake)
- *Dog and pony show* (marketing that has style and class but no real content)
- *Dog days* (hot summer days)
- *Dog-eat-dog* (intense competition and rivalry where everyone thinks only of themselves)
- *Don't judge a book by its cover* (do not judge people by appearances, look deeper)
- *Don't hold your breath* (do not have expectations that are too high)
- *Double-edged sword* (using an argument that could either help or hurt)
- *Down to earth* (someone who is realistic and practical)
- *Drag your feet* (taking too long to finish because they do not want to do it)
- *Dressed to the nines* (dressed in very best clothes)
- *Drive someone up the wall* (to annoy someone greatly)
- *Drop in the bucket* (an effort so small that it would not make a difference)
- *Drop the ball* (someone who is not doing his/her job or taking responsibilities seriously)
- *Ducks in a row* (well-organized, ready to go)

E:

- *Early bird catches the worm* (the earlier you begin, the better your chance at success)
- *Eat crow* (having to admit that you are wrong)
- *Egg on your face* (made to look foolish or to be embarrassed)
- *Eleventh hour* (something happens at the very last minute before a deadline)
- *Every cloud has a silver lining* (something positive that comes from an unfortunate situation)
- *Eye for an eye* (the punishment equals the crime)
- *Eyes are bigger than one's stomach* (someone who is greedy and takes more than he/she can eat or manage)

Practice IV

Directions: Write the **figurative** meaning of the idiom on the line provided.

EXAMPLE:

Egg on your face: <u>made to look foolish or to embarrass</u>.

1. Down to earth: _____

2. Ducks in a row: _____

3. Every cloud has a silver lining: _____

4. Drop the ball: _____

5. Dog and pony show: _____

6. Don't judge a book by its cover: _____

7. Eat crow: _____

8. Eleventh hour: _____

9. Dog days: _____

10. Drop in a bucket: _____

F:

- *Face the music* (to accept the negative consequences of a decision or action)
- *Fair-weather friend* (a friend who is there in good times but abandons you in difficult times)
- *Feather in your cap* (an achievement or success that will help in the future)
- *Fish out of water (like a)* (placed into an unfamiliar or new situation that is confusing)
- *Fit as a fiddle* (in perfect health)
- *Fly in the ointment* (something that prevents complete enjoyment of something else)
- *Fly off the handle* (to get extremely angry about something)

- *Food for thought* (something worth thinking about)
- *Forest for the trees (can't see)* (so caught up in small details that they do not understand the big picture)
- *From rags to riches* (to start life very poor and then make a fortune)
- *From the horse's mouth* (hear something directly from the person concerned or responsible)
- *Full circle* (when something ends up where it began)
- *Full of hot air* (someone who talks a lot about nothing)

G:

- *Get on your soapbox* (someone who talks about a subject he/she feels strongly about)
- *Get out of bed on the wrong side* (to begin the day in a bad mood for no real reason)
- *Get your feet wet* (to get your first experience about something)
- *Gild the lily* (to decorate something that is already ornate and elaborate)
- *Go Dutch* (pay equal share for a meal)
- *Go fly a kite* (tell someone to go away)
- *Gone to pot* (something that has gone wrong or not taken care of properly)
- *Grab the bull by its horns* (to deal directly with a problem)
- *Grain of salt (take something)* (do not necessarily believe the entire story or criticism)
- *Greek to me* (when you do not understand something)
- *Green thumb* (someone who is skilled as a gardener)
- *Green-eyed monster* (someone who is extremely jealous)
- *Gray area* (there is no clear right or wrong/not black and white)

Practice V:

Directions: Identify each of the idioms below.

EXAMPLE:

To be placed into a new situation or an uncomfortable position <u>Fish out of water</u>

1. Tell someone to go away _____

2. To become extremely angry _____

3. When you do not understand something _____

4. To begin the day in a bad mood _____

5. Placed into an unfamiliar situation _____

6. A friend who abandons you in difficult times _____

7. To start life poor and to gain wealth later _____

8. When something ends where it began _____

9. In perfect health _____

10. To pay an equal share _____

H:

- *Hang out to dry* (to abandon someone when he/she is in trouble)
- *Haste makes waste* (doing something too fast without planning will likely cause you to spend more time and money to do it right)
- *Hat trick* (three successes, one right after another)
- *Have your cake and eat it too* (someone who wants to have everything his/her way, especially when his/her wishes are contradictory)
- *Head is in the clouds* (someone who has unrealistic or impractical ideas)
- *Hear a pin drop* (complete silence in a room)
- *Hit the hay* or *hit the sack* (go to bed)
- *Hit the nail on the head* (exactly correct about something)
- *Hit the roof* (to lose your temper and become quite angry)
- *Hold your horses* (slow down, not so fast)
- *Hook, line, and sinker* (accepting completely)
- *Hop, skip, and a jump* (short distance away)
- *Hornet's nest* (something that is controversial and causes trouble and anger)
- *Horse of a different color* (a different matter or issue altogether)
- *Hotheaded* (someone who angers easily)

I:

- *In one ear and out the other* (someone who listens but forgets or does not pay close attention)
- *In the doghouse* (in trouble)
- *In the pink* (healthy)
- *In the red* (bank account is overdrawn/no money)
- *Indian summer* (a period of warm weather in late autumn)
- *Irons in the fire* (someone who has a number of things going in his/her favor)
- *It never rains but it pours* (when things go wrong, they really go wrong)
- *It takes two to tango* (when things go wrong with two sides, neither party is innocent)
- *It's no use crying over spilled milk* (getting upset after something has gone wrong is pointless because it cannot be changed, just accept it)
- *Ivory tower* (those who live in an ivory tower are said to be detached from the world around them)

J:

- *Joined at the hip* (people who are closely connected or think the same way)
- *Jump the gun* (start before the appropriate time)
- *Jump through hoops* (to make great efforts and sacrifices for something or someone)
- *Jungle out there* (a dangerous situation where there are no rules)
- *Jury's out* (there is no general consensus or agreement)
- *Just desserts* (someone getting the punishment of suffering the consequences that he/she deserves)
- *Just off the boat* (someone who is naive and inexperienced)

K:

- *Keep it under your hat* (keep a secret, do not tell anyone)
- *Keep your chin up* (an encouragement—do not give up)
- *Keep your fingers crossed* (hope for a positive outcome)
- *Keep your nose to the grindstone* (stay focused and work hard)
- *Kettle of fish (a fine)* (a difficult problem or situation)
- *Kick the bucket* (to die)
- *Kick up your heels* (to be in a celebratory or partying mood)
- *Kid gloves (handle with)* (handle a situation very delicately or with great care)
- *Knight in shining armor* (someone who saves you when you are in great danger)
- *Knock on wood* (to hope for good luck by knocking on wood)

Practice VI

Directions: Write a sentence using each of the idioms listed below.

EXAMPLE:

When asking mom for a new outfit, you better handle it <u>with kid gloves</u> because she just gave you money for the trip.

1. The jury's out _____

2. In the doghouse _____

3. Hold your horses _____

4. Hear a pin drop _____

5. Too many irons in the fire _____

6. Knight in shining armor _____

7. Jump through hoops _____

8. In the red _____

9. Hit the hay _____

10. Keep your chin up _____

L:

- *Leave no stone unturned* (look at every angle when trying to achieve something)
- *Leopard can't change its spots* (people cannot change various aspects of their personalities, especially negative ones)
- *Let sleeping dogs lie* (do not disturb the situation as it will result in more complications or trouble)
- *Like a fish out of water* (being uncomfortable in the current situation)
- *Like the back of your hand* (knowing something very well)
- *Like two peas in a pod* (very similar or identical)
- *Lily-livered* (a coward)
- *Lion's share* (the biggest and the best part)
- *Look before you leap* (consider carefully the possible results or consequences before doing something)
- *Look what the cat dragged in* (a person who arrives flustered and looking a mess)
- *Lose your marbles* (gone mad or crazy)
- *Luck of the draw* (winner chosen by chance, not intentionally)

M:

- *Make a mountain out of a molehill* (do not exaggerate the importance or seriousness of a problem)
- *Man's best friend* (a dog)
- *Memory like an elephant* (having a good memory)
- *Mind your Ps and Qs* (behave yourself and be polite)
- *More than one way to skin a cat* (there are different ways to achieve the same result)
- *Music to my ears* (exactly what you wanted to hear)

N:

- *Needle in a haystack* (very difficult to find if not impossible)
- *Nest egg* (money saved for the future)
- *New York minute* (something that happens very quickly)
- *No skin off my nose* (something that does not affect or bother you)
- *No spring chicken* (not young)
- *Not my cup of tea* (not something that you are interested in)
- *Nothing to crow about* (not something to be proud of, not particularly good or special)

Practice VII

Directions: Match the idiom to its definition by writing the letter of the correct definition on the line to the left.

1. _____ No spring chicken   A. Cowardly

2. _____ Luck of the draw   B. Nearly impossible to find

3. _____ Lily-livered   C. A dog

4. _____ Needle in a haystack   D. Happens very quickly

5. _____ Man's best friend   E. The biggest and the best share

6. _____ New York minute   F. Not as young as he used to be

7. _____ Nothing to crow about   G. Nothing to be proud of

8. _____ Lose your marbles   H. Chosen by chance or luck

9. _____ Music to my ears   I. To go crazy

10. _____ Lion's share   J. Exactly what I wanted to hear

O:

- *Off the beaten track* (not a normal route or path)
- *Offer an olive branch* (to offer peace)
- *On pins and needles* (excited or extremely worried about something)
- *Once bitten, twice shy* (someone who has been hurt or had something go wrong will be far more careful the next time)
- *Once in a blue moon* (once in a rare occasion)
- *One bad apple can spoil the whole bunch* (one bad person or policy can ruin everything)
- *Out of the frying pan and into the fire* (going from one bad situation to a worse situation)
- *Out on a limb* (at risk or taking a chance at something)
- *Out to lunch* (someone who is crazy, not particularly aware of things)
- *Over the hill* (older and not able to perform as before)

P:

- *Pandora's box* (something that causes all sorts of trouble that was not anticipated)
- *Pass the buck* (place the blame or responsibility onto someone else)
- *Pay the piper* (accept the consequences for something that you have done wrong)
- *Pie in the sky* (an impractical scheme)
- *Piece of cake* (easy, really easy)
- *Pigs might fly* (something that will never happen or succeed)

- *Pot calling the kettle black* (criticizing someone for something that the person does him/herself)
- *Preaching to the choir* (trying to convince an audience who already agrees)
- *Pull the wool over someone's eyes* (to fool, deceive, or cheat someone)
- *Push the envelope* (go to the limits, do something to the maximum)
- *Put someone out to pasture* (force someone to resign or give up responsibility)
- *Put a foot in your mouth* (say something embarrassing or stupid)
- *Putting the cart before the horse* (doing something in the wrong order, backward)

Q:

- *Quiet as a mouse* (make no noise at all)

Practice VIII

Directions: Write the definition of the idiom on the line.

EXAMPLE:

Pass the buck—place the blame or responsibility onto someone else.

1. Push the envelope _____

2. Pigs might fly _____

3. Out to lunch _____

4. Preaching to the choir _____

5. Off the beaten track _____

6. Put your foot in your mouth _____

7. Pie in the sky _____

8. Over the hill _____

9. Piece of cake _____

10. Once in a blue moon _____

R:

- *Rags to riches* (from poor beginnings to wealth)
- *Rat race* (competitive struggle for success in work)
- *Read someone the riot act* (to warn about stopping an activity or risk the consequences)
- *Real McCoy* (the real thing)
- *Red-letter day* (a good luck day when something special happens to you)

- *Reinvent the wheel* (do not waste time doing something that has already been done before)
- *Rest on your laurels* (someone who relies on past achievements rather than attempting to achieve new things)
- *Rise from the ashes* (something that recovers after serious failure)
- *Roll out the red carpet* (welcome someone in a special way)
- *Rose-colored glasses* (see things in a more positive manner)
- *Rub shoulders* (meet and spend time with those who are powerful or famous)
- *Ruffle a few feathers* (to annoy someone when making changes)
- *Rule of thumb* (approximately)
- *Run of the mill* (ordinary, nothing exceptional about it)

S:

- *Sacred cow* (something so esteemed that it cannot be criticized or attacked)
- *Salad days* (the happiest days of your life)
- *Salt in your wound* (adding more pain to an already painful or embarrassing situation)
- *Scraping the barrel* (to make do with what is left when everything/everyone is used up)
- *Set in stone* (cannot be changed)
- *Set the wheels in motion* (get something started)
- *Shape up or ship out* (improve or leave the organization/job)
- *Silence is golden* (better not to say anything)
- *Sink or swim* (without help, either you succeed or fail)
- *Sit on the fence* (in the middle, not supporting either side of an issue)
- *Skate on thin ice* (taking a great risk of failing)
- *Skeleton in your closet* (a dark or shameful secret in the past)
- *Sleep like a log* (sleep very soundly)
- *Spill the beans* (reveal a secret or to confess)
- *Square peg in a round hole* (the feeling that you do not fit in somewhere)
- *Squeaky wheel gets the grease* (the loudest and most frequent complaints get attention)
- *Squeeze blood out of a turnip* (cannot get something out of someone, especially money, that he/she does not have)
- *Step up to the plate* (take on responsibility or a new challenge)
- *Still waters run deep* (quiet people tend to be more interesting than those who require a lot of attention)
- *Stitch in time saves nine* (do the best that you can now to save time from having to do it again later)
- *Storm in a teacup* (someone who exaggerates a problem, making it bigger than it is)
- *Straw that broke the camel's back* (the cause or situation that finally brought about a collapse or to lose one's temper)

- *Swan song* (final achievement or public appearance)

Practice IX

Directions: Write a sentence using the idioms listed below.

EXAMPLE:

Storm in a teacup: <u>You are making such a storm in a teacup about this; it is not a big deal, get over it</u>.

1. Sleep like a log _____

2. Swan song _____

3. Rule of thumb _____

4. Rat race _____

5. Spill the beans _____

6. Step up to the plate _____

7. Red-letter day _____

8. Roll out the red carpet _____

9. Rub shoulders _____

10. Sink or swim _____

T:

- *The grass is always greener* (what others have seems better than what we have)
- *Thick as thieves* (good friends who have no secrets)
- *Think outside the box* (be creative, think beyond the sedate or normal)
- *Thorn in your side* (something that causes trouble or makes life difficult)
- *Throw the book at someone* (punish someone to the full extent possible)
- *Thumbs up* or *thumbs down* (thumbs up is good/ok, thumbs down is not ok)
- *Tighten your belt* (try to save money, economize)
- *Tip of the iceberg* (the problems that can be seen are obvious, but the underlying problems that cannot be seen are worse)
- *Tongue in cheek* (teasingly, not serious)
- *Too many cooks spoil the broth* (when too many people try to do something, the results are not always good)
- *Turn over a new leaf* (start over fresh, make a new start)
- *Twist someone's arm* (convince or persuade someone)
- *Two left feet* (someone who is clumsy)

U:

- *Ugly duckling* (a child who shows little promise but later develops into a talented or beautiful person)
- *Up in the air* (no decision has been made, uncertain)
- *Up the creek without a paddle* (in real trouble)
- *Up to your neck* (involved deeply in something like work)

V:

- *Velvet glove* (someone who appears gentle but who is determined and inflexible underneath)
- *Vicious circle* (a series or sequence of unfortunate events, each worse than the one before)

W:

- *Wake-up call* (warning of a threat or challenge forcing someone to change his/her behavior)
- *Warts and all* (accepting people for who they are, faults and everything)
- *Water under the bridge* (the past is not important and not worth worrying about)
- *Wear your heart on your sleeve* (someone who shows emotions or feelings easily)
- *Wet behind the ears* (someone who is young or inexperienced)
- *Wet blanket* (someone who spoils other people's fun)
- *What goes around comes around* (if you do bad/good things, bad/good things will happen in return)
- *When in Rome, do as the Romans* (follow the customs and culture of a place that you are visiting)
- *Where there is a will, there is a way* (if there is a strong desire to do something, there is a way to get it done)
- *Which came first? The chicken or the egg?* (when it is not clear who or what caused something)
- *White elephant* (something that stands out as a burden or an expense)
- *Wild-goose chase* (wasting time chasing after something that will not be successful)
- *Wolf in sheep's clothing* (on the surface it looks fine, but underneath lies evil)
- *Worth your salt* (deserving of respect)
- *Writing's on the wall* (something that is doomed to fail)

Y:

- *Yellow bellied* (cowardly)
- *You can lead a horse to water, but you can't make it drink* (you can offer good advice, but you cannot make them follow it)
- *You can't have your cake and eat it too* (you cannot have things both ways)

Practice X

Directions: Underline the idioms used in the following sentences.

EXAMPLE:

You are going to be <u>up a creek without a paddle</u> if you do not get your bills paid every month.

1. That man is nothing more than a wolf in sheep's clothing; he is not a good person.
2. She has been up to her neck in phone calls and requests for information.
3. Once you leave your job, you are going to have to tighten your belt.
4. Thank you for asking me to dance, but I have two left feet.
5. Marika was sent on a wild-goose chase looking for that special fabric.
6. If she does not find a job soon, she will get a real wake-up call when she cannot pay her bills.
7. Not having a back-up plan proved to be a real thorn in my side.
8. He is nothing but a yellow-bellied loser.
9. Lindsay decided to marry him, warts and all.
10. Although Dakota is making millions now, she was quite the ugly duckling as a child.

Chapter 20 Review Quizzes

Vocabulary Review Quiz

Directions: Write the definition of the vocabulary word on the line.

1. bawl _____

2. civilize _____

3. effigy _____

4. flux _____

5. horror _____

6. loathing _____

7. modus operandi _____

8. posterior _____

9. stomp _____

10. vagrant _____

Idiom Definitions

Directions: Select the correct definition, and write the letter of the answer on the line to the right of the number.

1. _____ To put the cart before the horse means _____.
   a. to plan ahead
   b. to do things in the wrong order
   c. to make something out of nothing
   d. none of the above

2. _____ Which of the following is NOT an idiom?
   a. row your boat
   b. it is raining cats and dogs
   c. the lion's share
   d. the black sheep of the family

3. _____ Which of the following is NOT an idiom?
   a. to bite the dust
   b. kick the bucket
   c. bite the bullet
   d. take me to the mall

4. _____ Which of the following is an idiom?
   a. weigh it on the scale
   b. a swarm of bees
   c. a hornet's nest
   d. everything is blue

5. _____ *To face the music* means to_____.
   a. face up to your punishment
   b. listen to it carefully to hear the melody
   c. escort the boy to the office
   d. none of the above

6. _____ *Wet behind the ears* means to_____.
   a. young and innocent
   b. old and experienced
   c. temperamental
   d. crabby

7. _____ Which of the following is NOT an idiom?
   a. wild-goose chase
   b. to leave high and dry
   c. father, man, host, count, rooster
   d. to turn over a new leaf

8. _____ True or False? Idioms are strange figures of speech.
   a. True
   b. False

9. _____ Someone who is *yellow-bellied* is_____.
   a. a friend
   b. a coward
   c. brave
   d. a loser

10. _____ A *hat trick* is _____.
   a. three successes in a row
   b. a losing streak
   c. a card game
   d. none of the above

Idioms

Directions: Write sentences using the idioms shown on the lines below.

EXAMPLE:

Birthday suit: <u>Make sure you take a robe to the sauna, you do not want to get caught in your birthday suit in front of strangers.</u>

1. To put one's foot in one's mouth _____

2. To go Dutch _____

3. To bite the dust _____

4. Go to pot _____

5. A rule of thumb _____

6. Take it with a grain of salt _____

7. Skeleton in one's closet _____

8. The straw that broke the camel's back _____

9. Double-edged sword _____

10. The writing's on the wall _____

11. Warts and all _____

12. Dog days _____

13. The die is cast _____

14. Set in stone _____

15. Rub shoulders with _____

16. To get cold feet _____

17. Cold shoulder _____

18. A piece of cake _____

19. The black sheep _____

20. Off the beaten track _____

Real-World Practice Activities

Reading and Listening

Directions: This is going to be a more-challenging assignment. Because idioms are seldom used in formal language, you will need to pay attention to conversations and entertainment television and radio broadcasts. Over the next week or so, listen for idioms. There are hundreds of them. After reviewing the idioms in this chapter, you will recognize them when you hear them. Idioms are odd little sayings. Try your best to read/hear ten (10) of them and write them on the lines below. If they are new to you, look them up in a dictionary or online.

1. _____
2. _____
3. _____
4. _____
5. _____
6. _____
7. _____
8. _____
9. _____
10. _____

Writing

Directions: Using some of the idioms that you discover, write a one-paragraph story that may or may not make sense. Have fun with it.

_____
_____
_____
_____
_____
_____
_____
_____
_____
_____

Chapter 21

ALLUSIONS

Allusions are references to a variety of different things that readers will encounter almost every day. Like the idioms that we explored in the previous chapter, allusions are often unique to a language or culture. For instance, in the English language, nursery rhymes or fairy tales are often referred to in a reading. One such curious little rhyme is *Humpty Dumpty sat on a wall, Humpty Dumpty had a great fall. All the King's horses and all the King's men couldn't put Humpty together again.* Unless you were exposed to these strange little ditties as a child in an English-speaking country, the possibility exists that the meaning or significance of the reference might escape you and leave you confused. However, like idioms, there are hundreds of allusions in many different categories (literary, Biblical, Latin, Greek, mythological, popular culture, and so on.) Covering them all would be nearly impossible. Therefore, the goal of this chapter is to provide a broad exposure to allusions.

Vocabulary Development

1. **aloha** (a low ha) A Hawaiian word that means hello or good-bye.
2. **bauble** (baw bul) A showy trinket or toy of little or no value.
3. **countrified** (cun tri fyd) Rural or rustic.
4. **expletive** (ecks ple tiv) A swear word or other expression used in an exclamation.
5. **giddy** (gid dee) Having a sensation of whirling or spinning; overexcited.
6. **insular** (inn soo lar) Separate or remote; of or like an island.
7. **ogle** (o gul) To eye lecherously or amorously.
8. **poker** (po ker) A card game in which a bluff is used as players bet on the game.
9. **rotisserie** (row tis ser ee) An appliance with a rotating spit for roasting or barbecuing meat.
10. **shard** (shard) A broken piece of pottery or glass.

Literary Allusions

A broad variety of literary allusions are in English, ranging from various characters to nursery rhymes to classic literature. Nursery rhymes are written in italics and noted with an (NR).

- Ahab—Captain from Herman Melville's *Moby Dick*. He is obsessed with the capture of the great white whale.
- Aladdin's lamp—refers to magic from a lamp in the *Arabian Nights*.
- Alger, Horatio Jr.—An author who is known for his writings of characters who begin as poor boys but through much hard work and diligence become successful. Typically referred to as a "Horatio Alger story."
- *Baa, baa black sheep,/Have you any wool?/Yes sir, yes sir,/Three bags full./One for my master,/and one for my dame,/and one for the little boy who lives down the lane.* (NR)
- Bard of Avon—a name for Shakespeare, one of the most respected and well-known writers of the English language.
- Big Bad Wolf—enemy of the *Three Pigs* who threatens to "huff and to puff and to blow their house down."
- *Catch-22*—a war novel written by Joseph Heller from where the figurative phrase "*catch-22*" comes; referring to any situation that puts someone in a double bind no matter what they do.
- Cheshire Cat—alluding to Lewis Carroll's *Alice's Adventures in Wonderland*. The cat has a long-lasting and rather mischievous smile.
- *Dr. Jekyll and Mr. Hyde, The Strange Case of*—a novel by Robert Louis Stevenson with a character who has a dual personality (good and evil).
- Dracula—vampire character from the novel of the same title.
- *Et tu, Brute?*—a Latin sentence that means "even you Brutus," which is the last thing that Julius Caesar said before he died. He is shocked that his friend has had a hand in his murder.
- *Face that launched a thousand ships, Was this the*—a line from the play *Doctor Faustus* by Christopher Marlowe; referring to Helen of Troy, the most beautiful woman in history and the cause of the Trojan War.
- *Goldilocks and the Three Bears*—a children's story about a girl who wanders into the bears' house and eats their porridge, sits in their chairs, and sleeps in their beds.
- Grinch—from the Dr. Seuss story *How the Grinch Stole Christmas*. A Grinch is someone who is stingy and unpleasant and who ruins everyone's fun.
- *Hey diddle diddle/The cat and the fiddle,/The cow jumped over the moon;/The little dog laughed/To see such sport/And the dish ran away with the spoon.* (NR)
- *Hickory, dickory, dock,/The mouse ran up the clock,/The clock struck one,/The mouse ran down;/Hickory, dickory, dock.* (NR)
- Hook, Captain—the villain in the play *Peter Pan*.
- Huck Finn—title character of Mark Twain's novel *The Adventures of Huckleberry Finn*. Huck is a boy who runs away and rafts down the Mississippi River with an African-American runaway slave named Jim.
- Iago—mean, evil, and conniving character from Shakespeare's play *Othello*.
- *Jack be nimble;/Jack be quick;/Jack, jump over the candlestick.* (NR)
- *Jack and Jill went up the hill,/To fetch a pail of water;/Jack fell down, and broke his crown,/And Jill came tumbling after.* (NR)

- *Jack Sprat could eat no fat;/His wife could eat no lean,/And so betwixt them both,/They licked the platter clean.* (NR)

- Lilliput—the land that Gulliver, the title character from Jonathan Swift's writing called *Gulliver's Travels*. The people of Lilliput are only 6 inches (15 cm) tall.

- *Little Bo-Peep has lost her sheep,/And can't tell where to find them;/Leave them alone, and they'll come home,/Wagging their tails behind them.* (NR)

- *Little Boy Blue, come blow your horn,/The sheep's in the meadow, the cow's in the corn;/But where is the boy who looks after the sheep?/He's under the haystack fast asleep.* (NR)

- *Little Jack Horner sat in the corner,/Eating his Christmas pie;/He put in his thumb, and pulled out a plum,/And said "What a good boy am I!"* (NR)

- *Little Miss Muffet/Sat on a tuffet,/Eating some curds and whey./Along came a spider,/And sat down beside her,/And frightened Miss Muffet away.* (NR)

- Mrs. Malaprop—a character from a play called *The Rivals* who is constantly mixing up words, now referred to as malapropisms.

- *Mary Mary quite contrary,/How does your garden grow?/With silver bells and cockle shells,/And pretty maids all in a row.* (NR)

- Mitty, Walter—a character from the short story written by James Thurber of a man who is repressed and ordinary but dreams of doing great things.

- *Mother Goose Rhymes*—most of the (NR) listed are from this children's book of rhymes. The author of the rhymes is unknown.

- Neverland (or Never-Never Land)—the home of Peter Pan from the play of the same name, it is a place where children never grow up.

- *Old Mother Hubbard/went to the cupboard/To fetch her poor dog a bone;/And when she got there/the cupboard was bare,/And so the poor dog had none.* (NR)

- *Parting is such sweet sorrow*—line from Shakespeare's play *Romeo and Juliet*.

- *Peter Piper picked a peck of pickled peppers. How many pecks of pickled peppers did Peter Piper pick?* (NR)

- Rip Van Winkle—the title character from a story by Washington Irving. The man goes to sleep for 20 years and wakes up to find that everything has changed.

- Robin Hood—title character about a man and his band of merry men who steal from the rich and give to the poor.

- Shylock—a merciless money lender from Shakespeare's play *The Merchant of Venice* who demands a pound of flesh cut from the merchant who defaults on a loan.

- *Simple Simon met a pieman/Going to the fair:/Says Simple Simon to the pieman,/"Let me taste your ware."/Says the pieman to Simple Simon,/"Show me first your penny,"/Says Simple Simon to the pieman,/"Indeed I have not any."* (NR)

- *Star-crossed lovers*—a phrase from *Romeo and Juliet* referring to the doomed relationship between a couple whose parents dislike each other.

- *There was an old woman who lived in a shoe./She had so many children, she didn't know what to do./She gave them all broth, without any bread,/Then whipped them all soundly, and sent them to bed.* (NR)

- *Thirty days hath September, April, June and November: All the rest have thirty-one, except February that stands alone with twenty-eight days and twenty-nine at Leap Year.* A rhyme to help remember the number of days in each month.

- *To be or not to be*—well-known quote from Shakespeare's play *Hamlet.*

- *Wizard of Oz*—well-known story about Dorothy who is carried off by a tornado to the Land of Oz. She meets many interesting characters, including the Scarecrow, the Cowardly Lion, and the Tin Man and eventually gets back to Kansas with a pair of magic red shoes.

- Yahoos—the crude and uncouth "brutes" from the land of the Houyhnhnms in Jonathan Swift's *Gulliver's Travels* and who represent the worst side of human nature. A yahoo is an uncouth and ill-mannered person.

Practice I

Directions: Identify the source of the following allusions. Write the name of the source or an explanation of the character on the line provided.

EXAMPLE:

___Robin Hood___   A man and his band of merry men who steal from the rich and give to the poor

1. _____   *To be or not to be.*

2. _____   The woman who continually mixes up words and misspeaks

3. _____   *There was an old woman who lived in a shoe . . . .*

4. _____   Captain Ahab

5. _____   Yahoos

6. _____   Cheshire Cat

7. _____   The story of an oppressed man who dreams of doing something great someday

8. _____   The story of a boy who works his way up from poor to rich

9. _____   The Bard of Avon

10. _____   The place where children never grow up

Mythological and Folkloric Allusions

These include major characters, gods and goddess, and various events from Greek, Roman, and other areas of the world. In the English language, Greek and Roman gods were often referred to in writings, especially in earlier writings such as those of Shakespeare, Marlowe, and beyond. Learning Latin and Greek and also classical literature was part of a young man's education. (Girls were not allowed to attend school, and any education they received was at home.)

- Achilles—great Greek warrior, with a weak spot, his Achilles heel.
- Adonis—extraordinarily good-looking boy
- Amazons—tribe of warrior women
- Aphrodite—Greek goddess of love and beauty
- Apollo—god of poetry, prophecy, medicine, and light
- Argonauts—companions of Jason who search for the golden fleece
- Athena—goddess of wisdom
- Blarney Stone—a stone/rock in Ireland that legend holds that those who kiss it will be blessed with the gift of gab (talking/eloquence)
- Bunyun, Paul—American/Canadian legendary giant lumberjack
- Charon—the boatman who carried the souls of the dead across the River Styx and into Hades, the underworld
- Cinderella—fairy tale of a beautiful young girl with a wicked step mother and stepsisters
- Cupid—god of love
- Cyclops—one-eyed giant
- Daedalus—designer of the labyrinth in mythology; a symbol of inventiveness
- Diana—goddess of the hunt and the Moon
- Elysian Fields—the place where the souls of the good went; a place of supreme happiness and bliss
- Eros—god of love
- Godiva, Lady—legend of an English noblewoman who rides naked on horseback, covered, only by her long hair
- Grim Reaper—a cloaked, solemn-looking man who carries a scythe and takes the lives of people as though he is harvesting grain
- Groundhog Day (February 2)—if the groundhog who comes out of his hole sees his shadow, then there will be six more weeks of winter
- Hades—god of the underworld
- Hansel and Gretel—a fairy tale about a boy and girl who are going to be eaten by a witch
- Helen of Troy—the most beautiful woman in history for whom the entire Greek army sailed to get her back; her abduction was the cause of the Trojan War
- Hercules—strongest man on Earth
- Icarus—by using artificial wings to escape the labyrinth, he flew too close to the Sun and the wax holding the feathers together melted and he fell to his death
- Io—one of the many maidens seduced by Zeus and who eventually escaped to Egypt
- Janus—Roman god of doors and gateways, new beginnings
- Jason—a man with a checkered life who lived many adventures while looking for the golden fleece with his friends the Argonauts
- Jupiter—the most powerful god in Roman mythology; his equal is Zeus in Greek mythology

- Labyrinth—a maze built on the island of Crete by Daedalus, who was kept in the maze until he escaped with his son Icarus
- Leda and the swan—the story of the rape of a queen of Sparta by Zeus, who had taken the form of a swan
- Leprechauns—in the folklore of Ireland, these are little men who are capable of revealing the location of buried treasure
- *Little Red Riding Hood*—a fairy tale of a little girl wearing a red-hooded cloak who visits her grandmother and finds a wolf disguised as her grandmother instead
- Medusa—anyone who looks at this monster turns to stone
- Mercury—messenger of the gods, someone who is quick, very fast
- Narcissus—a young man who, while looking at his reflection in a pond, fell in love with himself, we call those who are self-absorbed narcissists
- Odysseus—Greek hero from the Trojan War who wandered for ten years trying to return home
- Oedipus—the king who unknowingly killed his father and married his mother, one of the Theban plays by Sophocles
- Olympus, Mount—the highest mountain in Greece and the home of the Greek and Roman gods
- Pan—the Greek god of flocks, forests, meadows, and shepherds; he is depicted with a reed pipe, horns, and the feet of a goat
- Pandora's box—a curious woman opened a box that she was instructed not to open and all the evils of the world flew out, hence the common saying that to open Pandora's box will cause a grievous situation
- Pegasus—a winged horse
- Phoenix—a mythical bird that upon occasion would burn itself to death and then proceed to rise from the ashes
- Pluto—the Roman name for the god of the underworld
- Poseidon—the Greek god of the sea
- Prometheus—the Titan who stole fire from the gods and gave it to humans
- Pygmalion—a sculptor who hated women but fell in love with a statue that he made of one and prayed to Venus to help him find a woman like it, and she brought the statue to life
- Quetzalcoatl—represented as a plumed serpent, he is the god of nature to Native-American tribes in Mexico
- Romulus and Remus—twin brothers who were raised by a she-wolf and founded the city of Rome
- Saturn—the Roman name for one of the Titans, the father of Zeus
- Scylla and Charybdis—Scylla, was a six-headed monster who lived on a rock on one side of a narrow strait, and Charybdis was a whirlpool on the other side; when ships tried to pass through, they would be seized, which is what is referred to when you are "caught between a rock and a hard spot" (or between two difficult situations)

- Sirens—evil creatures who sang in beautiful voices to lure sailors to shipwreck and their deaths
- Sisyphus—punished for offending Zeus, he was forced to roll a boulder up a hill and once it was almost at the top, it would roll back down and he would have to begin again, the labor of Sisyphus"
- *Sleeping Beauty*—a fairy tale about a beautiful young woman who is put into a deep sleep by a jealous fairy/witch but who is awakened eventually with the kiss of a young prince
- *Snow White and the Seven Dwarfs*—another wicked stepmother and deep-sleep story, Snow White hides in the forest to avoid her wicked stepmother and finds herself in the cottage of the seven dwarfs
- Sphinx—a winged monster with the head of a woman and the body of a lion
- Styx—one of the rivers in Hades that Charon had to cross carrying the souls of the dead
- Tell, William—hero of Switzerland famous for his archery skills and who was forced to shoot an apple off of his son's head
- Thor—god of thunder in Norse mythology
- Tiresias—blind prophet who revealed the truth about Oedipus
- Titans—rulers of the universe until they were overthrown by Zeus
- *Tortoise and the Hare*—one of Aesop's fables (there are many) that tells of a race between the tortoise and the hare; of course, the hare, knowing he would win, fools around and does not focus and the tortoise, who plods away diligently, wins the race (there is a moral to the story, can you guess it?)
- Trojan Horse—a hollow horse made by the Greeks that held soldiers; it was left at the gates as a gift to the Trojans who accepted it with open arms; once they had fallen asleep, the Greek soldiers opened up the horse, sacked the city, and won the Trojan War
- Trolls—from Norse mythology, these are ugly little dwarfs who live in caves, steal children and property, and hate any kind of noise
- Troy—the site of the Trojan War
- *Ugly Duckling*—a children's story by Hans Christian Anderson of a young bird who is made fun of constantly because he is so ugly but who eventually turns into a beautiful swan
- Unicorn—small, horselike creature with a horn growing out of its forehead
- Vampire—a corpse who leaves its coffin at night to suck blood from a victim
- Venus—goddess of love and beauty
- Werewolves—human beings who are transformed into wolves and who prowl at night, dig up graves, and eat babies
- Zephyr—god of the west wind
- Zeus—the chief god who defeated the Titans

Practice II

Directions: Matching—write the letter of the definition of the character, concepts, or place on the line to the left of the entry.

EXAMPLE:

   A   Venus   A. goddess of beauty

1. _____ Elysian Fields   A. Chief god who conquered the Titans
2. _____ Adonis   B. Goddess of love and beauty
3. _____ Trojan Horse   C. Giant lumberjack
4. _____ Zeus   D. Boatman who carried souls of the dead
5. _____ Labyrinth   E. God of love
6. _____ Mercury   F. Killed his father/married his mother
7. _____ Aphrodite   G. Hollow horse with hidden soldiers
8. _____ Paul Bunyun   H. Fell in love with his reflection
9. _____ Icarus   I. Where the souls of good people went
10. _____ Scylla/Charybdis   J. Ugly dwarfs who hate noise
11. _____ Charon   K. Ugly duck/beautiful swan
12. _____ Eros   L. Founders of Rome
13. _____ Medusa   M. A very fast messenger of the gods
14. _____ Oedipus   N. River in Hades or the underworld
15. _____ Ugly Duckling   O. Son of Daedalus who flew to the Sun
16. _____ Trolls   P. Stole fire from the gods/gave to humans
17. _____ Styx   Q. An extraordinarily handsome man/boy
18. _____ Prometheus   R. Anyone who looks at her turns to stone
19. _____ Romulus/Remus   S. Monster and a whirlpool
20. _____ Narcissus   T. A maze designed by Daedalus

Biblical Allusions

Just as allusions to mythology is/were common in the English language because it was a part of a classical education, so too are references to the Bible. In the past, the Bible was one of the few (sometimes the only) books that the majority of people had in their possession. As you read more and more English and American literature, you will experience many references to Biblical characters and events. The following is a brief sampling. Again, there are hundreds of them—too many to list here.

- Adam and Eve—the first man and woman created as noted in the book of Genesis
- Angels—spirits who live in Heaven with God
- Apocalypse—a final catastrophe from the New Testament
- Apostles—twelve men chosen by Jesus to spread the gospel after his death
- Babel—the tower being built to reach to heaven, but God confused the languages of the men building it and the task was left unfinished; that is how different languages began
- Babylon—a place of sin and corruption
- Burning bush—God revealed Himself to Moses through a burning bush that was not consumed by the fire
- Cain and Abel—sons of Adam and Eve; Cain killed Abel and was exiled
- Coat of many colors—the coat that Jacob gave to his son Joseph, which made his other sons envious
- Creation—the beginning of the world, which took six days and the seventh day was considered a day of rest
- Crown of thorns—crown made of thorn branches that Jesus was forced to wear before the crucifixion
- Damascus—an ancient city in Syria where "on the road to Damascus," the apostle Paul underwent a dramatic conversion and now refers to a turning point in one's life
- Daniel in the lions' den—thrown into a den of lions to be eaten for his belief in God, Daniel was spared and emerged from the den unharmed
- David—a small boy who was granted permission to fight the giant Goliath, a Philistine warrior; David killed Goliath with a rock from a sling shot
- Eden—the beautiful garden containing the tree of life where God had intended Adam and Eve to live in peace
- Exodus—led by Moses, the Exodus describes the departure of the Israelites from slavery in Egypt and the plagues that they endured
- Golden Rule—do unto others as you would have them do unto you, from the Sermon on the Mount
- Hebrew—the language of the Hebrews in which the Old Testament was written
- Jacob's ladder—a ladder that Jacob saw in a dream of God, who stood at the top of the ladder and promised to bless Jacob and to bring his descendants into the Promised Land
- Job—a man whose faith was severely tested by Satan but who remained steadfast in his beliefs and would not curse God; God rewarded Job by giving him twice as much as he had before; anyone who endures any long suffering is considered to have the "patience of Job"
- John the Baptist—a hermit and preacher who baptized followers of Jesus and who was beheaded at the wish of Salome, the daughter of Herod the ruler of Galilee
- Jonah and the whale—the story of a man who refused God's wish to become a prophet; while at sea, God raised a storm and Jonah was swallowed by a whale where he lived for three days; once the whale vomited him up on dry land, Jonah accepted God's mission for him

- Joseph—the husband of Mary, Jesus's mother
- Judas Iscariot—the disciple who betrayed Jesus
- Last Supper—a Passover meal that Jesus ate with his disciples the night before he was crucified
- Lazarus—a man raised from the dead by Jesus
- Loaves and fishes—the feeding of thousands of hungry followers by Jesus, who multiplied the five loaves of bread and two fish to satisfy everyone's hunger
- Lucifer—another name for Satan
- Magi—the wise men who visited Jesus shortly after he was born
- Mary—mother of Jesus
- Mary Magdalene—a cursed woman who became a follower of Jesus
- Messiah—the anointed one; Christians believe that the Messiah is Jesus; the Jews do not believe that the Messiah has arrived yet
- Moses—a great leader and prophet of the Israelites who, after forty years of wandering, led his people to the Promised Land
- Nazareth—the hometown of Jesus
- Noah and the Flood—Noah was commanded to build an ark that would accommodate his family and two of every creature on Earth; it rained for forty days and nights, destroying everything except those on the ark
- Olive branch—the branch brought by the dove to Noah's ark, which was a sign that the Flood was receding; it is now regarded as a sign of peace
- Original sin—the eating of the forbidden fruit by Adam and Eve, which led to their exile from the Garden of Eden
- Philistines—enemies of the Israelites; a Philistine has come to mean that a person is uncultured and ignorant
- Promised Land—the land that God promised to the descendants of Abraham, Isaac, and Jacob; a land flowing with milk and honey
- Parting of the Red Sea—an act of God to help Moses and his people escape from Egypt and from the forces in pursuit of them
- Sabbath—day of rest, which is Saturday among the Jews
- Samson and Delilah—a man with incredible strength but whose strength lies in his uncut hair; he was betrayed by his lover Delilah, who cut his hair while he was sleeping and then called the Philistines, who then captured him
- Satan—the devil, Lucifer
- Sodom and Gomorrah—two evil cities that were destroyed by fire and brimstone (sulfur); God sent his angels in the form of men to warn them to leave, but they found only one good man, named Lot; they warned Lot not to look back or be turned into a pillar of salt; Lot's wife looked back, and she was turned into a pillar of salt

- Song of Solomon—a collection of poems about sexual love and courtship that have been interpreted as allegories of God's love for Israel; they are attributed to Solomon, a Hebrew king and son of David
- Ten Commandments—the commandments that were engraved on stone tablets given to Moses on Mount Sinai
- Tree of knowledge of good and evil—the tree from which Adam and Eve ate the forbidden fruit
- Walking on water—a miraculous feat performed by Jesus to catch up with his disciples who had left in a ship ahead of him

Practice III

Directions: Using the Word Bank below, write the name of the person or the event on the line that matches its definition. The words from the word bank will be used only once.

EXAMPLE:

  Sodom and Gomorrah   Two evil cities destroyed by fire and brimstone.

1. _____ Wise men who visited Jesus shortly after he was born

2. _____ Brought by a bird to Noah's ark as a sign that the Flood was receding

3. _____ Swallowed by a whale

4. _____ Beheaded at the request of Salome

5. _____ Do unto others as you would have them do unto you

6. _____ Killed the giant Goliath

7. _____ Enemies of the Israelites; ignorant and uncultured people

8. _____ Betrayed by Delilah, who cut his hair

9. _____ Sons of Adam and Eve

10. _____ A man with great patience

Word Bank: Philistines, Jonah, Job, David, Samson, Magi, John the Baptist, Cain and Abel, olive branch, the Golden Rule

Chapter 21 Review Quizzes

Vocabulary Review Quiz

Directions: Write the definition of the vocabulary word on the line.

1. aloha _____

2. bauble _____

3. countrified _____

4. expletive _____

5. giddy _____

6. insular _____

7. ogle _____

8. poker _____

9. rotisserie _____

10. shard _____

Allusion Definitions

Directions: Select the correct definition, and write the letter of the answer on the line to the right of the number.

1. _____   An allusion is a _____ in a piece of literature
   a. reference to a myth, historic event, and so on
   b. question
   c. comment about a catastrophe
   d. none of the above

2. _____   Which of the following is NOT an allusion to a nursery rhyme?
   a. Mary had a little lamb
   b. Humpty Dumpty
   c. The old woman in the shoe
   d. John the Baptist

3. _____ Which of the following is NOT an allusion to mythology?
   a. Icarus
   b. Humpty Dumpty
   c. Zeus
   d. Mercury

4. _____ Which of the following is a Biblical allusion?
   a. Job
   b. Burning bush
   c. Adam and Eve
   d. all of the above

5. _____ The hollow horse filled with soldiers is the _____ .
   a. ghostly horse
   b. Trojan Horse
   c. unicorn
   d. none of the above

6. _____ The Bard of Avon is a reference to _____ .
   a. James Baldwin
   b. T. S. Eliot
   c. Chaucer
   d. Shakespeare

7. _____ Which of the following is NOT an allusion?
   a. Wild-goose chase
   b. *Catch-22*
   c. Baa, baa black sheep
   d. Horatio Alger

8. _____ True or False? Allusions are references found in various pieces of literature.
   a. True
   b. False

9. _____ A story about a young girl and three bears is titled_____.
   a. *Little Red Riding Hood*
   b. *Cinderella*
   c. *Goldilocks and the Three Bears*
   d. *Hamlet*

10. _____ An evil, conniving, and contemptuous character in Shakespeare's play *Othello* is _____.
   a. Solomon
   b. Iago
   c. Samuel Johnson
   d. Jane Eyre

Allusions

Directions: Write the meanings or the references to the allusions on the lines below. The answers in the word bank will be used only once.

EXAMPLE:

    Judas Iscariot   *a disciple who betrayed Jesus*

1. _____ *Et tu, Brute?*
2. _____ A bloodthirsty vampire
3. _____ The goddess of the hunt and the moon
4. _____ Protected Noah, his family, and the animals
5. _____ *Sleeping Beauty*
6. _____ *Humpty Dumpty*
7. _____ Grew up to be a beautiful swan
8. _____ *Parting is such sweet sorrow*
9. _____ Shot an arrow off of his son's head
10. _____ A tale from Aesop about a race

> **Word Bank:** Diana, William Tell, a fairy tale, quote from *Romeo and Juliet,* last words of Julius Caesar, Tortoise and the Hare, a nursery rhyme, Count Dracula, Noah's Ark, the Ugly Duckling

Real-World Practice Activities

Reading and Writing

Directions: Locate an article or a book of Aesop's Fables. Skim through the book or article first, and then choose one or two of the fables to read. Write a summary about one of the two fables. What is the moral of the story? Is the story applicable to everyday life?

_____

_____

_____

_____

_____

_____

_____

_____
_____
_____
_____
_____
_____
_____
_____
_____
_____
_____
_____
_____
_____
_____

Listening

Directions: Take time to listen for allusions. During the course of the day, whether it is on television, in a film, on the radio, or in the lyrics of a song, someone will mention an allusion. It may not be to a piece of literature or to mythology or to the Bible—it could be to a political event (Watergate), a historical event (the Vietnam War), or a famous person or celebrity (Paris Hilton). Begin listening for allusions, and write them down when you hear them. If you are not certain of its history, research the background.

_____
_____
_____
_____
_____
_____
_____
_____
_____
_____

STUDY SKILLS, READING AND WRITING IMPROVEMENT

Being able to focus on studying and improving reading and writing involve understanding a few basic principles and applying them to life. In this chapter, we will focus on tips that will help in all of the areas. Some of them will work for you, others will not. Give them a try, and see if things improve in areas that you might need improving.

Vocabulary Development

1. **ail** (ail) To be sick or ill.
2. **bald** (bald) Hairless, without hair.
3. **cent** (cent) A penny, one hundredth of a dollar.
4. **mourning** (morn ing) Remembering the dead.
5. **neigh** (nay) Sound of a horse.
6. **precedents** (pres i dents) An established course of action.
7. **queue** (kue) A line or series of people waiting their turn.
8. **wade** (wade) Walk in shallow water.
9. **whine** (wine) An annoying cry or request for something.
10. **yolk** (yoke) The yellow part of the egg.

Study Skills

Setting up a quiet place to study is the first thing to do. Then work at focusing on each subject.

Studying

- Find a quiet place to study with a desk, plenty of light, and few distractions.
- Turn off the television, cell phones, and so on, and limit interruptions.
- Gather all of the materials that you need—paper, pens, pencils, dictionary, and so on.
- Be positive.
- Set goals. What are you trying to accomplish—short term and long term?
- Be flexible and realistic.
- Know your assignments—what are they and when are they due?
- Plan ahead. Get a calendar, and schedule specific time periods for working on each class or project.
- Do not forget to schedule outside activities/jobs as well.
- Stick to the plan—do NOT procrastinate.
- Prioritize tasks—complete what is most important first.
- Break larger tasks into smaller pieces/chunks, and complete each smaller piece before moving on to the next.
- Work on the most difficult or time-consuming tasks first (while you are fresh).

Listening and Taking Notes in Class

- Be prepared with paper/pens/pencils.
- Keep focused on the teacher and what he/she is saying—be attentive.
- Listen for cue words such as "the most important point" or "remember."
- Write down what is written on the board.
- Write a "?" next to any information that you need to clarify later.
- Review your notes and rewrite if necessary.

Remembering Information

- Use mnemonics—word associations, alliteration, rhymes, songs, and so on to master a sizeable amount of information that you need to remember.
- Invent an acronym (a word formed from the first letter of several words—BRICK = black, red, indigo, coral, and khaki).

Strategies for Taking Tests

- Review material at least three times, and avoid cramming the night before.
- Get a good night's sleep.
- Eat a good breakfast with protein (protein is brain food), and avoid foods high in sugar.
- Arrive on time—or earlier; try not to be hurried or rushed.
- Relax, take a deep breath, and focus.
- Look at the entire exam to see what you have to do and in what time period.
- Read the instructions carefully—do not risk assuming that you know what to do. (What if the instructor writes, "After you have read these instructions, put your pen down and wait quietly until the end of the period, and you will get an automatic *A*")?
- If it is a multiple-choice test, eliminate obvious wrong answers. If the correct answer does not jump out at you, rely on intuition.
- Avoid changing answers later; often your first choice is correct.
- For essay exams, brainstorm, think ahead, and organize your thoughts before jumping into an essay. Structure is important.
- Make sure you have a good thesis statement and will be able to prove it.

Practice I

Directions: Write ten (10) study skill tips on the lines below.

EXAMPLE:

Find a quiet place to study.

1. _____
2. _____
3. _____
4. _____
5. _____
6. _____
7. _____
8. _____
9. _____
10. _____

Reading Skills

Improving reading skills is a lifelong process. Reading thick, jargon-laden textbooks in high school and college is a fact of life and can seem overwhelming. It does not have to be, though. Follow the suggestions below, and life in the reading world will go much smoother.

Reading Comprehension and Improvement

- Visualize as you read. Imagine drawing a picture of what you are reading, sentence by sentence.

- Do not read words individually; consume them as groups (sentences to several lines and eventually a paragraph). The more you practice this visualization technique, the more you will be able to grasp larger portions of text and understand it.

- Use your finger or a bookmark to help you to read faster; do not tediously linger by reading each word slowly.

- Use visualization techniques to help comprehension.
  - Just as you might use a brainstorming web for writing an essay, use a similar web for reading.
  - Draw a circle, and write the chapter heading in the center of it.
  - Draw branches of the web with each new idea or subheading that is introduced in the text. Add important notes to these branches as you read.

- Be positive.

- Become motivated—look at reading as a simple hoop to jump through to get to the next level, not as drudgery.

- Find a good place to read. Make sure that you are not too hungry or that you bring a healthy snack (protein is brain food—nuts, peanut butter sandwich, cheese, and so on).

- Reading nonfiction is vital—newspapers or news magazines are written at a higher reading level for the most part.

- Reading nonfiction will help vocabulary skills.

- Oftentimes novels or other fictional pieces of literature have intentional grammatical errors and dialogue that is confusing to second language learners.

Strategies for Reading Textbooks or Other Nonfiction Works

- If you are reading for a class such as history, science, or math, know the assignment, the due date, and what exactly is needed from the reading.

- Gather any materials you may need to complete the assignment: paper, sticky notes, highlighters, pens, pencils, handouts, dictionary, and so on.

- Be prepared and focused—know what your learning goals are.

- Avoid distractions (such as television, telephones, your little brother, and so on).
- Get the big picture first. Skim the chapter, and look at titles, subheadings, any words in boldface type, photographs and their captions, graphs, and any questions at the end of the chapter.
- Once you have the big picture in mind, go back and begin the actual reading.
    - o Read actively and quickly.
    - o Participate with the text.
    - o If it helps, read out loud.
    - o Read through the entire assignment.
    - o If you need to reread a confusing portion, go ahead.
- After reviewing for the big picture and reading fairly quickly, go back and re-review.
    - o Look at passages within the big picture—where is this information taking you?
    - o If you own the book, underline or highlight as you read.
    - o If it is not your book, use sticky notes to mark areas that you might want to review later or need to remember.
- Go back a third time.
    - o Make a rough outline of the chapter using headings, subheadings, and boldface words for the outline.
    - o Draw pictures; make flashcards, whatever it is that helps you remember information, just do it. Become an active participant with your textbook.

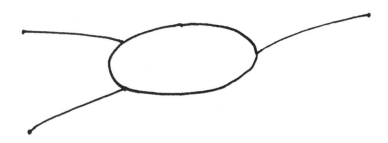

Strategies for Reading Novels

- A novel is more complex than a short story.
- In a novel, there is a better-developed plot and characters. It is intended to entertain, instruct, or amuse the reader.
- To understand novels, the reader must understand how they are written.
- Setting is the time and place of the story. Determine when and where the story takes place. It could take place in the future, past, or present. It could be set in the city, in the countryside, on Mars, or under the ocean.

- Be aware of characters as they appear in the story. Keep mental notes (or notes on paper) of each of them.
  o Determine who is the protagonist (the main character) and the antagonist (someone who goes against the main character—it could be another person, an idea, or an emotion).
  o If there are a number of characters, force yourself to keep them straight.
  o Separate the main characters from the minor characters in your mind.
- Events or plot—keep track of the events in the story.
- How does the story evolve?
- Are there many stories interwoven into the plot or is the plot focused around the happenings of one character?
- Identify the problem or conflict and the solution (denouement) at the end of the novel. What exactly is going on, and how is the situation resolved?
- Sometimes it helps to investigate the background information of the author. When was the novel written? Was there something going on historically when the author wrote the book such as the French Revolution or industrialization?
- Examine the author's style of writing.
- Does the style of writing seem modern and succinct (to the point), or are the passages laden with detail?

Strategies for Reading Poems

- Poems are intended to be heard and not read silently. However, if reading a poem aloud is not possible (or embarrassing when you are in a public place), then read visually (draw images in your mind).
- Read through the entire poem. Do not stop to try to analyze—read for the big picture or general image.
- Read the poem a second time, slowly and purposefully.
- Examine individual words, punctuation, and space. How does the poet lay the poem out on paper—stanzas—lots of white space—varied line lengths?)
- Read the poem again and again, as many times as you need to understand it.
- Some poems are more complex and metaphorical, while others are to the point and express an idea or purpose clearly. That is the interesting thing about poetry. There are many styles and hundreds of ways to express something.

Good Readers Continually Improve Their Vocabulary

- Write unfamiliar words in a word log.
- Try to learn word meanings through context. How are they used in the sentence?

- Look up unfamiliar words in a dictionary.
- Use them in your conversation or in journal writing.

Practice II

Directions: Write a variety of reading improvement tips as suggested on the lines below.

EXAMPLE:

Improving vocabulary: <u>Keep a log of unfamiliar words that you can look up later and study</u>.

1. Reading comprehension: _____

_____

2. Reading comprehension: _____

_____

3. Reading novels: _____

_____

4. Reading nonfiction: _____

_____

5. Reading nonfiction: _____

_____

6. Reading nonfiction: _____

_____

7. Improving vocabulary: _____

_____

8. Reading poems: _____

_____

9. Reading poems: _____

_____

10. Reading novels: _____

_____

Writing Skills

General Writing Tips

The following suggestions will help all of your writing assignments. Various types of academic writings will be introduced in the following chapter.

- Vary sentence beginnings—there are thousands of words in the English language, so there is no need to repeat the same word at the beginning of each sentence. The only time a writer might repeat a sentence beginning is to make a point or draw attention to something, which is called echoing.

- Vary sentence length—to make your writing more interesting, vary the lengths of your sentences; 5-word, 8-word, 10-word, 7-word, and even a 1-word sentence now and then will make your writing more interesting. Repeating 7-word sentences over and over again is boring. Give the reader something interesting to read.

- Word choice #1—choose the right word for your writing. If you are writing an academic paper for school, increase your sophistication or maturity with proper word choice. Do not overdo it, though. You want to sound intelligent without sounding too erudite (overeducated or bookish) or over the top. For instance, the word *selection* is far more sophisticated than the word *pick*. *Enormous* is a far better choice than the elementary school word *big*. Do you get the point?

- Word choice #2—choose a word that sounds better. Poets tend to choose words that have pleasant sounds—or grating sounds—depending upon the subject. The word *ugly* sounds less pleasing than the word *unattractive*. *Stunning* or *attractive* sounds better than *pretty*.

- Do not end your sentences with prepositions—*over, under, above, beyond*. You may begin your sentences with prepositions, but avoid using them at the end.

- If you are using first person—avoid flooding your paper with *I*, especially at the beginning of the sentences. Of course, you have to use the pronoun, but alternate it with the word *my*.

- If you are writing about a person, alternate the person's name with a pronoun such as *he* or *she*, *his* or *her*.

The Writing Process

For all types of writing, the process is generally the same. Whether you are writing an in-class essay, an autobiographical piece, or a persuasive essay or are doing a research paper, you have got to think about the topic before you write.

- Brainstorm—think about the topic. Jot down everything you know about the subject—everything. You may or may not use it all, but sometimes random ideas blossom into full-blown ideas or topics. If you are writing an essay, try to choose three main points or topics about the subject that will be the basis for your body paragraphs.

o Use lists with a different heading for each.

o	Topic A	Topic B	Topic C
o	idea	idea	idea
o	idea	idea	idea
o	idea	idea	idea

o Use a web with three different ovals—one for each topic.

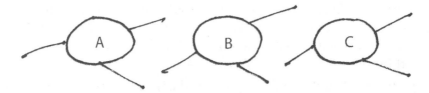

- Organize information—The structure and organization of your writing is extremely important. The reader needs to know where you are going and that the information follows what you have promised them in the thesis statement. A simple or informal outline is fine and not time-consuming.
  - o Introduction = hook, topic sentences and THESIS STATEMENT
  - o Body paragraph 1 = Topic/support 1
  - o Body paragraph 2 = Topic/support 2
  - o Body paragraph 3 = Topic/support 3
  - o Conclusion
- Write—compose the essay in the following order.
- Introduction—one of the most important parts of the paper. This is the reader's first impression of you. Make it a good one. The introduction contains the following components:
  - o Hook—an attention-grabbing sentence. It could be a strong statement, a quote (try to avoid in most cases unless it really works for the subject of your essay), a definition (do not overuse), or an anecdote (an extremely brief but effective story pertaining to the topic).

    —*Do not walk away from responsibility. Your help is needed now!*

    —*There comes a time in everyone's life when opportunity comes knocking upon the door.*

    —*I will never forget the time I walked into the lobby with my skirt tucked into my underwear. Was I embarrassed? What do you think?*
  - o Topic Sentences—usually two to three of them. They explain or introduce the points you want to make about the topic. These sentences coincide with the body paragraphs that follow.

    —*1) Exercising a dog, feeding it, brushing it, bathing it, picking up after it; 2) buying food and supplies; and 3) taking it to a vet; all take time and money.*

    —*1) The highways driven were varied and long. 2) Staying in frightening hotels and motels was strange and not to mention the 3) odd people that you meet on the road.*

—1) Not only is it poisonous and 2) has unique markings, 3) it has an interesting relationship background in that upon occasion, the female will actually eat the male black widow once he has fertilized the eggs. I guess we now know why the species is called "black widow."

o   Thesis Statement—THE MOST IMPORTANT PIECE OF INFORMATION IN YOUR ESSAY. This sentence tells the reader exactly where you are going in the essay. This is what you are going to prove. Thesis statements are most often located at the bottom of the introductory paragraph, but that depends upon your instructor. He/she may prefer that it be the first line of the essay.

—Taking care of a dog is a time-consuming and expensive endeavor that should be thoroughly thought through before taking on the responsibility.

—Driving to Nova Scotia from California was a road trip that no one would be able to forget: the highways, the hotels, the people all strange, but exciting.

—The black widow spider is a creature that should not be taken lightly.

- Body paragraph 1—is about topic # 1
- Body paragraph 2—is about topic # 2   } 3 to 5 sentences each
- Body Paragraph 3—is about topic # 3
- Conclusion—restates the points you are trying to prove. Leave the reader thinking about your topic. End with a strong statement or point.

Practice III:

Directions: In the space below, write a brainstorm and an outline for an essay on a topic of **your choice**, such as your favorite sport, car, or TV show; caring for pets; or traveling.

BRAINSTORM: Think of three main topics or ideas about your subject.

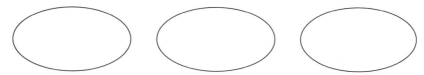

OUTLINE: Briefly organize the information from your brainstorm in the space below.

Chapter 22 Review Quizzes

Vocabulary Review Quiz

Directions: Write the letter of the definition on the line next to the word that it defines.

1. _____ ail	A.	The yellow part of the egg.
2. _____ bald	B.	Hairless, without hair.
3. _____ cent	C.	Walk in shallow water.
4. _____ mourning	D.	To be sick or ill.
5. _____ neigh	E.	An annoying cry or request for something.
6. _____ precedents	F.	A line or series of people waiting their turn.
7. _____ queue	G.	Sound of a horse.
8. _____ wade	H.	Remembering the dead.
9. _____ whine	I.	An established course of action.
10. _____ yolk	J.	A penny, one hundredth of a dollar.

Study Skills, Reading and Writing Improvement Definitions

Directions: Select the correct definition, and write the letter of the answer on the line to the right of the number.

1. _____ Which of the following is important when beginning to study?
   a. Finding a quiet place
   b. Gathering all materials and supplies needed
   c. Knowing the assignment or task details
   d. all of the above

2. _____ Identify a strategy for reading textbooks or other nonfiction.
   a. Get the big picture or general idea first.
   b. Write an introduction.
   c. Underline the thesis statement.
   d. Focus on word choice.

3. _____ The most important part of the introductory paragraph is the _____.
   a. topic sentences
   b. hook
   c. thesis statement
   d. none of the above

4. _____ True or False? Reading a poem more than once will help the reader improve understanding.
   a. True
   b. False

5. _____ The solution or the resolution of a novel is also called the _____.
   a. plot
   b. setting
   c. denouement
   d. place

6. _____ Exploring the _____ background can often help the reader better understand the novel.
   a. character's
   b. author's
   c. antagonist's
   d. protagonist's

7. _____ Beginning each _____ with a different word makes an essay more interesting.
   a. sentence
   b. paragraph
   c. topic
   d. none of the above

8. _____ The _____ of an essay should leave the reader thinking about the subject matter.
   a. introduction
   b. body paragraph 1
   c. thesis statement
   d. conclusion

9. _____ Topic sentences are used to support the _____.
   a. thesis statement
   b. the pronouns
   c. the verbs
   d. all of the above

10. _____ True or False? Brainstorming is an important part of the writing process.
    a. True
    b. False

Study Skills, Reading and Writing Improvement

Directions: Identify each of the following suggestions by category. Write *SS* for study skill, *RI* for reading improvement, and *WI* for writing improvement.

EXAMPLE:

   __RI__ Continually learn new words

1. _____ Avoid distractions

2. _____ Write an outline

3. _____ Visualize

4. _____ Brainstorm

5. _____ Read aloud

6. _____ Get the big picture first

7. _____ Introductory paragraph

8. _____ Gather all needed materials

9. _____ Make sure there is good light

10. _____ Topic sentences

11. _____ Plot

12. _____ Thesis Statement

13. _____ Characters

14. _____ Body paragraphs

15. _____ Find a quiet place

16. _____ Conclusion

17. _____ Denouement

18. _____ Hook

19. _____ Conflict or problem

20. _____ Use a calendar, plan ahead

Real-World Practice Activities

Reading, Writing, and Listening

Directions: Find a topic that interests you on a current event. Read an article or two or three. Listen to news programs. Discover as much as you can about the topic. Once you feel comfortable enough with the knowledge that you have obtained, write a brainstorm and then an outline on your topic. Think of **three** points that you want to prove or discuss in an essay. What exactly do you want to express about this subject? Once you have completed the brainstorm and outline, write a thesis statement. What do you want to prove to your reader?

BRAINSTORM:

OUTLINE:

THESIS STATEMENT:

Chapter 23

ACADEMIC WRITING

Over the course of your education, there will be a number of opportunities to write essays, reflections, formal letters, and other types of academic writing. In this chapter, we will address a broad spectrum of writing skills: the formal letter, news and feature stories, autobiographical essays, and comparison/contrast, descriptive, expository, narrative, persuasive, and problem/solution essays.

Vocabulary Development

1. **bistro** (bis tro) A small bar or restaurant in Europe or something like it elsewhere.
2. **cataclysm** (kat a kliz im) A violent disaster or upheaval.
3. **conga** (cong ga) A dance in which people form a long, winding line.
4. **easel** (ee zil) A wooden or metal support to hold a painting, blackboard, and so on.
5. **gape** (gape) To open the mouth wide; to stare with open eyes and mouth in disbelief.
6. **gratuity** (gra too i tee) A tip, money given in recognition of services rendered.
7. **marshmallow** (marsh mel ow) A soft, sticky candy made of sugar, egg white, and gelatin.
8. **peevish** (pee vish) Irritable, grumpy.
9. **reproach** (ree proach) To express disappointment or disapproval to a person for a fault or offense.
10. **teem** (teem) To be full of or present in large numbers.

Formal Letters

In writing a formal letter or business letter, there is a protocol or set of rules to follow. A formal letter is written for a specific reason: regarding business issues; to discuss, to announce, to clarify, or to present a problem; and so on. Review the following suggestions for writing formal letters.

- Follow the form/format of a business letter.
- Be clear and succinct in what you have to say. Business people do not have extra time for wordiness, so get to the point quickly.
- Grammar and spelling should be impeccable—no errors.
- Present yourself as knowledgeable, not wishy-washy, flaky, or inarticulate.

Business Letter Form

The business letter form is professional looking and follows a strict format. It should be typed and then neatly printed on quality paper. The following form is called full block form. Notice the strict spacing rules between each section. All of the sections are aligned to the left.

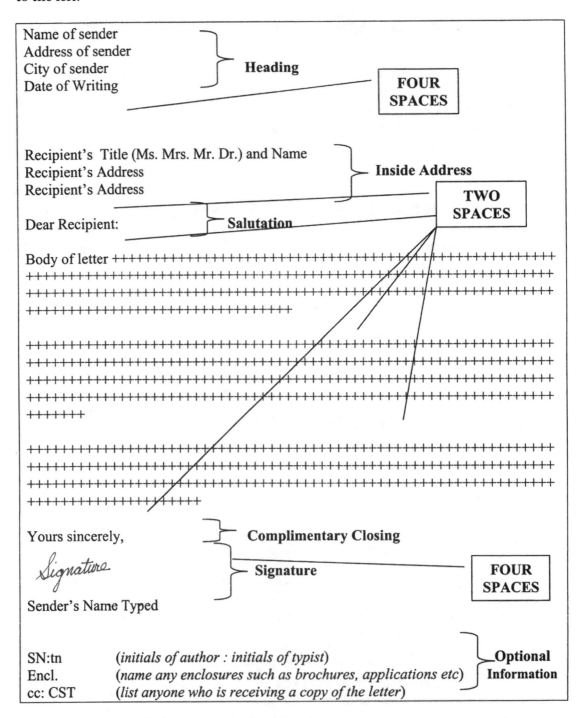

Name of sender
Address of sender
City of sender   } **Heading**
Date of Writing

FOUR SPACES

Recipient's Title (Ms. Mrs. Mr. Dr.) and Name
Recipient's Address   } **Inside Address**
Recipient's Address

TWO SPACES

Dear Recipient: } **Salutation**

Body of letter +++
+++
+++
+++++++++++++++++++++++++++++++++++

+++
+++
+++
+++
+++++++

+++
+++
+++
++++++++++++++++++++++

Yours sincerely,   } **Complimentary Closing**

Signature   } **Signature**

FOUR SPACES

Sender's Name Typed

SN:tn   *(initials of author : initials of typist)*
Encl.   *(name any enclosures such as brochures, applications etc)*   } **Optional Information**
cc: CST   *(list anyone who is receiving a copy of the letter)*

R. S. Bradley
1234 Minor Street
Plaza Mejor, NM 89984
30 April 2010

Mr. Adrian LaMar:
5656 Main Street
Fulawin, MN 67890

Dear Mr. LaMar:

In regards to our phone conversation of 28 April 2010, I want to assure you that our company will do everything in our power to help resolve your recent dispute with Rapid Arrival Trucking Company. Although the company has an untarnished reputation, errors do happen. We are in the process of locating the missing box and will deliver it to you as soon as possible. It was placed on another truck, and that truck is on its way back to the warehouse. Again, I apologize for any inconvenience, and you should have the missing item within one week.

Sincerely,

R. S. Bradley

R. S. Bradley

Practice I

Directions: Refer to the diagram on page 336 to answer the following questions about writing formal or business letters. Write the answers in the spaces provided in the sentences.

1. How many spaces are there between the complimentary closing and the sender's typed name? _____

2. What is the title of the area where the recipient's title, name, and address appear in the letter? _____

3. The style of this type of letter is called _____.

4. All of the information, including body paragraphs and heading, are aligned to the _____ of the page.

5. The date of the writing is placed below the _____.

6. The salutation states _____.

7. There are _____ spaces between the heading and the inside address.

8. There are _____ spaces between the body paragraphs.

9. The letter should be written _____ and to the point.

10. It should be printed on _____ paper.

Addressing an Envelope

The first thing the person receiving your letter sees is the envelope that you have addressed. Make certain that you do it right and that it is done neatly. There is only one way to address an envelope, regardless of to whom you are sending the letter. When sending a formal letter to a business associate, a friendly letter to your aunt, or a letter or brief note to your best friend, follow this format. The postal service will thank you.

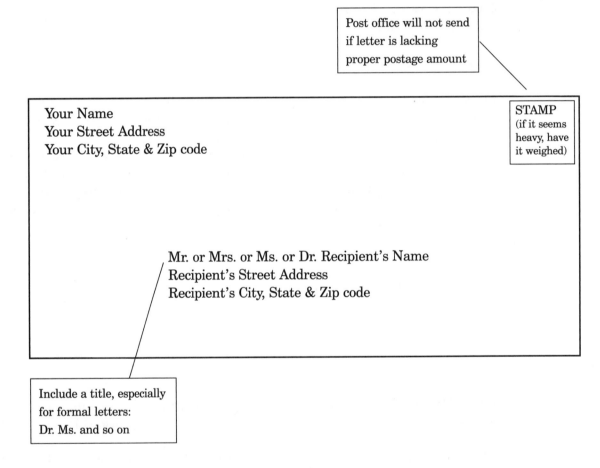

Post office will not send if letter is lacking proper postage amount

Your Name
Your Street Address
Your City, State & Zip code

STAMP
(if it seems heavy, have it weighed)

Mr. or Mrs. or Ms. or Dr. Recipient's Name
Recipient's Street Address
Recipient's City, State & Zip code

Include a title, especially for formal letters:
Dr. Ms. and so on

Journalistic Writing

Writing journalistically is a unique form of writing. This writing is nonfiction and factual. There are specific rules to follow in writing a news story and in writing a feature story or an editorial piece.

- News stories are current events. These are what you see on the front pages of the newspapers or current event magazines.
  - o Accuracy, accuracy, accuracy—the most important and vital of all tips for news writing is accuracy. Names, dates, places, events—all of them MUST be accurate. Always double-check your facts and sources.
  - o Unbiased—avoid opinions and editorializing. Write just the facts.

o News stories include a great deal of information right up front. The first sentence, or the lead of the story, tells the reader all of the main facts. Good leads relate the "5Ws" and an "H": *who, what, where, when, how,* and *why* of the story.

—*"Last night the local community joined together in honoring Mr. T. Han for his quick thinking and bravery in saving six of his fellow lacrosse teammates from what would have been a fatal automobile accident last month when they were returning from an out-of-town game."*

• The remainder of the story relates additional information according to its relevance. The most important information is first. Support detail follows. This format is known as an inverted pyramid ▼ with the most important information at the top and the least important information at the bottom.

NEWS STORY FORM:

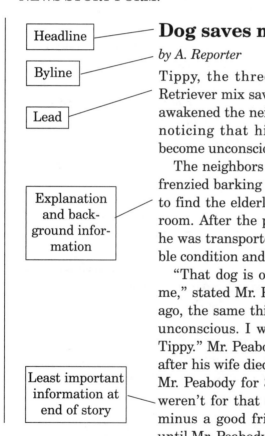

Headline ——————— **Dog saves master's life, again**

Byline —————— *by A. Reporter*

Lead —————— Tippy, the three-year-old chocolate-haired St. Bernard-Retriever mix saved his master from death last night when he awakened the neighbors with frantic barking apparently after noticing that his owner, who suffers from diabetes, had become unconscious.

Explanation and background information —————— The neighbors immediately called 911 when they heard the frenzied barking and quickly went into their neighbor's home to find the elderly man unconscious on the floor of his living room. After the paramedics arrived and treated Mr. Peabody, he was transported to St. Peter's Hospital, where he is in stable condition and expected to return home in a few days.

"That dog is one of the best things that ever happened to me," stated Mr. Peabody from his hospital bed. "Two months ago, the same thing happened with my blood sugar and I fell unconscious. I wouldn't have survived if it hadn't been for Tippy." Mr. Peabody adopted the dog from a local shelter soon after his wife died. The neighbors, who have lived next door to Mr. Peabody for 35 years, believe the dog is a godsend. "If it

Least important information at end of story —————— weren't for that dog looking out for George, we would all be minus a good friend." The neighbors are dog-sitting Tippy until Mr. Peabody returns home.

• Feature stories are intended to inform or to be entertaining and interesting. Like news stories, there are specific procedures to consider when writing. There are many different types of feature stories and many reasons for them being included in a newspaper or magazine.

o Feature stories have hooks instead of leads. The first sentence in the story usually grabs the reader's attention and causes the reader to want to continue reading.

o Information is presented in a more stylized form of writing, which is different than news story writing.

o Accuracy, accuracy, accuracy is just as important in a feature story.

o Readers expect to learn something and/or to be entertained.

- Types of feature stories

   o Firsthand account—evolves from the writer's personal experiences, such as experiencing a traumatic or humorous event. For instance, the elderly man in our simple news story above or a writer assigned to the feature might write a story about dogs that save lives.

   o Informative feature is as the title states: informative. This type of story is not linked to current news events; it is simply written for interest. An example of an informative feature story might be one that explores the back roads and alleys of a large urban region.

   o Historical feature is a story that is most often tied to a current event. For instance in the news, a hurricane hits a region that has been devastated many times before by similar natural disasters. The feature story may revisit the cycle or incidence of the previous events. From a different angle, the feature may interview those who have survived and why they continue to stay.

   o News features are stories directly tied to a current event or situation. The news may be reporting an incident that is scientifically linked to global warming. The feature story might explore the phenomenon of global warming, what scientists are saying, and what nations around the globe are doing to resolve the problem.

   o Personality feature is a story on an individual or group of individuals. A personality feature might explore the strength and courage of a young woman's journey in surviving a debilitating disease or a group of immigrants who are struggling to survive in a country that is so culturally different than their homelands that their daily struggles would humble even the most daring of souls.

Man and Woman's Best Friend
by B. Reporter

It is a common cliché heard around the world that a dog is a man's (and woman's) best friend. As sure as history repeats itself, history also tells us over and over again that what may be a silly little cliché is indeed true. Our furry little friends who take so much of our time, attention, and money are the same creatures that often save our lives.

The words loyalty and dog are synonymous. Loyal dogs are reported to have gone to extraordinary lengths, literally to save their masters. Gina, a five-year-old German Shepherd was out on a hike with her master when part of the trail gave way and her master fell down a steep, rocky slope and lay unconscious. Gina leaped down to her master and began barking. The continual howling, which echoed throughout the area, alerted park officials. Gina's master was rescued, Gina was lauded as a hero, and the two reunited to continue a relationship that would be difficult to disavow.

The story of Sammy the tiny little Chihuahua and his master . . . .

- Editorial or opinion writing is what it appears: an opinion. Editorial or opinion writing is persuasive, clearly written, and intended to entertain, satirize, convince, or prove a point regarding a specific issue. Editorials are found in the latter pages of the first section of a newspaper or in the earlier pages of a magazine. Editorials are obviously written by the editors or assistant editors and are intended to relay a message or opinion on behalf of the newspaper or magazine in general. However, newspapers (and sometimes magazines) are obliged to print both sides of the issue. These opinions are printed on the opposite page of the editorial—it is called the op-ed page for "opposite the editorial." This is where a varied group of editorial-like pieces are printed. They often oppose the opinions of the editors. There may be one writer (not a staff member) who agrees and another who disagrees—kind of like a battle of opinions or a "he said" "she said" skirmish. Editorial or opinion pieces, however, are strongly written. Pronouns are rarely used, particularly first-person pronouns (I, me, my). Instead, the column reads as though what is being written is the way it is, convincingly so.

Saving Our Schools

While participating in what is considered everyone's civic duty, tomorrow the voting public will visit their polling places. As is tradition, the editorial staff of this newspaper publishes its recommendations for various candidates and propositions. Without a doubt, our children and our community need your vote. On tomorrow's ballot rests Proposition H. In short, this has to pass in order to save our award-winning public schools. Proposition H will bring millions of dollars to public education with minimal sting (twenty dollars per year) to us, John Q Public. It is a win-win situation. We here at the Newspaper recommend a YES vote on Proposition H.

Practice II

Directions: Answer the following questions regarding journalistic styles of writing by filling in the blank with the correct answer. Use each word in the Word Bank only once (although one word is used twice, it is listed twice).

1. News stories are _____ events that have occurred in the past 24 hours.

2. _____ stories are those written for human interest, to entertain and to inform.

3. The _____ is the first long line/paragraph of a news story.

4. A _____ is the first line of a feature story that sucks the reader into the story.

5. The 5Ws and an H are covered in the first paragraph of a _____ story.

6. _____ are columns written by the editors of a newspaper or magazine.

7. The _____ _____ is a form that demonstrates the relevance of information that is given in a news story.

8. The _____ is the line that gives the author or writer credit.

9. A headline is written in boldface at the _____ of an article.

10. Historical, news, personality, and informative are types of _____ stories.

Word Bank: current, feature, top, byline, inverted pyramid, news, feature, lead, editorials, hook

---

Autobiographical/Personal Essays

In an autobiographical or personal essay, the subject of the essay is you and only you.

- Review and implement the writing tips in Chapter 22.
- Understand and review the assignment.
- Autobiographical writing is generally less-formal writing than other types of essays.
- Brainstorm about personal traits, personal events or tragedies, characteristics, strengths, weaknesses, hobbies, family, and extracurricular activities.
- Be attentive to your audience. Who is going to be reading this? Your peer? An admissions officer? Write accordingly.
- Often you are asked to explain an incident or an event in your life, your personality, or your goals.
  - o Ensure that the reader feels your emotions without being overly dramatic. Use vivid language.
  - o Write to inform or to entertain.
- This type of writing is often used in college applications. And you often need to address an obstacle you have faced in your life, a life-changing event, or to focus on future goals.

A Strange New City, A Close Call

By the time I reached my bicycle, I was out of breath and my heart was racing. Never in my life had I run that fast to get away from someone or something. However, it was an incident that I would never forget as long as I live and a time when I was thankful for trusting my intuition.

It was a beautiful day for a bike ride. After ending up downtown in an area that was unfamiliar to me, I locked up my bike and started to explore the city. While wandering and enjoying the new sights, I was approached by a young girl about my age. She seemed nice, and I noticed immediately that she had an accent. When asking her where she was from, I immediately began speaking her language. Although I had not spoken it in awhile, we both enjoyed the conversation. Feeling comfortable with who I thought might be a new friend, the young woman invited me to her house. She explained that she was having a bunch of kids over that were our age. I agreed. My new "friend" gave me her address, and I continued my exploration of the new city.

Soon enough, it was time to head off to find the young girl's home. After locking my bike, I walked the six blocks to my destination. When I reached the well-tended older home, I walked up to the door and knocked. Two young men, well groomed and friendly, greeted me; they invited me in. Noticing the lack of furniture and an extremely large framed picture of a foreign man hanging on the wall, my stomach suddenly jumped. "What is this place?" I thought to myself and asked for the young girl that I had met earlier. They told me she would be here soon and asked me to sit at a long table and join all of the other kids in a meal. I politely sat down but declined to accept any food. I had a very strange feeling inside. Before long, the meal was over and the group of young people was escorted into another room. There was that odd picture hanging on the wall again. "This is very strange," I thought, but I politely sat down along with the other ten or fifteen young people.

A young man began to speak about an unfamiliar religion. He was charismatic, and the small audience was enthralled with his message. However, I became more and more uncomfortable as he continued to refer to the strange man whose picture was hanging on the wall. "How do I get out of here?" I thought. My gut feeling became so strong that I suddenly decided to start coughing—I could not think of anything else to do. All I knew was that I had to get out of there. After standing up, I headed toward the door. The speaker stopped me and asked where I was going. I pretended to cough severely and hurriedly left the room. In the next room, the two well-dressed men stood between the door and me. They tried to stop me and shouted, "No, don't go, give us your address first," but I continued to feign a coughing spell that probably saved my life. I ran for the door and did not stop until I reached my bike.

*As fast as my legs could peddle, I made it to my apartment, carried my bike in, locked the door, and sat down with a sigh of relief. That was frighteningly strange, I thought, and was content to be safe at home. Years later, I saw the same picture of the man I had seen at the house—**in the newspaper**. The article was about a cult that the man had started so many years ago targeting young people on their own in large cities. Sigh. What a close call.*

Comparison/Contrast Essays

The primary purpose in a comparison/contrast essay is to compare two different but similar things. For instance, you could compare two movies, two friends, or two seasons.

- Brainstorm and organize your thoughts.

- A Venn diagram (two overlapping circles) is helpful to focus thoughts and ideas on similarities and differences.
- The introduction should include mention of both topics.
- The thesis statement should be clearly defined. What are you going to prove by comparing the two topics?
- The essay can be organized in one of two ways as follows:
  - o Block arrangement (4 paragraphs)
    - —Introduction
    - —Body 1: Supporting details (similarities)
    - —Body 2: Supporting details (differences)
    - —Conclusion
  - o Alternating Arrangement (5 paragraphs)
    - —Introduction
    - —Body 1: Element #1
    - —Body 2: Element #2
    - —Body 3: Element #3
    - —Conclusion

Colossal Cities, Goliath Opportunities

The City of Angels or the Big Apple: two completely different cities on opposites ends of the country. Los Angeles is on the west coast where it seems the Sun never ceases to shine. New York, on the other hand, is on the east coast and suffers through weather changes of one extreme to the other: cold to hot and hot to humid. However, Los Angeles and New York City have more similarities with their culture, size, and varied opportunities than with their extreme differences in location and weather.

Museums, symphonies, theaters, hotels, parks, art galleries, sports venues, and infinite restaurants are but a few of the cultural attractions that the City of Angels and the Big Apple have in common. The opportunity to be entertained with such a broad spectrum of temptations could keep anyone busy for years on end. It seems impossible to become bored while living in either New York or Los Angeles. All of these potential entertainment spots would be less probable in cities with less population and physical size.

The larger the city in size and population, the more potential there is for developing culturally and economically. Small cities have less people to draw talent from, less funding or tax base, and limited business growth. Large cities like New York and Los Angeles draw people like magnets. Their large populations and physical size allow the development of better transportation systems with international airports that draw people not only from within the city itself but from an extended area beyond. Beyond transportation and economic benefits, the bonuses of living in a large area and with an extensive population provide many additional opportunities as well.

Opportunity. Cities the size of New York and Los Angeles provide unlimited opportunities for their citizens. The job market is especially varied in large urban areas. With millions of people to provide services for, job seekers have more opportunity in a large city than in a small community. Consider as well the opportunities for higher education, health care, and other social services that are extensive in Los Angeles and New York compared with cities and towns with limited population. Opportunity is definitely a plus in large cities.

Although these two great cities are situated in different corners of the United States, their similarities in culture, size, and opportunity make New York and Los Angeles appear related in many aspects. Life in these two enormous cities, varied as they are in some respects, is something to celebrate and to appreciate.

Problem/Solution Essays

These essays present a problem and then offer one or more solutions.

- Brainstorm the problem, and list everything that you can possibly think about it. EVERYTHING.

- Brainstorm possible solutions—attempt to find at least two viable solutions. How will these actually solve the problem?

- Format the essay as follows:
  - Introduction
  - Problem
  - Solution #1
  - Solution #2
  - Conclusion

- Begin the essay with a strong statement followed by a general introduction of the problem—and a focused thesis statement.

Taxes Not Underage Tattoos

Tattooing has become a renewed, tangible, and almost inerasable fad of the new millennium. Although tattooing has been around for thousands of years, the extent of its popularity in modern culture has exceeded any era since the process began. Tattooing is permanent, and that is the problem, especially for the parents of underage children who manage to obtain tattoos without permission. How does society deal with what historically is the eventual regret of body art for the underage? Raising taxes on services in tattoo parlors and forcing clients to sign a contract that has a one-month waiting period before proceeding with the tattoo are solutions to a worrisome situation.

> *Taxes. Everyone dislikes them. Tattoo establishments, like all businesses, are taxed. They are legitimate businesses and deserve the right to succeed economically just like any other business. However, the problem that exists is the negligence in regulating the age requirement of customers. Of course all customers' identifications should be checked, but that does not always happen. Increasing taxes or presenting a penalty by 10 percent as a punishment for establishments that neglects to screen their customers should become a national standard. In addition to the economic punishment, part of the responsibility should be accountable to customers as well.*
>
> *Formulating a contract, similar to those used in gun purchases, should be established and enforced. The contract would allow the tattoo business to check the legitimate age of the customer before proceeding with the body art. Underage children would be screened out, and their parents could breathe a sigh of relief. Furthermore, not only would this contract eliminate the underage problem, but also customers would have an opportunity to rethink their design choices and whether or not to go ahead with the tattoo. A contract would eliminate underage customers and those who jump into a permanent body change at a whim.*
>
> *Tattoo art and the businesses that provide the service deserve the freedom to survive economically. However, eliminating troublesome underage customers could be resolved by establishing a monetary punishment and a legitimate procedural contract. The underage children who frequent these businesses without permission would be held accountable and the businesses themselves less liable with the implementation of such commonsense solutions.*

Narrative Essays

A narrative essay tells a story. It is told from a specific point of view, usually first person, but third-person point of view is effective too. NOTE: See the writing example for the descriptive essay below. With minor modifications, this would also work as a narrative essay.

- Use precise detail and events. Describe the scene, the person, or the event thoroughly
- It must have a thesis statement—something to prove.
- Provide the reader with vivid images by using descriptive details.
- Conflict and dialogue may be used effectively.
- The writing is usually less formal, leaning toward lively and creative.
- Narratives have a plot—use a chronological time line to move your story.

Descriptive Essays

These are intended to provoke a response from the reader. They present an impression of something through sensory detail—details that represent one of the five senses: vision, touch, taste, hearing, or smell.

- Brainstorm the topic—what do you want to describe? Describe a person, place, event, memory, or thing.
- Think of adjectives, verbs, and adverbs.
- Focus on details—anything that will spark an image in the readers' mind.
- Word choice is colorful and visual—let the reader feel your experience through your words.
- It could be a boring topic, but make it interesting with description.
- Essays can be objective (literal) or subjective (emotional level).

Mesmerizing Moments

When I first walked into the room, all I can say is that I was mesmerized by the sudden overwhelming sense of peace that enveloped me. It was my first visit to Prague, and I wandered into a medieval convent that was the site of an exhibit that displayed the works of a fifteenth-century monk. I do not know if it was the exhibit, the background music, or the chilling and almost spiritual ambience of the convent itself, but the feeling was unforgettable.

The first thing I sensed was calm. While walking into the aged stone building, there was not a sound to be heard. The quiet was loud, if that makes any sense. After strolling through what appeared to be an austere and endless labyrinth of corridors, I entered a large cavernous room with a slightly dank and musty odor. The lighting was subtle as if modern-day electronics had returned to the wick and wax illumination of the past. Instead of being alarmed by the eerie darkness as a child might be, the delicate light set a serene mood.

Once my eyes had adjusted to the light, the display of paintings seemed to appear out of nowhere. The compositions were positioned on what appeared to be papier-mâché-textured walls that were painted a deep charcoal color. Although there were a number of other visitors, the greatness of the room and the loftiness of the walls made them almost disappear. In looking at the richly earth-toned art, that sense of peace continued to occupy my psyche. The paintings of centuries-old revered religious figures returned my gazes as if to underscore their sympathies and to substantiate my feelings of inner tranquility.

After settling into the room and enjoying the exhibit, suddenly it occurred to me that I was hearing voices. At first I thought, of course, that I was imagining things. Soon the sweet sound of unadorned but deep-toned and harmonious voices became evident. It was a recording of a choir of monks chanting their morning petitions. The sound, the serenity of the surroundings, and the presence of the beautiful art resulted in an experience that brought chills to my soul.

At an unhurried pace, walking from painting to painting and savoring the understated chanting and the diffuseness of light, I eventually noticed the time. I had spent several hours in the exhibit. With hesitation, I inhaled the ambience and wandered back down the corridors and out into the streets filled with cars and buses and more people than I could count. My experience in the convent was unforgettable, touching, and healing in a sense. The subtle light and sounds and the richness of the art is as lucid now as the day I experienced it—what a mystifying and exhilarating encounter.

Expository Essays

The primary purpose of an expository essay is to define, explain, or otherwise provide information on a specific topic. With often a "how to" focus, the expository essay explains such things as how to repair a car, grow tomatoes, or cook a gourmet meal.

- Review and continue to implement the writing tips from Chapter 22.
- Understand the topic or prompt given, and brainstorm thoroughly.
- Organize/structure your essay—it is easy to keep to the five-paragraph structure unless the required length of the paper is beyond that.
- Make certain that your thesis statement is focused: not too broad as to lose sight of your paper's purpose and not too narrow as to be too confining.
- Write in third person, not first person.
- Write without emotion or editorializing, state facts nothing more.
- Each paragraph should support or add additional information to your topic.
- The conclusion should refocus on the thesis and, without being trite, restate briefly your main support points. It should leave the reader with a strong statement—something to think about. Do not introduce new material in the conclusion.

The Care and Feeding of a Dog

Taking care of a dog is not as simple or as uncomplicated as it may seem. A dog needs proper care and feeding. A dog needs attention. A dog needs exercise. So before you visit an animal shelter or a pet store and begin begging your parent for that cute little or big dog that you have fallen in love with, my advice is to read this first. Dogs are loyal friends. However, proper care and plenty of time and exercise are really needed to earn that loyalty.

First of all, the care and feeding of dogs cost money, lots of it. Most of you think, "Yeah, that's ok, I can buy inexpensive food and water out of the tap is cheap. "There is more involved than that. Dogs need healthy diets, and good dog food adds up money wise. In addition to food and water, dogs need to have checkups and shots just like humans, only different kinds of shots. Veterinary visits are NOT cheap. Our hairy little friends also need to be bathed, brushed, and de-fleaed on a regular basis. Are you getting the picture? Food, vet bills, bathing, brushing, de-fleaing—oh and less we forget, cleaning up their droppings—all add up to a huge time commitment.

Time. Hope you have lots of it. Little Fido or Sparky needs your attention. Of course, you have other things to do with your time: homework, school, work, friends, television, volunteering at the old-folks home—all of that adds up. How do you fit a dog into the big picture of time commitment? YOU HAVE TO MAKE TIME, that is how. What is your dog going to do while you are away? Who is going to take care of it while you do your chores? That is another something to think about—always something to think about with a dog! Dogs need your time commitment. If you do not have the time, do not get a dog, get a fish. Fish require attention but not like dogs that, also by the way, need exercise.

Exercise! Another thing to add to the list of caring for a dog! Sitting around the house all day while you are gone is fine but not fair. Would you like that? Waiting, sitting, sleeping, waiting, sitting, and sleeping. BORING! Take your dog for a walk down the street, around the block a few times, or to the dog park or a city park if it is allowed. Whatever you do—get the dog out for some exercise EVERY DAY, not just when you feel like it!

As you can see, the proper care and feeding of a dog is expensive and time-consuming. That is not to say that the effort is not worth it because it is. Owning a dog is a serious responsibility and not to be taken lightly. Owning a dog takes time, money, and a major commitment to one of the best friends you will ever have. Think before you fall in love with a dog and then discover the effort is more than you can handle. Be kind. Be thoughtful. Most of all, do not neglect your dog.

Persuasive Essays

A persuasive essay is written with the intent to convince the reader of a certain position. The position may or may not be one you actually agree with, but your obligation is to present evidence so convincingly as to win over the reader. Compare it to an attorney defending a client he/she knows is guilty, but his/her job is to defend that person to the best of his/her ability.

- The topic chosen must have more than one side—it must be a debatable topic.
- Do not use personal pronouns—be firm about your viewpoint.
- Brainstorm and then organize your position.
- Your thesis statement should be a strong statement that you are going to prove in the rest of the essay.
- A persuasive essay should be organized in the following manner:
  o   Introduction
  o   Body 1 = Support topic 1
  o   Body 2 = Support topic 2, but add clear information regarding the opposition; avoid turning the reader against you with this information—keep the reader on your side
  o   Body 3 = Support topic 3
  o   Conclusion = restates or supports your views—leaves the reader thinking

A New Wave Social Disease

Trash. Have you ever just sat yourself down and seriously thought about trash? Where does all the trash come from? Where does it go? Well, you probably have no idea. Think about it. Trash is an epidemic. Almost everything we buy comes in some sort of wrapper or container. Do you know where that plastic sandwich container goes after you put it into the trash? Do you know where that soda pop can ends up if you do not recycle it? Well, now is the time to sit down and think about it. Millions of tons of reusable trash are being dumped into landfills when it could be recycled. Recycling is a solution, not a problem. Our efforts to decrease the amount of trash and increase our recycling efforts should not be optional; they should be mandatory.

Plastic containers, cardboard boxes, tin cans, aluminum cans, glass bottles, and glass jars, all of these can be recycled. Considering the amount of packaging that goes on in the world, one would think the entire world is hovering beneath one giant piece of plastic wrap. Recycling all of this packaging should be mandatory and not merely an option for those who are ecologically minded. Miles and miles of valuable lands are being filled up with trash—much of which can be recycled. Rregrettably and erroneously, trash lies festering in the ground when it could be reused.

How do we begin to regulate, to enforce something that should be common sense? Recycling should be a habit for everyone. It should be a class in school that we all have to take to graduate from high school. Of course, there are those who are too busy to recycle, or those who rationalize their nonrecycling habits with the ideation that "there is no room to store the recycling." Well, guess what? Mother Earth is running out of places to store perfectly good recyclables, too. Cities should be fined for not recycling at least 85–90 percent of their trash. Neighborhoods, apartment buildings, businesses, and all areas of the public and private sector should, in turn, be fined by the cities. Everyone is to blame for this crisis. We should all hang our heads in shame.

Recycle. Recycle. Recycle. That should be a mantra playing through our heads every time we go to the grocery store. Every time we buy something, it should be wrapped in a container that will be reused. Trash is a plague, an epidemic that is destroying the planet. Recycle; do not wait for these giant piles of trash to swallow us up. Recycle.

Practice III

Directions: Fill in the blanks with words from the essay explanations above.

1. There are about _____ sentences in each paragraph.
2. Academic essays should have strong _____ statements.
3. An _____ explains something.
4. Persuasive essays are written with the intent to _____ the reader of something.
5. Descriptive essays are written to _____.
6. An essay that is about you is called an _____ essay.
7. Narrative essays _____ stories.
8. A _____ essay compares two similar topics.
9. Essays that present a problem and probable solutions are called _____ essays.
10. Academic essays usually have about _____ paragraphs.

Chapter 23 Review Quizzes

Vocabulary Review Quiz

Directions: Write the letter of the definition on the line next to the noun that it defines.

1. _____ bistro

2. _____ cataclysm

3. _____ conga

4. _____ easel

5. _____ gape

6. _____ gratuity

7. _____ marshmallow

8. _____ peevish

9. _____ reproach

10. _____ teem

A. A soft, sticky candy made of sugar, egg white, and gelatin.

B. A tip, money given in recognition of services rendered.

C. To open the mouth wide; to stare with open eyes and mouth in disbelief.

D. To express disappointment or disapproval to a person for a fault or offense.

E. A dance in which people form a long winding line.

F. A violent disaster or upheaval.

G. To be full of or present in large numbers.

H. A small bar or restaurant in Europe or something like it elsewhere.

I. A wooden or metal support to hold a painting, blackboard, and so on.

J. Irritable, grumpy.

Academic Writing Definitions

Directions: Select the correct definition, and write the letter of the answer on the line to the right of the number.

1. _____ An editorial is a short writing that the _____ write.
   a. staff writers
   b. editors
   c. reporters
   d. feature writers

2. _____ True or False? Problem/solution essays present a problem without doing anything about it.
   a. True
   b. False

3. _____ Which of the following is NOT an example of an essay?
   a. Expository
   b. Persuasive
   c. Feature story
   d. Narrative

4. _____ Which of the following is NOT found in a newspaper?
   a. editorial
   b. news story
   c. feature story
   d. formal letter

5. _____ Identify the thesis statement below.
   a. The wheelbarrow is red.
   b. Recycling should be mandatory and not optional.
   c. He went to the circus with his sister yesterday.
   d. Blanca has a new friend.

6. _____ Identify the section of a formal letter that contains the recipient's address.
   a. Salutation
   b. Heading
   c. Inside address
   d. Signature

7. _____ Formal letters use _____ grammar and language.
   a. colloquial
   b. casual
   c. proper
   d. all of the above

8. _____ The Five Ws and an H are found in the _____.
   a. library
   b. grocery store
   c. essay
   d. lead

9. _____ A(n) _____ essay is intended to convince the reader.
   a. expository
   b. narrative
   c. persuasive
   d. formal letter

10. _____ A(n) _____ essay relates a story.
    a. expository
    b. narrative
    c. persuasive
    d. formal letter

Formal Letters

Directions: In the space below, outline the format for a formal letter. Identify and label each of the sections.

Journalistic Writing

Directions: Identify the 5Ws and an H in each of the leads that are listed below. Note: in some leads, not all of the questions will be answered.

1. Early this morning, six students intending to pull an end-of-the-year prank were arrested for attempted vandalism as security guards caught them breaking into the local high school.

   a. who _____

   b. what _____

   c. where _____

   d. when _____

   e. how _____

   f. why _____

2. Twenty residents were left homeless and seven hospitalized for burns and smoke inhalation from a fire caused by a dropped cigarette that destroyed an apartment building last night in the 2000 block of Main Street.

   a. who _____

   b. what _____

   c. where _____

   d. when _____

   e. how _____

   f. why _____

3. Sixteen visitors from Spain were rescued by the fire department at Disneyland yesterday when a ride they were on was disabled.

   a. who _____

   b. what _____

   c. where _____

   d. when _____

   e. how _____

   f. why _____

4. After suffering burns over 20 percent of his body, a twenty-five-year-old man was taken by helicopter to the burn center in Alameda after the car he was driving suddenly caught fire and burst into flames.

   a. who _____

   b. what _____

    c. where _____

    d. when _____

    e. how _____

    f. why _____

5. The local police and county sheriffs are conducting a search for a missing three-year-old girl who wandered away from her babysitter at the wilderness park this morning.

    a. who _____

    b. what _____

    c. where _____

    d. when _____

    e. how _____

    f. why _____

Academic Essays

Directions: Identify each of the following academic essays by writing a definition of each.

1. Persuasive

_____

2. Comparison/Contrast

_____

3. Expository

_____

4. Descriptive

_____

5. Problem/Solution

_____

6. Narrative

_____

7. Autobiographical

_____

Real-World Practice Activities

Reading

Directions: Read the headlines of a newspaper, and list the titles of five (5) news stories and five (5) feature stories.

News stories:

1. _____
2. _____
3. _____
4. _____
5. _____

Feature stories

1. _____
2. _____
3. _____
4. _____
5. _____

Writing

Directions: Write an introductory paragraph to a descriptive essay.

_____

_____

_____

_____

_____

_____

_____

_____

_____

_____

_____

_____

_____

_____

_____

_____

Listening

Directions: Listen carefully to a news program on the radio, on television, or on the Internet. Then write the 5Ws and an H (who, what, where, when, how, and why) for one of the news events.

Who:

_____

What:

_____

Where:

_____

When:

_____

How:

_____

Why:

_____

BASICS OF WRITING A RESEARCH PAPER

During the course of your education, there will be a time when you are asked to research something. It could be a historical event, a scientific process, or a societal malady such as poverty or health care—there are literally over a million possible things to research. The key to research is to do it well, to be organized, and to allow plenty of time. Procrastination is NOT going to help on this type of assignment.

Vocabulary Development

1. **diploma** (di ploh ma) A certificate awarded by a school or college to a person who has successfully completed a course of study.
2. **fillet** (fill eh) A boneless piece of meat or fish.
3. **gnaw** (naw) To bite persistently at something hard.
4. **hamlet** (ham let) A small village.
5. **hijack** (hi jack) To seize control of a vehicle by force.
6. **impeach** (im peech) To charge a public official with misconduct in office before a tribunal.
7. **leech** (leech) A small, bloodsucking worm that usually lives in water.
8. **meld** (meld) To blend together or merge.
9. **oedipal** (ed i pal) Of or relating to the Oedipus complex (attraction of a child to the parent of the opposite sex—related to the Greek legend of Oedipus).
10. **sesquipedalian** (sess kwi ped a lee ann) Having many syllables.

General Format and Style

Depending on the format of your assignment or the demands of your instructor, the information below is globally accepted. However, make certain that you **follow the specific directions of your instructor.** Everyone asks for different information or style; no two research paper assignments are the same.

- Type using 12-point font such as Times, Geneva, Bookman or Helvetica.
- Double space with 1" (2.5 cm) margins, single sided on 8-1/2" × 11" (22 cm × 28 cm) paper.
- Number pages consecutively beginning after title page.
- Adhere to the page limit of the assignment.
- Follow the MLA (Modern Language Association) or other style guide that is recommended by your instructor—there are many (Chicago, APA, and so on).
- Indent the first line of each paragraph.
- Present your points in logical order.
- Use present tense.
- Avoid informal wording. Do not use jargon, slang terms, or superlatives.
- The title page should address specifics that your instructor requests but usually includes:
  - o Paper title
  - o An illustration
  - o Your name/course number/date

The Twelve-Step Research Paper

1. Choosing a Topic

The first step and one of the most difficult things about a research paper is choosing a topic.

- Ensure that you clearly understand the assignment.
- Brainstorm ideas that interest you within the confines of the assignment.
- Topic ideas should be broad enough to be able to find information but not too broad as to be overwhelming.

2. Preliminary Topic Research

The second step is to research your topic choice, making certain that you are able to find enough information to cover your topic.

- Look for resources with information about your topic—periodicals, encyclopedias, books, and online searches.
- Go to the library or complete an online search for information.
- Make certain that you can find enough information to fulfill the breadth and depth of the assignment.

- Did your instructor ask for sources in all areas or will he/she allow information from one area (such as online information)?

- If there is not enough material or sources for your topic, you will need to broaden the scope of the topic or choose another.

- Once you are positive that the resources that you have found will cover the assignment, either move on to the next step or go back to the beginning and embark on a new topic.

3. Bibliography Cards

Each resource that you use will need to be listed on either a works cited page or a bibliography page, depending on your assignment. If you complete one of these bibliography cards on each source that you actually use for information for your paper, making your bibliography page at the end of the assignment will be much easier.

- Purchase (or make your own) 3" × 5" (7 cm × 12 cm) cards.

- Complete a card as directed below for each resource from which you actually acquire information. Do not bother to complete a card on books or other materials that you are not going to use.

- In general, always write down the following: author, title of book/publication, the publication date, the publisher, the first city listed on the title page, the pages on which you found the information (not always needed for documentation, but it is good information for you), volume numbers (if any). If this is an online source, write down the date you accessed the information.

- The following examples are general formatting rules for works cited or a bibliography page. You will need to consult the specific resource that your instructor suggests for additional information.

  - Books—most books are formatted as follows, but note the indentation of the second line and not the first line. Be particular about punctuation. All entries are alphabetized according to last name.

> Gardner, John. <u>Grendel</u>. New York:
> Vintage Books, 1971.

- Encyclopedias—articles in an encyclopedia differ from entries for books. Name the author of the article (if there is one noted), the title of the article, the title of the work, the date of publication, and the edition number.

> Smith, Robert W. "How to Eat Chocolate Without the Mess."
> <u>Encyclopedia of Modern Chefs</u>. Ed. Kenneth Jones.
> Chicago: Chicago Press, 1964.

- Periodicals—the information varies according to the publication of the periodical. If it is a scholarly journal, it may be paginated continuously throughout the year. In that case, you will see a number such as 365 when the journal itself is only 50 pages long. You will need to note the volume number and pages of the article as well as the date of the publication. Otherwise, the following is a typical documentation for a periodical.

> Kahnke, Erik. "Sipping Soda on the Yacht." <u>Journal of the American Yachtsman</u> 43 (2004): 32–37.

- Newspapers—documenting newspaper sources is similar to a periodical. Author, title of article, name of the newspaper, date, section letter or number, and the page number are required.

> Hale, Joseph. "Going the Way of the Wayward Child."
> The Los Angeles International 14 Mar. 1976: C2.

- Online sources—these are more challenging because not all of the information is available. However, good sites will have a "how to cite this article" link. Use it. Otherwise, format the information as shown.

> Author, Article. Title of Article. Website Name. Posting Date
> Organization affiliated with the site and the date
> you accessed the site and finally, the electronic
> address of the site < *www. weireuioosdfoi.com* >

4. Thesis Statement and Initial Information Search

Now that you know the topic and are positive that there is enough information to cover it, begin the real search for knowledge that will prove your thesis statement. Write your thesis statement right now.

- Write a thesis statement—what exactly are you going to prove in this research paper? (Refer back to Chapter 22 for information on writing a thesis statement.)
- Your thesis must be provable and supported by a variety of facts.
- Once your thesis is set, redo your information search from Step 2 but with your thesis statement in mind.
- Look at each source.
  - o Check the table of contents and the index for specific information about your topic.
  - o If the resource looks promising, check it out of the library, copy the article, or print off the online information.
  - o Once you have enough resources, go on to Step 5.

5. Information Gathering

Take all of your resources, with your blank bibliography cards and note-taking paper, and find a quiet place to begin the more tedious process of gathering actual facts and information.

- Look through all of your materials.
- Focus on what information is in what source.
- Use sticky notes or bookmarks to mark the pages of the information that you are going to use.
- If the source has what you need, *complete a bibliography card* for it and keep it in a stack. Make sure you have all of the bibliographic information that you need.
- NOTE: Write the page numbers of where the information that you are going to use is on the note card.

6. Reading and Note Taking

Now that you have found the information that you need, begin reading the material and taking notes.

- Optional Idea—Use a different-colored card for each resource or for each subtopic of your paper. When you begin writing, you will be able to locate what you need more quickly this way.
- Read material thoroughly, looking for information that will allow you to prove your thesis statement.
- Take notes by bulleting fragments of important information in *your own words. Avoid writing word for word* to avoid accidental plagiarism.
- If you need to use quotes, make sure you know the page number of where you found the quote, whose quote it is, and of course from which book you found it.

7. Organization of Information/Outlining

Once you have found the needed information and facts and have completed the reading and taken notes, organize the research paper by setting up an outline.

- Revisit your thesis statement.
- Have you collected enough information to prove what you set out to prove?
- Take the information that you have gathered, and organize the paper logically point by point, being cognizant of how the paper is going to flow for the reader. You do not want to jump around from topic to topic. Be organized in your progression of points to prove.
- Write an outline of all of the subtopics that will assist you in proving your thesis.
- Organize your notes according to your outline (see the example below).

OUTLINE

Introduction—Includes the thesis statement and introduces the reader to your topic. The introduction lays the groundwork for the rest of the paper. It should be clearly stated and organized.

Body (Subtopics are optional)

    A. Body Topic 1

        1. Subtopic

        2. Subtopic

    B. Body Topic 2

        1. Subtopic

        2. Subtopic

    C. Body Topic 3

        1. Subtopic

        2. Subtopic

        3. Subtopic

    D. Body Topic 4

        1. Subtopic

    E. Body Topic 5

        1. Subtopic

        2. Subtopic

Conclusion—restate or reword your thesis. Summarize your arguments. Explain why you have come to this conclusion. Leave the reader thinking.

8. Writing the Paper

With everything in órder (notes, outline) begin writing your paper.

- Begin with the introduction, which includes your thesis statement. Prepare the reader for what you are going to prove.
- Continue through each body paragraph/topic area logically.
- Transition logically from one topic to the next with transition sentences.
- Write from the heart the first time through. You will go back over the paper to correct logic and other things later.

9. Footnotes or Endnotes

Again, depending on the style or format of your paper, the assignment may ask for footnotes or endnotes. Footnotes are used to explain or clarify information that is either too lengthy or too distracting to parenthesize ( ) within the text of the paper.

- Footnotes are numbered.[1] These superscript numbers appear at the end of a sentence and the explanations appear at the bottom of the page.
- Endnotes, like footnotes, are numbered with superscript numbers at the end of a sentence.[2] However, instead of being located at the bottom of the page, the explanations are listed on a separate page located before the bibliography or works cited page.

10. First Edit (The First Rough Draft) and Rewrite

Print a copy of your paper and read it.
- Mistakes are easier to find if you can hear them. Reading your paper aloud helps.
- Correct errors in grammar and spelling as you go.
- Does the paper move logically from topic to topic? If not, rearrange sections.
- Have someone else read the paper if possible to catch errors in grammar and organization.
- Rewrite any parts that need clarification.
- Set the paper aside for a day or two. Looking at it too much sometimes causes you to overlook mistakes. Return to it fresh and rested.

11. Bibliography or Works Cited Page

Gather all of your bibliography cards. Depending on your assignment, you may have to follow the demand of a specific entity—such as Modern Language Association (MLA), the American Psychological Association (APA), *The Chicago Manual of Style*, and so on.

- Alphabetize your 3" × 5" (7 cm × 12 cm) cards. Type the page in that alphabetical order. This is simple if you followed the suggestions in Step 3.

12. Second Edit, Title, Publication, and Submission

Read the paper again, and correct any errors in grammar, spelling, and organization.

- Title the paper appropriately. Although titles can be clever and humorous, this probably is not the time to take a chance on that.
- Go through the following checklist before you print.
  - ☐ Are all errors in spelling and grammar corrected?
  - ☐ Does your paper look good visually?

- ☐ Are your paragraphs indented and page numbers inserted if necessary?
- ☐ Correct any orphaned words—words that for some reason are left on their own. Move them forward or backward as necessary.
- ☐ Recheck the formatting—spacing and margins.
- After rereading and making all of the final corrections and if you feel that finally your paper is perfect, print the final copy.
- Relook at all of the pages—make certain that they are in order.
- Make certain that the printing is well-done.
  - o The ink must be clear.
  - o All pages must be printed.
- Follow the instructor's instructions for submission. Some just want it stapled, and some want it in a binder or folder. Make this person happy. Follow directions and remember— he/she will be assigning the grade.

Chapter 24 Review Quizzes

Vocabulary Review Quiz

Directions: Write the letter of the definition on the line next to the noun that it defines.

1. _____ diploma

2. _____ fillet

3. _____ gnaw

4. _____ hamlet

5. _____ hijack

6. _____ impeach

7. _____ leech

8. _____ meld

9. _____ oedipal

10. _____ sesquipedalian

A. Of or relating to the Oedipus complex (attraction of a child to the parent of the opposite sex—related to the Greek legend of Oedipus).

B. To blend together or merge.

C. A small, bloodsucking worm that usually lives in water.

D. To bite persistently at something hard.

E. A boneless piece of meat or fish.

F. A certificate awarded by a school or college to a person who has successfully completed a course of study.

G. A small village.

H. To seize control of a vehicle by force.

I. To charge a public official with misconduct in office before a tribunal.

J. Having many syllables.

Basics of Writing a Research Paper Definitions

Directions: Select the correct definition, and write the letter of the answer on the line to the right of the number.

1. _____ A research paper must contain _____.
   a. one paragraph
   b. a thesis statement
   c. footnotes
   d. none of the above

2. _____ The bibliography page or the works cited page lists _____.
   a. quotes used in the paper
   b. banquet dates
   c. spelling errors in the paper
   d. resources used in writing the paper

3. _____ Which of the following is NOT required in writing a research paper?
   a. Chaperone
   b. Editing
   c. Writing
   d. Resource information

4. _____ Which of the following words is NOT a formatting style for a research paper?
   a. Modern Language Association
   b. American Psychological Association
   c. *Oxford American Dictionary*
   d. all of the above

5. _____ A thesis statement tells the reader what is going to be _____ .
   a. described in the conclusion
   b. proven in the paper
   c. edited in the final draft
   d. none of the above

6. _____ The conclusion of the paper _____.
   a. restates the thesis
   b. reviews major points
   c. leaves the reader thinking
   d. all of the above

7. _____ True or False? It is vital that the author of the research paper find enough resources to cover the topic.
   a. True
   b. False

8. _____ In organizing the information for the paper, _____ is helpful.
   a. an editor
   b. an outline
   c. a note taker
   d. a teacher

9. _____ The paper should be organized _____.
   a. foolhardily
   b. haphazardly
   c. logically
   d. at random

10. _____ _____ and correcting spelling and grammar errors should be completed at least twice.
    a. Editing
    b. Copying
    c. Printing
    d. Negotiating

Real-World Practice Activities

Reading and Writing

Directions: Think about the possibilities of having to write a research paper. Visit the library or search online for research topics and various resources that will help in completing the task. On the lines below, write a list of topics that you might be interested in researching. Do you think that you will be able to find enough information to write perhaps a 10-page paper? Check all the resources to find out.

_____

_____

_____

_____

_____

_____

_____

_____

_____

_____

_____

_____

_____

_____

_____

Listening

Directions: Listen to the news on television or on the radio. What topics are being discussed? Write down any that interest you and might be a possible topic for further study.

_____

_____

_____

_____

_____

_____

_____

Chapter 25

COMPREHENSIVE VOCABULARY REVIEW EXERCISES

REVIEW EXERCISE I

Directions: Using the Word Bank, fill in the blanks with the correct vocabulary word that best completes the thought of the sentence.

1. The philharmonic's new cellist studied at a music _____ in Germany.
2. Despite being invaded by the Spanish many centuries ago, the indigenous tribe remained true to the _____ of their ancestors.
3. After volunteering for two weeks in Honduras, we left with a sense of _____ that we had contributed to the devastated community.
4. The queen wears her spectacularly jeweled_____ only for special occasions.
5. Right now he is working in a research _____ for a company that is investigating cures for cancer.
6. When we joined together the two _____, the end result surprised us.
7. The high school _____ team began fund-raising to build a new swimming pool that they so desperately needed.
8. During her _____, she was taken away from her parents and sent to France, where her grandparents raised her.
9. The _____ in the Middle Ages was a man of noble birth.
10. Yesterday our _____ handed out city maps of London.

Word Bank: pride, elements, tiara, laboratory, childhood, water polo, ideologies, conservatory, knight, chaperone

---

REVIEW EXERCISE II

Directions: Underline the correct pronoun that best fits the meaning of the sentence.

1. *She/Her* was named the queen of the prom last night.
2. The coffee plant, which is native to Ethiopia, is the source of coffee beans but *they/it* are now grown in the tropics, especially Brazil.
3. William O. Douglas was an associate justice of the U.S. Supreme Court. *He/Him* was a strong supporter of civil rights.
4. In referring to Donne, *we/she* are referring to the English poet who wrote many love poems, elegies, and satires.
5. November 5 is Guy Fawkes Day in England, the anniversary of *its/hers* namesake's plot against James I and Parliament that went awry.
6. Lead *us/its* to the opening of the cave where the bats enter.
7. There is an exhibit of *your/he* favorite artist, Chagall, at the county museum.
8. The professor believes that *For Whom/We the Bell Tolls* is one of Hemingway's best novels.
9. That is *theirs/shes* and this is ours.
10. That cannot be *ours/shes,* it is theirs.

REVIEW EXERCISE III

Directions: Using the Word Bank, fill in the blanks with the correct vocabulary word that best completes the thought of the sentence.

1. This artist's work almost seems to _____ the works of Renoir and Gauguin.
2. Our funds continue to _____ by the day; we will need to increase our belt cinching or raise more funds.
3. Over time, the river slowly _____ the rock and carved a unique canyon that is now known as the Grand Canyon.
4. _____ the roadway signs or you will find yourself lost.
5. The surgeon decided to _____ despite the fact that her chances of survival were minimal.
6. Mark Twain wrote the story of Huck Finn, a boy who travels down a river on a _____.
7. Believe me, my mother will _____ me about this one little mistake until the day I die.
8. The _____ of the light tones with the dark causes a striking and bold effect in the painting.

9. Eating protein before an exam is like _____ your brain with energy and power.

10. The end results will be _____ if you take a more conservative approach to the process.

> **Word Bank:** heed, operate, raft, admonish, fortifying, unite, shrink, eroded, minimized, juxtaposition

REVIEW EXERCISE IV

Directions: Using the Word Bank, fill in the blanks with the word that best completes the thought of the sentence.

1. The Portuguese man-of-war is considered a _____.

2. An _____ is a musical piece that is primarily known in classical music.

3. His experiences seem almost _____ and extraordinary.

4. One of the most famous _____ artists is Walt Disney, who made Mickey Mouse famous the world over.

5. Tibet is an _____ nation.

6. It has a lion's body and the head and the wings of an eagle; the _____ is an interesting mythological creature.

7. A humorous five-lined rhymed stanza is a _____.

8. The percussion section is set at the very back of an _____.

9. The seventh planet from the Sun is called _____.

10. _____ are architectural and structural features of a building.

> **Word Bank:** animation, cnidarian, columns, griffin, limerick, opus, orchestra, quixotic, autonomous, Uranus

REVIEW EXERCISE V

Directions: Underline the word that best completes the meaning of the sentence.

1. The *magnification/lengthening* of the bacteria under the microscope looked like something from a science fiction film.

2. When she hiked up the mountain too high, *spelling/vertigo* set in from lack of oxygen and she nearly fell.

3. Rossetti was a member of the *clowns/pre-Raphaelites* who disliked formal academic art.

4. The *monkey/albatross* is a long-winged bird that inhabits areas of the Pacific Ocean.

5. He never makes any sense; his thoughts flow just like a *stream-of-consciousness/river* novel.

6. The weather was *cheerful/bleak* at the beach this morning, and then it began to pour down rain.

7. The *worried/frail* old woman had difficulty walking because she was so weak and fragile.

8. The *fusion/separation* of the colors red and blue produces purple.

9. The *persecution/melting* of the tribe of indigenous people led to an upheaval that caused thousands to die.

10. Whenever we have a disaster drill at school, it causes a *plow/disturbance* and focusing on our work becomes difficult.

REVIEW EXERCISE VI

Directions: Using the Word Bank, fill in the blank with the word that best completes the thought of the sentence.

1. After Tanisha went away to college, she became more and more _____ , bizarre and eclectically behaved.

2. Avery believed that his partner for the group project was _____ and bold because he so outspoken.

3. His business was _____; it was a sham, and he was a fraud.

4. Oftentimes the army hires _____ to teach their recruits.

5. After losing so much weight, his jeans were quite _____.

6. My mother's apple pies were never too _____; they were always the perfect degree of sweetness.

7. The spy bleached her dark _____ hair to blonde to evade the enemy.

8. Twenty emaciated dogs were found in her home when she died; they were extremely _____.

9. You can never accuse her of being too _____; she seems to always know what is fair and what is not fair.

10. The _____ disease was torturous to endure.

> **Word Bank:** civilian, roomy, tart, auburn, audacious, bogus, bohemian, diplomatic, malignant, malnourished

REVIEW EXERCISE VII

Directions: Write a sentence using each of the vocabulary words listed.

1. tranquilly _____

_____

2. serpentinely _____

_____

3. dramatically _____

_____

4. meticulously _____

_____

5. extravagantly _____

_____

6. artistically _____

_____

7. boastfully _____

_____

8. offensively _____

_____

9. poetically _____

_____

10. whimsically _____

_____

REVIEW EXERCISE VIII

Directions: Using the Word Bank, complete the sentence with the vocabulary word that best fits the meaning.

1. _____ your last memo, we will address that issue at the next board meeting.
2. I wanted to talk to you _____ your son.

3. If you will step _____ , the train will be departing soon.

4. Going _____ all odds, our team came from behind and won the championship.

5. _____ losing twenty of our fifty games this season, we consider the season a success.

6. _____ two months, she will be moving permanently to her new home.

7. Lift that rock, and you will find all sorts of bugs _____.

8. _____ one small detail, I would consider the task complete.

9. The next time we take that lengthy of a road trip, we will travel _____ first class and not economy.

10. With that _____, the trip went well considering the delays at the airport.

Word Bank: aboard, against, concerning, despite, excepting, notwithstanding, regarding, underneath, via, within

---

REVIEW EXERCISE IX

Directions: Underline the word that best completes the meaning of the sentence.

1. The detective will *ravel/unravel* the mysterious crime.
2. Everything that the principal said was *redundant/reclusive* because he had said it all before.
3. Suddenly Joshua felt a sharp *tear/pang* in his abdomen.
4. Many jailed *informants/moles* are unreliable.
5. Reverend Desmond's morning *kick/homily* was inspiring.
6. I cannot wait to see the *jaundice/kabuki* theater while we are in Kyoto.
7. *Crater/Hole* Lake in Oregon is a spectacular sight.
8. This is where our paths *diverge/jaunt*; you go that way, and I will go this way.
9. All of that work was *tiny/superfluous*, but thank you for working so diligently.
10. Our school talent show will have a large section of students who like to *push/pantomime*.

REVIEW EXERCISE X

Directions: Using the Word Bank, fill in the blanks with a vocabulary word that best fits the context of the sentence.

1. The basement was creepy; it was _____ and damp and full of scary spiders.
2. If you do that, you are going to _____ all of your efforts to change a bad habit.

3. A large part of the population of Central America is _____, part Spanish and part indigenous peoples.

4. Sometimes I think she is a real _____ the way she changes her personality depending upon who she is with.

5. Most _____ are completely boring and difficult to stay awake through, but his speech was spectacular and moving.

6. My favorite thing on a Sunday morning is a _____ along with taking my time to read the Sunday paper.

7. After a long day at work, it is relaxing to come home and listen to the _____; it relieves stress.

8. Julius Caesar was very much liked by the _____ despite what Brutus and Cassius had to say.

9. I have never heard of anyone ever wanting to become a _____ when they grow up. Who wants to start a dishonest business?

10. It never fails that when the plane _____, my ears begin to pop.

> **Word Bank:** chameleon, dank, legatos, mestizo, mocha, descends, orations, plebians, racketeer, sabotage

REVIEW EXERCISE XI

Directions: Underline the word that best completes the meaning of the sentence.

1. In hiring employees, it is best to avoid *patriarch/nepotism* because that often leads to problems.

2. It was common in the 1700s for men to wear *wigs/pathos*.

3. They are going to *disband/orbit* the company and divide the employees as well.

4. When you speak with him, he presents himself with such *proximity/pathos* that it makes you want to cry.

5. The astronaut's final *fizz/orbit* was uneventful.

6. The building was designed like a *honeycomb/patriarch*, similar to the six-sided cells of a bee's nest.

7. The *fizzy/glorifying* sound of champagne fills the air during New Year's Eve.

8. The houses were built within such close *nepotism/proximity* that the neighbors could practically reach out and touch the house next door.

9. The *patriarch/orbit* of the family still resides in Italy.

10. They will begin to *pathos/glorify* the servicemen's commitments as soon as they return from Iraq.

REVIEW EXERCISE XII

Directions: Write a sentence using the vocabulary word in the proper context.

1. trailblazer _____

_____

2. steppe _____

_____

3. radiate _____

_____

4. gullible _____

_____

5. beacon _____

_____

6. learned _____

_____

7. pedigree _____

_____

8. egotism _____

_____

9. cosmopolitan _____

_____

10. anopheles _____

_____

REVIEW EXERCISE XIII

Directions: Underline the word that best fits the meaning of the sentence.

1. The opening of the play was *heron/premature* because the audience had not arrived.
2. Before you leave for the island, check the *virgule/barometer* to make sure the weather is going to be pleasant.
3. *Seasonable/Lasagna* is my favorite Italian dish.
4. Did you know that a *virgule/heron* is the slanted line that separate words or lines?
5. Jefferson Davis was the president of the *Confederacy/lasagna*.
6. Her dress was far too *jinx/flamboyant* for my tastes.

7. A long-legged *seasonable/heron* gracefully wades in the marshes.

8. Do not *jinx/tintinnabulation* it!

9. I have got to get my ears checked; this *tintinnabulation/barometer* continues to annoy me.

10. The Smith's decorations are certainly *jinx/seasonable*.

REVIEW EXERCISE XIV

Directions: Using the Word Bank, write the vocabulary word on the line next to its definition.

1. _____ To add notes to explain or clarify.

2. _____ To win the attention or the interest of.

3. _____ The orange or red substance occurring in carrots, tomatoes, and other vegetables and that is a source of vitamin A.

4. _____ To mend by weaving yarn across a hole.

5. _____ A part or extract of a film, book, or song.

6. _____ Aimed or shot at a very close range.

7. _____ An artificial or natural lake that is used to store a water supply.

8. _____ To rebound or bounce off a surface.

9. _____ A series of giant waves caused by a disturbance in the ocean floor.

10. _____ Cloudy, muddy, not clear.

> **Word Bank:** reservoir, turbid, ricochet, darn, excerpt, annotate, tsunami, beguile, carotene, point-blank

REVIEW EXERCISE XV

Directions: Write a sentence using the vocabulary word in the proper context.

1. abrasive _____

_____

2. asteroid _____

_____

3. chanteuse _____

_____

4. fallow _____

_____

5. kinetic _____

_____

6. peccadillo _____

_____

7. self-preservation _____

_____

8. summon _____

_____

9. trance _____

_____

10. vesicle _____

_____

REVIEW EXERCISE XVI

Directions: Using the Word Bank, write the vocabulary word on the line next to its definition.

1. _____ Before the Civil War in the United States.
2. _____ An area of ground that is permanently wet and spongy from decayed plants.
3. _____ A large cave.
4. _____ To behead.
5. _____ To keep in confinement or to cause delay.
6. _____ The blocking of light of either the sun or the moon.
7. _____ To cause a person to feel disgraced or embarrassed.
8. _____ A connoisseur of wines.
9. _____ A nation ruled by the wealthy.
10. _____ Long, or tall and thin.

> **Word Bank:** bog, spindly, plutocracy, eclipse, antebellum, decapitate, detain, humiliate, oenophile, cavern

REVIEW EXERCISE XVII

Directions: Using the Word Bank, fill in the blanks with the vocabulary word that best fits the context of the sentence.

1. The nurse will instruct you on how to continue to _____ the wound with ointment.

2. _____ racing was an exciting pastime in ancient Rome.

3. The grass _____ after the rain.

4. The librarian looked stereotypical with her _____ clothes and old-fashioned hairstyle.

5. Allison's jeans were a lovely dark _____ blue.

6. I want to win the _____!

7. The letters of complaint to the publisher were _____, and the mailroom employees could not keep up.

8. Allow your _____ to judge; they will know better how to dress.

9. Tibet is a _____ country.

10. Shylock, a character from Shakespeare's *Merchant of Venice,* practiced _____; he lent money with high interest.

> **Word Bank:** anoint, peers, voluminous, lottery, chariot, mountainous, usury, indigo, glistens, dowdy

REVIEW EXERCISE XVIII

Directions: Using the Word Bank, fill in the blanks with a vocabulary word that best fits the context of the sentence.

1. The little boy was _____ when his mother would not buy him a new GI Joe.

2. The creepy old man that lives above me _____ around like an elephant and makes all kinds of noise.

3. Their behavior was quite _____ after the teacher decided to make them write an essay.

4. The English burn a model of Guy Fawkes in _____ on Guy Fawkes Day.

5. The state of economics is in a constant state of _____; it is always changing.

6. "The _____! The _____!" is a famous line from the *Heart of Darkness,* a novel by Joseph Conrad.

7. *Fear and _____ in Las Vegas* is the name of a film starring Johnny Depp.

8. That, my friend, is not my _____; I do not work like that.

9. The architect designed the house so that the bedrooms were located in the _____ portion of the house where it is the quietest.

10. You will become a _____ if you do not settle down and find a job.

> **Word Bank:** vagrant, modus operandi, horror, bawling, civilized, effigy, flux, loathing, posterior, stomps

REVIEW EXERCISE XIX

Directions: Using the Word Bank, fill in the blanks with a vocabulary word that best fits the context of the sentence.

1. The _____ of the egg contains cholesterol.
2. The children love to go _____ in the shore breakers at the beach.
3. _____ says the horse!
4. The elderly woman was _____ and had not felt well in ages.
5. One hundred pennies or one hundred _____ make one dollar.
6. Many men tend to go _____ as they age, and for some, this sign of aging is a nightmare.
7. Line up in the _____ please.
8. She set the _____ by being such an honorable employee.
9. Do not _____ and complain; do something about it!
10. Olivia, the character in Shakespeare's *Twelfth Night,* is in _____ for her dead brother.

> **Word Bank:** ailing, bald, precedents, queue, wading, yolk, whine, cents, mourning, neigh

REVIEW EXERCISE XX

Directions: Using the Word Bank, fill in the blanks with a vocabulary word that best fits the context of the sentence.

1. The character Scrooge in Charles Dickens's novella *A Christmas Carol* is a _____ and grumpy old man.
2. The _____ and sidewalk cafes in Paris are like nothing else in the world.
3. Hurricane Katrina was one of the most _____ events in the history of natural disasters in the U.S.
4. The long, winding line of people dancing the _____ was exciting to witness.
5. He could not help but _____ at her beauty and charm.
6. Vincent van Gogh used an _____ when he painted.
7. Our camping favorite is s'mores (short for some more), which are made with chocolate, graham crackers, and roasted _____ all melted together.
8. The jungle is _____ with snakes and other wild things.
9. With large groups at a restaurant, the _____ is included with the meal.
10. Her integrity was beyond _____.

> **Word Bank:** peevish, reproach, teeming, easel, gape, cataclysmic, bistros, conga, gratuity, marshmallow

REVIEW EXERCISE XXI

Directions: Using the Word Bank, write the vocabulary word next to its definition.

1. _____ A certificate awarded by a school or college to a person who has successfully completed a course of study.

2. _____ A boneless piece of meat or fish.

3. _____ To bite persistently at something hard.

4. _____ A small village.

5. _____ To seize control of a vehicle by force.

6. _____ To charge a public official with misconduct in office before a tribunal.

7. _____ A small bloodsucking worm that usually lives in water.

8. _____ To blend together or merge.

9. _____ Of or relating to the Oedipus complex (attraction of a child to the parent of the opposite sex—related to the Greek legend of Oedipus).

10. _____ Having many syllables.

> **Word Bank:** diploma, meld, sesquipedalian, impeach, hamlet, gnaw, fillet, oedipal, leech, hijack

REVIEW EXERCISE XXII

Directions: Using the Word Bank, fill in the blanks with the vocabulary word that best fits the context of the sentence.

1. Let me _____ on that for awhile; I will make a decision by tomorrow.

2. Parker's new toy is _____; he broke it already!

3. I do not really think Fred is a _____ by nature, although he has spent time in jail for driving without a license.

4. In order to do well on this major exam, I need to _____ the information into my brain.

5. The process will be _____ if each step is thoroughly completed.

6. They invited us over to dinner last month, and I feel it is my duty to _____ and have them over this week.

7. That was the season finale, the _____. What an ending!

8. The beach cities are filled with _____ who move from bench to bench and use the public restrooms and other facilities.

9. The answer to this dilemma is _____; there is not a clear solution.

10. The Smiths hired a new _____ to look after Amanda and Emily.

> **Word Bank:** desperado, engrain, facilitated, governess, nebulous, omega, reciprocate, kaput, ruminate, vagrants

REVIEW EXERCISE XXIII

Directions: Using the Word Bank, write the vocabulary word next to its definition.

1. _____ Rural or rustic.

2. _____ A showy trinket.

3. _____ Broken piece of pottery or glass.

4. _____ Overexcited; feeling of spinning or twirling.

5. _____ To eye lecherously.

6. _____ A swear word or other expression used with an exclamation.

7. _____ Separate or remote.

8. _____ Hawaiian word that means hello or good-bye.

9. _____ is a card game in which a bluff is used as players bet on the game.

10. _____ an appliance with a rotating spit used to roast or barbecue meat.

Word Bank: aloha, bauble, countrified, expletive, giddy, insular, ogle, poker, rotisserie, shard

Chapter 26

COMPREHENSIVE ENGLISH EXAM

1. _____ Two clauses together make a _____ sentence.
   a. simple
   b. compound
   c. complex
   d. compound-complex

2. _____ "Confronting a problem honestly is the best way to deal with it" is a sentence that has a _____ phrase.
   a. verbal
   b. adverb
   c. participial
   d. gerund

3. _____ Identify the sentence with the compound predicate.
   a. An aurora is a sporadic display of light in the night sky.
   b. It is caused by charged particles from the Sun interacting with air molecules in Earth's magnetic field.
   c. Auroras occur in polar regions.
   d. They are known as aurora borealis in the north or as aurora australis in the south.

4. _____ Delayed subjects are those that appear _____ the verb.
   a. between
   b. before
   c. after
   d. all of the above

5. _____ Parentheses are used to enclose _____ within a sentence.
   a. additional or explanatory information
   b. slang
   c. added words to a quote
   d. spelling errors

6. _____ Identify the homonyms.
    a. way, whey, weigh
    b. better, worse
    c. easy, hard
    d. fantastic, great

7. _____ The root *mono* means _____.
    a. six
    b. five
    c. two
    d. one

8. _____ Identify the prepositional phrase below.
    a. without going into the water
    b. just a minute
    c. she is going
    d. the stock market crashed

9. _____ Which of the following sentences has an adverb that modifies another adverb?
    a. Her car and driver were waiting outside the restaurant.
    b. The spending habits of the heiress were entirely too extravagant.
    c. She was dressed in the latest fashions.
    d. all of the above

10. _____ Imperative sentences _____.
    a. give commands or make requests
    b. make statements
    c. ask questions
    d. none of the above

11. _____ Which of the following words has a long *i* sound?
    a. lid
    b. film
    c. fill
    d. fight

12. _____ Identify the indefinite articles below.
    a. the
    b. an, a
    c. the, a
    d. an, the

13. _____ Identify the sentence that is incorrectly capitalized.
    a. j. d. salinger is noted for his depictions of lonely characters.
    b. His characters are bored and frustrated with a conformist world.
    c. Salinger is reclusive and shuns all publicity.
    d. *The Catcher in the Rye* is his only novel.

14. _____ *After, against,* and *before* are _____.
    a. nouns
    b. adverbs
    c. prepositions
    d. verbs

15. _____ When you hope for a positive outcome, you_____.
    a. kick the bucket
    b. keep your fingers crossed
    c. leave no stone unturned
    d. look before you leap

16. _____ True or False? Action verbs can be either physical or mental activities.
    a. True
    b. False

17. _____ The root *helio* means _____.
    a. sun
    b. carry
    c. see
    d. help

18. _____ A complex sentence contains _____.
    a. two independent clauses
    b. a dependent clause and an independent clause
    c. three simple sentences
    d. two independent clauses and three predicates

19. _____ Identify the synonyms.
    a. green/black
    b. indigo/blue
    c. red/orange
    d. yellow/chartreuse

20. _____ Identify the sentence with the compound subject.
    a. The three sisters first wrote under male pseudonyms.
    b. The Brontë sisters were born in England.
    c. Anne, Emily, and Charlotte Brontë were sisters.
    d. All three sisters were novelists and poets.

21. _____ Which of the following is a common noun?
    a. Horatio
    b. hothouse
    c. Hernandez
    d. Winslow Homer

22. _____ Identify which of the following digraphs has a long *a* sound.
    a. moat
    b. boat
    c. rain
    d. oar

23. _____ True or False? Brackets are used when words are added to a quote that are not the author's original words.
    a. True
    b. False

24. _____ Identify the singular indefinite pronouns.
    a. another
    b. either
    c. each
    d. all of the above

25. _____ Identify the interrogative sentence below.
    a. Jaffa is a city in Israel.
    b. It is a suburb of Tel Aviv.
    c. Did you know it was captured by Alexander the Great in 332 B.C.?
    d. The city was settled in 1948 by Israelis.

26. _____ The use of the pronoun *I* in a story is known as ____.
    a. second-person narrative
    b. third-person narrative
    c. first-person narrative
    d. fourth-person narrative

27. _____ Which of the following words is misspelled?
    a. timing
    b. hopeful
    c. primeing
    d. skated

28. _____ *Wow!*, *Oh no!*, and *Watch it!* are _____.
    a. interjections
    b. prepositions
    c. nouns
    d. conjunctions

29. _____ The root of the words *liberation/liberty/libertarian* means
    a. fire
    b. animal
    c. write
    d. free

30. _____ A(n) _____ verb connects the noun or pronoun of a sentence with another word or group of words.
    a. action
    b. linking
    c. first person
    d. present tense

31. _____ Which of the following is correctly punctuated?
    a. henri rousseau was a french painter and best known for his scenes from a tropical jungle.
    b. jean Jacques rousseau was a French philosopher whose ideas helped shape the political events that caused the French revolution.
    c. Theodore Rousseau was a French painter and a leading member of the Barbizon School, a nineteenth century school of landscape.
    d. all of the above

32. _____ Identify the indirect object below.
    a. He conducts for the <u>Los Angeles</u> orchestra.
    b. There are <u>many instruments</u> in an orchestra.
    c. <u>The cello</u> is my favorite instrument.
    d. The French horn <u>sounds beautiful</u>.

33. _____ The indefinite pronouns *all, any, half, most, none,* and *some* can be
    _____.
    a. French or English
    b. depressed or happy
    c. singular or plural
    d. only singular

34. _____ An *allusion* is _____.
    a. a reference to something
    b. an influence
    c. a false impression
    d. none of the above

35. _____ Adverbs modify _____.
    a. nouns
    b. articles
    c. prepositions
    d. verbs

36. _____ Identify the gerund.
    a. swimming
    b. golf
    c. tennis
    d. ski

37. _____ *That, these, this,* and *those* are pronouns that can also be used as
    _____.
    a. verbs
    b. adverbs
    c. prepositions
    d. adjectives

38. _____ Identify the masculine noun below.
   a. hostess
   b. friend
   c. rooster
   d. education

39. _____ When *y* is the last letter of a word and it is preceded by a consonant, _____.
   a. change the *y* to *e* and then add the suffix
   b. change the *y* to *i* and then add the suffix
   c. change the *y* to *s* and then add the suffix
   d. none of the above

40. _____ Infinitive phrases begin with the word _____.
   a. *this*
   b. *taken*
   c. *to*
   d. *those*

41. _____ Which of the following diphthongs has an *oy*-like sound?
   a. house
   b. hook
   c. oil
   d. recoup

42. _____ True or False? Roots carry the primary meaning of a word.
   a. True
   b. False

43. _____ Identify the compound-complex sentence.
   a. Miles Davis was a jazz trumpeter and composer who played bebop with Charlie Parker, and then he formed a quintet with the famous saxophonist John Coltrane.
   b. Bette Davis, an American actress, is noted for strong character portrayals.
   c. Jefferson Davis was an American statesman and president of the Confederate States during the Civil War.
   d. Stuart Davis was a painter who favored cubism.

44. _____ Which of the following is an exclamatory sentence?
   a. Look out for the jaguar.
   b. It is a large spotted cat found in North and South America.
   c. You're mean!
   d. Jaguars eat large mammals, turtles, and fish.

45. _____ A neuter noun is _____ masculine or feminine.
   a. always
   b. continually
   c. absent
   d. neither

46. _____ Identify the common adjective in the list below.
  a. French
  b. Bohemian
  c. yellow
  d. English

47. _____ *Lily-livered* and *yellow-bellied* mean _____
  a. bravery
  b. noble
  c. cowardly
  d. flustered

48. _____ Which of the following is the correct plural form of the word?
  a. geese
  b. glasses
  c. teeth
  d. all of the above

49. _____ *Who, whom, whose, which,* and *what* are _____ pronouns.
  a. collective
  b. interrogative
  c. possessive
  d. objective

50. _____ *Here, there,* and *outside* are adverbs of _____.
  a. time
  b. place
  c. manner
  d. degree

51. _____ *And, so, but, nor, yet, or,* and *for* are _____.
  a. prepositions
  b. interjections
  c. conjunctions
  d. verbs

52. _____ True or False? Nouns that are used as adjectives are words that individually can stand alone as nouns.
  a. True
  b. False

53. _____ Identify the R-controlled word whose sound changes radically with an added vowel
  a. store
  b. chore
  c. sore
  d. fire

54. _____ Identify the singular verbs below.
    a. works, builds, spends
    b. work, build, spend
    c. take, supply, bake
    d. none of the above

55. _____ An ellipsis is a series of _____.
    a. five periods and a comma
    b. three semicolons
    c. two periods
    d. three periods

56. _____ Identify the misspelled word below.
    a. embarrass
    b. receive
    c. unique
    d. yeild

57. _____ True or False? The predicate is the noun or pronoun part of the sentence.
    a. True
    b. False

58. _____ Which of the following is the future tense of the word *squeeze*?
    a. I squeeze.
    b. She will squeeze.
    c. I had squeezed.
    d. They will have squeezed.

59. _____ The use of a noun as a direct object is called a_____ noun.
    a. predicate
    b. possessive
    c. object
    d. subject

60. _____ To *put your foot in your mouth* means that_____.
    a. you are very old
    b. you have a big mouth
    c. your foot tastes good
    d. you said something stupid or embarrassing

61. _____ The number of a pronoun includes _____ pronouns.
    a. singular and plural
    b. possessive and interrogative
    c. nominative and collective
    d. none of the above

62. _____ Identify the sentence that does NOT agree in number.
    a. Barcelona is a beautiful and interesting city.
    b. Traveling around London is easy because of the subway.
    c. Paris are the city of love.
    d. Dublin is a busy and cosmopolitan city.

COMPREHENSIVE ENGLISH EXAM **391**

63. _____ The pronoun *I* is _____ capitalized.
    a. never
    b. seldom
    c. occasionally
    d. always

64. _____ *Seldom, yearly,* and *quarterly* are adverbs of _____.
    a. time
    b. place
    c. manner
    d. degree

65. _____ Periods are used _____.
    a. to end a sentence that makes a statement
    b. to end a question
    c. to end an exclamation
    d. on top of a comma

66. _____ Identify the compound pronoun below.
    a. I
    b. she
    c. yourself
    d. each other

67. _____ Adding a suffix _____.
    a. changes nothing about the word
    b. changes the meaning of the word
    c. cancels out the word
    d. destroys the word

68. _____ Identify the complex sentence below.
    a. Chihuahua is the largest state in Mexico.
    b. Chihuahua is the capital of Chihuahua.
    c. The climate and terrain vary in Chihuahua from mountainous to desert.
    d. none of the above

69. _____ Identify the idiom.
    a. Go to the doctor.
    b. Once in a blue moon.
    c. Pigs eat garbage.
    d. Over the river and through the woods.

70. _____ True or False? Imperative sentences can be punctuated with a period or with an exclamation point.
    a. True
    b. False

71. _____ There are _____ types of conjunctions.
    a. one
    b. six
    c. three
    d. twelve

72. _____ Identify the dependent clause below.
    a. and lived until 1877.
    b. Yesterday we sailed to Catalina,
    c. They collaborated on many books.
    d. none of the above

73. _____ True or False? Interrogative pronouns ask a question.
    a. True
    b. False

74. _____ The _____ receives the action of the predicate.
    a. direct object
    b. subject
    c. noun
    d. indirect object

75. _____ Identify which of the following is incorrectly capitalized.
    a. new year's day
    b. empire state building
    c. sunday
    d. all of the above

76. _____ Identify the first-person pronoun.
    a. you
    b. he
    c. she
    d. I

77. _____ Which of the following is the plural of mouse?
    a. mouses
    b. mice
    c. mices
    d. mouse

78. _____ Identify the antonyms.
    a. random/arbitrary
    b. clock/timepiece
    c. decrease/add
    d. peaceful/calm

79. _____ The superlative form of the word *low* is _____.
    a. low
    b. lower
    c. lowest
    d. most low

80. _____ A paragraph should be _____
    a. well structured and organized
    b. simple
    c. plain
    d. redundant

81. _____ Topic sentences _____.
  a. follow the conclusion
  b. support the main idea
  c. introduce a topic
  d. all of the above

82. _____ There is/are _____ idea(s) supported in each paragraph.
  a. six
  b. twelve
  c. one
  d. nine

83. _____ A transitional sentence _____ moves the reader from one idea to another.
  a. sincerely
  b. smoothly
  c. hastily
  d. austerely

84. _____ A _____ adds detail and interest to a paragraph.
  a. topic sentence
  b. concluding sentence
  c. transitional sentence
  d. support sentence

85. _____ Identify the three forms of adverbs.
  a. positive, comparative, negative
  b. positive, comparative, insignificant
  c. positive, negative, superlative
  d. positive, comparative, superlative

86. _____ A *piece of cake* means that _____.
  a. you pass the blame
  b. it is easy
  c. you say something stupid
  d. you criticize someone

87. _____ *Within, upon,* and *without* are _____.
  a. compound prepositions
  b. simple prepositions
  c. phrasal prepositions
  d. none of the above

88. _____ Independent clauses express a complete thought and _____.
  a. cannot stand alone
  b. can stand alone
  c. never express good ideas
  d. all of the above

89. _____ Identify the complex sentence below.
    a. Chicory is a perennial weedy plant whose leaves are often cooked and eaten.
    b. Chicory is a plant.
    c. Its fleshy roots are dried and ground up to mix with coffee.
    d. Chicory has bright blue flowers.

90. _____ Which of the following sentences below uses a colon correctly?
    a. The dogs: ate spinach and meatballs.
    b. The menu includes: steak, garlic mashed potatoes, asparagus and chocolate mousse.
    c. Never take: medicine.
    d. Getting to the zoo takes: hours.

91. _____ Identify the declarative sentence.
    a. Jamaica is an independent island nation in the Caribbean.
    b. Did you know that Jamaica's capital is Kingston?
    c. Its beaches are beautiful!
    d. All of the above

92. _____ Which of the following should be capitalized?
    a. titles
    b. days of the week
    c. awards
    d. all of the above

93. _____ Identify the words with the silent consonants.
    a. rhythm, wrap, thigh
    b. sing, abuse, lay
    c. rise, mellow, life
    d. never, rode, off

94. _____ The root *astro* means _____.
    a. study of man
    b. field
    c. cave
    d. star

95. _____ The word *who's* is a _____.
    a. preposition
    b. noun
    c. contraction
    d. verb

96. _____ *Jack Sprat* is a _____.
    a. Greek myth
    b. fairy tale
    c. nursery rhyme
    d. Biblical allusion

97. _____ The Blarney Stone is located in _____.
    a. Switzerland
    b. Mexico
    c. Massachusetts
    d. Ireland

98. _____ The _____ are large, strong warrior women.
    a. Amazons
    b. Nymphs
    c. Unicorns
    d. Argonauts

99. _____ The money lender named _____ demanded a pound of flesh from the title character in this Shakespearean play.
    a. Iago
    b. Desdemona
    c. Shylock
    d. Bard

100. _____ The story of the loaves and fishes is a _____ allusion.
     a. mythological
     b. folkloric
     c. historical
     d. Biblical

APPENDIX

Chapter 1 English Pretest

1. C	31. D	61. A	91. D
2. A	32. A	62. B	92. B
3. A	33. C	63. A	93. D
4. D	34. A	64. C	94. C
5. B	35. C	65. D	95. A
6. C	36. A	66. B	96. D
7. D	37. C	67. A	97. B
8. A	38. C	68. B	98. C
9. C	39. A	69. D	99. C
10. A	40. D	70. C	100. A
11. A	41. B	71. C	
12. B	42. A	72. D	
13. D	43. B	73. A	
14. A	44. D	74. A	
15. C	45. B	75. C	
16. D	46. B	76. C	
17. A	47. A	77. A	
18. A	48. A	78. B	
19. C	49. B	79. C	
20. B	50. D	80. A	
21. B	51. A	81. B	
22. C	52. C	82. D	
23. B	53. D	83. C	
24. A	54. D	84. D	
25. C	55. A	85. B	
26. C	56. B	86. C	
27. A	57. D	87. A	
28. D	58. A	88. D	
29. C	59. C	89. C	
30. A	60. D	90. A	

Chapter 2 Nouns

Practice I

1. A	6. A	11. A	16. C
2. C	7. A	12. C	17. A
3. C	8. C	13. C	18. A
4. C	9. C	14. C	19. C
5. A	10. A	15. A	20. A

Practice II

1. batch
2. United Nations
3. crowds
4. orchestra
5. swarm
6. Seattle Supersonics
7. congregation
8. pride
9. flocks
10. team

Practice III

1. person
2. idea
3. thing
4. thing/idea
5. person
6. thing
7. place/thing
8. idea
9. place/thing
10. place/thing

Practice IV

In medieval <u>Europe</u>, a knight was a man of some noble status. <u>King Arthur</u> led a group of knights of the highest order called the <u>Knights</u> of the <u>Round Table</u>. As knights, these men were admired for their battle skills, honesty, and bravery. Each year, <u>King Arthur</u> asked the knights to return to <u>Camelot</u> (the site of <u>King Arthur's</u> court) on <u>Pentecost</u> (a religious festival celebrated in <u>May</u> or <u>June</u>). There were twenty-five knights whose names are inscribed on the <u>Winchester Round Table</u>; <u>Sir Galahad</u>, <u>Sir Gawain,</u> and <u>Sir Lancelot du Lac</u> are three of the twenty-five knights.

Practice V

1. stages
2. concert
3. melodies
4. necklaces
5. dinner
6. New York Knicks
7. counselor
8. assistants
9. litters
10. calendar

Practice VI

Answers may vary

1. Frenchman
2. onion ring
3. bookmark
4. grandfather
5. newspaper
6. oceangoing
7. North Atlantic
8. Mexican-American
9. university student
10. Buddhist monk

Practice VII

1. indefinite
2. masculine
3. feminine
4. neuter
5. feminine
6. indefinite
7. neuter
8. indefinite
9. indefinite
10. indefinite

Practice VIII

1. possessive
2. objective
3. subject
4. subject
5. predicate
6. subject
7. possessive
8. predicate
9. objective
10. predicate

Practice IX

Sentences will vary

1. Winning the gold medal in long-distance running is my life-long goal.
2. Without a doubt, traveling is my favorite hobby.
3. Writing is relaxing
4. Whispering while someone is speaking is impolite.
5. Swimming without a life jacket in the ocean is risky.
6. Snoring is a strange and annoying habit.
7. Canning takes a great deal of time and patience.
8. Spelling correctly is a good skill to practice.

9. Sleeping is good.
10. Walking relieves stress.

Chapter 2 Review Quizzes: Vocabulary Review Quiz

1. D   6. G
2. B   7. J
3. H   8. E
4. A   9. F
5. I   10. C

Noun Definitions

1. B   6. B
2. C   7. B
3. A   8. C
4. C   9. D
5. A   10. A

Common and Proper Nouns

The Dominican Republic is an independent nation that is located in the West Indies. The small country occupies the eastern two-thirds of the island called Hispaniola. The western third of the island is Haiti. The island was visited by Christopher Columbus in 1492. At that time, a Spanish settlement was established in Santo Domingo, which is the Dominican Republic's present-day capital. In 1697, the western third of the country was ceded to France. In 1795, the entire island was ruled by the French, but the eastern side was returned to Spain in 1809. The Dominican Republic won its independence a second time in 1844 after being annexed to Haiti in 1821.

Abstract and Concrete Nouns

Transcendental meditation is a form of relaxation. This technique is partly based on ancient Hindu ideology, and it was rediscovered in the twentieth century by an Indian spiritual teacher. Those who practice meditation concentrate on a mantra, a word or phrase that they repeat over and over to achieve a state of relaxation. Physiologically, meditation decreases oxygen consumption and heart rate.

Singular and Plural Nouns

1. The flies enjoyed our picnic as much as we did. fly picnics
2. Swimming in the ocean off the coast of Florida is dangerous because of a record number of shark attacks. oceans coasts sharks
3. A neuron is a basic structural element of the nervous system. neurons elements
4. The Masai are characteristically tall and slender Africans from Kenya and Tanzania. Masai African
5. A clock is an instrument for measuring time. clocks instruments
6. The little pig squealed when it was taken from its mother. pigs mothers
7. Tiny Tim is the handicapped son of Bob Cratchit in Charles Dickens's *A Christmas Carol.* sons Carols
8. Kitsch, pronounced *kich*, is any work of art or other objects such as furniture that are intended to look expensive but are actually ugly or in bad taste. works object

9. One of the most famous movie <u>monsters</u> is named King Kong, a giant <u>ape</u> that terrorizes New York City. _____ monster _____ apes

10. Chicken pox is a mild but contagious <u>dis-ease</u> that causes <u>blisters</u> on the skin. diseases _____ blister _____

Feminine, Masculine, Neuter, and Indefinite Nouns

<u>Michel Foucault</u> _M_ was a French <u>philosopher</u> _I_ and <u>historian</u> _I_. He studied the historical and social <u>contexts</u> _N_ of *ideas* _N_ and *institutions* _N_ such as <u>prison</u> _N_, <u>school</u> _N_, <u>asylum</u> _N_, and the <u>police force</u> _N_. His basic <u>premise</u> _N_ was that <u>systems</u> _N_ of knowledge, like <u>psychology</u> _N_, have changed <u>humans</u> _I_ into <u>subjects</u> _I_.

Noun Usage
1. possessive noun
2. object noun
3. subject noun
4. subject noun
5. object noun
6. predicate noun
7. object noun
8. subject noun
9. subject noun
10. predicate noun

Gerunds
Answers will vary
1. Dancing
2. Swimming
3. Protesting
4. Flying
5. Snoring
6. Laughing
7. Fishing
8. Practicing
9. Skiing
10. Buying

Chapter 3 Pronouns

Practice I
1. The <u>shark</u> is determined to capture [its] next victim, the sea lion.
2. The <u>volunteers</u> worked day and night to meet [their] goals for the opening of the New Globe Theatre.
3. <u>Geology</u> is a broad field of science; [it] incorporates many areas of study, from rock to ice.
4. In a mural painted by Mexican muralist Diego Rivera, the <u>woman</u> seemed captivated by [her] surroundings.
5. <u>Samuel Beckett</u> was born in Ireland in 1906, but [he] emigrated to Paris in the 1920s.
6. <u>Tennis</u> is a game played by either two or four players, and [it] is sometimes known as lawn tennis.
7. The <u>Theater of the Absurd</u> developed from the philosophy of Albert Camus. However, [it] was applied to modern drama in 1961, which demonstrated the irrationality of life.
8. <u>Terra-cotta</u> is absorbent but rigid earthenware. [It] is used in building, sculpture, and pottery.
9. <u>Shakespeare</u> wrote plays that were performed in the Globe Theatre, and [he] was part owner as well.
10. Although jazz trumpeter <u>Miles Davis</u> played with Charlie Parker, [he] formed a new band in 1955 that included saxophonist John Coltrane.

Practice II

The continent of Asia is the home of the famous Terra Cotta Warriors, *which* __S__ are found in China. Asia is the largest continent in the world. *It S* extends in the north from a part of Russia that is in the area of the Arctic Circle to south of the equator in Indonesia. However, *its* __S__ western boundary with Europe follows a line that runs through the Ural Mountains, west of the Caspian Sea, and along the Caucasus. Asia's eastern border includes the islands of Japan. Although Europe and Asia form one large continent, *they* __S__ have always been considered two continents. The people *who* __S__ inhabit Asia make up half the world's total population. Mandarin Chinese has more speakers than *any other* __P__ language of the continent. Economically, agriculture is important to Asia. Although less than 10 percent of the continent is cultivated, *it* __S__ produces more than 90 percent of the world's rice, rubber, cotton, and tobacco.

Practice III

Paragraphs using pronouns will vary

Practice IV

1. It was Nostradamus, the French prophet and astrologer, <u>who</u> was afraid of being persecuted during the Inquisition for heresy.
2. Jazz music consists of syncopated rhythms <u>that</u> are based on improvisation or creative, spur-of-the moment interpretations.
3. Mao Zedong is the Chinese statesman to <u>whom</u> credit is given for helping to establish the People's Republic of China.
4. The novella is a highly structured, short narrative <u>that</u> is longer than a short story but shorter than a novel.
5. Artists Diego Rivera and José Clemente Orozco, <u>whose</u> murals are known internationally, are both from Mexico.
6. The U.S. Open is now played at Arthur Ashe Stadium, <u>which</u> was named after the respected African-American tennis player.
7. Terra-cotta is known as "baked earth," <u>which</u> is fired in a kiln at fairly low temperatures.
8. The name *Canaveral* is Spanish for "canebreak" and is derived from <u>those</u> explorers who discovered the area.
9. The theory of continental drift and the concept of seafloor spreading <u>that</u> were replaced by the theory of plate tectonics are fairly new to the field of geology.
10. The original Globe Theatre was built in an area known as Southwark on the bank of the Thames (pronounced "tems") River, <u>which</u> is now known as Bankside.

Practice V

1. Who	6. Who
2. whom	7. who
3. who	8. who
4. who	9. whom
5. whom	10. whom

Practice VI

1. which	6. which
2. that	7. that
3. which	8. which
4. that	9. that
5. which	10. that

Practice VII

you	him	that	your
her	<u>no one</u>	theirs	his
hers	<u>nothing</u>	them	yourselves
<u>one</u>	these	<u>other</u>	they
<u>another</u>	himself	<u>others</u>	this
any	many	our	those
<u>both</u>	he	<u>nobody</u>	their
itself	she	which	yours
<u>each</u>	neither	some	who
<u>either</u>	<u>anybody</u>	I	ours
<u>anyone</u>	it	ourselves	we
<u>anything</u>	its	<u>several</u>	what
me	<u>somebody</u>	whom	herself
everyone	mine	<u>someone</u>	whose
everything	my	<u>something</u>	yourself
few	such	<u>all</u>	us

Practice VIII
Sentences will vary

Practice IX
Sentences may vary

1. After this theater was demolished in 1644, it was rebuilt and then reopened in 1995.
2. That will be sent to the museum's laboratory for further study.
3. In 1980, Arthur Ashe became the non-playing captain of that team.
4. Those musicians and many others are legendary in the field of jazz and blues.
5. These plays, *Waiting for Godot, Endgame, and Happy Days,* explore ideas of survival, paralysis, and suffering.
6. That street in the ancient city of Teotihuacán is called the Avenue of the Dead.
7. That absurdist play by Samuel Beckett was first performed in French at a theater in Paris.
8. This plot symbolizes the meaninglessness of human life and connects the play to the themes of existentialist philosophy.
9. Considered literary existentialists, these authors wrote about characters who struggle with hopelessness and absurdity.
10. This is the first building with a thatched roof since the Great Fire of London in 1666.

Practice X

1. I	6. it
2. his	7. we
3. They	8. they
4. our	9. his
5. they	10. Her

Practice XI

1. third	6. first
2. second	7. second
3. first	8. third
4. third	9. first
5. first	10. third

Practice XII
Sentences will vary

1. you	6. they
2. he	7. we
3. she	8. they
4. it	9. she
5. we	10. you

Practice XIII

1. It was <u>my</u> understanding that <u>your</u> area of expertise would be the subject of a debate on ancient Mexico.
2. <u>Her</u> record for writing absurdist plays surpasses any that have preceded <u>her</u>.
3. That is not <u>yours</u>! Give it back! It belongs in <u>his</u> grandfather's ancient artifacts collection.
4. Mexico is proud of <u>its</u> historic achievements that date back to pre-Columbian times.
5. <u>His</u> newest piece of art is definitely more outlandish than <u>yours</u>.
6. <u>Your</u> wish to become the first to research the life expectancy of sharks may be a dream come true.
7. <u>Their</u> music originates not only in the southern regions of the United States but from Africa as well.
8. <u>Its</u> name is Spanish for "canebreak."
9. Much to <u>her</u> surprise, the award for best new artist was given to a young woman who was inspired by blues music.
10. <u>His</u> works are often linked to the Theater of the Absurd.

Practice XIV

1. them
2. her
3. me
4. him
5. us
6. it
7. you

Practice XV

Sentences will vary

Practice XVI

1. M
2. N
3. M
4. M
5. N
6. N
7. N
8. F
9. F
10. N

Chapter 3 Review Quizzes: Vocabulary Review Quiz

1. B
2. C
3. D
4. F
5. J
6. A
7. G
8. I
9. E
10. H

Pronoun Definitions

1. C
2. B
3. D
4. C
5. A
6. D
7. C
8. D
9. A
10. B

Pronoun Antecedents

The <u>Bogside Artists</u> are mural painters [who] live and work in Northern Ireland. [Their] names are <u>Tom Kelly</u>, <u>William Kelly</u>, and <u>Kevin Hasson</u>. After working together since 1993, [they] finally completed what is known as the *People's Gallery* in 2004. [It] is a tribute to the local residents and the struggles [they] have endured in the name of human rights. The ten large <u>murals</u> are located in the area of Bogside, [which] is a neighborhood outside the city of Derry in Northern Ireland. [They] span the entire length of Rossville Street. [This] <u>area</u> was the site of intense political unrest between the British Army, and the Irish Republican Army, including the Battle of the Bogside and Bloody Sunday. Thousands of <u>people</u> visit the murals each year and pay tribute to lives lost in the name of human rights.

Pronoun Types

Answers may vary

The other day while Tim and __*I*__ were hanging out at home, and mostly because _*we*_ had nothing better to do, _*we*_ started a discussion about sharks of all things. _*I*_ told Tim that there are more than 360 different species of sharks. Then _*he*_ told _*me*_ that sharks normally swim at about 5 miles (8 km) per hour, but when _*they*_ attack _*they*_ reach speeds up to about 30 miles (48 km) per hour. _*It*_ was interesting to discover that _*each*_ of us knew facts about sharks that the _*other one*_ did not. So by the end of the discussion, _*we*_ were quite proud of _*ourselves*_. That was not only because _*we*_ both managed to learn a great deal more about sharks, but because the subject is _*something*_ _*that*_ neither one of us would ever bring up in a normal day-to-day conversation.

Pronoun Classes

1. RX
2. P
3. D
4. IT
5. RL
6. ID
7. D
8. IT
9. D
10. ID

Forms of Personal Pronouns

1. FPS
2. TPP
3. TPS
4. SPS
5. TPS
6. TPP
7. TPS
8. FPP
9. TPS
10. FPS

Pronoun Cases

1. P
2. O
3. P
4. N
5. P
6. N
7. O
8. P
9. O
10. N

Pronoun Genders

1. F
2. M
3. N
4. N
5. N
6. F
7. N
8. M
9. N
10. N

Chapter 4 Verbs

Practice I

1. kill/physical
2. ascend/physical
3. inspired/mental
4. flows/physical
5. hoped/mental
6. believed/mental
7. ended/physical
8. is known/mental
9. established/physical
10. planned/mental

Practice II

1. Lech Walesa, a Polish statesman and labor leader, <u>organized</u> an independent, self-governing labor union known as Solidarity in 1980.

2. In Greek mythology, dryads are nymphs of the woodland and guardian spirits of trees.

3. Scarlet fever, an acute infectious disease affecting children, is caused by bacteria.

4. Parvati, the wife of the Hindu god Shiva, is also the mother of the elephant-headed god Ganesh.

5. Lyme disease <u>causes</u> pain in the muscles and joints, a red rash, fever, and headache.

6. Paul McCartney <u>cowrote</u> most of the Beatles's hit songs with John Lennon.

7. The various forms of energy <u>include</u>: kinetic, potential, electrical, nuclear, thermal, light, and chemical.

8. The Lumière brothers, Louis and Auguste, are considered pioneers of cinematography with their invention of a combined motion picture camera and projector.

9. Salicylic acid, the colorless, crystalline ingredient used in aspirin, <u>occurs</u> naturally in plants such as willow bark and wintergreen oil.

10. The United States government <u>financed</u> the completion of the Panama Canal to use as a passage for war ships.

Practice III

1. operate
2. erodes
3. raft
4. speeds
5. shouts
6. collide
7. trusts
8. fly
9. maps
10. wave

Practice IV

1. third person/singular
2. third person/singular
3. third person/plural
4. first person/plural
5. third person/plural
6. third person/singular
7. third person/singular
8. third person/singular
9. third person/singular
10. third person/plural

Practice V

1. P
2. P
3. A
4. A
5. P
6. A
7. P
8. P
9. A
10. P

Practice VI

CONJUGATION OF THE VERB *TALK*	
Singular	**Plural**
Present Tense	
I talk you talk he/she/it talks	we talk you talk they talk
Past Tense	
I talked you talked he/she/it talked	we talked you talked they talked
Future Tense	
I will talk you will talk he/she/it will talk	we will talk you will talk they will talk
Present Perfect Tense	
I have talked you have talked he/she/it has talked	we have talked you have talked they have talked
Past Perfect Tense	
I had talked you had talked he/she/it had talked	we had talked you had talked they had talked
Future Perfect Tense	
I will have talked you will have talked he/she/it will have talked	we will have talked you will have talked they will have talked

Practice VII

Sentences will vary

1. The effects of global warming will have been attributed to human activities.

2. They have discovered that increased amounts of carbon dioxide and other greenhouse gasses are the leading cause.

3. The chemist Arrhenius had first speculated about the greenhouse effect in 1887.

4. It has released carbon dioxide and other greenhouse gasses by burning fossil fuels, agriculture, and land clearing.

5. The results of global warming will have caused rising sea levels and changes in the amounts and patterns of precipitation.

6. Scientists had believed that these changes would increase the frequency and intensity of extreme weather events such as flooding, droughts, hurricanes, and tornadoes.

7. They will have discussed the possibility of the destruction of ecosystems and the decline of various species due to global warming.

8. They saw negative glacier mass or glacier retreat from 1900 to 1980 in 142 of the 144 mountain glaciers with records.

9. Global glacier retreat is a significant concern.

10. Global warming has increased the reproduction rate of mosquitoes and the number of blood meals that they take; it has prolonged their breeding season and shortened their maturation period.

Practice VIII

1. indicative
2. indicative
3. imperative
4. indicative
5. indicative
6. indicative
7. indicative
8. indicative
9. indicative
10. imperative

Practice IX

1. auxiliary
2. intransitive
3. intransitive
4. intransitive
5. intransitive
6. auxiliary
7. transitive
8. auxiliary
9. intransitive
10. transitive

Practice X

	IRREGULAR VERB FORMS							
Present Tense	**Past Tense**	**Past Participle**	**Present Tense**	**Past Tense**	**Past Participle**	**Present Tense**	**Past Tense**	**Past Participle**
am, be	**was, were**	been	awake	**awoke**	awoke	beat	beat	**beaten**
become	**became**	become	begin	began	**begun**	bite	**bit**	bitten
blow	blew	blown	break	broke	broken	**bring**	**brought**	brought
burst	**burst**	burst	**catch**	caught	caught	choose	chose	chosen
climb	climbed	climbed	come	came	**come**	cut	cut	cut
dive	dived	dived	do	did	done	drag	**dragged**	dragged
draw	drew	**drawn**	drink	drank	drunk	**drive**	drove	driven
drown	drowned	drowned	eat	ate	eaten	fall	fell	**fallen**
flow	flowed	flowed	fly	**flew**	flown	forget	forgot	**forgotten**
freeze	froze	frozen	get	got	got/ gotten	give	**gave**	given
go	went	gone	hang (picture)	hung	hung	hang (criminal)	hanged	hanged
know	**knew**	known	lay (to place)	laid	laid	lead	led	led
leave	left	left	lend	lent	lent	let	let	let
lie (to recline)	lay	lain	lie (to tell a falsehood)	lied	lied	lose	lost	lost
ride	rode	**ridden**	ring	rang	rung	**rise**	**rose**	risen
run	ran	run	say	said	said	see	saw	seen
send	sent	sent	shake	shook	shaken	shine (give light)	shone	shone
shine (polish)	shined	shined	shrink	**shrank**	shrunk	sing	sang	sung
sink	**sank**	sunk	sit	sat	sat	spring	sprang	sprung
steal	**stole**	stolen	swear	**swore**	sworn	swim	**swam**	swum
swing	swung	swung	take	took	**taken**	teach	taught	taught
tear	tore	torn	**tell**	told	told	think	**thought**	thought
throw	**threw**	thrown	try	tried	**tried**	understand	understood	**understood**
wake	waked/ woke	waked	wear	**wore**	worn	weave	wove	woven
weep	wept	**wept**	wind	wound	**wound**	wring	**wrung**	wrung
write	wrote	written						

Practice XI

Sentences will vary

Chapter 4 Review Quizzes:
Vocabulary Review Quiz

1.	H	6.	C
2.	E	7.	B
3.	I	8.	F
4.	J	9.	D
5.	A	10.	G

Verb Definitions

1.	A	6.	D
2.	C	7.	B
3.	D	8.	C
4.	B	9.	B
5.	A	10.	D

Action and Linking Verbs

The emu (pronounced "ee myoo") $\boxed{\text{is}}$ the largest bird that is native to Australia. After its relative, the ostrich, the emu $\boxed{\text{is}}$ the second-largest bird in the world. It $\boxed{\text{is}}$ a soft-feathered brown bird that reaches a height of up to 6 feet 6 inches (200 cm). Although the birds cannot fly, they $\boxed{\text{can}}$ travel great distances at speeds over 30 miles (50 km) per hour. Emu <u>feed</u> on plants and insects, and they are farmed for their meat, oil, and leather. Considered the unofficial national bird of Australia, the emu <u>appears</u> on the coat of arms of Australia, on a 50-cent coin, and on various postage stamps. However, equally as important, the emu <u>holds</u> a prominent place in the myths of the Australian indigenous peoples, the Aborigines. They say that the Sun $\boxed{\text{was}}$ made when an emu's egg $\boxed{\text{was}}$ thrown into the sky. The emu $\boxed{\text{is}}$ an important bird in Australia both culturally and as a national treasure.

Verb Numbers

1.	P	6.	S
2.	S	7.	S
3.	S	8.	P
4.	P	9.	S
5.	P	10.	S

Person of a Verb

1.	FP	6.	SP
2.	TP	7.	TP
3.	TP	8.	TP
4.	SP	9.	TP
5.	TP	10.	TP

Voice of a Verb

1.	A	6.	P
2.	P	7.	P
3.	A	8.	A
4.	P	9.	P
5.	A	10.	P

Tenses of a Verb and Verb Conjugation

CONJUGATION OF THE VERB *EXIST*	
Singular	**Plural**
Present Tense	
I exist you exist he/she/it exists	we exist you exist they exist
Past Tense	
I existed you existed he/she/it existed	we existed you existed they existed
Future Tense	
I will exist you will exist he/she/it will exist	we will exist you will exist they will exist
Present Perfect Tense	
I have existed you have existed he/she/it has existed	we have existed you have existed they have existed
Past Perfect Tense	
I had existed you had existed he/she/it had existed	we had existed you had existed they had existed
Future Perfect Tense	
I will have existed you will have existed he/she/it will have existed	we will have existed you will have existed they will have existed

Mood Forms of a Verb
Sentences will vary

Classes of a Verb
Definitions and sentences will vary

Auxiliary or helping verbs are verbs that help to form tenses, mood, and voice.

Transitive verbs are verbs that indicate action and are always followed by an object that receives the action.

Intransitive verbs are verbs whose action is complete—there is no object that receives the action.

Irregular Verbs

Present Tense	Past Tense	Past Participle
1. send	sent	sent
2. swing	swung	swung
3. break	broke	broken
4. blow	blew	blown
5. wring	wrung	wrung
6. ring	rang	rung
7. draw	drew	drawn
8. forget	forgot	forgotten
9. weave	wove	woven
10. forsake	forsook	forsaken

Verbals—Gerunds, Infinitives, and Participles

1. participle
2. participle
3. gerund
4. infinitive
5. gerund
6. infinitive
7. participle
8. gerund
9. participle
10. infinitive

Chapter 5 Subject + Predicate = Simple Sentences

Practice I
1. <u>Animation</u> is time-consuming and therefore expensive to produce.
2. <u>Walt Disney</u> was a pioneer in the field of animation.
3. <u>Animation</u> is not only used for entertainment, but it is used for educational purposes as well.
4. A <u>storyboard</u>, which looks similar to a comic strip, is the early production stage of traditional animation.
5. Because the <u>cels</u> have to be synchronized with the drawings, the dialogue is recorded first.
6. For every second of film, there are twenty-four <u>drawings</u>.
7. In one minute of animation there are 1440 <u>drawings</u>.
8. The <u>cartoon</u> backgrounds are painted on cardboard or celluloid.
9. <u>Rotoscoping</u> is a method of animation that traces the movement of actors and scenery from actual film footage.
10. Some <u>films</u> use a combination of live-action footage and animation: actors appear to interact with cartoon characters.

Practice II
<u>The Portuguese man-of-war</u> is a member of the Cnidaria phylum. <u>It</u> is a part of the class of hydrozoa within this phylum. <u>The Portuguese man-of-war</u> looks like a blue jelly-fish-like bubble or bottle and is often called

a blue bubble or blue bottle. The hydrozoa's name comes from its air bladder, which looks like a "man of war"—a sailing vessel with cannons. Its long tentacles are used to hunt for prey and are dangerous to humans. The sting from the tentacles causes excruciating pain. Stings from the Portuguese man-of-war have been linked to several deaths. They are particularly dangerous to children, the elderly, asthmatics, and those with allergies. The tentacles are capable of stinging even if they are detached from the blue bottle's body. The best treatment for the sting is first of all to remove the barb with tweezers and then to apply ice or hot water.

Practice III

1. and	6. or
2. and	7. or
3. or	8. and
4. and	9. and
5. or	10. and

Practice IV

1. are	6. were
2. is	7. lay
3. is	8. is
4. are	9. is
5. say	10. was

Practice V

Sentences will vary

1. A soldier carries weapons if he or she is in combat.
2. The librarian's book was lost in the vast expanse of the library.

3. His daughter Nan took a trip to Nanking.
4. A maiden from Wales spent her life tending to the milk cows.
5. Forrest's music is loud and obnoxious.
6. After Natalie was accepted into the pre-med program, she felt relief.
7. A mathematician is not afraid of numbers.
8. Baseball season lasts from April to October.
9. Candy wrappers are colorful and attractive to buyers.
10. Permanent ink is not easy to get off of your face.

Practice VI

Sentences will vary

1. The Jet Propulsion Laboratory is a NASA installation and the command center for the deep-space program.
2. The Dark Ages is a term applied to the early Middle Ages and the first few centuries following the fall of Rome.
3. Herodotus is an ancient Greek historian and often referred to as the father of history.
4. The collapse of the Roman Empire in the fifth century was caused by a tribe that invaded the city and the abdication of the last Roman emperor, Romulus Augustulus, in 476.
5. The Medici were a family of politicians and patrons of the arts who lived in Florence, Italy.
6. Oxford and Cambridge Universities in England hold positions of high esteem, and many of their graduates gain eminence in public life.

7. Germany, Italy, and Japan were allied and known as the axis powers before and during World War II.

8. Alexander Hamilton, James Madison, and John Jay wrote a series of eighty-five essays called the *Federalist Papers*, which were intended to persuade the voters of New York to adopt the Constitution and are considered a classic example of practical political principles.

9. Panic among residents and the loss of billions of dollars was the result of the Three-Mile Island Nuclear Plant meltdown and subsequent leakage of radiation into the atmosphere.

10. Refugees and others who flee their countries often leave for political reasons or to avoid punishment for their political affiliations.

Practice VII

1. The woodwinds include <u>flutes, piccolos, oboes, clarinets, and bassoons</u>.

2. The brass section consists of <u>horns, saxophones, trumpets, trombones, and tubas</u>.

3. Timpani, snare drums, and bass drums, are <u>percussion instruments</u> in an orchestra.

4. The string section includes <u>harps, violins, violas, cellos, double bass, and pianos</u>.

5. Beethoven's symphonic works were <u>influential to orchestration</u>.

6. All instrumental sections have <u>one soloist except for the violin section, which has two</u>.

7. The first violinist is considered <u>the concertmaster</u> and is ranked next to the conductor.

8. In the fifteenth and sixteenth centuries, most nobles had <u>court musicians</u>.

9. Monteverdi, Pachelbel, Vivaldi, Handel, Scarlatti, Bach, and Telemann are considered <u>composers of the baroque period</u>.

10. Johann Sebastian Bach composed music for <u>choirs, orchestras, and solo instruments</u>.

Practice VIII

1. Mozart wrote the king <u>an opera</u>.
2. Bach left the world <u>a legacy of music</u>.
3. He gave us <u>over 300 cantatas</u>.
4. Handel bought his son <u>a new clavichord.</u>
5. She practically fed her daughter <u>music morning, noon, and night</u>.
6. Monteverdi gave his friend <u>music lessons</u>.
7. His son returned Jason's <u>guitar</u>.
8. Stradivari built his sons <u>the finest violins in the entire world</u>.
9. Beethoven influenced composers <u>the world over</u>.
10. Frederic Chopin devoted his life <u>to composing piano music</u>.

Practice IX
Sentences will vary

Chapter 5 Review Quizzes:
Vocabulary Review Quiz

1. G	6. F
2. H	7. J
3. I	8. D
4. B	9. A
5. E	10. C

Subject, Predicate, and Simple Sentence Definitions

1. B	6. A
2. C	7. D
3. C	8. D
4. A	9. D
5. C	10. B

Subjects

<u>Uranus</u> is the seventh planet from the Sun and the fourth largest in mass. <u>It</u> was the first planet that was discovered in modern times. Although <u>it</u> was seen by astronomers as early as 1690, it was always mistakenly documented as a star. <u>Sir William Herschel</u> discovered the planet in 1781, but he initially reported it to be a comet. <u>It</u> was first named Georgium Sidus which means "Georgian star" after King George III of England. When <u>Herschel</u> was told that sidus means "star," he renamed it the Georgian Planet. However, <u>that name</u> was not accepted outside of England. *It* was suggested that the newly discovered planet be named after Herschel, the discoverer. There were as many as <u>nine additional names</u> suggested by astronomers all over the world, but finally the name Uranus was settled upon.

Simple, Complete, and Compound Subjects

1. simple/complete
2. compound
3. simple/complete
4. simple/complete
5. compound
6. simple/complete
7. compound
8. simple/complete
9. complete
10. simple

Predicates

1. Tibet <u>is an autonomous region in southwest China.</u>
2. <u>Surrounded by mountains,</u> Tibet <u>is historically inaccessible.</u>
3. It <u>is rich in mineral resources such as gold, copper, and uranium.</u>
4. The principal religion of Tibet <u>is Tibetan Buddhism.</u>
5. The country <u>flourished in the seventh century.</u>
6. Early in the thirteenth century, Genghis Khan <u>conquered the region. It remained under Mongol rule until 1720.</u>
7. The Chinese Qing Dynasty <u>claimed sovereignty in 1720. By 1912 and with the fall of the Qing Dynasty, Tibet reasserted its independence.</u>
8. In 1950, China <u>sent its new communist forces to invade Tibet.</u>
9. The country <u>was declared an autonomous region in 1951 and was governed by the Dalai Lama.</u>
10. China <u>launched a full-scale invasion in 1959, but the Dalai Lama managed to flee the country.</u>

Simple, Complete, and Compound Predicates

Sentences will vary

1. The orchestra sounds fantastic in the new Disney Music Hall.
2. Uranus is a planet.
3. An animated cartoon is a complicated form of filmmaking.
4. Limericks are fun to read and to write.
5. An opus is a musical composition or a set of compositions.
6. A Doric column is used in various types of architecture.
7. Cnidarians are sea creatures.
8. A mythological griffin has a varied history and purpose.
9. An autonomous country is one that is difficult to explain.
10. A quixotic person or character is usually kind of crazy or bizarre.

Direct and Indirect Objects

In 1965, China formally annexed <u>Tibet</u> as an autonomous region. <u>During this time,</u> the Cultural Revolution was occurring in China. <u>Because of the new laws and regulations dictated</u> by the revolution regarding religion, over 4,000 monasteries in Tibet were destroyed. Thousand of Tibetans were forced <u>into exile.</u> Rallies <u>for proindependence in 1987–1989</u> were suppressed by the Chinese army. Human violations continue in the region <u>despite restoration of some of the monasteries and a return of Tibetan as the official language.</u>

Chapter 6 Subject-Verb Agreement

Practice I

1. P	6. S
2. S	7. P
3. S	8. S
4. P	9. S
5. P	10. P

Practice II

1. has	6. have
2. are	7. have, are
3. are	8. consists
4. soar	9. are
5. is	10. live

Practice III

1. was	6. surrounds
2. is	7. searches
3. seems	8. take
4. is	9. are
5. C	10. destroyed

Practice IV

1. was	5. wanted
2. were	6. have been
3. wanted	7. found
4. were	

Practice V

Sentences will vary

Practice VI

1. was invented
2. was born
3. won
4. became (or was)
5. was (or became)
6. used
7. adapted
8. was not used
9. invented
10. died

Practice VII

1. are	6. needs
2. bites	7. has
3. is	8. was
4. tell	9. are
5. are	10. is

Chapter 6 Review Quizzes: Vocabulary Review Quiz

1. F	6. G
2. C	7. I
3. D	8. A
4. J	9. E
5. B	10. H

Subject-Verb Agreement Definition Review

1. B	6. A
2. A	7. D
3. D	8. B
4. B	9. D
5. A	10. C

Singular and Plural Subjects

The Harlem Renaissance was a movement or period of creativity in literature, art, and music among African Americans in the 1920s. The movement centered in the Harlem area of New York City. The participants of the movement were children of parents who, for the most part, had endured the injustices of slavery. Many of them were a part of what was known as the "Great Migration" out of the South and into the less divisive regions of the North after the Civil War. The Harlem Renaissance represented a "new negro" and served to negate stereotypes often held. It allowed a new sense of self-worth and intellectualism to develop and evolve. Countee Cullen, Zora Neale Hurston, Langston Hughes, and Claude McKay were exemplary writers of the movement. Louis Armstrong, Duke Ellington, Ethel Waters, and Paul Robeson were well-known entertainers of the era.

Singular and Plural Verbs

Stream-of-consciousness __S__ is a literary technique in which the thought processes of a character __P__ are presented in a chaotic, disconnected, and illogical manner by the author. Also called interior monologue, stream-of-consciousness writings __P__ are challenging for the reader to follow. The character's thoughts __P__ appear to be quite random and disconnected. Although the technique __S__ gained prominence in the twentieth century, prominent writers such as Leo Tolstoy and Edgar Allan Poe used similar techniques in their works in the 1800s. James Joyce, Virginia Woolf, and William Faulkner __P__ are best known for their works using stream-of-consciousness.

Collective Nouns and Compound Subjects

1. CN
2. CS
3. CS
4. CN
5. CN
6. CN
7. CS
8. CS
9. CN
10. CN

Pronoun Agreement

1. Raskolnikov, the protagonist in the novel *Crime and Punishment*, plans to murder the pawnbroker to solve his money problems.
2. The Russian author Fyodor Dostoevsky began writing his famous novel in 1864.
3. St. Petersburg is where the novel is set; it is a city in Russia.
4. Raskolnikov believes that he is above the law and is doing everyone a favor by murdering the old woman.
5. In addition to murdering the old pawnbroker, Raskolnikov murders her sister, who innocently stumbles onto the murder scene.
6. Marmeladov is a friendly drunkard, and he has a daughter named Sonya.
7. Sonya is forced into prostitution to help support her father's young family, but she is extremely religious.
8. Dunya is Raskolnikov's sister, who agrees to marry Luzhin to save her family from financial ruin.
9. Razumihkin is a friend of Raskolnikov's who falls in love with Dunya.
10. Porfiry is a clever police detective who investigates the murders of the two women.

Indefinite Pronouns

1. __S__ Each of the students is going to give a presentation.
2. __P__ Most of the neighbors are in agreement with the proposal for new sidewalks.
3. __S__ Someone needs to take responsibility for the mistake.
4. __S__ Everything is going to be okay.
5. __P__ All of the titles are misspelled and need to be corrected.
6. __P__ Neither of the women likes the food at the newly opened restaurant.
7. __S__ Another beautiful place to visit is Prague in the Czech Republic.
8. __S__ Anyone with any common sense knows not to shout out answers like that.
9. __P__ Some shall be banished, and some shall be punished.
10. __S__ Any laptop computer will do at this point.

Chapter 7 Adjectives

Practice I

1. definite
2. indefinite
3. indefinite
4. definite
5. indefinite
6. definite
7. definite
8. definite
9. definite
10. indefinite

Practice II

Words will vary

Common Adjective	Proper Adjectives
1. dumb	French
2. crazy	English
3. little	Cornish
4. red	Jamesonian
5. orange	Laotian
6. first	South American
7. bold	Mexican
8. thin	Chinese
9. atrocious	Indian
10. primary	Iranian

Practice III

The word Bohemian can be used in either of ___these___ two ways. First of all, it can be used to describe the people who live in the Bohemia region or area now known as the Czech Republic. The term for __this__ area comes from a Latin term for the original Celtic tribe that once lived there. Secondly, the term bohemian in modern-day usage represents any person who lives an unconventional and artistic life. __Those__ subscribing to a bohemian lifestyle believe that self-expression is vital to their existence and that art (dancing, painting, writing, singing, and so on) is the primary focus of __this__ lifestyle. __This__ term was originally applied to a group of "bohemians" known as the Bloomsbury group in London and a group of writers in Carmel-by-the-Sea, California, in the early 1900s.

Practice IV

1. lung		6. wardrobe
2. cream		7. nurse
3. earth		8. television
4. cat		9. perfume
5. Office		10. entry

Practice V

	Positive	Comparative	Superlative
1.	loud	louder	loudest
2.	high	higher	highest
3.	tart	more tart	most tart
4.	grand	more grand	most grand
5.	easy	easier	easiest
6.	gloomy	gloomier	gloomiest
7.	expensive	more expensive	most expensive
8.	happy	happier	happiest
9.	late	later	latest
10.	roomy	roomier	roomiest

Chapter 7 Review Quizzes:
Vocabulary Review Quiz

1. J		6. C
2. E		7. A
3. D		8. G
4. B		9. H
5. F		10. I

Adjective Definitions Review Quiz

1. D		6. A
2. C		7. C
3. A		8. B
4. D		9. B
5. C		10. B

Articles: Definite and Indefinite

Rolling Stone Magazine published an article in 2004 that listed the top 500 greatest songs of all time. Over 170 musicians, music critics, and other officials in the music industry voted for the songs. The list caused a reasonable amount of controversy because the only song that is not sung in English is a song called *La Bamba* by Ritchie Valens. Of the 500 songs listed, 357 are from the United States, 117 are from the United Kingdom, 10 are from Canada, and 8 are from Ireland. The list includes 202 songs from the 1960s and 144 are from the 1970s. Although there are 24 songs from the 1980s, there is an extremely limited number from the twenty-first century (one by Outkast and two by Eminem). The oldest song is from 1948, which is a song titled "Rollin' Stone" by Muddy Waters. The Beatles have the most songs on the list, 23. The Rolling Stones, Bob Dylan, and Elvis Presley each have more than 10 songs listed. The top song is by Bob Dylan, "Like a Rolling Stone." The remainder of the top 10 songs are "(I Can't Get No) Satisfaction" by the Rolling Stones, "Imagine" by John Lennon, "What's Going On" by Marvin Gaye, "Respect" by Aretha Franklin, "Good Vibrations" by the Beach Boys, "Johnny B. Goode" by Chuck Berry, "Hey Jude" by the Beatles, "Smells Like Teen Spirit" by Nirvana, and the last of the top ten is "What'd I Say" by Ray Charles.

Common and Proper Adjectives

1. pearl
2. legend
3. clam
4. Filipino
5. story
6. life
7. token
8. family

Demonstrative Adjectives or Pronouns Used as Adjectives and Nouns Used as Adjectives

Sentences will vary

Forms of Adjectives: Positive, Comparative, Superlative

1. largest
2. C
3. C
4. most popular
5. most threatening
6. greatest
7. C
8. warmest
9. C
10. C

Chapter 8 Adverbs

Practice I

Sentences will vary

Practice II

Words will vary

Pasteurization is a heat treatment of food that is used _primarily_ to kill bacteria and other microorganisms. The treatment was _initially_ discovered by a French chemist named Louis Pasteur in the 1860s, for whom the process is named. He is known as one of the founders of microbiology. Pasteur also discovered that he could _deliberately_ weaken certain disease-causing microorganisms and then use the weakened culture to vaccinate against the disease. Milk is _mechanically_ pasteurized by heating it to 161.6°F. (72°C) for 16 seconds. Today, a process known as ultrapasteurization is used to produce milk that is called UHT (ultra-heat-treated) milk. It is heated to 270°F. (132°C) for one second to __potentially__ __add__ a shelf life of several months to the product.

Practice III
Words will vary
1. <u>outrageously</u>   narrow
2. <u>extraordinarily</u>   ordinary
3. <u>unusually</u>   scrawny
4. <u>excruciatingly</u>   roasted
5. <u>dramatically</u>   tall
6. <u>environmentally</u>   green
7. <u>sparingly</u>   nutritious
8. <u>frighteningly</u>   ugly
9. <u>delicately</u>   frail
10. <u>gregariously</u>   nasty

Practice IV
Words will vary
1. almost
2. never
3. Most
4. very
5. only
6. too
7. Most
8. Less
9. very
10. far

Practice V
1. time
2. degree
3. degree
4. degree/manner
5. place
6. place
7. degree/manner
8. time
9. manner
10. time

Practice VI
1. most artistically
2. whimsically
3. farthest
4. happily
5. most inquisitive
6. well
7. fastest
8. worst
9. aggressively
10. better

Chapter 8 Review Quizzes: Vocabulary Review Quiz
1. C   6. G
2. E   7. A
3. B   8. H
4. F   9. J
5. I   10. D

Adverb Definitions
1. D   6. B
2. B   7. D
3. B   8. A
4. D   9. C
5. C   10. A

Adverbs That Modify Verbs, Adjectives, or Other Adverbs
1. verb   6. verb
2. adjective   7. adjective
3. verb   8. verb
4. adverb   9. verb
5. adjective   10. verb

Adverbs of Time, Place, Manner, and Degree
Answers will vary

Adverbs of Time	Adverbs of Place	Adverbs of Manner	Adverbs of Degree
yesterday	here	anxiously	greatly
hourly	there	badly	very
yearly	under	cautiously	highly
quarterly	below	quickly	extremely
annually	nearby	weakly	immensely

Forms of Adverbs: Positive, Comparative, Superlative

Positive	Comparative	Superlative
fast	<u>faster</u>	fastest
quietly	more quietly	<u>most quiet</u>
seriously	<u>more serious</u>	most seriously
<u>late</u>	later	latest
well	better	<u>best</u>
<u>tranquilly</u>	more tranquilly	most tranquilly
<u>artistically</u>	more artistically	most artistically
little	less	<u>least</u>
far	<u>farther</u>	farthest
stately	<u>more stately</u>	most stately

Chapter 9 Prepositions, Conjunctions, and Interjections

Practice I

1. S
2. C
3. S
4. P
5. S
6. C
7. P
8. S
9. C
10. S

Practice II

1. of
2. in
3. between
4. about
5. by
6. on
7. Without
8. by
9. from
10. on

Practice III

1. <u>Since</u> the ancient Greek Olympics, running competitions have been part of history.
2. The effects of running are felt <u>not only</u> in the body <u>but</u> in the mind as well.

3. Running is a complex physical activity <u>that</u> requires the use of many muscles.

4. <u>Although</u> walking is less stressful to the body, running can burn 50 percent more calories <u>than</u> walking.

5. Because it is a high-impact sport, <u>there</u> are many injuries associated with running.

6. Jogging is a slow type of running <u>that</u> used to be called roadwork.

7. There are many different running events, <u>and</u> they are ranked according to distance.

8. Sprints are short but very fast events <u>when</u> the runner runs his or her fastest for the entire race.

9. Marathons are long-distance events <u>and</u> measure 26 miles (42 km) and 385 yards (352 m) long.

10. <u>Although</u> running is a competitive sport itself, it is also an important part of other team sports such as soccer (football), American football, basketball, lacrosse, and rugby.

Practice IV

1. subordinate
2. coordinate
3. correlative
4. correlative
5. coordinate
6. subordinate
7. subordinate
8. subordinate
9. subordinate
10. coordinate

Practice V

There once was a sailor named Naylor, who sat on a tack and said "<u>Quack!</u>" Not knowing the meaning he started repeating, five hundred and fifty one "<u>Quacks!</u>" His commander named Ander heard the commotion on board and hurriedly went to discover. "<u>Oh my!</u>" said Ander, "What's got into your dander, and when are you going to stop?" "I don't know what's wrong," said Naylor the sailor as he continued to bellow the word. But drawing a crowd by shouting out loud caused a ruckus that definitely turned into a fruckus. The last that we heard, Naylor was swimming the sea, shouting "<u>Quack</u>" at the top of his lungs. His only friends now are the ducks that scream "<u>Wow!</u>" And that is the end of our sailor.

Chapter 9 Review Quizzes: Vocabulary Review Quiz

1. E	6. C
2. H	7. G
3. D	8. A
4. J	9. F
5. I	10. B

Preposition, Conjunction, and Interjection Definitions

1. C	6. B
2. A	7. C
3. D	8. C
4. A	9. C
5. A	10. A

Prepositions

Bob Dylan is a popular singer and composer <u>from</u> the United States. He was born <u>in</u> 1941, and his real name is Robert Allen Zimmerman. Dylan changed his name <u>to</u> Bob Dylan when he began his music career and originally was going <u>to</u> call himself Robert Allen. However, he decided <u>upon</u> Bob Dylan after reading the works <u>of</u> poet Dylan Thomas. Although Dylan is known <u>for</u> rock and roll, gospel, hard rock, folk music, blues, jazz, and rockabilly, some <u>of</u> his most memorable works are the protest/social commentary songs such as "Blowin' <u>in</u> the Wind" and "The Times They Are a-Changin'." He has won many awards including the Grammy, Academy Award, and Golden Globe. Dylan is listed not only as one <u>of</u> *Time Magazine's* one hundred most influential people <u>of</u> the twentieth century but also as one of *Rolling Stone Magazine's* one hundred greatest artists <u>of</u> all time.

Conjunctions

Sentences will vary

1. <u>and</u> Let's go to the zoo and then on to Sea World.
2. <u>while</u> Playing around at the park while she is working at home is not fair.
3. <u>not only, but also</u> Not only are you going to be rewarded monetarily, but also sent on a dream vacation.
4. <u>although</u> This hardly makes sense, although I am beginning to see your point.
5. <u>yet</u> To be honest yet diplomatic, you've got to tone down the rhetoric.
6. <u>when</u> Tomorrow will be fine when the laborers are here to help.

7. <u>but</u> There will always be another opportunity to prove yourself, but just don't let that chance slip by again.
8. <u>neither, nor</u> Neither you nor Sheila are allowed to swim in the pool without supervision.
9. <u>in order that</u> In order that the contents of the container be disguised, you will have to recover the box.
10. <u>since</u> Perhaps the order of the tasks will have to be changed since Parker will no longer be available to help.

Interjections

Answers will vary

1. Please!
2. Don't do that!
3. You can't!
4. Yes, I can!
5. Stop!
6. Buckle up!
7. Switch!
8. Excuse me!
9. Oh no!
10. Ouch!

Chapter 10 Phrases and Clauses

Practice I

1. Belize, <u>a Republic in Central America</u>, is located on the Caribbean Sea.
2. Between 300 B.C. and A.D. 1000, Belize was a part of the Mayan empire, <u>an outstanding and highly skilled culture</u>.
3. Shipwrecked sailors from Britain, <u>who eventually took control of the country</u>, founded the first European settlement in 1638.
4. Belize, <u>previously known as British Honduras</u>, achieved independence in 1981.

5. Guatemala, <u>a neighboring country to the east</u>, claimed Belize at that time, but British troops remained in Belize to discourage an invasion.

6. Belmopan, <u>the capital of Belize</u>, is the site of its government, a constitutional monarchy.

7. The economy of Belize, <u>a lower-middle-income developing country</u>, is based on agriculture.

8. Agriculture, <u>particularly sugar cane</u>, is the chief commercial crop of Belize.

9. Mestizos, <u>a mix of Spanish-Indian ethnicities</u>, make up 44 percent of the population.

10. Creoles, <u>those who are primarily African American</u>, represent about one-third of the population.

Practice II

1. <u>An impact crater</u> is a depression or hole found in the surface of a planet .

2. <u>It</u> is caused by two bodies hitting each other, such as a meteorite, asteroid, or a comet hitting the moon's surface .

3. <u>The moon</u> has about one-half-million craters on its surface .

4. <u>The largest-known crater in the solar system</u> is on the moon .

5. <u>This crater</u> is called the South Pole-Aitken basin and is 1,388 miles (2,240 km) in diameter and 8 miles (13 km) deep .

6. <u>A crater</u> generally has a circular shape with steep sides .

7. <u>A volcanic crater</u> is also called a caldera .

8. <u>It</u> is caused when a vent of lava is expelled explosively .

9. <u>Craters</u> can also be caused by human-made explosives .

10. <u>An example of a human-made explosive</u> is underground nuclear tests .

Practice III

Paragraphs will vary

Practice IV

1. _G_ By <u>covering nearly one-third of Africa's land area</u>, the Sahara Desert is the world's largest desert.

2. _I_ <u>To understand the desert's expanse</u>, it has an area of about 3,500,000 square miles (9,065,000 sq km).

3. _G_ <u>Extending west to east for 3,000 miles (4,800 km)</u>, the Sahara reaches from the Atlantic Ocean in the west to the Red Sea in the east.

4. _G_ <u>Being less than 4 inches (10 cm)</u>, the annual rainfall of the Sahara makes it one of the driest areas in the world.

5. _P_ <u>Covered with sand and stone</u>, there is little natural vegetation in the desert.

6. _I_ <u>To be exact</u>, two-thirds of the Sahara is stony desert.

7. _P_ Tibesti Massif, <u>rising to 11,000 feet (3,350 m)</u>, is the highest point in the Sahara.

8. _P_ Qattara Depression, the lowest point of the desert, is <u>located at 436 feet (133 m) below sea level</u>.

9. _P_ <u>Nurturing civilizations for thousands of years</u>, oases are important centers for water, crop farming, and transportation.

10. _P_ Two main ethnic groups, <u>including the Tuareg and the Tibu</u>, inhabit the Sahara, but Nomads continue to herd goats and sheep.

Practice V

_I_ Hernando De Soto was a Spanish explorer. After taking part in the conquest of Central America under Francisco Pizarro, he was appointed the governor of Cuba in 1537. Given permission to conquer the North American mainland, _I_ his expedition landed in Florida in 1539. De Soto advanced north _D_ until he reached the Carolinas. _I_ Later the expedition traveled as far west as the Mississippi River. _D_ Because his ruthless search for treasure proved to be nonsuccessful, coupled with his extremely brutal treatment of the native inhabitants, a battle was fought in 1540 at Maubila. _I_ Thousands of native inhabitants were killed either through fighting, fire, or suicide. De Soto lived until 1542, _D_ when he died of a fever.

Practice VI

Answers will vary

Adverb Clauses	Noun Clauses
1. after	1. that
2. although	2. when
3. though	3. whenever
4. unless	4. what
5. until	5. who

Adjective Clauses that Tell *What Kind* or *Which One*

Sentences will vary

Chapter 10 Review Quizzes: Vocabulary Review Quiz

1. G	6. C
2. I	7. E
3. F	8. H
4. J	9. A
5. B	10. D

Phrase and Clause Definitions

1. A	6. C
2. B	7. A
3. A	8. A
4. A	9. B
5. C	10. D

Appositive Phrases

Genghis Khan, the word *Khan* means ruler, was born about 1165. He was a political and military leader, who united the Mongol tribes in 1206. Later he demonstrated his military genius by conquering Peking, now known as Beijing, in 1215 and continuing to annex Iran and invading Russia as far as Moscow. Although he is often thought to be a bloodthirsty and ruthless ruler because of his many military successes, he is also appreciated and respected for establishing the Mongol nation, the largest empire ever known. After his death in 1227, his sons and grandsons continued to rule the empire, which endured for another 150 years.

Noun and Verb Phrases

Sentences will vary

1. The facilities are not available during December.
2. *Hombre* is the Spanish term for "man."
3. Chardonnay is a variety of white grape that is used in wine making.
4. The Celts were a group of people who inhabited western Europe in the pre-Roman era.
5. A relic is an object of interest primarily because of its age or association with something.
6. There are over 2,000 species of rodents, constituting the largest order of mammals.
7. A sidecar is a small car for a passenger that is attached to a motorcycle.
8. Yoga is a Hindu system of philosophic meditation that incorporates a variety of postures.
9. Quetzals are a variety of colorful birds that are found in Central and South America.
10. Lasers generate an intense beam of radiation and are used for a variety of medical procedures.

Prepositional Phrases

Wales is a constituent member of the United Kingdom. It is located on the southwest side of Great Britain and is bordered by England on the east. The capital of Wales is Cardiff, and it is located in the south. During the eleventh century, the Celtic-speaking Welsh were conquered by the English Norman King Edward I. In 1301, Prince Edward (later King Edward II) became the Prince of Wales. Today, Prince Charles is the Prince of Wales. North Wales has the greatest density of sheep in the world. The economy relies on agriculture now, although in the past, it was the leading producer of coal. With the decline of its traditional heavy industries of coal and steel, lighter industries such as electronics are partially offsetting the loss.

Gerund, Infinitive, and Participial Phrases

1. Winning the lottery is the only excitement that remains constant in my life.
2. To write down those five little numbers makes me want to shout, "This is it! The winning ticket!"
3. To walk up to the counter with my numbers and my money sends chills down my spine.
4. After wishing me luck, the clerk calls me by name. He has seen me many times before.
5. Carefully, I place my ticket in my wallet and I wait; waiting can be torture.
6. My hands tremble with anticipation to turn the pages of the newspaper where the winning numbers are printed.

7. <u>While holding my breath</u>, I compare the numbers, one by one.

8. <u>After reading the numbers</u>, I slowly reread, recheck, and compare the numbers to my ticket.

9. Quickly, <u>disappointment hangs heavy in my heart</u> when the numbers do not match.

10. Then soon enough <u>the excitement begins welling up again</u> the following week with one little dollar and the hope that someday it will turn into millions.

Independent and Dependent Clauses
Answers will vary

1. <u>You should go home</u> because you seem exhausted.

2. Going to the market yesterday was entertaining <u>and fruitful.</u>

3. When you make fresh noodles, <u>hang them up on a rack to dry.</u>

4. Monty works in a bakery <u>that specializes in wedding cakes.</u>

5. <u>Rewrite the information</u> because the message was superfluous.

6. Gardening can be relaxing and useful <u>in a backbreaking kind of way.</u>

7. If I speak French with my neighbors, <u>they become homesick for Paris.</u>

8. <u>I jumped for joy</u> when I heard my favorite song on the radio.

9. <u>You're teasing me</u>, which is really not funny because it hurts.

10. <u>You cannot go out to play</u> until you finish washing the dishes.

Adjective, Adverb, and Noun Clauses
Sentences will vary

1. Adjective Clause The team member <u>who enjoys debating the most</u> is Tommy.

2. Noun Clause <u>Whomever you want to choose</u> will be fine with me.

3. Adverb Clause <u>After misspelling the last word at the spelling bee</u>, I wanted to dig a hole and bury myself from embarrassment.

4. Adverb Clause <u>Wherever you are,</u> there you are!

5. Adjective Clause We saw a cage full of lions <u>that seemed extraordinarily hungry</u> when we walked by.

6. Noun Clause <u>What do you think is going to happen next</u>?

7. Adjective Clause The art gallery <u>where we saw the exhibit</u> is now closed.

8. Noun Clause Herman finally learned <u>what the answer to the math problem was.</u>

9. Adverb Clause <u>As long as you remember to feed the cat while I am gone</u>, I will be happy.

10. Noun Clause When going to Canada or Mexico from the United States the border guards will check the passport of <u>whoever visits.</u>

Chapter 11 Sentence Structure and Classification

Practice I

1. <u>Although today's popular musicals are a genre of light entertainment that embody a plot, strong songs, and energetic dance numbers</u>, 1 <u>they developed in the late nineteenth century combining elements of light opera, revue, and burlesque.</u> 2

2. A chameleon is an arboreal lizard found primarily in Madagascar, Africa, or Asia, 1 but it is known for its ability to change color. 2

3. Cafe mocha is a combination of espresso, steamed milk, and chocolate, 1 and although it is a popular beverage served in the U.S., 2 it is not as popular in Europe. 3

4. A guitar is a plucked string instrument first associated with the Moors, a group of medieval Muslim inhabitants of the western Mediterranean area 1 and the people who first introduced it to Spain as early as the twelfth century. 2

5. Baja California means "Lower California," 1 and it is a peninsula located in Northwest Mexico 2 and it consists of two states, Baja California Norte and Baja California Sur. 3

6. Agronomy is the science of soil management and improvement, 1 but it also includes the studies of the interrelationships of plants and soils. 2

7. Click language is any of several southern African languages belonging primarily to the Khoisan group 1 and characterized by the use of suction speech sounds known as clicks. 2

8. Goldfish are freshwater carp that were originally found in China 1 but were domesticated about 1,000 years ago 2 and have become one of the most popular aquarium fish. 3

9. Jimi Hendrix was an influential and innovative guitarist and rock musician 1 and is renowned for his colorful and improvisational live performances. 2

10. Today, Osaka, Japan, is the third largest city in Japan as well as a major transportation hub and principal industrial port, 1 but it was heavily bombed during World War II. 2

Practice II

Mount Rushmore is a giant granite sculpture of four U.S. presidents located in South Dakota. Known as a presidential memorial, it represents 150 years of American presidential history. The four presidents included in the monument are George Washington, Thomas Jefferson, Theodore Roosevelt, and Abraham Lincoln. Each of the sculptures is 60 feet (18 m) high and rises 5,725 feet (1.745 m) above sea level. Historian Doane Robinson, who convinced sculptor Guntzor Borglum to visit the site to be certain that the project could be accomplished, conceived the idea for the sculpture. Congress authorized the project in 1925. Calvin Coolidge, the sitting president at the time, insisted that in addition to George Washington, two Republicans and one Democrat be included in the memorial. Borglum and 400 assistants worked on the sculpture from October 4, 1927 until October 31, 1941. Borglum died of an embolism in 1941, and his son Lincoln Borglum continued the project, but funding was exhausted and the project halted. Originally, the sculptures were going to continue to the waist of each man, but that did not come to fruition. The total cost of the sculpture was nearly $990,000. Although there were a few injuries, no deaths occurred with the work.

Practice III

Answers will vary

1. (SC) Dividing the United States from Mexico,
   (IC) the Rio Grande River flows from Colorado to the Gulf of Mexico,
   (IC) and it has been the source of commerce in several states.

2. (IC) Charlemagne was the first emperor of the Holy Roman Empire
   (IC) and his name means "Charles the Great,"
   (SC) a model for Christian rulers.

3. (IC) O Henry's real name was William Sydney Porter,
   (SC) an American writer,
   (IC) and he was known for the surprise endings in his stories.

4. (SC) Known as the Scottish play,
   (IC) *Macbeth* is a tragedy,
   (IC) and it is a play of a man and his wife who go to great lengths for power.

5. (SC) A famous poem,
   (IC) "O Captain, My Captain" was written by Walt Whitman,
   (IC) and it tells the story of Lincoln's death through seafaring metaphor.

6. (IC) The Crusades was a series of wars fought between the eleventh and thirteenth centuries,
   (IC) where European kings and warriors fought for control of the Holy Lands,
   (SC) but also exposed Europeans to goods from Asia.

7. (SC) A scientist and agricultural inventor,
   (IC) George Washington Carver aided the economy of the South in the late nineteenth and early twentieth centuries,
   (IC) as he developed hundreds of uses for crops such as the peanut and sweet potato.

8. (IC) The NAACP stands for the National Association for the Advancement of Colored People,
   (IC) and it is an organization that promotes the rights and welfare of people of color,
   (SC) founded in 1909.

9. (IC) Liechtenstein is a Constitutional Monarchy
   (SC) located between Austria and Switzerland,
   (IC) and it is one of the smallest European countries.

10. (IC) Being afraid of heights is not unusual,
    (IC) it is a phobia that is called acrophobia,
    (SC) or the abnormal fear of heights.

Chapter 11 Review Quizzes: Vocabulary Review Quiz

1. G	6. A
2. B	7. D
3. E	8. J
4. C	9. H
5. I	10. F

Sentence Definitions

1. D	6. B
2. B	7. C
3. C	8. B
4. A	9. A
5. B	10. C

Compound, Complex, and Compound-Complex Sentences

1. CD-CX
2. CD
3. CX
4. CX
5. CX
6. CD-CX
7. CX
8. CD
9. CX
10. CX

Chapter 12 Punctuation

Practice I

1. Have you ever been to Disneyland?
2. It is supposed to be the happiest place on Earth.
3. My favorite ride is the Pirates of the Caribbean.
4. I could go on that ride all day . . . hey, watch it!
5. Ouch!
6. You stepped on my toe!
7. What is your favorite ride?
8. I have never been on that, and I am afraid of roller-coaster rides.
9. For some reason they make me . . .well, let us just say nauseous.
10. When shall we go?

Practice II

Sir Isaac Newton was an English physicist, mathematician, astronomer, natural philosopher, and alchemist. Born in 1643, he is well regarded as one of the most influential figures in the history of science. Newton is most noted for his treatise *Philosophiae Naturalis Principia Mathematica,* which was published in 1687. In it, he describes universal gravitation and the three laws of motion, both of which laid the groundwork for classical mechanics. Newton was the first to demonstrate that the motion of objects on Earth and of celestial bodies is governed by the same set of natural laws. Newton is also credited with the advancement of heliocentrism and the principles of conservation of momentum and angular momentum. He invented the reflecting telescope and developed a theory of color. He based his observations on a prism that he discovered decomposes white light into a visible spectrum. Calculus, the speed of sound, the origin of stars, and many other areas were advanced because of Newton's work.

Practice III

1. There are many reasons for hiking: enjoying the scenery, exercise, exploring unfamiliar territory, and silence.
2. Yesterday we hiked the 5-mile (8-km) loop up into the Olympics in the rain; getting soaked and muddy was worth the view.
3. Hiking supplies that should always be carried include the following: compass, water, snacks, warm clothes, and first aid supplies.

4. When hiking alone, take precautions; it can be very dangerous.

5. She has hiked in British Columbia, Canada; Northern Cascades, Washington; and Mt. McKinley, California.

6. Hiking in Tibet and Nepal is known as trekking; it is often strenuous and steep.

7. The Pacific Crest Trail is 2,650 miles long (4,260 km); it extends from Canada to Mexico and parallels the Pacific Ocean.

8. Distress signals used in the mountains include: three blasts on a whistle with a one-minute pause, three fires, or piles of stone in a triangle.

9. In open air, the most heat is lost through the head; hypothermia can be prevented by covering the head.

10. "Leave No Trace" is a list of principles that hikers should follow: carry out all trash, respect nature and wildlife, plan ahead, be prepared, and be considerate of other visitors.

Practice IV

1. The disbanding of the 1960's rock group caused great turmoil.

2. The orbit's path appeared to curve.

3. The wig's color did not blend well with the original.

4. The honeycomb's texture disintegrated in the extreme heat.

5. A deacon is an ordained minister who serves as a priest's assistant.

6. Samuel Goldwyn's commercially successful films included *Wuthering Heights, Guys and Dolls,* and *Porgy and Bess.*

7. Plato was a Greek philosopher. The writer's greatest work was *The Republic.*

8. New York's state capital is Albany.

9. One of Marvin Gaye's most famous single recordings was "I Heard It Through the Grapevine."

10. King Henry VIII's court imprisoned Sir Thomas Wyatt because he was allegedly the former lover of Anne Boleyn and a friend of Thomas Cromwell.

Practice V

1. "Ten persons who speak make more noise than ten thousand who are silent." (Napoleon)

2. What did Kahlil Gibran mean when he wrote, "Even as love crowns you so shall he crucify you. Even as he is for your growth so is he for your pruning"?

3. John Keats wrote "Ode on a Grecian Urn" and "Ode to a Nightingale."

4. "Love built on beauty, soon as beauty, dies." (John Donne)

5. The meaning of William Blake's "Expect Poison from Standing Water"escapes me.

6. "A man may die," said John F. Kennedy, "nations may rise and fall, but an idea lives on. Ideas have endurance without death."

7. The song she sang was titled "Concrete Angel."

8. "Friends show their love in times of trouble, not in happiness." (Euripides)

9. "Rudeness" writes Eric Hoffer, "is the weak man's imitation of strength."

10. "The youth of a nation are the trustees of posterity." (Benjamin Disraeli)

Practice VI

1. "Let us not burden [groan] our remembrance with a heaviness that's gone." (Shakespeare)

2. Toxicology is the study of poisonous substances (and their effects on living things).

3. Computer software (as opposed to computer hardware or equipment) is the coded programs and their associated files.

4. The osprey (or hawk) lives in coastal regions or around lakes.

5. Daniel Ortega (a Nicaraguan president and statesman) joined the Sandanistas and was then exiled to Cuba.

6. The Battle of Hastings (fought in Southeast England in 1066) brought an end to the Anglo-Saxon monarchy.

7. "Trees are the earth's endless effort to speak to the listening heaven [sigh]." (Rabindranath Tagore)

8. Sorghum (the most widely cultivated grain in Africa) is far more tolerant of hot climates than corn or other grains.

9. The ant (a social insect) belongs to a family that also includes bees and wasps.

10. "There is no harbor of peace from the changing waves of joy [hee hee] and despair." (Euripides)

Practice VII

1. Irving Berlin (1888-1989), a songwriter and composer, wrote nearly 1,000 songs.

2. The proximity of the pollution-spewing factory is unacceptable.

3. That loud crackle-fizz sound is coming from the soda pop can.

4. Aunts, uncles, cousins, grandparents—it does not matter who—just get some volunteers to help.

5. Rain or shine—the show will go on.

6. Roses are red/Violets are blue/Sugar is sweet/And so are you.

7. They will have to dig $10\frac{1}{2}$ feet to find the pipe.

8. The Spanish-speaking woman tried to find her way through the maze of traffic.

9. Whatever you do, always buy a self-cleaning oven. They are the best!

10. My mother-in-law makes the best casseroles.

Practice VIII

Englishman Charles Dickens was a prolific writer who lived from 1812–1870. He began his writing career as a parliamentary reporter for the Morning Chronicle. Dickens's earliest success was a satirical piece titled Sketches by Boz, but The Pickwick Papers launched his early literary career. All of Dickens's novels appeared in serial form before being published in their entirety. His early novels include Oliver Twist, Nicholas Nickleby, and Barnaby Rudge. After a trip to America, he completed Martin Chuzzlewit and then wrote A Christmas Carol. Dickens's more sophisticated novels include David Copperfield, Bleak House, Hard Times, Little Dorrit, and A Tale of Two Cities. Great Expectations, Our Mutual Friend, and the incomplete The Mystery of Edwin Drood are his last novels. He provided literature with some of its most memorable characters and was able to capture the mood of Victorian England very descriptively.

Chapter 12 Review Quizzes:
Vocabulary Review Quiz

1. E
2. D
3. G
4. F
5. I
6. B
7. J
8. A
9. H
10. C

Punctuation Definitions

1. C
2. D
3. A
4. C
5. A
6. B
7. B
8. C
9. A
10. B

Punctuation

1. As a child, one of my favorite song lyrics, "When the moon hits the sky like a bigga pizza pie that's amore," was popular.
2. Oh no!
3. One of the best books that I have ever read is <u>Crime and Punishment</u> by Fyodor Dostoevsky.
4. Where do you think you are going?
5. Martin Scorsese, a film director who recently won an Oscar for his film <u>The Departed</u>, is passionate about his work.
6. America Ferrera, who plays Betty in the television program "Ugly Betty," is the daughter of Honduran immigrants.
7. Garry Kasparov is a well respected chess player who grew up in the former Soviet Union, but is opposed to the way things are going in Russia at present.
8. Michael J. Fox, famous for his acting in both television and film, was diagnosed with an early onset of Parkinson's disease in 1991.
9. Alas!
10. Screenwriter Shonda Rhimes is a single mom whose Emmy-winning show "Grey's Anatomy" has taken the world by surprise.
11. The remarkable thing about Pepsi's new boss is that she is a woman, she is from India, and she is concerned about communities, energy use, and health.
12. Virgin Galactic is one of the first commercial airlines to envision space flight for everyone.
13. Elizabeth Windsor is also known as Queen Elizabeth II, Britain's head of state.
14. How many commonwealth countries does Britain oversee?
15. Charles and Mary Lamb, a brother and sister collaboration team, are most remembered for their children's books <u>Tales from Shakespeare</u>.
16. Ennio Morricone, an Italian film composer, wrote scores for: <u>A Fistful of Dollars</u>, <u>The Good the Bad and the Ugly</u>, <u>Once Upon a Time in the West</u>, <u>The Untouchables</u> and <u>The Mission</u>.
17. Robert Oppenheimer, a theoretical physicist, headed the Manhattan Project to develop the atomic bomb.
18. Wernher von Braun, a rocket engineer who was born in Germany, is largely responsible for launching the first U.S. satellite <u>Explorer I</u> and later worked on the development of the Saturn rocket for the Apollo program.
19. Nightshade is a deadly, poisonous plant with purple leaves.
20. Watch out!

Chapter 13 Sentence Purpose

Practice I

1. imperative
2. declarative
3. interrogative
4. declarative
5. interrogative
6. declarative
7. exclamatory
8. declarative
9. exclamatory
10. declarative
11. imperative
12. exclamatory
13. declarative
14. declarative
15. exclamatory
16. interrogative
17. exclamatory
18. imperative
19. imperative
20. declarative

Chapter 13 Review Quizzes: Vocabulary Review Quiz

1. G		6. B
2. E		7. J
3. H		8. A
4. D		9. F
5. I		10. C

Sentence Type Definitions

1. D		6. A
2. B		7. D
3. B		8. C
4. A		9. B
5. C		10. C

Declarative, Exclamatory, Imperative, and Interrogative Sentences

1. interrogative
2. declarative
3. declarative
4. interrogative
5. imperative/declarative
6. interrogative
7. interrogative
8. declarative
9. interrogative
10. declarative
11. declarative
12. declarative
13. declarative
14. exclamatory
15. declarative

Chapter 14 Capitalization Rules

Practice I

1. |o|n our vacation, we will be visiting the |s|outheast, the |g|reat |l|akes area, and then on to |y|ellowstone |n|ational |p|ark.
2. |t|he |naacp| stands for the |n|ational |a|ssociation for the |a|dvancement of |c|olored |p|eople.
3. |t|he |n|*ina*, the |p|*inta*, and the |s|*anta* |m|*aria* were the ships that |c|olumbus sailed.
4. The US. |p|urple |h|eart |m|edal is awarded to those who have been injured or killed while serving in the military.
5. She was selling |a|frican goods in her shop on 331st |s|t.

6. |d|uring the |g|reat |d|epression, work and food were at a premium.

7. After church services, we will celebrate |e|l |d|ia de la |v|irgin |g|uadalupe with a grand feast.

8. |t|he entries in the |c|annes |f|ilm |f|estival seem outstanding this year.

9. |t|he |nfl| will reevaluate their decision.

10. |m|y sister will fly to |o|ahu first and then on to |n|ew |z|ealand.

11. Take |h|ighway 101 until you get to |h|ighway 67 and then go east.

12. Next |s|eptember and |o|ctober, they are taking a trip to |r|ussia.

13. |t|he |n|ile |r|iver flows through |e|gypt and other |a|frican countries.

14. Who do you think is going to win, the |d|emocratic |p|arty or the |r|epublican |p|arty?

15. |n|ame the men who signed the |d|eclaration of |i|ndependence.

16. |m|y |j|ewish friends will fly to |i|srael for |c|hanukah next year.

17. |w|e did not get to see the |c|liffs of |m|oher on our trip to |i|reland.

18. |c|inco de |m|ayo is on a |s|aturday this year.

19. |f|rom |s|an |a|ntonio, |i| plan on flying to |c|hicago and then on to |m|ontreal.

20. |i|f you will please read this passage from the |k|oran, you will better understand what we are discussing.

Practice II
Sentences will vary

Chapter 14 Review Quizzes: Vocabulary Review Quiz

1. B	6. E
2. G	7. J
3. C	8. A
4. F	9. H
5. I	10. D

Capitalization Rules

1. A	6. B
2. D	7. A
3. A	8. B
4. D	9. B
5. C	10. D

Capitalization

|l|awrence |f|erlinghetti, an |a|merican poet, was born on |m|arch 24, 1919. |h|e was born in |y|onkers, |n|ew |y|ork, where he attended high school and earned the rank of |e|agle |s|cout. Later he attended the |u|niversity of |n|orth |c|arolina at |c|hapel |h|ill. |f|erlinghetti served as an officer in the |n|avy during |w|orld |w|ar II and afterward earned a master's degree at |c|olumbia and a doctorate at the |s|orbonne in |p|aris. While in |p|aris, he met a man who convinced him to go to |s|an |f|rancisco, where |f|erlinghetti taught |f|rench, painted, and wrote literary criticism. |i|n 1953, he and |p|eter |d|. |m|artin opened |c|ity |l|ights |b|ookstore, which was named after the |c|harlie |c|haplin film |c|ity |l|ights. |f|erlinghetti opened a publishing company when |m|artin left for |n|ew |y|ork and began to publish the early works of poets who are known as the |b|eat |g|eneration. |p|oets |j|ack |k|erouac and |a|llen |g|insberg were among

this group. $\boxed{f}$erlinghetti's $\boxed{a}$ $\boxed{c}$oney $\boxed{i}$sland *of the* $\boxed{m}$*ind* is his best-known collection of poetry and has been translated into nine languages.

Chapter 15 Writing Paragraphs

Practice I
Answers will vary

Practice II
Answers will vary

Practice III
Answers will vary

Chapter 15 Review Quizzes: Vocabulary Review Quiz

1. H	6. F
2. E	7. B
3. G	8. D
4. C	9. J
5. I	10. A

Paragraph Writing Definitions

1. D	6. A
2. C	7. C
3. A	8. A
4. B	9. A
5. D	10. C

Writing Paragraphs
1. topic sentence
2. support sentence
3. support sentence
4. support sentence
5. concluding sentence

Chapter 16 Pronunciation Review

Practice I

1. S	6. L
2. L	7. L
3. S	8. L
4. L	9. S
5. S	10. L

Practice II
Answers will vary

1.	eigh	neigh, weight, sleigh
2.	ea (long e)	eat, beat, meat
3.	ow (long o)	bow, tow, sow
4.	ee	wee, sleep, meet
5.	ey (long e)	money, key, turkey
6.	ai	straight, sail, mail
7.	ie (long i)	tie, pie, lie
8.	oa	oar, boar, oat
9.	ea (short e)	head, read, spread
10.	ay	stay, hay, away

Practice III

Once there was a <u>sow</u>, named <u>Chow</u>, who seemed to be able to <u>plow</u>. She <u>toiled</u> in the <u>oil</u> and ended up <u>stewing</u> in the <u>house</u>, and then her husband named <u>McCoy</u> brought home some bok <u>choy</u>. Not long in the <u>soup</u>, the <u>room</u> filled with <u>straw</u>, and then the <u>raccoon</u> started skipping until <u>noon</u>. Once he was <u>subdued</u>, the <u>mouse</u> <u>threw</u> a <u>louse</u>, and the Mr. and Mrs. finally <u>subdued</u> the <u>coy boy</u>.

Practice IV

Answers will vary

1. m__ar__ket
2. st__or__k
3. t__ur__key
4. terr__or__
5. __ur__ban

6. g__ar__den
7. s__ir__e
8. maj__or__
9. m__er__chant
10. c__er__emony

Practice V

Answers will vary

Beginning Y Consonant Sound	Ending Y Vowel Sound	One-syllable Ending Y = Long I Sound	Multisyllable Ending Y = Long E Sound
yeast	*treaty*	*spy*	*duplicity*
year	meaty	sly	lovingly
yoke	stinky	ply	jokingly
yellow	penny	sty	lovely
yield	money	buy	carelessly
yoga	every	fly	flawlessly
yoghurt	berry	fry	tediously
yolk	very	by	needlessly
yodel	merry	pry	carefully
yogi	scary	cry	randomly

Practice VI

Answers will vary

C S Sound	C K Sound	G J Sound	G G Sound	S S Sound	S Z Sound
circus	*couch*	*ginger*	*grate*	*side*	*muse*
celestial	cat	ginseng	get	salvage	lose
celebrate	cattle	giraffe	ghost	salute	excuse
celery	caucus	gipsy	gimmick	salutation	amuse
ceiling	caught	gin	gill	saint	bemuse
cedar	cauliflower	gerund	gear	sales	peruse
ceasefire	caulk	gestation	gas	salad	choose
cellar	cauterize	gesture	garrulous	seem	newsy
cellophane	caution	germ	garnet	sill	bluesy
censor	cave	geometry	garment	season	abuse

Practice VII

Answers may vary

1. After fighting for his true love's life, t h e _knight_ rode off on his white horse.

2. The _tomb_ was dark and full of spider webs, but we continued our search for ancient relics.

3. The _rhythm_ of the Cuban music is exotic.

4. Please hang the _wreath_ on the door.

5. The baker has to _knead_ the _dough_ for about ten minutes before he allows it to rise.

6. Tomorrow I am going to _wrap_ all of the gifts for the party.

7. A _synonym_ is a word that means the same or close to the same as another word.

8. I told Tina not to suck her _thumb_ any more, but she will not listen.

9. _Knock_ on the door to see if they are home.

10. The _bright_ Sun caused the fabric to fade.

Practice VIII

quick   antique   boutique

oblique   croquet   quiz

quaint   clique   turquoise

quarter   unique   queasy

squint   quadrant   opaque

quill   mystique   pique

Practice IX

1. sw   swear, swim, sweep
2. br   bring, brisk, brought
3. spr   spring, sprite, spray
4. gr   green, gravy, gravel
5. cr   creed, creek, crate
6. dr   drink, dry, drip
7. tr   travel, trade, tried
8. tw   twist, twelve, twirl
9. sn   snail, snarl, snip
10. gl   glove, glisten, glare

Practice X
Answers will vary

1. –sp   crisp, lisp, wisp
2. –dge   drudge, grudge, fudge
3. –pt   kept, wept, swept
4. –lk   milk, bilk, silk
5. –ng   bang, gang, tang
6. –nd   round, sound, pound
7. –ft   soft, loft, thrift
8. –nk   link, mink, sink
9. –nt   mount, taunt, aunt
10. –st   mist, pest, crest

Practice XI
Sentences will vary

Chapter 16 Review Quizzes:
Vocabulary Review Quiz

1. carotene
2. darn
3. tsunami
4. reservoir
5. excerpt
6. annotate
7. point-blank
8. ricochet
9. beguile
10. turbid

Pronunciation Definitions

1. B   6. A
2. D   7. C
3. B   8. D
4. A   9. A
5. D   10. D

Long and Short Vowel Sounds

1. mules   2. dock   3. life   4. deal
5. sunshine 6. mate   7. fifty   8. wayside
9. punish   10. ruler   11. throw   12. coach
13. rat   14. grow   15. peach   16. joy
17. bay   18. cut   19. slow   20. timid

Vowel Digraphs and Diphthongs

1. digraph
2. diphthong
3. digraph
4. digraph
5. digraph
6. digraph
7. digraph
8. diphthong
9. diphthong
10. digraph

R-Controlled Vowel Sounds
Answers may vary

1. terr__or__
2. hamb__ur__ger
3. th__ir__sty
4. w__ar__ned
5. g__ar__den
6. st__ar__dust
7. sc__ar__let
8. conc__er__t
9. f__or__mally
10. t__ir__e

The Letter Y

Y Consonant Words	Y Vowel—Long I Sound	Y Vowel—Long E Sound
yearn	*try*	*baby*
yell	buy	sleekly
yore	cry	weakly
yacht	fry	weekly
yellow	dry	really
yarn	demystify	wealthy
yeas	testify	healthy
yes	disqualify	bleakly
yield	preoccupy	chiefly
yoke	purify	briefly

Consonants

Sentences will vary

Silent Consonants

<u>gnaw</u>	ship	<u>comb</u>
<u>column</u>	left	silt
music	<u>wrap</u>	tell
<u>bomb</u>	swim	<u>wreath</u>
<u>knapsack</u>	mellow	forgive
elbow	<u>tomb</u>	<u>hymn</u>
homonym	<u>dough</u>	<u>spaghetti</u>
silent	mischief	<u>sigh</u>
star	<u>gnu</u>	swear
<u>thumb</u>	money	wheat

Consonant Blends and Digraphs

1. CB	6. CB
2. CB	7. CB
3. CD	8. CD
4. CB	9. CD
5. CB	10. CB

Chapter 17 Prefixes, Suffixes, and Spelling Improvement

Practice I

Answers will vary

1. hyper- <u>*hyperactive, hyperbola, hyperthermia*</u>
2. dys- dysfunctional, dysentery, dyspepsia
3. pro- provide, promotional, protect
4. tri- triangular, triad, triple
5. quad- quadrant, quadriplegic, quadratic
6. bi- biped, bipolar, binocular
7. retro- retrograde, retroactive, retrospective
8. anti- antibacterial, antisocial, antiwar
9. mal maleficent, malicious, mallow
10. un unsung, undone, unfinished

Practice II

Confucius, a revered <u>Chinese</u> philosopher and thinker, was born in 551 B.C. His philosophies, which emphasize <u>morality</u> in both governmental and personal areas as well his beliefs in justice and <u>sincerity,</u> have influenced many people for centuries. In fact, Confucius's philosophies have been developed into a system of thought known as <u>Confucianism</u>. A collection of his teachings titled *Analects of Confucius* were compiled many years after his death in 479 B.C.

Born into a poor family, Confucius's <u>family</u> at one time held a noble ranking. However, the <u>family</u> fled from the State of Song to the State of Lu, which is now a part of Shandong Province. According to records, his father was <u>seventy</u> and his mother <u>eighteen</u> when he was born. His father died when he was three. Confucius married Qi Quan at the age of <u>nineteen,</u> and his wife had their first child, Kong Li, one year later. Confucius worked at various jobs, including sheepherding, cow herding, clerking, and bookkeeping. Later he became an <u>administrative</u> manager and eventually the justice minister in the State of Lu. At the age of fifty-five, he quit the position because of philosophical and moral differences between himself and the <u>politics</u> of the duke.

Soon after Confucius's departure from his job in the State of Lu, he began a long journey of teaching his beliefs. He did not return home until he was sixty-eight, where he spent his last years teaching his disciples and transmitting old <u>wisdoms</u> into a set of books called the *Five Classics*. His beliefs and philosophies, known as <u>Confucianism</u>, dominated China until the early twentieth century and influenced the <u>Japanese</u>, Koreans, and <u>Vietnamese</u>.

Practice III

1. waigh | weigh | waygh
2. ceeling | ceiling | cealing
3. neibor | neighbor | naghbor
4. deseet   deciet | deceit |
5. baige | beige | baje
6. | chief | cheaf   cheif
7. anchent | ancient | anchint
8. beleeve   beleave | believe |
9. | seize | seeze   sieze
10. feald   fild | field |

Practice IV

1. drag + -ed =   dragged
2. stop + -ing =   stopping
3. sag + -ing =   sagging
4. brag + ing =   bragging
5. shop + ed =   shopped
6. drop + ing =   dropping
7. throb + ed =   throbbed
8. wrap + ing =   wrapping
9. strap + ed =   strapped
10 pin + ing =   pinning

Practice V

1. skated   skatted | skated |
2. fileing   filleing | filing |
3. | flameless | flaimless   flammless
4. timeing | timing | timeeing
5. | priming | primeing   primming
6. hopefull   hoppful | hopeful |
7. | judgment | judgement   jugment
8. | stated | statted   stateed
9. careing | caring | carring
10. placment   placeement | placement |

Practice VI

1. triing — trying
2. varyous — various
3. fairries — fairies
4. succeed — Correct
5. daisyies — daisies
6. prying — Correct
7. ladyies — ladies
8. candyied — candied
9. universitys — universities
10. crying — Correct
11. plentyful — plentiful
12. merryment — merriment
13. beautyful — beautiful
14. marriage — Correct
15. happyness — happiness
16. interceed — intercede
17. scaryiest — scariest
18. companion — Correct
19. acceede — accede
20. excede — exceed

Practice VII

1. tooth — teeth
2. glasses — glasses
3. synopsis — synopses
4. potato — potatoes
5. man — men
6. shelf — shelves
7. box — boxes
8. deer — deer
9. goose — geese
10. scissors — scissors

Chapter 17 Review Quizzes: Vocabulary Review Quiz

1. G   6. E
2. D   7. C
3. H   8. F
4. B   9. A
5. I   10. J

Suffixes, Prefixes, and Spelling Rules

1. A   6. C
2. B   7. B
3. D   8. A
4. C   9. D
5. A   10. A

Suffixes and Prefixes

1. non- — nonjudgmental, nonabrasive, nonsense
2. -ed — stormed, judged, abraded
3. -ment — judgment, encouragement, cement
4. pre- — prevent, present, presentation
5. para- — parameter, parakeet, paramedic
6. -est — interest, starkest, best
7. -ing — interesting, besting, judging
8. un- — unethical, untoward, uncooperative
9. anti- — anti-inflammatory, antibiotic, antismog
10. -er — tamer, schemer, temper

Spelling Rules

1. generashun   generation   generacion
2. takeing   takking   taking
3. possession   poscession   poccession
4. terifing   terrifying   tarrifying
5. preceed   precead   precede
6. presence   presense   presens
7. sweatting   sweating   sweeatting
8. flame   flaime   flayme
9. babyies   babees   babies
10. triangle   tryangle   triangyle
11. glasses   glases   glass
12. boxs   boxes   boxxes
13. trowsers   trousers   troussers
14. etiquette   etickette   etikette
15. ernest   earnest   errnest
16. subbtel   subtel   subtle
17. playwrite   playright   playwright
18. assassin   asassin   assassyn
19. vakume   vackum   vacuum
20. sponcer   sponsor   sponsir

Chapter 18 Word Roots and Vocabulary Improvement

Practice I

1. cardio — cardiograph, cardiopulmonary, cardiology
2. bio — biology, biochemistry, biography
3. liber — liberty, libertine, liberation
4. pend — pendant, pending, pendulous
5. agri — agriculture, agronomy, aground
6. pyro — pyromaniac, pyrotechnics, pyrolysis
7. ject — conjecture, project, inject
8. helio — heliograph, heliocentric, heliotrope
9. anthro — anthropology, anthropomorphic, anthropologist
10. dem — democracy, democrat, demonstrate

Practice II
Sentences will vary

Practice III
Sentences will vary

Chapter 18 Review Quizzes: Vocabulary Review Quiz

1. humiliated
2. oenophile
3. Antebellum
4. eclipses
5. plutocracy
6. decapitating
7. spindly
8. bog
9. detained
10. cavern

Roots Word and Vocabulary Improvement Definitions

1. C
2. A
3. C
4. A
5. A
6. D
7. C
8. C
9. C
10. C

Root Identification

1. sus<u>pend</u>
2. anti<u>bio</u>tic
3. e<u>ject</u>
4. <u>ped</u>estrian
5. <u>vide</u>otape
6. <u>dem</u>ocracy
7. <u>gen</u>etic
8. <u>educ</u>ate
9. <u>gen</u>uine
10. <u>miss</u>ion
11. <u>port</u>able
12. <u>pend</u>ing
13. <u>liber</u>ate
14. auto<u>graph</u>
15. <u>dict</u>ionary
16. <u>voc</u>ation
17. <u>mal</u>ice
18. <u>om</u>it
19. con<u>struct</u>
20. re<u>ject</u>

Vocabulary Improvement
Tips will vary

Chapter 19 Homonyms, Synonyms, Antonyms, and Confusing Words

Practice I

1. _Bread_/Bred is a staple food that is made by mixing flour, salt, yeast, and water.
2. They will be using the _altar_/alter for a special ceremony.
3. We will need to trim the bows/_boughs_ before the next big storm.
4. They say that eating carat/_carrots_ is good for your eyesight.
5. Our team bold/_bowled_ their best game yet.
6. The _berry_/bury pie was delicious.
7. They were attacked by a bare/_bear_ while hiking.
8. _Eye_/I really do not know what to say about your predicament.
9. The strange cent/_scent_ coming from the closet was sickening.
10. She will be air/_heir_ to an extremely large corporation.

Practice II

1. Get plenty of sleep and eat healthy, thus avoiding the flue/_flu_.
2. The ship was made of led/_lead_.
3. Once the jam/_jamb_ is built, the door can be hung.
4. _Hey_/hay, don't you think you should be doing your homework?
5. Be careful when you drive at night, the dear/_deer_ seem to jump into the streets out of nowhere.
6. William _lacks_/lax motivation; he needs to improve his study habits.
7. There was no room at the in/_inn_, and they had to continue their travels.
8. The links/_lynx_ slept peacefully in its cage.
9. Shannon injured her heal/_heel_ and was unable to compete in the finals.
10. The _fir_/fur trees drop needles and cones most of the year.

Practice III

Sentences will vary

Practice IV

1. David's long and mysterious _tale_/tail seemed far-fetched and untrue.
2. All _week_/weak, Loomee forced herself to study for the exam.
3. Valerie is going to _sew_/sow a project for art class.
4. _Would_/wood you please tell me where to find the museum?
5. "Oh no!" she side/_sighed_, "We missed the last train to Kilarney."
6. Avoid eating the yoke/_yolk_ of the egg; it is full of cholesterol.
7. As a response to the story, there were _tears_/tiers falling from everyone in the audience.
8. The rescue team arrived on the seen/_scene_ before the police.
9. Queen Elizabeth II continues on the _throne_/thrown of Great Britain.
10. The large _toad_/towed hopped from one lily pad to another.

Practice V

Answers will vary

1. strong   tough
2. distant   remote
3. knave   rogue
4. clever   intelligent

5. sharp	pointed
6. prey	victim
7. glisten	shine
8. assistant	aide
9. boring	dull
10. coarse	rough

Practice VI

1. fast/quick
2. buy/sell
3. hate/love
4. sloppy/neat
5. before/after
6. narrow/thin
7. decrease/add
8. tardy/late
9. jabber/babble
10. clear/muddy
11. far/close
12. harmless/harmful
13. hate/despise
14. beautiful/ugly
15. include/contain
16. narrow/wide
17. powerful/strong
18. tardy/early
19. lazy/ambitious
20. peaceful/calm
21. dim/bright
22. pull/push
23. dumb/stupid
24. hot/cold
25. outside/inside
26. today/present
27. wave/ripple
28. rascal/knave
29. disagreement/agreement
30. free/imprisoned

Practice VII

1. Will you *sit*/ set the flower vase onto the kitchen table?
2. You have completely mistaken our true *principals*/ principles in your response.
3. Which / *That*/*Who* of the chemical experiments will Mrs. Hescox demonstrate today?
4. Nick did *good*/ well on the test today.
5. The effect /*affect* of the smog on his lungs was disturbing.
6. *Your*/ You're going to spend the holidays with your grandmother in Guadalajara.
7. Jinny needs to fix the clasp on her necklace or else she will *loose*/ lose the pendant.
8. Sara will investigate the meanings of the *illusions*/ allusions in the novel *Crime and Punishment*.
9. Buddy has a /*an* pleasant personality.
10. There are a *lot* /*alot* of students who do not read their books.

Chapter 19 Review Quizzes: Vocabulary Review Quiz

1. I	6. B
2. C	7. H
3. G	8. D
4. F	9. E
5. A	10. J

Homonyms, Synonyms, Antonyms, and Confusing Words Definitions

1. C	6. A
2. B	7. B
3. A	8. C
4. D	9. C
5. B	10. D

Homonyms

1. The mane idea of the sentence is not always easy to find. main
2. During the rush, the isle was blocked and no one could leave. aisle
3. At the sound of a loud noise, the hair ran into its burrow. hare
4. The dents cloud formation is a certain sign of rain. dense
5. Anthony will become a night at the Queen's command. knight
6. Olivia was in morning for her dead brother for many years. mourning
7. Nun of the waiters is paying any attention to us. None
8. Going back home at this point doesn't make any scents. sense
9. James will urn a living by designing a unique computer program. earn
10. It is going to take me a month to rap all of those gifts. wrap

Synonyms and Antonyms

1. A petite/large
2. S repeat/duplicate
3. A drizzle/pour
4. A avoid/encounter
5. S clever/intelligent
6. A dull/shiny
7. S error/mistake
8. A distrust/trust
9. S total/sum
10. S ponder/think
11. A stare/glance
12. A minor/major
13. A fasten/unlock
14. A peaceful/warlike
15. A gentle/harsh
16. S merry/happy
17. A hasty/slowly
18. S vacant/empty
19. S friend/pal
20. A adore/despise

Confusing Words

1. C Do not forget, your purse is under the table.
2. E The school principle was given an award for bravery. (principal)
3. E I am going to go to the post office anyways; I might as well stop at the dry cleaners too. (anyway)
4. E Whether you approve or not, there is an new necklace in your jewelry box. (a)
5. C Global warming is having a disturbing effect on the climate patterns around the world.
6. E Between thousands in the crowd watching the game, there were dozens of celebrities. (Among)
7. E They were cent to visit the museum. (sent)
8. C Your mother is waiting.
9. C Which animal in the zoo do you like best?
10. E To who shall we send the invitation? (whom)

Chapter 20—Idioms

Practice I

1. G
2. J
3. F
4. I
5. C
6. D
7. E
8. H
9. B
10. A

Practice II

Answers will vary

1. Resolve old problems or issues
2. Getting over first meeting awkwardness
3. Some find beauty in things that othes do not
4. Good luck
5. An outsider/someone different
6. Family relationships are stronger than other relationships
7. Naked
8. Something good comes from something that seems bad
9. Understand beyond what is written or stated
10. Either one way or the other, very clearly presented

Practice III

1.	F	6.	H
2.	E	7.	I
3.	B	8.	D
4.	J	9.	A
5.	G	10.	C

Practice IV

Answers will vary

1. Unpretentious, level-headed
2. Being prepared, ready, organized
3. Something good comes from what appears to be ominous
4. Become irresponsible suddenly
5. Showing off, bragging about something
6. Not all things appear the way they seem
7. Having to admit that you are wrong
8. At the very last minute
9. Easy, carefree, but hot summer days
10. Effort/amount so small that it will not make a difference

Practice V

1. Go fly a kite.
2. Fly off the handle.
3. It's Greek to me.
4. Get up on the wrong side of the bed.
5. Like a fish out of water.
6. Fair weather friend.
7. From rags to riches
8. Going full circle
9. Fit as a fiddle
10. To go Dutch.

Practice VI

Sentences will vary

Practice VII

1.	F	6.	D
2.	H	7.	G
3.	A	8.	I
4.	B	9.	J
5.	C	10.	E

Practice VIII

Answers will vary

1. Go to the limits
2. Nearly impossible
3. Insane or crazy
4. Trying to convince an audience that already agrees
5. Not the normal route
6. To say something stupid or embarrassing
7. An impractical scheme or idea
8. Old, not as young as before
9. Easy
10. Seldom or very rarely

Practice IX

Sentences will vary

Practice X

1. That man is nothing more than <u>a wolf in sheep's clothing</u>; he is not a good person.
2. She has been <u>up to her neck</u> in phone calls and requests for information.
3. Once you leave your job, you are going to have to <u>tighten your belt.</u>
4. Thank you for asking me to dance, but <u>I have two left feet</u>.
5. Marika was sent on <u>a wild-goose chase</u> looking for that special fabric.
6. If she does not find a job soon, she will get a real <u>wake-up call</u> when she cannot pay her bills.
7. Not having a back-up plan proved to be a real <u>thorn in my side</u>.
8. He is nothing but a <u>yellow-bellied</u> loser.
9. Lindsay decided to marry him, <u>warts and all</u>.
10. Although Dakota is making millions now, she was quite the <u>ugly duckling</u> as a child.

Chapter 20 Review Quizzes:
Vocabulary Review Quiz

1. Loud weeping, to shout or cry loudly
2. To cause an improvement in behavior from savage to a more developed society
3. A sculpture or model of a person
4. Constant or continuous succession of changes
5. Extreme feeling of fear or loathing
6. Feeling of extreme dislike, hate
7. A person's way or method of working
8. Situated in the back or behind
9. To tread heavily or loudly
10. A person who has no settled home or regular work

Idiom Definitions

1. B
2. A
3. D
4. C
5. A
6. A
7. C
8. A
9. B
10. A

Idioms

1. To say something stupid or embarrassing
2. To share the cost of something (usually a meal)
3. To die
4. To let get out of shape or out of order
5. As a general rule or estimate
6. Don't take it too seriously, take it lightly
7. Something to hide or to be embarrassed about
8. To lose patience, something that finally makes you angry
9. Using an argument that could help or hurt, either way
10. Something that is not likely to succeed, doomed to fail
11. With all of its/his/her faults
12. Hot summer days
13. An unalterable decision, only fate will decide the consequences
14. Very difficult or can't be changed
15. Spend time with important people
16. To suddenly get nervous or change one's mind about something
17. Someone who is rude or unfriendly to you
18. Easy
19. An outsider, someone different
20. Not the usual route

Chapter 21 Allusions

Practice I

Answers will vary slightly

1. Hamlet/Shakespeare
2. Mrs. Malaprop
3. Nursery Rhyme/Mother Goose
4. from *Moby Dick* by Herman Melville
5. crude and uncouth people/*Gulliver's Travels*/Jonathan Swift
6. from *Alice's Adventures in Wonderland*/Lewis Carroll
7. Walter Mitty
8. a Horatio Algier story
9. Shakespeare
10. Neverland or Never-Never Land from the play *Peter Pan*

Practice II

1. I	11. D
2. Q	12. E
3. G	13. R
4. A	14. F
5. T	15. K
6. M	16. J
7. B	17. N
8. C	18. P
9. O	19. L
10. S	20. H

Practice III

1. Magi
2. olive branch
3. Jonah
4. John the Baptist
5. Golden Rule
6. David
7. Philistines
8. Samson
9. Cain and Abel
10. Job

Chapter 21 Review Quizzes:
Vocabulary Review Quiz

1. A Hawaiian word that means hello or good-bye
2. A showy trinket or toy of little or no value
3. Rural or rustic
4. A swear word or other expression used in an exclamation
5. Having a sensation of whirling or spinning; overexcited
6. Separate or remote; of or like an island
7. To eye lecherously or amorously
8. A card game in which a bluff is used as players bet on the game
9. An appliance with a rotating spit for roasting or barbequing meat
10. A broken piece of pottery or glass

Allusion Definitions

1. A	6. D
2. D	7. A
3. B	8. A
4. D	9. C
5. B	10. B

Allusions

1. the last words of Julius Caesar
2. Count Dracula
3. Diana
4. Noah's Ark
5. a fairy tale
6. a nursery rhyme
7. the Ugly Duckling
8. lines from Shakespeare's *Romeo and Juliet*
9. William Tell
10. Tortoise and the Hare

Chapter 22 Study Skills, Reading and Writing Improvement

Practice I
Answers will vary

Practice II
Answers will vary

Practice III
Answers will vary

Chapter 22 Review Quizzes: Vocabulary Review Quiz

1. D   6. I
2. B   7. F
3. J   8. C
4. H   9. E
5. G   10. A

Study Skills, Reading and Writing Improvement Definitions

1. D   6. B
2. A   7. A
3. C   8. D
4. A   9. A
5. C   10. A

Study Skills, Reading and Writing Improvement

1. SS   6. RI   11. RI   16. WI
2. WI   7. WI   12. WI   17. RI
3. RI   8. SS   13. WI   18. WI
4. WI   9. SS   14. RI   19. RI
5. RI   10. WI   15. WI   20. SS

Chapter 23 Academic Writing

Practice I
1. four
2. inside address
3. block
4. left
5. heading
6. Dear _____
7. four
8. two
9. succinctly
10. quality

Practice II
1. current
2. feature
3. lead
4. hook
5. news
6. editorial
7. inverted pyramid
8. byline
9. top
10. feature

Practice III
1. five
2. thesis
3. expository essay
4. convince (answer varies)
5. provoke a response (answer varies)
6. autobiographical
7. tell
8. comparison/contrast
9. problem solution
10. five

Chapter 23 Review Quizzes:

Vocabulary Review Quiz		Academic Writing Definitions	
1. H	6. B	1. B	6. C
2. F	7. A	2. B	7. C
3. E	8. J	3. C	8. D
4. I	9. D	4. D	9. C
5. C	10. G	5. B	10. B

Formal Letters

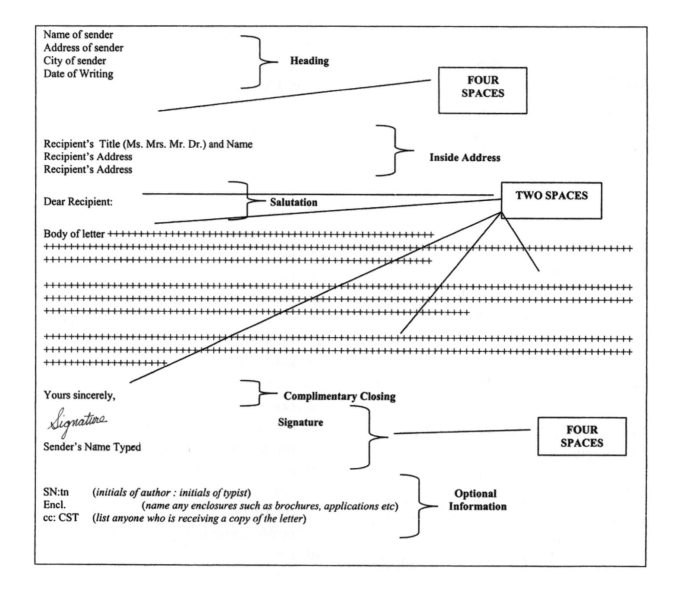

Name of sender
Address of sender
City of sender
Date of Writing ——— Heading

FOUR SPACES

Recipient's Title (Ms. Mrs. Mr. Dr.) and Name
Recipient's Address
Recipient's Address ——— Inside Address

Dear Recipient: ——— Salutation

TWO SPACES

Body of letter ++

Yours sincerely, ——— Complimentary Closing

Signature ——— Signature

Sender's Name Typed

FOUR SPACES

SN:tn (*initials of author : initials of typist*)
Encl. (*name any enclosures such as brochures, applications etc*) ——— Optional Information
cc: CST (*list anyone who is receiving a copy of the letter*)

Academic Essays

1. Persuasive—to convince the reader of a certain position, idea, or concept
2. Comparison/Contrast—to compare and contrast, find the similarities and differences between two topics
3. Expository—to explain
4. Descriptive—to provoke a response; to describe an event/happening
5. Problem/Solution—to present a problem and a solution to the problem
6. Narrative—to tell a story
7. Autobiographical—a personal event or happening

Chapter 24 Basics of Writing a Research Paper

Chapter 24 Review Quizzes: Vocabulary Review Quiz

1. F	6. I
2. E	7. C
3. D	8. B
4. G	9. A
5. H	10. J

Basics of Writing a Research Paper Definitions

1. B	6. D
2. D	7. A
3. A	8. B
4. C	9. C
5. B	10. A

Chapter 25 Comprehensive Vocabulary Review Exams

Review Exercise I

1. conservatory
2. ideologies
3. pride
4. tiara
5. laboratory
6. elements
7. water polo
8. childhood
9. knight
10. chaperone

Review Exercise II

1. She
2. they
3. He
4. we
5. its
6. us
7. your
8. Whom
9. theirs
10. ours

Review Exercise III

1. unite
2. shrink
3. erodes
4. heed
5. operate
6. raft
7. admonish
8. juxtaposition
9. fortifying
10. minimized

Review Exercise IV

1. cnidarian
2. opus
3. quixotic
4. animation
5. autonomous
6. griffin
7. limerick
8. orchestra
9. Uranus
10. Columns

Review Exercise V

1. magnification
2. vertigo
3. pre-Raphaelites
4. albatross
5. stream-of-consciousness
6. bleak
7. frail
8. fusion
9. persecution
10. disturbance

Review Exercise VI

1. Bohemian
2. audacious
3. bogus
4. civilian
5. roomy
6. tart
7. auburn
8. malnourished
9. diplomatic
10. malignant

Review Exercise VII

Sentences will vary

Review Exercise VIII

1. regarding (or #2)
2. concerning (or # 1)
3. aboard
4. against
5. despite
6. within
7. underneath
8. excepting
9. via
10. notwithstanding

Review Exercise IX

1. unravel
2. redundant
3. pang
4. informants
5. homily
6. kabuki
7. Crater
8. diverge
9. superfluous
10. pantomime

Review Exercise X

1. dank
2. sabotage
3. mestizo
4. chameleon
5. orations
6. mocha
7. legatos
8. plebians
9. racketeer
10. descends

Review Exercise XI

1. nepotism
2. wigs
3. disband
4. pathos
5. orbit
6. honeycomb
7. fizzy
8. proximity
9. patriarch
10. glorify

Review Exercise XII

Sentences will vary

Review Exercise XIII

1. premature
2. barometer
3. Lasagne
4. virgule
5. Confederacy
6. flamboyant
7. heron
8. jinx
9. tintinnabulation
10. seasonable

Review Exercise XIV

1. annotate
2. beguile
3. carotene
4. darn
5. excerpt
6. point-blank
7. reservoir
8. ricochet
9. tsunami
10. turbid

Review Exercise XV

Sentences will vary

Review Exercise XVI

1. antebellum
2. bog
3. cavern
4. decapitate
5. detain
6. eclipse
7. humiliate
8. oenophile
9. plutocracy
10. spindly

Review Exercise XVII

1. anoint
2. chariot
3. glistens
4. dowdy
5. indigo
6. lottery
7. voluminous
8. peers
9. mountainous
10. usury

Review Exercise XVIII

1. bawling
2. stomps
3. civilized
4. effigy
5. flux
6. horror; horror
7. *Loathing*
8. modus oprandi
9. posterior
10. vagrant

Review Exercise XIX

1. yolk
2. wading
3. neigh
4. ailing
5. cents
6. bald
7. queue
8. precedents
9. whine
10. mourning

Review Exercise XX

1. peevish
2. bistros
3. cataclysmic
4. conga
5. gape
6. easel
7. marshmallow
8. teeming
9. gratuity
10. reproach

Review Exercise XXI

1. diploma
2. fillet
3. gnaw
4. hamlet
5. hijack
6. impeach
7. leech
8. meld
9. oedipal
10. sesquipedalian

Review Exercise XXII

1. ruminate
2. kaput
3. desperado
4. engrain
5. facilitated
6. reciprocate
7. omega
8. vagrants
9. nebulous
10. governess

Review Exercise XXIII

1. countrified
2. bauble
3. shard
4. giddy
5. ogle
6. expletive
7. insular
8. aloha
9. poker
10. rotisserie

Chapter 26 Comprehensive English Exam

1. **B**	26. **C**	51. **C**	76. **D**
2. **D**	27. **C**	52. **B**	77. **B**
3. **D**	28. **A**	53. **D**	78. **C**
4. **C**	29. **D**	54. **A**	79. **C**
5. **A**	30. **B**	55. **D**	80. **A**
6. **A**	31. **C**	56. **D**	81. **C**
7. **D**	32. **A**	57. **B**	82. **C**
8. **A**	33. **C**	58. **B**	83. **B**
9. **B**	34. **A**	59. **C**	84. **D**
10. **A**	35. **D**	60. **D**	85. **D**
11. **D**	36. **A**	61. **A**	86. **B**
12. **B**	37. **D**	62. **C**	87. **A**
13. **A**	38. **C**	63. **D**	88. **B**
14. **C**	39. **B**	64. **A**	89. **A**
15. **B**	40. **C**	65. **A**	90. **B**
16. **A**	41. **C**	66. **C**	91. **A**
17. **A**	42. **A**	67. **B**	92. **D**
18. **B**	43. **A**	68. **C**	93. **A**
19. **B**	44. **C**	69. **B**	94. **D**
20. **C**	45. **D**	70. **A**	95. **C**
21. **B**	46. **C**	71. **C**	96. **C**
22. **C**	47. **C**	72. **A**	97. **D**
23. **A**	48. **D**	73. **A**	98. **A**
24. **D**	49. **B**	74. **A**	99. **C**
25. **C**	50. **B**	75. **D**	100. **D**

INDEX